THE COMPLETE ILLUSTRATED ENCYCLOPEDIA OF

BUDDHISM

THE COMPLETE ILLUSTRATED ENCYCLOPEDIA OF
BUDDHISM

A COMPREHENSIVE GUIDE TO BUDDHIST HISTORY, PHILOSOPHY AND PRACTICE,
MAGNIFICENTLY ILLUSTRATED WITH MORE THAN 500 COLOUR PHOTOGRAPHS

CONSULTANT EDITOR: IAN HARRIS, PhD

HELEN VARLEY • PETER CONNOLLY • STEFANIA TRAVAGNIN

HERMES HOUSE

CONTENTS

p1 The Buddha descending to his last incarnation, 3rd–4th-century relief; p2 Wat Mahathat, Sukhothai, Thailand; p3t Kinkaku-ji, Kyoto, Japan; p3b Amitabha-Buddha, 11th–12th century; p4l Monks at Bumthang monastery, Bhutan; p4r Monks in Diskit monastery, India; p5l The meditation gesture, dhyana mudra; p5r Prayer wheels at Swayambhunath stupa, Nepal.

CHAPTER 5:
BUDDHIST TRADITIONS

INTRODUCTION

Buddhism is believed to be the world's fifth largest religion today, as ranked by numbers of adherents, and there are also signs that it is one of the fastest-growing religions. Part of Buddhism's appeal is that it has doctrine – a set of principles and beliefs that all practitioners seek to follow – but its teachings are not dogmatic. The Buddha enjoined his followers to question all that he had taught them, so debate is part of Buddhist practice. Further, although he exhorted his followers to go forth and preach the Dharma (his teachings, literally 'the Truth'), Buddhism is not a fervently evangelical faith.

PHILOSOPHY OR RELIGION?

The Buddha did not present himself as the messenger of a supreme God. In fact, Buddhism denies the existence of a creator-god and teaches that no sentient being has a soul, or core identity, that lives on after death. Arguably the oldest and most orthodox of the three main traditions of Buddhism, the Theravada, which claims to follow the Buddha's original teachings, holds that the Buddha was human, not divine. Buddhism has been defined as a 'philosophy and psychology wrapped around a moral code of mind-training'. Many people follow it with the aim of self-transformation, by achieving altered states of consciousness through meditation.

However, Buddhism does not deny the supernatural – the Buddha accepted the existence on Earth of other buddhas before him and of spirit beings, good and evil. Buddhism also has a cosmology. Its universe consists of 31 realms, with hells at the bottom and, above the lower realms inhabited by beings such as animals and humans, a succession of heavens. These hells and heavens are not places of eternal damnation or reward, but temporary staging posts in the cyclical path of birth–death–rebirth.

The concept of 'samsara' – a Sanskrit word that, as it is understood in Buddhism, means not

Left Green Tara, a Buddhist saviour-goddess popular in Tibet, Nepal and Mongolia. She is the feminine counterpart of Avalokiteshvara, the bodhisattva of compassion.

reincarnation, but rebirth or 'rebecoming' – did not originate with the Buddha. It was an idea current in the religions of the 5th century BCE (during the Buddha's lifetime), and one that the Buddha accepted, along with a belief in karma. This is the theory that the balance of good and bad acts committed during a lifetime determines how a being is reborn – in the form of an animal, a human, or a god. These ideas form the core doctrine of Buddhism as a religion.

Mahayana, the second major Buddhist tradition, which emerged in the 1st century BCE, teaches that the Buddha is an earthly manifestation of a celestial buddha. Mahayana schools revere bodhisattvas – semi-divine figures who, through compassion and wisdom, dedicate themselves to the salvation of all sentient beings. Followers of the many Mahayana schools – which include Zen, Nichiren-derived teachings and most other schools popular in the West today – see Buddhism very much as a religion.

Tibetan (Vajrayana or Tantric) Buddhism, a third major tradition, which branched off from the Mahayana during the 1st millennium CE, developed mystic practices as a way of eliminating the fetters that tie beings to samsara. The blend of animism and symbolic Vajrayana ritual practices, employed in Tibetan Buddhism and its various schools and sects, make it fundamentally distinct from the Mahayana and Theravada traditions.

Right Two Japanese Zen monks practise Zazen (seated meditation). Eyes open, they face a blank wall in order to diminish the sensory world. In time, this practice overcomes the mind's defences against total concentration.

Above Thai bhikkhunis carry the Buddha's sacred remains, brought from Sri Lanka during Buddha Day celebrations in Bangkok. This annual festival honours the Buddha's birth, enlightenment and death.

Nevertheless, the goal of all Buddhists is to end the cycle of birth–death–rebirth and to eliminate suffering.

MEDITATION

To meditate is to calm the mind. The Buddha taught that meditation, combined with the observance of a moral code and the development of wisdom, is the path to enlightenment. Through meditation, Buddhists strive to experience what the Buddha experienced – loss of self and ego, the ability to see things as they really are, and the self-transformation that goes with the attainment of enlightenment. Meditation therefore offers potential for personal growth, spiritual advancement through the conquest of psychological obstacles, and the possibility of greater happiness.

This partly explains the great surge of interest in Buddhism in the Western world in the second half of the 20th century. The image of the Western follower of Buddhism is of a well-educated, often affluent person, who turns to Buddhism in a quest for inner calm.

HOW THIS BOOK IS ORGANIZED

This book begins with the birth of the Buddha and the stories that developed around this exceptional figure. The following chapter delves into the Buddha's teachings and explains the doctrines and concepts that have been central to Buddhism from the very start.

The third and fourth chapters discuss the spread of Buddhism over the ensuing centuries, both chronologically and geographically. The dissemination of Buddhism across the world, and its transformation as it engaged with new cultures, is explored, all the way to the 21st century. The final, fifth chapter looks in more detail at the separation of Buddhist philosophy into distinct traditions, schools and sects over time.

TIMELINE

FROM THE BUDDHA'S LIFETIME DURING THE 5TH CENTURY BCE, THIS TIMELINE SHOWS THE EVOLUTION OF BUDDHISM AND ITS SPREAD THROUGH ASIA DURING THE 1ST MILLENNIUM TO ITS EVENTUAL ESTABLISHMENT IN THE HIMALAYAN KINGDOMS.

6th century BCE
- Life of the Buddha Shakyamuni, according to traditional sources.

5th century BCE
- Life of the Buddha Shakyamuni, according to modern sources.
- First Buddhist Council, held at Rajagriha, codifies the rules of the Sangha and establishes the Buddhist canon by oral tradition.

4th century BCE
- Second Buddhist Council is held at Vaishali.

3rd century BCE
- The Sangha splits into Sthaviravada and Mahasamghika schools, which later subdivide into smaller schools.
- Ashoka ascends the throne of India's Mauryan empire in 268. He converts to Buddhism, establishes the first Buddhist state and sends missionaries across the known world.
- Ashoka convenes the Third Buddhist Council (c.250).
- Ashoka's son Mahinda heads the first Buddhist mission to Sri Lanka.

2nd century BCE
- Buddhist missionaries reach South-east Asia and convert the Mon and Lao peoples.
- Emergence of the Theravada tradition.

1st century BCE
- The *Tripitaka*, the Buddhist canon, is written down in Pali by monks in Sri Lanka.

- Buddhist monks follow trading caravans into Central Asia along the Silk Route.
- Emergence of the Mahayana tradition and the *Prajñaparamita*, or 'Perfection of Wisdom' sutras.

1st century CE
- Buddhism enters China.

100s
- The Buddhist Emperor Kanishka expands the Kushan empire into Central Asia.
- An Shigao, a Parthian monk, crosses Central Asia into China, where he translates Buddhist texts into Chinese.
- The *Mulamadhyamakakarika* is written by the philosopher Nagarjuna.
- Emergence of the Madhyamaka school.

200s
- Buddhist monasteries are founded at Taxila, an ancient centre of traditional learning situated in Gandhara, in north-western India.
- Emperor Kanishka convenes the Fourth Buddhist Council in Gandhara.

300s
- Emergence of the Yogacara school.
- Chinese pilgrims visit India in search of Buddhist scriptures.
- Chinese Mahayana monks reach Korea in 372.
- Vasubandhu, founder of the Yogacara school, writes a

critical commentary on the *Abhidharma* of the Sarvastivadin tradition in Kashmir.
- The first Chinese Buddhist schools are founded.

400s
- Pure Land Buddhism becomes prominent in China.
- Nalanda flourishes as a seat of Buddhist learning.
- The Chinese pilgrim Faxian travels to India in search of Buddhist texts.
- Buddhaghosa, an Indian monk and scholar, writes commentaries on Theravada texts in Sri Lanka.
- The White Huns invade northern India c.440. Buddhism on the Indian subcontinent begins to decline.
- The Khmer kingdom in Cambodia expands.
- Bamiyan, where monks have carved two colossal Buddha statues into a cliff-face, becomes a flourishing centre of Buddhism.

500s
- Bodhidharma, an Indian monk, transmits teachings of Chan Buddhism to China.
- Monks are appointed to political positions in China, and Buddhism is diffused throughout the state.
- The Tiantai sect emerges.
- Mahayana monks establish Buddhism in Japan.
- The Buddhist kingdoms of Dvaravati and Haripunchai are founded by the Mon in South-east Asia.

600s
- The Chinese pilgrim Xuanzang journeys to India in search of Buddhist scriptures.
- The Tang dynasty (618–907) introduces a 'golden age' of Chinese Buddhism.
- The Chan meditative school is founded.
- Buddhism first reaches Tibet.
- The first Buddhist monasteries are founded in Bhutan.
- Ho-ling, a Buddhist state, occupies central Java from 640.
- Arab armies invade Bactria and Gandhara.
- Tantric Buddhism emerges from the Mahayana school.

700s
- The Vajrayana tradition develops as a form of Tantric Buddhism at Nalanda, now an international Buddhist university.
- Buddhism becomes the official religion of Tibet.
- Samye monastery is founded in Tibet.
- The states of Srivijaya and Mataram in Malaysia and Indonesia have become centres of Mahayana learning. Their rulers build Borobudur on the island of Java.

800s
- Zen Buddhism emerges in Japan from the teachings of Chinese Chan masters.
- Tribal groups from the Buddhist kingdom of Nanzhao, around modern Yunnan in China, begin migrating into South-east Asia.

- The Burmese found the kingdom of Bagan, which becomes a centre of Theravada study.
- King Indravarman II founds a Mahayana Buddhist dynasty in the kingdom of Champa in central Vietnam.

900s
- Vikramashila in north-eastern India becomes the centre for Tantric Buddhism.
- Ladakh becomes a sanctuary for Tibetan Buddhists fleeing persecution.
- The first Chinese Buddhist canon is compiled in 983.

1000s
- Atisha, a monk from Nalanda, translates Sanskrit texts into Tibetan. The Tibetan schools of Buddhism emerge.
- The Ly dynasty establishes a Buddhist state in Vietnam, where Chan Buddhism prevails.

1100s
- Muslim armies invade and conquer northern India.
- Khmer King Jayavarman VII completes the great city of Angkor Thom.

1200s
- Kublai Khan makes Buddhism the court religion of Tibet, now part of the Mongol empire, in 1253.
- The Buddhist kingdom of Sukhothai is founded by an alliance of Thai chiefdoms.

Far left The Buddha in parinirvana, *3rd century BCE, Isurumuniya temple, Anuradhapura, Sri Lanka;* **top left** *Ananda temple, 11th–12th centuries, Bagan, Burma (Myanmar);* **top middle** The Tale of Musashibo Benkei, *15th century;* **top right** *Young monks chanting during a festival at Bangalore, India, 21st century.*

1300s
- Buddhist Shan people found the kingdoms of Ava in Burma (Myanmar), Lanna and Ayutthaya in Thailand, and Lan Xang in Laos.
- Indonesia is rapidly converting to Islam.

1400s
- The monk Tsongkhapa founds Ganden monastery outside Lhasa in 1409.
- The first edition of the Tibetan Buddhist canon is compiled.
- Buddhism in Vietnam begins to decline under the Le dynasty.

1500s
- Altan Khan founds an independent Buddhist kingdom in Mongolia.
- Burmese kings reunite Burma and forge a Buddhist empire in South-east Asia.

1600s
- The 5th Dalai Lama unites Tibet under the Geluk school, which was founded in the 15th century by Tsongkhapa.
- Tibetan lamas establish Buddhist monarchies in Bhutan and Sikkim.

CHAPTER 1

THE BUDDHA

The historical Buddha, Siddhartha Gautama, was born in India in the 5th century BCE. During the 1st century BCE, the story of his life was written down in the Pali language by monks in Sri Lanka. By that time, the facts of the Buddha's life had been overlaid with folk tales and religious symbolism, so the story that has come down to us contains much myth.

From central India to Central Asia and eastern China, the life of the Buddha is depicted in paintings made by Buddhist monks on the walls of remote caves. As an act of religious merit and to provide teaching aids, they portrayed scenes from the Buddha's life that had been recalled after his death by his disciples. The oldest paintings, at Ajanta in India's Maharashtra province, date from the 2nd century BCE.

Since the 19th century, archaeologists and historians have tried to determine the historical facts behind the story of the Buddha, and they have made many revealing discoveries regarding the origins of Buddhism. However, the 2,500-year-old chronicle of the Buddha's life remains not so much a historical record as an allegory – a story that can be read in many different ways and that is believed by millions of Buddhists to reveal universal truths about the mind, life, death and cosmology.

Opposite A novice Buddhist monk presents an offering of flowers to a Buddha head carved into a tree at Wat Phra Mahathat, Ayutthaya, Thailand. The majority of Thai people are adherents of Buddhism.

Above A scene from the Jataka Tales, a series of stories about the previous life of the Buddha. In this Indonesian relief, Siddhartha Gautama rides in a royal carriage from one palace to another.

INDIA BEFORE THE BIRTH OF THE BUDDHA

THE HISTORICAL BUDDHA, SIDDHARTHA GAUTAMA, WAS BORN INTO A SOCIETY THAT REVERBERATED WITH RELIGIOUS IDEAS. THE ANCIENT RELIGION OF THE BRAHMANS WAS IN DECLINE, BUT BRAHMANISM WAS SPAWNING RADICAL NEW SECTS, INCLUDING JAINISM.

The Buddha lived during the 5th century BCE, in India. The Indus Civilization cities of Harappa and Mohenjo-daro, which flourished in the north-west during the Indian Bronze Age, had declined more than 1,000 years earlier, and many once-nomadic tribal groups had spread across the subcontinent. They settled in agricultural communities called *janapadas*, which evolved over the centuries into small kingdoms and city-states.

THE OLDEST RELIGION
The first religious scriptures, the Vedas, emerged as a Sanskrit oral tradition in *c.*1500BCE. The elite Brahmans, whose priestly religion followed instructions for carrying out various rites described in the Vedic Brahmana scriptures, transmitted their knowledge from father to son. Only they knew how to conduct the rituals, which involved fire, the sacred drink known as 'soma' and the slaughter of many animals.

Brahmanism was an early form of Hinduism, and left its mark on Hindu society in the rigid caste system. The four main castes were the Brahmans (priests, teachers and scholars), the Kshatriyas (warriors and kings), the Vaisyas (traders) and the Sudras (farmers, herders, artisans and others).

THE GREAT NATIONS
By the 6th century BCE, the northern *janapadas* had coalesced into 16 or more large states called *mahajanapadas*, or 'great nations',

Above Scenes from the Mahabharata, *one of the two major ancient Hindu epics, are depicted on the walls of many Hindu temples. The bas-reliefs shown above adorn the walls of Angkor Wat in Cambodia.*

governed by elite groups or dynasties of kings. By 500BCE, rivalry and fighting had reduced the *mahajanapadas* to four. Two great epic poems in Sanskrit, the *Ramayana* and the *Mahabharata*, describe wars among the kingdoms that inhabited the Gangetic plain. They are part of the Hindu canon and are thought to have been transmitted as an oral tradition for centuries before they were written down starting in 400BCE.

The kings of Maghada, a *mahajanapada* south of the Ganges (in modern Bihar), had raised armies and conquered surrounding *janapadas*. Mahavira, the sage who reformed and revivified the ancient religion of Jainism, was born in the town of Vaishali in this north-eastern Indian state sometime during the first half of

Left The birth of Mahavira, the Jain Tirthankara, or leader, is depicted in this illustration from the Kalpasutra, *a text first written toward the end of the 5th century* BCE, *which recounts the story of his life.*

Above This 17th-century illustration depicts a scene from the Ramayana, *one of the two great epics of India. The poem recounts the story of Rama, a legendary king in ancient India and an important deity in Hinduism.*

the 6th century BCE. Probably around 30 years after the birth of Mahavira, the Buddha was born in northern Maghada.

NEW RELIGIONS

The 5th and 6th centuries BCE saw many new sects challenge the power of the Brahmans. Of these, the two that had the greatest impact were Buddhism and Jainism. Their ideas were a radical departure from the orthodox views of the time. Many rejected the animal sacrifice that was central to Brahmanism. Mahavira and the Buddha taught non-violence toward all other living creatures as a central tenet, the Jains believing that every thing, even inanimate objects, has a soul. Both sects also rejected the need to worship deities.

They also shared many other beliefs, among them the concept of karma – that moral decisions and actions individuals take today determine their destiny. While the Brahmans imparted the sacred knowledge of the Vedas only to privileged castes, Jainism and Buddhism taught that people were responsible for their own spiritual destiny.

Their ideas had more in common with Hinduism, which interpreted the concluding Veda scriptures, the *Upanishads*. These focused on meditation as a means of merging one's spiritual self with the Ultimate Reality. The concept of samsara, the cycle of birth-death-rebirth, to which every soul is subject until it attains moksha, or release, also first appears in the *Upanishads*.

Right Images of meditating yogis have been found by archaeologists excavating the ruins of Harappa and Mohenjo-daro, cities of the Indus Civilization in India, which lasted from about the 3rd to the 2nd millennium BCE.

THE BUDDHA'S BIRTH

THE BUDDHA WAS BORN IN THE 5TH CENTURY BCE IN THE FAR NORTH OF INDIA (MODERN-DAY NEPAL). THE STORY OF HIS BIRTH HAS BEEN EMBELLISHED BY FOLKLORE AND MYTHOLOGY, AND THERE ARE MANY LEGENDS SURROUNDING HIS CONCEPTION AND BIRTH.

Siddhartha Gautama, who became known as the historical Buddha, was born in what is now southern Nepal in *c*.485BCE. His traditional birth date is earlier – some sources say 624BCE and others 566 or 563BCE – but scholars who have recently studied the chronologies of the Buddha and his contemporaries conclude that if, as the texts state, he lived to the age of 80, he must have died sometime between 410 and 400BCE.

There is little historical evidence for the events of the Buddha's life as recorded in the scriptures. The latter were first written down during the 1st century BCE in Pali, an ancient Indian vernacular, but historians are unable to separate fact from fiction in the stories of the Buddha's life told in either the Pali canon or later Buddhist texts. Over centuries, the accounts were coloured by mythology and laden with symbolism, and different versions of the Buddha's story – all a mixture of scripture, legend and folklore – are told in different places. The story of the Buddha's life, as traditionally recounted, is outlined over the following pages.

THE BUDDHA'S ANCESTRY

Siddhartha Gautama was born into the Shakya clan and is often known as Shakyamuni, 'the sage of the Shakyas'. Although he is said to have been a king's son, the Shakyas were in fact governed not by a monarch but by a small council, perhaps of elders.

Above The Buddha is said to have sprung from Mahamaya's right side, where he was caught in a golden net by mythical beings called *devas*.

The clan belonged to the Kshatriya, or warrior caste, and its territory centred on Kapilavastu on the northern edge of the state of Maghada. Whether or not Siddhartha's family were of royal descent, it is thought that his

EXCAVATING BUDDHA'S BIRTHPLACE

During the 1st millennium CE, pilgrims from countries as distant as China, Tibet, Burma and Indonesia braved sea and mountain crossings to visit Lumbini, birthplace of the Buddha. However, pilgrimages ceased after the 13th-century Muslim conquest of India, when Buddhist sites and monuments were sacked and razed. The site was abandoned and forgotten, and even its name had changed by 1896, when Dr Alois A. Fuehrer, a German archaeologist, discovered an ancient stone pillar inscribed with a homage to the Buddha's birth. The pillar was identified as one erected at Lumbini in the 3rd century BCE by Ashoka, the great Indian emperor of the Mauryan dynasty. The site was excavated and pilgrims flocked to it. In the early 1990s, Japanese archaeologists unearthed a stone slab said to mark the exact spot of the Buddha's birth, and found a bas-relief that portrayed Mahamaya giving birth. In 1997, Lumbini was made a World Heritage Site. Work continues on landscaping and conserving the many ancient buildings and the thousands of artefacts found during excavations.

Left The emperor Ashoka made a pilgrimage to Lumbini in about 250BCE and erected a stone pillar there. Centuries later, lightning broke the pillar in half.

father, who is traditionally called Shuddhodana, and his mother, Mahamaya, may have been nobles, because the records emphasize Shuddhodana's wealth.

BIRTH OF THE BUDDHA

Some versions of the Buddha's birth story claim that he was conceived when his mother dreamt of his descent from heaven in the form of a white elephant. The dream denoted not only the purity of the Buddha's conception, but also that he would become a Universal Monarch – an upright and benevolent world ruler – or a buddha, that is, a spiritually enlightened being. (In Indian mythology, the white elephant was a sign of royal power.)

Ten months later, Mahamaya travelled from Kapilavastu with her retinue of women to give birth at her mother's house in nearby Devadaha, as was the

Right Legend recounts that Mahamaya, the Buddha's mother, conceived during a dream, in which a white, four-tusked elephant penetrated her right side and entered her womb. The dream symbolizes the purity of the Buddha's conception.

custom. On the day of the full moon, the party stopped to rest in a grove of sal trees in the lovely Lumbini Park, where Mahamaya bathed in the Pushkarni Pool. Afterward, catching hold of a sal branch that miraculously swept down within her reach, and facing east, she gave birth.

Many miracles are said to have attended the birth: the newly reborn infant looked in each of the eight cardinal directions, then took seven steps to the east,

Above The Pushkarni Pool, the sacred tank in which Mahamaya is said to have purified herself before giving birth, can still be seen among the ruins at serene Lumbini.

symbolizing the future path of Buddhism, while a lotus flower, signifying enlightenment, sprang up at each of his steps. In a godlike voice, the child is said to have proclaimed, "I am the Leader of the World; I am the Guide of the World. This is my final birth."

EARLY LIFE

NAMED SIDDHARTHA ('HE WHO ATTAINS SUCCESS AND PROSPERITY')
BY HIS FATHER, SIDDHARTHA GAUTAMA IS PORTRAYED AS A
COSSETED AND PROTECTED INFANT, BUT ALSO AS A CHILD WITH
EXTRAORDINARY ABILITIES AND UNUSUAL SENSITIVITIES.

Many tales of the Buddha's birth and early life were recorded in the *Lalitavistara Sutra*, a text believed to have been written around the 3rd century CE, some 700 years after his death.

"Legend is often a poetic form of history, and lifts the story to a plane above the accidents of time and place", wrote Christmas Humphreys, founder of Britain's Buddhist Society, in *Buddhism*, published in 1951. He interpreted the Buddha's life as it is presented in the Pali canon and later scriptures as a hagiography (a religious biographical account), a great symbolic story, like that of Jesus Christ or Moses. He believed that the writers of the scriptures were

more concerned with conveying the meaning of the big events in the Buddha's life than their chronological accuracy and that their aim was to relate a wider truth than could be told by an accurate historical record. Thus, everything in the Buddha's life may be read as an allegory – "the mystery story", as Christmas Humphreys put it, "of the evolution of man from birth to final attainment".

CHILDHOOD

Five days after Siddhartha's birth, an ascetic and seer called Ashita came down from his mountain retreat to see the child. Renowned for his supernatural gifts, Ashita had already seen many portents of a great event, such as a vision of gods in the sky, around the tenth month of Mahayama's pregnancy. When he saw Siddhartha's body, the sage recognized all the signs of

Above A Nepalese gilded bronze statue of Mahayama, the moment before she gave birth to the Buddha, dating from the 18th century. Seven days after her delivery she died, symbolizing her purity. The young Siddhartha was cared for by her devoted sister.

a *mahapurusha,* or 'Great Man': the 32 major signs – for example, tightly curled hair circling to the right on his head – and the 80 minor signs. Ashita cried to think that he would be gone when Siddhartha began to reveal his wisdom.

Despite the relative modesty of the Sakka state, the Pali chroniclers emphasize Siddhartha's luxurious upbringing and his education in the 64 spiritual arts, as well as in skills such as archery and horsemanship. They also describe his heroic qualities – how as a youth he defeated all in an archery competition and how, during a ceremony, he fell into a deep meditative trance, although he was untrained in meditation.

The young Siddhartha displayed unusual sensitivities. The scriptures highlight his kindness

Below This ancient stone relief depicts the visit of the sage Ashita to the infant Buddha, and his revelation to his parents, Shuddhodana and Mahayama, that their newborn son would become a great leader.

to animals and recount an incident when he saved a swan that his cruel cousin Devadatta had shot.

Forewarned by the sage Ashita's prediction that Siddhartha might turn to the *shramana* tradition of wandering ascetics and leave the Shakya clan in search of spiritual enlightenment, his father resolved to protect him against life's uglier realities, such as ageing and decay. The scriptures recount that members of the household who fell ill were kept away from Siddhartha, and that gardeners even removed flowers before they began to wilt.

MARRIAGE

At 16, Siddhartha, now of marriageable age, was presented to eligible young women of his clan and won the hand of the desirable Yashodhara by defeating rival suitors in a contest of strength and martial prowess. Siddhartha married Yashodhara and the couple lived in luxury,

THE SEARCH FOR KAPILAVASTU

After the Buddha's birthplace, Lumbini, was rediscovered in 1896, archaeologists, guided by chronicles written in the 5th and 7th centuries by the Chinese pilgrims Faxian and Xuanzang, identified a site 25km (16 miles) west of the village of Tilaurokot as Kapilavastu, the place where Siddhartha Gautama grew up.

Excavations led by Dr Robin Coningham and Dr Armin Schmidt of the University of Bradford, England, began in 1997, and the team identified moated fortifications, streets and houses, and found jewellery, toys and pottery shards dating from before the 5th century BCE.

Piprawha, a village 93km (58 miles) south of Lumbini in Uttar Pradesh, India, may have been the site of the old Kapilavastu city, before it was moved, or part of Kapilavastu's territory. Excavations of the site by the Archaeological Survey of India during the 1970s located several stupas and a building some believe to be the palace of Shuddhodana. Like many other places associated with the Buddha's life, the site has become a focus of pilgrimage.

moving their household as the seasons changed among three palaces built for them by Shuddhodana in a vast enclosed park on his estates. Yashodhara later gave birth to a son, Rahula. According to some scriptures, Siddhartha had four wives, of whom Yashodhara was the second, and was surrounded by sensual pleasures.

Below Drawing a bow was one of the feats Yashodhara's suitors had to accomplish in order to win her hand in marriage.

THE GREAT DEPARTURE

SUPERNATURAL BEINGS CALLED DEVAS APPEARED AT SPECIAL POINTS DURING SIDDHARTHA GAUTAMA'S LIFE. IN HIS YOUTH, THEY MADE HIM AWARE OF HUMAN SUFFERING TO ENSURE THAT HE FULFILLED HIS DESTINY: TO SEARCH FOR A WAY TO OVERCOME IT.

Above Siddhartha Gautama's great encounter with old age, sickness and death showed him that his perception of life had been flawed. His youth, health and happiness would not last, but, inevitably, he would grow old, become ill and die.

One day, the Buddha's story continues, Siddhartha was riding in his chariot beyond his father's estate when, approaching the city, he passed an old man shuffling along, bent over a stick, weak and vulnerable. Startled, Siddhartha turned for an explanation to Channa, his charioteer, who told him that the man was aged, and explained that old age, with its infirmities, is the lot of all humanity. Siddhartha returned home, but his thoughts troubled him, preventing him from enjoying the pleasures of his life.

The next day, he drove out again. This time the devas placed in his path a man afflicted with disease. Siddhartha's life had been so sheltered that he knew nothing of illness, but he learned from his charioteer that disease and pain are the burden of humankind. Saddened, he returned home.

Below This illustration from a Chinese sutra (scripture) depicts the Buddha's dissatisfaction with his comfortable life and his decision to leave home to live as an ascetic in the forest.

The following day, Siddhartha set out once more, and at the city gate, he saw a corpse that was being carried to the funeral pyre by grieving mourners. Channa informed him that death is the ultimate, inescapable fate of all living beings.

THE *SHRAMANA*

Distraught, but still wanting to learn about life, Siddhartha made a fourth journey with Channa. This time they passed a poor man who, though he was begging for alms, seemed calm, self-possessed and free from malice. Channa explained that this man was a *shramana*, a wandering ascetic who had renounced the attachments of society and had gone into the world alone to live a homeless existence in search of spiritual fulfilment.

Shuddhodana was anxious that his only son should gain influence in society and become a leader, and he had filled Siddhartha's life with entertainments and other distractions. He also hoped that Siddhartha's newborn son, Rahula

(the name means 'tie' or 'impediment'), would bind him to his home and family. However, Siddhartha was deeply impressed by the demeanour of the renunciant he had met and was becoming increasingly disillusioned with his own life of ease.

RENUNCIATION

Among many religious and philosophical trends that arose in India during the 1st millennium BCE was the *shramana* movement. These 'wanderers', many of whom rejected the beliefs of the Brahmans and their rigid adherence to sacrifices described in the Vedas, were forging new beliefs and philosophies. Foremost among them was Mahavira, the reformer of Jainism and a near-contemporary of the Buddha. Many *shramanas* sought to end the cycle of birth-death-rebirth by achieving purity of the soul, or oneness with the Ultimate Reality. *Shramanas* engaged in public debates with orthodox Brahmans and with each other on these issues.

By the 5th century BCE, it had become an established tradition in northern India that, having performed their social duty by marrying and supporting a family, men would renounce family life and caste privileges and seek enlightenment through study and meditation and by living the austere life of a mendicant.

FINAL DEPARTURE

On Siddhartha's 29th birthday, beautiful dancing girls entertained him until he fell asleep. Later that night, he awoke to find that the women asleep around him were no longer so attractive. He was overcome with revulsion at his pointless existence, and his mind filled with thoughts of impermanence, suffering and death.

The idea that a person's soul is reborn after death to live another life was a widely held belief at that time, but to Siddhartha, the prospect of repeated lives and deaths now seemed abhorrent. He therefore resolved to abandon his home and family to search for a way to end this cycle of suffering by living the meditative existence of a *shramana*.

Before leaving, he visited his sleeping wife and son. Resisting the temptation to hold Rahula and awaken them both, he vowed to revisit his son after his enlightenment. He then left his home, riding his horse, Kanthaka, with Channa, his charioteer, clinging to its tail. Devas intervened to silence the sound of the horse's hooves.

Heading south-east, the men reached the River Anoma. There, Siddhartha cut off his hair, exchanged his rich apparel for a mendicant's garb and returned his horse and charioteer to his father as evidence of his renunciation.

Above Seated on his horse Kanthaka, Gautama Siddhartha takes the first step on his path to enlightenment, as shown in this 19th-century painting of the Great Departure from Wat Ratchasitaram in Thon Buri, Bangkok.

Below By abandoning his fine clothes and jewellery and cutting off his hair, Siddhartha renounced his privileged life and signalled that he would follow the path of an itinerant mendicant.

THE AWAKENING

SIDDHARTHA'S QUEST WAS TO END THE ETERNAL CYCLE OF DEATH–
BIRTH–REBIRTH AND THE SUFFERING OF ALL SENTIENT BEINGS, BUT
HE COULD NOT ACHIEVE ENLIGHTENMENT UNTIL HE HAD FOUND A
MIDDLE WAY BETWEEN HEEDLESS LUXURY AND ASCETIC SELF-DENIAL.

After cutting himself off from his family and making himself homeless, Siddhartha Gautama sought teachers. From the first, he learned the doctrine of the non-existence of all things, and from the second, he learned that there is neither consciousness nor unconsciousness. They taught him techniques such as slow beathing and holding the breath to help control the mind, but these, once learned, did not seem to bring him greater insight. The beliefs of these Brahmans did not resonate with him or help him find his real self. Moreover, he did not manage to conquer his cravings for food, sleep, sensual pleasure and sex.

Siddhartha joined a group of strict ascetics living in the open, quickly adopting a regime of fasting and meditation. He mastered all they knew, and achieved deep trancelike states, but the years of extreme asceticism had weakened him, and by this time he was wasting away. The 32 marks of the 'Great Man', noted at his birth, had disappeared from his body, and he almost died.

THE MIDDLE WAY

Siddhartha decided that asceticism was not the way to enlightenment. As he meditated in a forest beneath a banyan tree, a young mother, Sujata, offered him a bowl of milk rice. Sujata had been visiting the forest in order to supplicate a tree spirit for the gift of a son. Now pregnant, she

Left This 6th-century stele from China shows the enlightened Buddha as abhayadana, *the bestower of fearlessness, seated on a lotus, symbol of purification and enlightenment, with his disciples and bodhisattvas.*

Above Monks, princes and bodhisattvas surround the Buddha as he sits beneath the Bodhi tree in this 2nd-century BCE *Kushan stone relief carving in the Indian Museum at Sarnath.*

returned to give thanks with the rice and, mistaking Siddhartha for the tree spirit, she offered it to him. He accepted the gift, and divided it into 49 portions, on which he subsisted for 49 days. His strength returned and, with it, the bodily marks of the great man.

Below Assailed by the demons of Mara, whose name means 'killer', Siddhartha touched the Earth as a testament to his right to enlightenment. The Earth responded with a loud and vigorous tremor.

Disillusioned at his apparent loss of willpower, five disciples who had joined him went their separate ways and Siddhartha continued alone.

No one existed, Siddhartha realized, who could show him how to achieve enlightenment; he had to find his own way. He understood that this must be a 'middle way' between extremes of self-indulgence and asceticism. Keeping the body strong and healthy was one part of this; so too was cultivating attitudes of mind and behaviour that bring calm.

Working on putting these thoughts into practice, Siddhartha wandered toward the bank of the Niranjana River at Uruvela (now Bodhgaya in Bihar). Aware that the time of his enlightenment was near, he sat, facing east, beneath a pipal (sacred fig) tree, to meditate quietly, vowing to persist until he had attained spiritual awakening.

Below The reliefs at Borobudur in Indonesia tell stories of the Buddha's life from the Lalitavistara. *Here, Siddhartha Gautama bathes in the Niranjana River.*

MARA, 'THE EVIL ONE'

Mara is the name given to the ruler of the World of Desires, governor of the cycle of death and rebirth. Fearful that Siddhartha's enlightenment would illuminate his own shadowy realm, Mara struggled with him beneath the Bodhi tree. First, his demons taunted Siddhartha with fire and darkness, then his three beautiful daughters tried to distract Siddhartha from his meditations. But they failed.

In a final assault, Mara, as Lord of the World, claimed that Siddhartha's seat beneath the Bodhi tree and the gift of enlightenment were his by right. Siddhartha recalled the many compassionate deeds he had performed as proof of his own right to enlightenment. Mara called upon his demons, who shouted their support of their master's claim, then he challenged Siddhartha to find someone to testify to the truth of his words. In response, Siddhartha touched the Earth with his right hand, supplicating it to bear witness to his past acts of compassion.

ENLIGHTENMENT

As he meditated, he was attacked by the powers of Mara, the tempter, the deva or spirit associated with death and rebirth. Mara represents the forces of the mind that militate against liberation and enlightenment. Siddhartha refused to be disturbed by Mara's barbs, which turned to flowers in the face of his calm.

The Awakening took place in three phases. First, Siddhartha fell into progressively deeper stages of meditation; then he recalled his past lives and saw the past lives of others. Finally, he understood the Dharma, or law, the causes and effects that keep the cycle of death and rebirth in motion. From this point on, he was called the Buddha, 'the Awakened One'.

Below Sujata offered the meditating Siddhartha Gautama milk rice in a golden bowl. Since a monk may not keep any precious object, he threw the bowl into a river.

TURNING THE WHEEL OF THE DHARMA

THE SCRIPTURES MAKE CLEAR THAT THE BUDDHA, HAVING ATTAINED ENLIGHTENMENT, COULD HAVE LEFT THE WORLD FOREVER. INSTEAD, HE CHOSE TO REMAIN INCARNATE, IN ORDER TO TEACH THE LAW HE HAD DISCOVERED TO THOSE WHO WERE READY TO LISTEN.

After his awakening, the Buddha sat cross-legged in meditation beneath the pipal tree (the 'Bodhi' or 'Enlightenment' tree) at Uruvela for seven days. He then remained close to the tree for seven weeks as he contemplated his experience of enlightenment. During the third week, he walked up and down as he meditated. Today, stones at the Bodhgaya temple mark his footsteps.

During the fifth week, the Buddha turned his attention to the task of teaching the doctrine that had just been revealed to him. He had doubts about how successful he could be: "The truth remains hidden from him who is in the bondage of hate and desire," he mused. "Nirvana remains incomprehensible and mysterious to the vulgar, whose minds are beclouded with worldly interests. Should I preach the doctrine and mankind not comprehend it, it would bring me only fatigue and trouble." He was in half a mind to end his sojourn on Earth.

Above This 7th-century Tibetan mural shows the Buddha 'setting the Wheel of the Dharma in motion' by giving his First Sermon in the Deer Park at Isipatana, modern Sarnath.

At this point, a deity, Brahma Sahampati, appeared to the Buddha and urged him to teach. He received a vision of lotus flowers, some blooming above the water, others in bud, and some too far beneath the surface to flower. He realized that they were like people, and decided that those in the middle group – *shramanas* already on the path to enlightenment – would be most receptive to his message.

He ate his first meal since Sujata's offering of milk rice during the seventh week, when two foreign merchants approached and offered him food – a sign that the

Left The Buddha eats a meal after his awakening, from a bowl miraculously fashioned from four bowls of precious metals, presented to him by the guardian gods of each of the cardinal points.

Buddha had returned to human existence. He imparted his message to them, and the two men became his first lay followers.

THE SERMON IN THE DEER PARK

His 'divine eye' told the Buddha that the two *shramanas* who had taught him to meditate had died. But he also perceived that the five disciples who had separated themselves from him when he gave up the ascetic life were now in Isipatana (modern Sarnath, near the holy city of Varanasi). Having found them there, he instructed them that they must now call him 'Tathagata', a form of address reserved for those who have travelled the path to enlightenment.

The Buddha made this meeting the occasion for setting in motion the Wheel of the Dharma (his teaching of the law, or doctrine) by giving his first sermon in the Deer Park at Isipatana on the evening of the full moon in June/July.

He began by explaining why he had abandoned extreme asceticism, and how the path to enlightenment lies along the Middle Way. In conclusion, he elucidated the doctrine he had understood as a result of his enlightenment, beginning with the Four Noble Truths.

THE COMMUNITY

The five men, with their disciplined minds and bodies, were quickly able to understand the Buddha's explanation of the nature of reality and the truth. Five days later, he gave another sermon, this time on impermanence and the idea of the 'non-self'. One man rapidly attained enlightenment and the others soon followed. They became the first members of the first Buddhist Sangha, or monastic community.

THE DEER PARK AT SARNATH

The peaceful Deer Park at Isipatana, called Sarnath today, where the Buddha first taught and transmitted the Dharma and where the first Sangha (monastic community) was founded, became a sacred place of pilgrimage after his death. Stupas, shrines, viharas (monasteries) and temples were built. The Mauryan emperor Ashoka made a pilgrimage there during the 3rd century BCE, and erected a stupa to mark the spot where the Buddha is said to have given his first sermon, and a stone pillar with an inscription. During the Gupta empire, 4th–6th century CE, Ashoka's stupa, known as the Dhamekh stupa, which had by then been rebuilt and enlarged, was faced in beautifully carved stone, some sections of which survive.

During the 12th century, Turkish Muslims sacked and looted Isipatana and killed its monks. The site was later raided for building stone. It was revitalized after 19th-century archaeologists excavated an ancient brick stupa, dating from before the 3rd century BCE, ancient inscriptions, and a stone casket containing relics and precious stones. Later excavations revealed a vihara, a temple, with a magnificent large frieze, and hundreds of exquisite statues of the Buddha.

Below Sarnath is a peaceful spot full of stupas and other remains from the time of the Buddha. This photograph shows the main shrine at the site.

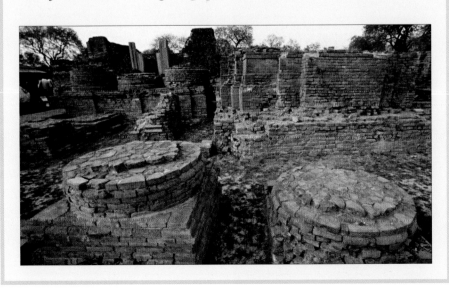

Above Meditating beside Muchalinda Lake six weeks after his enlightenment, the Buddha was sheltered from a storm by the Muchalinda, a naga, or snake spirit, which coiled around him.

THE BUDDHA'S TEACHINGS

FOR MORE THAN 40 YEARS, THE BUDDHA AND HIS FOLLOWERS
TRAVELLED THROUGHOUT EASTERN AND NORTHERN INDIA,
SPEAKING TO THE PEOPLE AND INSTRUCTING NEW CONVERTS IN THE
PATH TO ENLIGHTENMENT. HE ALSO PERFORMED MANY MIRACLES.

Above One year, the Buddha secretly ascended into the Heaven of the Thirty-three. There he found the reborn spirit of his dead mother. He stayed through a rainy season, teaching her, before descending a ladder to his followers waiting on Earth.

From a nucleus of six, the community that had formed around the Buddha at Isipatana (now Sarnath) quickly grew into a movement. One young convert was Yashas, a youth who, like Siddhartha Gautama years earlier, had realized the pointlessness of his comfortable existence. Yashas became the first lay person to join the Sangha and he went on to achieve enlightenment.

Yashas' father, likewise, became a lay follower, while his mother was the first female disciple. News of Yashas' enlightenment spread quickly, and more than 50 of the family's friends and acquaintances approached the Sangha and were eventually ordained. From

Below A 3rd-century Indian relief of the Buddha preaching, with women on the left and disciples in a seated meditation pose on the right.

this nucleus of adherents, the Buddha sent forth 60 to spread his teachings.

ON THE MOVE

The Sangha remained in Isipatana during the rainy season, when movement was difficult, then resumed the peripatetic life of a *shramana* group.

At Uruvela (now Bodhgaya), the Buddha approached a group of ascetics, the Kashyapa brothers and their more than 1,000 disciples, who were fire-worshippers. He persuaded their leader that fire-worship impeded their search for enlightenment because it did not free them from ignorance, craving and hatred. The brothers received his teaching and became converts.

Within a year of his awakening, the Buddha, accompanied by many monks, returned to his former home at Kapilavastu. Although his

family were initially shocked at his austere way of life, most of them eventually converted to his path. Many of the Shakya clan also became his followers.

The doctrine propounded by the Buddha was not restricted to people of particular classes or castes, unlike the religion of the Brahmans and others who followed the *Upanishads*. He shared the Dharma with all, from the barber Upali of the Sudra, or servant caste, to King Bimbisara of Rajagriha (modern Rajgir, Bihar) and his court. The Buddha's name spread, and many came to hear him preach.

THE FIRST MONASTERY

Followers of other religions and teachers sought out the Sangha while the monks rested in the Veluvana Bamboo Grove at Rajagriha, which had been given to them by King Bimbisara. Many of these *shramanas* were dissuaded from their extreme asceticism and were ordained.

Some time later, a rich merchant and convert, Anathapindika, invited the Buddha to his home

Left The Buddha spent long hours in meditation before he achieved enlightenment. This Tibetan thangka (painted or embroidered banner) shows him meditating with Mañjushri, the Bodhisattva of Wisdom, and Vajrapani, the Buddha's protector and guide.

SANSKRIT TERMS

arhat worthy one; a Buddhist or Jain who has gained insight into the true nature of existence and will not be reborn.

bhikkhu a fully ordained Buddhist monk. Nuns are bhikkhunis. (In Sanskrit, the corresponding terms are *bhikshu* and *bhikshuni*.)

Dharma the universal law, or truth, as proclaimed by the Buddha.

Sangha a Buddhist Order, or monastic community.

shramana a religious seeker; a person who avidly pursues spiritual knowledge, usually as a mendicant and homeless wanderer.

Tathagata the name the Buddha Shakyamuni used when referring to himself. The word literally means 'one who has thus come'.

at Shravasti, capital of Kosala, a *mahajanapada* bordering Maghada. A vihara (monastery) called Jetavana was founded there.

Jetavana became the home of the Sangha, and the Buddha gave most of his sermons and discourses there. The Buddha used his experience, gathered over several lifetimes, and his penetrating insight to make his teaching exactly suited to his students' capacities to understand the Dharma. His success was spectacular, since many travelled the path of enlightenment and became arhats. In time, Jetavana would also become the Buddha's final resting place.

GREAT MAGICAL WONDERS

The impact of the Buddha's teachings and his growing following aroused jealousy among other religious teachers. During the sixth year after his enlightenment, he was challenged by six leaders of other sects to a public debate in Shravasti. He announced that he would defeat them in the shade of a mango tree. He arrived to find all the mango trees cut down, but he cast a mango seed on the ground and a tree sprouted and grew tall.

The Buddha defeated the arguments of the teachers and made converts of them, then he performed 'twin miracles', making fire and water shoot out from his body. Finally, the Buddha projected simultaneous images of himself in four different postures. These and many other miraculous events in the Buddha's life became popular themes of Buddhist art in later centuries.

THE BUDDHA'S PASSING

IN HIS EIGHTIES, AND APPROACHING THE END OF HIS HUMAN LIFE, THE BUDDHA ENTERED A GROVE OF SAL TREES. THERE, SURROUNDED BY HIS DEVOTED MONKS, HE ACHIEVED PARINIRVANA — THE STATE OF ULTIMATE PEACE THAT FOLLOWS THE DEATH OF A BUDDHA.

Above Devadatta made three attempts on the Buddha's life: he sent assassins to kill him, then pushed a boulder over a cliff as the Buddha walked below. Finally, he set a raging elephant in his path, but, as shown here, the Buddha pacified the beast with his kindness.

The ancient texts tell few stories about the Buddha's last years, but the Pali *Mahaparinibbana Sutta*, or 'Sermon of the Great Passing', recounts in some detail the events of his last three months. Tradition says that the Buddha lived until he was 80, and by then his sect, although still small and scarcely known outside northern India, was established and respected for its doctrine of compassion and its strict precepts.

ATTACKS ON THE BUDDHA
The Buddha was challenged on several occasions during his later years, not only by the leaders of rival sects, but also by two beings, who, some commentators have theorized, symbolize the dark elements of the psyche that militate against change, success and liberation. One was Devadatta, the Buddha's cousin, who was ordained a monk but is portrayed as consumed with egotism and jealousy. One text tells how he tried, unsuccessfully, to take over the Sangha. Overcome with hatred and rivalry, he made three attempts to kill the Buddha. Finally, he caused a split among the monks.

Mara, 'the Evil One', had attacked Siddhartha during his spiritual awakening and tried to dissuade him from taking the gift of the Dharma to the people. As the Buddha approached the last months of his life, Mara appeared to him again, tempting him to free himself from human pain, to enter nirvana there and then. Until his task was complete, the Buddha replied, he would not seek release.

THE DEATH OF THE BUDDHA
During his final year, the Buddha travelled with Ananda, one of his chief disciples, who was his cousin and personal attendant of 25 years, through the northern states. In Maghada, he experienced a brief illness. Afterward, Ananda asked who would lead the Sangha when he had gone. The Sangha needs no central authority but the Dharma, was the reply, "...be ye islands unto yourselves....Hold fast to the Dharma as an island.... Look not for refuge to anyone besides yourselves...."

At Vaishali (near Pataliputra, modern Patna), the Buddha made his final address to his disciples. He urged them not to take his teachings on trust but rather to gain their knowledge directly, by experiencing the truth of them personally through meditation. He also appealed to them not to keep the joy of enlightenment to themselves, but to share it with the world.

Left The Buddha lay down on his right side between two sal trees, with his head facing the north, and withdrew into a meditative trance. Sacred texts state that at the moment of his passing, a violent tremor shook the Earth.

Right The young monks who were still searching for liberation and enlightenment expressed grief at the Buddha's passing, and at the loss of his guidance and teaching.

Travelling on, he stopped to dine with Cunda, a blacksmith, who prepared a special dish that is said to have contained pork. Afterward, the party continued northward and came to a grove of sal trees near Kushinara. The Buddha, ill with dysentery, caused, perhaps, by his last meal, lay down among the trees.

During his last hours, the Buddha asked his disciples whether they had any doubts about the Dharma. None did. He reassured the weeping Ananda that he would soon experience enlightenment. Then he uttered his final words, "Decay is inherent in all component things! Work out your own salvation with diligence."

Finally, he entered the highest states of consciousness and passed into parinirvana – the final nirvana of one who has experienced enlightenment, the final release from the cycle of rebirth.

BUDDHAS PAST AND FUTURE

'Tathagata', which means 'one who has thus come' or 'one who has thus gone', expresses the belief that Buddha Shakyamuni (the name given to Siddhartha Gautama) was the 25th in a line of buddhas, each of whom had resided on Earth for one historical cycle to teach the Dharma. The Jataka Tales are stories about the Buddha's previous lives. In one, Buddha Shakyamuni describes his encounter with Buddha Dipankara, whose admirable qualities so impressed him that he decided to cultivate them in himself.

When the current historical era has ended, Buddhists believe that a new buddha will be born, attain enlightenment, teach the Dharma and live a human life. That buddha is the Bodhisattva Natha (meaning 'Protector'), who will be born as the Bodhisattva Maitreya. Future buddhas reside in the Tushita heaven, one of many heavens in Buddhist teaching. In China, over the last two millennia, many individuals have declared themselves to be the Bodhisattva Maitreya, and their claims and cults have sparked political rebellions.

Right According to Buddhist teachings, the Bodhisattva Maitreya, depicted in this 2nd-century BCE sculpture, will succeed the Buddha Shakyamuni as the next buddha. He is an enlightened being who will, in a future age, come to Earth to teach the Dharma.

STUPAS

The buildings most closely associated with buddhism, stupas are shrines originally built to house relics of the Buddha, and are symbols of his mind and the path to enlightenment. Many are expressions of the finest architecture and art.

Before his death, the Buddha gave instructions for his funeral. His body was to be accorded the honours of a world ruler – washed, embalmed and carried in a coffin to the funeral pyre, and his ashes were to be buried in a stupa (a burial mound) at a crossroads.

With all the respect due to the ruler who brought the Dharma to the world, the funeral rites were carried out according to his wishes by the princes of Malla, the *mahajanapada,* where the Buddha died, and were accompanied by processions, music and dancing.

Disputes broke out among neighbouring rulers as to where the Buddha's ashes should rest.

Below These chortens (stupas) were erected in the mountains of Ladakh above the 17th-century Hemis gompa, *the largest and wealthiest monastery in Ladakh.*

To avoid conflict, they were divided among eight claimants. Each one erected a stupa over the relics given, and these stupas were venerated by the Buddha's followers.

THE FIRST STUPAS

Stupas did not originate with the Buddha, however. Archaeology has shown that from early Vedic times in India, the dead were cremated and their incinerated remains buried with ceremony in a funerary mound, known as a stupa.

The Buddha's wishes to be buried as a *chakravartin,* or world ruler, recall the tumuli at Lauriya Nandangarh, Bihar, dating from the 700s BCE. These grave mounds are so large that they are thought to belong to kings. Archaeologists believe that a wooden post at the apex of the dome may have supported a parasol, which was seen as a symbol of royal authority.

Above A hair of the Buddha is said to lie beneath this rock, which forms part of the Kyaiktiyo stupa in Burma. Pilgrims have covered it in gold leaf.

Buddhist stupas, built in brick and stone, have a cupola – representing the dome of heaven – which rests on a cylindrical base. Rising from the centre of the dome (or *anda,* literally 'egg', signifying the cycle of rebirth) is a *harmika* (platform), sheltered by a *chattra* (parasol), the two denoting enlightenment. Stupa architecture embodies many layers of complex Buddhist religious symbolism, so a stupa becomes a meditative focus for adherents walking the circumambulatory path around it.

Stupas are believed to radiate a beneficial influence over their locality, and they attract pilgrims. During the 3rd century BCE, the emperor Ashoka, a Buddhist convert, is said to have collected the Buddha's relics from seven of the eight original stupas, divided them into 84,000 portions, and vowed to send each portion to a different part of his empire and erect a stupa there. He had stupas erected all

Left The Buddha's all-seeing eyes gaze in all directions across the Kathmandu Valley in Nepal from the gilded and whitewashed Swayambhunath stupa. This stupa is said to have been built on the spot where a miraculous lotus was planted by an antecedent of the Buddha Shakyamuni. Between the eyes is the Sanskrit number one, symbolizing the single Buddhist path to enlightenment, and above it is the third eye, signifying wisdom.

Below The parasol of the 12th-century Kiri (White) vihara soars above the ancient city of Polonnaruwa, Sri Lanka's former capital. Its unrestored whitewashed plaster survived seven centuries of abandonment after the collapse of the Polonnaruwa kingdom.

over India and they became centres of pilgrimage and veneration. Large numbers were destroyed by later Hindu and Islamic dynasties, but many remain.

ARTISTIC TRADITIONS

Many early stupas are unadorned, but beautiful decoration, in the form of reliefs, sculpture, inscriptions, paintings and *torana*, or entrance gates, is a feature of later buildings. Artists expressed the architectural, artistic and folk traditions they knew in these religious structures. Thus, stupas contributed to the artistic development of many Asian countries where Buddhism spread and evolved. In Sri Lanka, the Himalayan kingdoms, and the countries of Central, East and South-east Asia, the stupa took on new architectural forms and different symbolism. 'Stupa' is a Sanskrit word. In Sri Lanka, it is called a dagoba, in Tibet a chorten, and in Thailand a chedi.

From the Buddha's time, stupas have been built to enshrine the relics of respected monks and teachers; over the last century, some have also been erected in the West.

BUDDHIST PILGRIMAGES

IN THE BUDDHA'S LAST DISCOURSE BEFORE HIS DEATH, HE URGED HIS FOLLOWERS TO MAKE PILGRIMAGES TO THE PLACES OF HIS BIRTH, ENLIGHTENMENT, FIRST SERMON AND DEATH. TO THESE FOUR HOLY SITES, BUDDHISTS LATER ADDED FOUR MORE 'GREAT PLACES'.

Above Rajagriha (modern Rajgir) was the capital of the kingdom of Maghada during the time of the Buddha, who preached many important sermons there.

Pilgrimage has had a significant place in the practice of Buddhism since at least the 3rd century BCE, when Ashoka the Great visited the Buddhist holy sites that lay within his empire. From ancient times, Buddhists visited the 'Eight Great Places' included in the texts and commentaries. After the 12th century, with the demise of Buddhism in India, many of the sacred sites were destroyed and subsequently forgotten. However, as Buddhism spread, new pilgrimage sites were established outside India: for example, the Chinese mountain monastery of Wutai Shan in north-eastern Shanxi province, where Mañjushri, Bodhisattva of Wisdom, resided.

From the 5th century CE, Chinese and, later, Tibetan pilgrims set out on long and dangerous journeys to India in search of Buddhist scriptures. Their accounts are a unique record of Buddhism and sacred sites in India during these centuries.

EIGHT GREAT PLACES

Traditionally, 'Eight Great Places' are visited by Buddhist pilgrims. The first four are major sites associated with key events in the Buddha's life; the others are sites of miraculous events.

- **Lumbini**, Nepal. The Buddha's birthplace.
- **Uruvela** (now Bodhgaya), Bihar, India. The place where the Buddha attained enlightenment.
- **Isipatana** (modern Sarnath, near Varanasi, India). The Buddha preached his first sermon, so turning the Wheel of the Dharma, in the Deer Park here.
- **Kushinara** (modern Kushinagar). The place where the Buddha passed away and entered nirvana.
- **Shravasti** (in north-eastern Uttar Pradesh). The Buddha performed 'Twin Miracles' here, sending fire and water from his body and appearing in several places at once. The remains of the Jetavana, the first Buddhist vihara, are here.
- **Rajagriha** (modern Rajgir, near Bihar). The Veluvana Bamboo Grove at Rajagriha was a retreat for the Sangha, a gift from King Bimbisara. A vihara was built and the Buddha delivered important sermons here.
- **Sankashya** (modern Sankissa). The Buddha ascended to the Tushita heaven, where his mother had been reborn as a male god. Following in the tradition of his predecessors, the Buddha taught the Dharma to his mother before descending to Earth at Sankashya.
- **Nalanda** (near Bihar). The Buddha preached for long periods at a mango grove here, where a tree miraculously grew from a toothpick he discarded. It became renowned as a great Buddhist centre of teaching.

Left Monks circumambulate the excavated remains of stupas and other ancient buildings at Lumbini, Nepal, the birthplace of the Buddha.

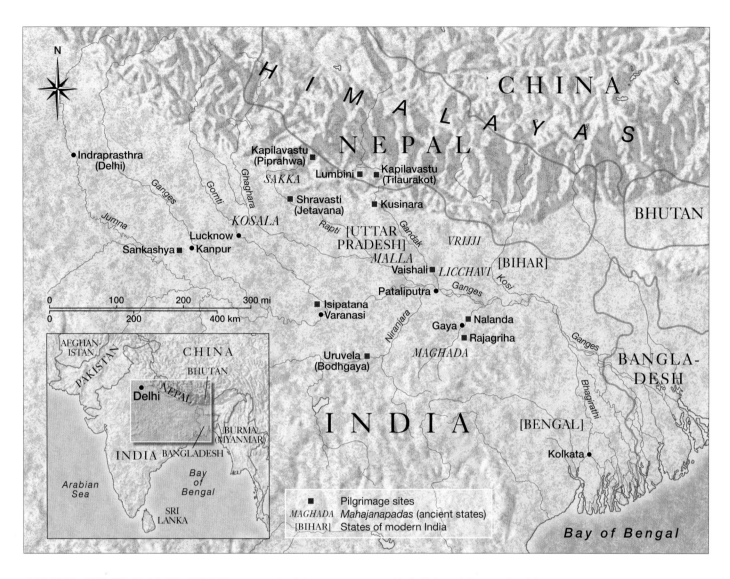

OTHER PILGRIMAGE SITES

Many other places in north–eastern India were visited by the Buddha and number among the holy places, including the sacred Hindu city of Varanasi (Benares). Other places have become pilgrimage sites in modern times, including the excavations at Kapilavastu (at Tilaurakot, Nepal, and Piprawha, Uttar Pradesh, India), the city where the Buddha grew up, and Vaishali (Bihar), where the Buddha miraculously cured a pestilence that was attacking the city's inhabitants. This was also the last place he visited before his death.

Right Sarnath, where the Buddha preached many sermons, was once the site of many monasteries, temples and stupas. It is still a sacred pilgrimage site.

NORTHERN INDIA AT THE TIME OF THE BUDDHA

The map above shows the mahajanapadas, or city-states, of northern India during the 5th century BCE, and the principal sites associated with the Buddha's life. Today these places have become major pilgrimage sites for Buddhists.

CHAPTER 2

WHAT THE BUDDHA TAUGHT

Siddhartha Gautama is believed to have achieved enlightenment by the age of about 30. Then, as the Buddha, he gathered a group of followers and travelled around northern India, teaching all who came to hear him, as well as debating with Brahmans, Jains and followers of other religions and belief systems. His teachings and discourses, as recalled by his disciples, were preserved by them after his death as the doctrine of the religion that later came to be called Buddhism.

Just eight weeks after his enlightenment, the Buddha delivered his key message to a group of ascetics, his former companions in his quest for spiritual awakening, in a deer park near Varanasi. That message, though profound, may be summarized in four simple statements – the 'Four Noble Truths' about the nature of reality – which form the foundation of Buddhist doctrine. In the fourth of these, the Buddha provides a way of ending repeated cycles of birth, death and rebirth – his 'Noble Eightfold Path' – which can lead to self-transformation and enlightenment. The Noble Eightfold Path provides guidelines for the practice of morality, mental training (or meditation) and insight – the three indispensable elements in the enlightenment process.

Opposite The spoked wheel, or Dharmachakra, *an ancient symbol of sovereignty and the law in Indian art, has been a symbol of the Buddha's teachings, or Dharma, since the early centuries* BCE.

Above Scriptures written in Sanskrit helped preserve the teachings of not only Buddhism but also Hinduism and Jainism. Some Sanskrit terms are common to all three religions, but the concepts ascribed to them vary.

THE DISCIPLES

SHORTLY AFTER THE BUDDHA'S DEATH 500 ARHATS CONVENED A COUNCIL IN A CAVE OUTSIDE RAJAGRIHA, CAPITAL OF THE HEARTLAND OF BUDDHISM, MAGHADA. THEIR MISSION WAS TO FIND A WAY OF PRESERVING THE BUDDHA'S TEACHINGS.

The Buddha's disciples were a loosely organized network of groups who lived in small communities or travelled across the Gangetic Plain, discussing and teaching the Dharma and practising meditation. During the rainy season, these groups converged at Jetavana or another of the retreats lay followers had donated to the Sangha for a few weeks of spiritual renewal. Their focus had been on the Buddha, and, obedient to his revelation that there should be no central authority but the Dharma, the disciples appointed no successor after his death. When the duties connected with the division and preservation of his relics were over, they drifted away from Kushinara, the place of his passing into parinirvana.

Above Mahakashyapa, like Siddhartha Gautama , had abandoned the life of a wealthy Brahman for an austere existence. He remained an ascetic even after accepting the teaching of the Buddha and attaining enlightenment.

THE FIRST BUDDHIST COUNCIL

Under the Buddha's inspiring guidance, many of his disciples had themselves achieved enlightenment. After his passing, these arhats preoccupied themselves with the question of how to preserve his teachings – his words as they had heard and remembered them – for future generations. They also realized the need to codify the rules of the Sangha in order to prevent any group from straying too far from the central core of the Dharma.

Within about a year of the Buddha's parinirvana, therefore, they decided to hold a meeting. According to tradition, 500 arhats assembled in a cave at Rajagriha, Maghada's capital, to review all of the Buddha's teachings. Perhaps by common consent, Mahakashyapa, an honoured elder of the Sangha who had assisted the Buddha, led the First Buddhist Council.

The Buddha had the gift of teaching according to the abilities and understanding of the listener or group to whom he was speaking. He would give examples, tell stories and put things in ways his listeners would understand. This meant that no one person had ever heard everything he had taught. Writing was a specialized skill in India in the 4th century BCE, and most Sangha members were probably illiterate, so nothing was written down. Mahakashyapa's plan was to ask each of the 500 arhats to repeat from memory the Buddha's teachings they knew.

THE BUDDHIST CANON

Ananda was asked to recount each of the Buddha's discourses he had personally heard. He began by saying where each discourse had taken place, then he repeated what he had heard the Buddha say. Others who had also been present verified or disputed Ananda's memory and a version was agreed.

Another of the disciples, Upali, who had formerly been a low-caste barber, recited the 227 rules that he recalled the Buddha imposing on the community

Above Two leading disciples – Sariputra, renowned for his wisdom, and Maudgalyayana, famous for mind-reading and other supernatural skills – stand on either side of the Buddha in this Thai painted silk banner.

Right Younger monks grieved at the Buddha's passing into parinirvana, as depicted in this 11th-century Japanese painting on silk. But the arhats reflected serenely on his liberation from the cycle of death and rebirth.

whenever he rebuked a monk for doing something that might harm someone or discredit the Sangha, or that did not fit the spirit of the Dharma.

Finally, Mahakashyapa repeated the Buddha's analyses of philosophy and metaphysics – how the human mind works, for instance, and the mechanisms that give rise to the cycle of death and rebirth.

Mahakashyapa then divided the assembly into three groups and charged each with memorizing one category of teachings. These later came to be called *Pitaka*, meaning 'baskets' or 'collections'. The teachings recited by Mahakashyapa, for example, were called the *Abhidharma Pitaka*, meaning 'The Basket of Higher Knowledge'.

The Saptaparni cave, the place where the Sangha held the First Buddhist Council, is among the many sites in Rajagriha (now Rajgir) that are today visited by Buddhist pilgrims.

THE DISCIPLE ANANDA

As the Buddha's personal attendant for many years, Ananda had heard more of the Buddha's teachings than anyone, so his presence was needed at the First Buddhist Council. However, only arhats could attend, and he had not attained enlightenment. It is written that Mahakashyapa pressed Ananda to practise meditation intensively to achieve enlightenment – and also that he charged him with having committed a disastrous misjudgement shortly before the Buddha's final illness. On the road to Vaishali, the Buddha may have suggested that Ananda could ask him to prolong his earthly existence until the end of the current era, more than two centuries hence. Perhaps because he did not grasp the significance of the Buddha's words, Ananda did not respond. Thereupon, the Buddha 'rejected his vital constituents'. As if to confirm his action, the Earth shook. Ananda, in crisis, threw himself into meditation and, it is recorded, successfully achieved enlightenment on the night that the Council opened.

Right The disciple Ananda, shown in this 6th-century marble sculpture from China, was the Buddha's cousin and his attendant for 25 years. He heard more of the Buddha's teachings than any other disciple and was famous for his ability to memorize.

THE DHARMA

IN HIS TEACHINGS, THE BUDDHA EXPLAINED HIS OWN INTERPRETATION OF THE DHARMA – THE LAW THAT GOVERNS THE UNIVERSE. HE SPOKE OF IMPERMANENCE, DEATH AND REBIRTH AND REVEALED THE PATH TO LIBERATION FROM THE TORMENTS OF EARTHLY LIFE.

Although it is a central part of Buddhism, the concept of Dharma existed long before the Buddha. The term derives from a Sanskrit word meaning 'to sustain' or 'uphold', and it appeared in the Vedas on law and customs. The Hindus interpreted Dharma as the law of the cosmos, which governs religious, social and individual action, and the Jains conceived of it as the life-force and as virtue.

The Dharma taught by the Buddha Shakyamuni (known as the Buddha-Dharma) includes many beliefs that were popular in 5th-century BCE India. For example, the Buddha accepted the Brahmanical pantheon of gods, devas and other supernatural entities, and their role became increasingly important as Buddhism spread across the East. The Buddha was also influenced by the Hindu belief in samsara, or reincarnation. Upon his enlightenment, he remembered his many previous lives and recalled that he was 24th in a line of buddhas, each of whom had been reborn for the purpose of teaching the Dharma. Over millions of years, knowledge of the Dharma faded,

Above The palm of this Siamese Hand of the Buddha is inscribed with the Wheel of the Dharma. The finger and thumb form a circle in the teaching sign, or vitarka *mudra.*

and the task of each buddha had been to teach it anew. The Buddha Shakyamuni fulfilled this task as much by example as by teaching. The very pattern of his life – renunciation, meditation and enlightenment – is also the Dharma, or spiritual truth, of earthly human existence.

SELF AND SOUL

The Buddha's unique contribution to Indian philosophy was an alternative to belief in a human soul. Central to Brahmanism was the idea that every living being has an eternal spiritual life-force, or soul, that survives unchanged after death and is reborn. This personal soul, called the *atman*, is part of a universal soul, called Brahma.

The Buddha searched but could find no evidence for the existence of a creator god or an eternal soul. He conceived of the

Left A Jain diagram of the universe. Jainism, established in the 7th–5th centuries BCE, shares many concepts with Buddhism, such as the idea of continual rebirth until the soul can achieve true liberation from the body.

Above The hands of this statue of the Buddha are in the Dharmachakra *mudra, or gesture, signifying that the Buddha is 'Turning the Wheel of the Dharma', or preaching the First Sermon in the Deer Park at Sarnath.*

components of all five aggregates change. Thus, although everyone has a personality, or self, there is no core, unchanging self, or immortal soul. *Anatman* is the Sanskrit term for the Buddhist idea of 'non-self'; it is *anatta* in Pali.

Throughout the course of their lives, individuals commit good and bad actions, and in so doing, they forge a moral identity, which, the Buddha taught, survives death and is reborn. He encapsulated this in his teachings on the Four Noble Truths.

Below A standing or walking buddha making the double abhaya *mudra usually signifies 'preaching'. The* abhaya *mudra – right hand raised, palm facing outward – is the gesture of friendship and protection.*

world and everything in it – trees, water, people – as made up of components or qualities such as colour, sight or youth. Humans are composed of five groups or aggregates of components, known as skandhas: the physical body

(called *rupa*); feelings, such as pleasure and pain (*vedana*); all that can be perceived and imagined (*samjna*); character traits and motivating forces, such as desire (*samskara*); and consciousness or mind (*vijñana*).

None of these aggregates is permanent, and while all are part of the 'self', none is, or becomes, the soul. Although the body is part of the self, the self is more than the body's shape or how it functions, and the body changes as a person ages. In fact, all through life, the

REPRESENTATIONS OF THE BUDDHA

BY THE EARLY CENTURIES OF THE COMMON ERA, IT HAD BECOME TRADITIONAL TO PLACE STATUES AND RELIEFS OF THE BUDDHA IN FRONT OF AND INSIDE STUPAS. THESE IMAGES OF THE LIVING BUDDHA WERE BELIEVED TO RADIATE HIS PRESENCE AND INFLUENCE.

In 2nd-century-BCE carvings on the *torana*, or gates, to the Great Stupa at Sanchi, the sculptors depicted Siddhartha Gautama before enlightenment, but they used symbols, such as a parasol or the Bodhi tree, to represent the enlightened Buddha. All early depictions were similarly aniconic – that is, there was no icon, or image, of the Buddha's person. Early Buddhists believed that his

Below The anjali mudra is a gesture of offering seen only on bodhisattvas and other lesser figures, indicating devotion to the Buddha or to the Dharma. In many Buddhist countries, it is used as a gesture of greeting.

relics emitted the Buddha's live presence, and through them, pilgrims could visualize him. To meditate while walking round stupas containing his relics was to experience and be directly influenced by the Buddha.

EARLY SCULPTURES

Art historians have established that the first Buddha images were probably produced by the Gandharan school before the 1st century CE. Gandhara, centred on Purushapura (modern Peshawar in northern Pakistan), had been part of Cyrus the Great's Persian empire and had absorbed the artistic styles of Persia, Greece and India. Greek influence is clear in the anatomically realistic figures and elaborately draped clothing on the Gandharan stone reliefs.

The Gandharan school may have influenced the wider production of artistic images of the

Above This 3rd–4th century depiction of the Buddha performing miracles at Shravasti (The Buddha of the Great Miracle), shows him standing, one hand raised in the abhaya mudra, the gesture of fearlessness.

Below Representations of the Buddha generally depict him in one of three positions: standing (symbolizing authority), sitting cross-legged in the lotus position (signifying calm), or lying on his right side (reserved for representations of parinirvana).

Buddha. The Mathuran school, which arose in north-central India near Agra (modern Uttar Pradesh), produced more evolved Buddha figures with more accurate anatomical proportions. Their postures and expressions convey authority and calm, and their robes indicate simplicity.

SYMBOLISM

Even these earliest statues and paintings depicted the Buddha in postures that recalled transforming events in his life. A set of conventions evolved: the Buddha is shown standing or walking, one arm raised in a sign of protection, embodying supreme sovereignty; he sits cross-legged in meditation, his hands resting, palms upturned in his lap – a sign of concentration; he touches the Earth with his right hand, calling upon it to witness his right to enlightenment; or raises it in a gesture of teaching; or sometimes he lies in deep meditation, entering parinirvana. An *ushnisha,* or protruberance, on the crown of a statue's head – often prominent enough to resemble a halo or spire – identifies the figure as the Buddha Shakyamuni. A raised

Right The vadara *mudra signifies offering, giving, compassion and sincerity. The arm is directed downward and outward, the hand open, symbolizing the Buddha's gift of the Truth. This statue dates from the 7th century.*

spot in the centre of the forehead is one of the 32 signs of the *chakravartin,* or universal monarch, and the ear lobes are lengthened, symbolizing nobility (nobles then wore heavy earrings, which extended their ear lobes) and wisdom. The Buddha's palms and soles are marked with the Wheel of the Dharma.

ASIAN ICONOGRAPHY

As Buddhism spread, other Asian countries produced Buddhist images according to their own artistic style and developed their own iconography, so that today, representations of the Buddha display more than 100 different gestures in addition to the eight that are common to all.

In homage to the Buddha's supernatural achievements, artists carved colossal Buddha figures, some, such as the group at Polonnaruwa in Sri Lanka, out of solid rock. Bangkok's oldest temple, Wat Pho, houses the world's largest reclining Buddha, at 46m (151ft) long, while the tallest stone Buddha is the early 8th-century seated Buddha in Leshan, Sichuan, China, which is 71m (233ft) high. Strict proportions between the limbs have governed most representations of the Buddha, which, large or small, are often still designed on a grid.

THE BUDDHIST UNIVERSE

UNENLIGHTENED BEINGS INHABIT THREE SPHERES OF EXISTENCE IN THE BUDDHIST UNIVERSE, WHERE THEY DWELL IN SEPARATE REALMS. THE KARMA THEY ACCUMULATE DURING THEIR LIFETIME DETERMINES WHETHER THEY ARE REBORN INTO A LOWER OR A HIGHER REALM.

Above 'The Burning Cauldron', a section from the 12th-century Japanese Hell Scrolls, *which depict 7 of the 16 lesser hells described in the* Sutra of the World Arising.

Buddhists see the universe as consisting of three worlds or spheres, which are inhabited by beings living out their cycles of birth–death–rebirth. The lowest is the Sphere of the Senses and Desires; above it is the Sphere of Form – the world of subtle matter; and the highest is called the Sphere of Formlessness – the realm of incorporeal beings. The spheres are subdivided into 31 levels, or realms, each inhabited by a different category of being. The lowest realm is Hell, while at the top is a heaven of Neither Perception nor Non-Perception. Here consciousness is transcended and only the mind exists.

SPHERES OF REBIRTH

It is possible to be reborn into any realm, or sphere, of the Buddhist universe, since samsara, or the cycle of rebirth, takes place inside and between the three spheres. To be born into the Sphere of Formlessness is to be close to liberation, but it is also possible for inhabitants of the lower spheres to become enlightened. Those who attain enlightenment no longer inhabit the spheres of existence.

To be reborn as a human, high up in the Sphere of the Senses and Desires, is a beneficial destiny for any being, because humans have ample opportunity to make spiritual progress toward achieving enlightenment and thus ending the cycle of samsara. However, those who have accumulated 'good' karma may be reborn at a higher level. To be reborn into one of the many levels inhabited by the gods is a challenge: existence there is blissful, yet gods must still strive to attain enlightenment and escape samsara. If they do not, they may be reborn into a lower sphere.

Below the human realm are the realms of 'bad destiny', where beings who have accumulated

Left The six segments of the Wheel of Life represent the six realms of rebirth in the Buddhist universe. Clockwise: 1. Gods, 2. Titans, 3. Animals, 4. Hell, 5. Ghosts, 6. Humans.

Above This Thai temple painting shows the Buddha visiting his mother in one of the lower of the 26 heavens of the Buddhist universe, and afterward descending to Earth.

'bad' karma may be reborn. The lowest realm consists of various hells, where evil deeds are punished by torments such as fire and freezing. In the Buddhist universe, once evil deeds have been expiated, release follows, and beings are reborn into a higher realm.

To be reborn into the animal kingdom is undesirable, since animals, whose understanding is limited and whose lives may be naturally short, or shortened by predators, have little opportunity to achieve enlightenment. Ghosts – former humans driven by insatiable cravings – inhabit the third realm and, some scriptures claim, there is a fourth realm inhabited by warlike Titans, who are enslaved by attachment to violence and power.

LEVELS OF MEDITATION

Meditation is the central practice in almost every school of Buddhism because it provides a superhighway to enlightenment. Novices begin with exercises in concentration and mind control, but once they have achieved deep states of trance, called dhyanas, they enter the Sphere of Form. As they master advanced meditation techniques, they may pass from these lower levels and enter the Sphere of Formlessness, where they may attain the meditation levels of Infinite Space, Infinite Consciousness, or even higher.

The Pali texts and later scriptures record that the Buddha managed to reach the seventh and eighth levels – the Realm of Nothingness, where body and mind separate, and of Neither Perception nor Non-Perception – which are on the same plane as the highest levels of the Buddhist universe. From there, he passed into nirvana.

THE WHEEL OF LIFE

The Wheel of Life (Bhavacakra, literally 'Wheel of Becoming') represents samsara. At its hub are a pig, a snake and a cock. These are the 'Three Poisons' that hinder spiritual development. The pig symbolizes greed, the snake hatred and the cock delusion. Delusions are negative traits, such as ill will, stubbornness, worry and laziness. The three animals pursue each other, keeping the wheel in motion. Delusions are obstacles to enlightenment, and individuals must overcome their negative traits or remain in samsara.

Rebirths are shown in the circle around the hub of the wheel: the right, black half depicts figures falling into the 'bad destinies', from which rebirth is almost inevitable, and the left half shows the ascent into levels of existence that offer hope of liberation.

Yama, Lord of Death, whose three eyes symbolize impermanence, harm and non-self, grasps the wheel. His five skulls represent freedom from old age, sickness, death, decay and rebirth.

Below A detail from a Wheel of Life illustration shows the central disc and the black-and-white circle around it.

REBECOMING

CENTRAL TO THE DHARMA IS THE CONCEPT OF SAMSARA, THE CYCLE OF BIRTH, AGEING, DEATH AND REBIRTH — THE IDEA THAT, JUST AS THE FLAME OF A DYING CANDLE SETS A NEW CANDLE BURNING, AT THE DEATH OF A LIVING BEING A NEW ONE COMES INTO EXISTENCE.

"Whatever things have an origin must come to cessation", taught the Buddha. At the end of life, the body dies, and the components that make up the personality dissolve. He did not teach that the personality, or even the soul, lives on after death to be reborn in a new body. His words are often explained by the analogy of a candle: just as a dying flame can light a new candle, so the dissolution of one personality

Below Tibetan monks accompany a deceased lama (a Tibetan teacher of the Dharma) to the cremation oven. Attending cremations, and even autopsies, keeps Buddhist monks mindful of the teaching of anitya, *or impermanence.*

gives rise to another. "There is rebirth of character", explained the Buddha to a Brahmin who asked if his soul would be reborn, "but no transmigration of a self. The thought-forms reappear, but there is no ego-entity transferred. The stanza uttered by a teacher is reborn in the scholar who repeats the words."

IMPERMANENCE

Buddhism celebrates the happiness that youth, success, friendship, love and parenthood can bring, but happiness is not the Buddhist goal. The Buddha-Dharma instils the message of *anitya*, or impermanence: youth, excitement, joy, contentment pass away; sorrow and sickness dog the lives of many,

Above The cycle of samsara (which translates from Sanskrit as 'the wandering') is started again at birth. Being born into the human realm is fortunate, and offers the opportunity of eventual enlightenment.

and bereavement and death are inevitable. All these experiences are *duhkha* — forms of suffering that range from dissatisfaction to misery, pain and grief. If we wish to understand the reality of our existence, we must recognize, as

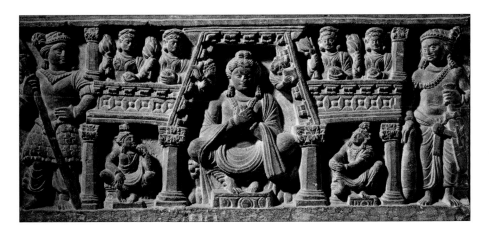

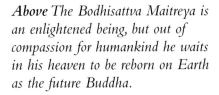

Above The Bodhisattva Maitreya is an enlightened being, but out of compassion for humankind he waits in his heaven to be reborn on Earth as the future Buddha.

did the young Siddhartha Gautama when he encountered old age, sickness and death, that suffering is inescapable. Further, if living and dying bring suffering, then repeated living and dying must bring the greatest suffering.

KARMA

Buddhist thought does not see suffering as punishment for having offended a god or gods. The Dharma teaches that people's unhappiness and suffering are the effect of their own harmful actions. The moral choices people make consciously and intentionally impact on their futures, and in this way individuals shape their own destinies. Bad actions, such as violence, greed, hatred and selfishness, harm others and also those who commit them. The resulting karma accumulates through a lifetime and must be expiated by suffering. No buddha can forgive it, and it does not expire when the body dies. It lives on after death, eventually to be reborn.

HEAVENS AND HELLS

The Buddha's last words were "Decay is inherent in all component things". Even death and rebirth are impermanent. After death, unenlightened living beings enter into one of five or six forms of rebirth, depending on their karma. They can be reborn in a hell – a place not of damnation but of purification, where evil deeds committed during earthly

Above Hells form the lowest level of existence in the Buddhist universe. This Khmer relief from Angkor Wat shows servants of Yama, Deva of Death, stringing up and beating those in debt to evil.

existence are punished by torment. When the evil is expiated, the being is released, to be reborn into a higher realm. Beings can be reborn as any kind of animal life, a ghost, a human or a god.

Reborn beings inhabit any of 31 realms, or states of existence, in the Buddhist universe. The upper realms are heavens, the mansions of the gods. Animals, humans, even the gods in their multi-level heavens, are all subject to the law of the Dharma and must attain enlightenment to end the cycle of death and rebirth that results from karmic cause and effect.

THE IDEA OF REINCARNATION

Buddhists speak of 'rebirth', 'rebecoming' or 're-death' rather than 'reincarnation', which has a narrower meaning: the rebirth of the soul in another body. In Hindu doctrine, for example, the immortal soul, or *atman*, is repeatedly reborn in the body of a living being. "Worn-out garments are shed by the body. Worn-out bodies are shed by the dweller within the body. New bodies are donned by the dweller, like garments", declares the *Bhagavadgita*, an important Hindu text. Achieving moksha, or enlightenment, frees the soul from reincarnation. The Buddha-Dharma shares the idea of rebirth with the Hindus, Jains and Sikhs, but rejects the idea of an immortal soul that lives on, unchanging, after death, as well as the belief that humans are reborn only as humans. They may be reborn as animals, or as ghosts – disembodied former humans whose worldly desires made them slaves to attachment.

Above Just as new star clusters, such as the Pleiades, form from the dust of dying stars, so everything in the Buddhist universe passes through a cycle of birth, death and rebirth.

CAUSE AND EFFECT

TO WIN FREEDOM FROM THE CONSEQUENCES OF PAST KARMA, A PERSON MUST BREAK, ONE BY ONE, EVERY LINK IN THE CHAIN OF KARMIC CAUSE AND EFFECT. THIS IS ACHIEVED BY MEANS OF MORAL DECISIONS, MERITORIOUS LIVING, DAILY PRACTICE AND MEDITATION.

Central to Buddhist thinking is the idea of karma, meaning 'deeds'. All actions have future consequences in terms of personal merit (*punya*, or 'good' karma) or demerit (*papa*, or 'bad' karma). A kindness to another person accumulates merit by building *punya*, while a selfish, unkind act will earn demerit through *papa*. However, Buddhists believe that for actions to have karmic consequences, they must be carried out consciously and intentionally.

The balance of karma at death determines in which of the six realms of the Buddhist universe (shown on the preceding pages) an individual will be reborn. Karma is also thought to determine one's physical appearance, health, mental abilities and character. Bad deeds, such as lying or theft, shape one's character and destiny after death. Thus, the Buddha taught, we are responsible for our own salvation.

Below An illustration from the Sutra of Cause and Effect, *detailing the incarnations of the Buddha. Here, men report to Siddhartha's father that he is following his new life of austerity.*

THE 12 STEPS TO REBIRTH
The Buddha analysed how karmic cause and effect works in his doctrine of *pratitya-samutpada*, a concept which is variously translated as 'dependent arising', or 'co-dependent origination', or 'origination-in-dependence'. This idea means that an event takes place only because other events exist in a chain of cause and effect that extends both into the past and the future. Thus, if X happens, Y will follow; if X does not happen, then Y will not follow.

The chain has 12 links or steps, each of which comes into existence because of the preceding one. The 12 segments in the outer circle of the Wheel of Life illustrate in sequence the links in this chain of cause and effect:

1 Cause and effect start from ignorance, the first link in the chain. Ignorance is represented by a blind man, because men are blinded by their own ignorance.
2 A potter at his wheel follows the blind man as the second link in the chain. The potter represents the individual shaping his life in ignorance by his actions.

Above The Wheel of Life depicts the sequence of 12 events in the chain of cause and effect. The sequence leads to samsara – the cycle of birth–death– rebirth. Samsara will end only if the chain is broken.

3 A monkey represents the imprints of actions taken in ignorance on the consciousness, parts of which survive death and carry them into a future life.
4 Travellers in a boat symbolize the consciousness ('name') that enters the embryo in the womb of the individual's future mother. The boat represents the body ('form') that the embryo will become.
5 Empty houses in link 5 represent the six soon-to-develop senses of the embryo.
6 A couple holding each other symbolizes contact. The six senses of the growing infant develop to the stage where communication becomes possible.
7 A man shot in the eye is the image on the seventh segment of the Wheel of Life. It symbolizes the ability of the embryo's maturing senses to transmit pain and pleasure. Through these feelings, individuals experience karma directly, by responding to the effects of their past actions, both good and bad.
8 An individual eating an apple symbolizes the feelings of desire caused by attachment.

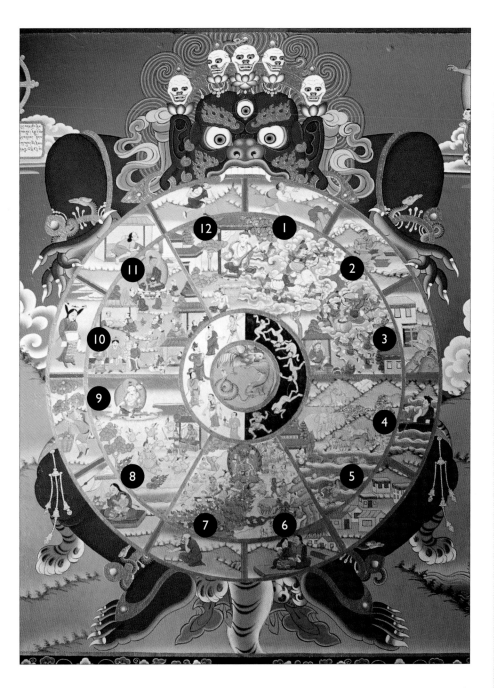

Above The outer circle of the Wheel of Life depicts the 12 links in the chain of causation that leads to samsara. Starting in the top right-hand segment (at one o'clock), the numbered links follow each other in sequence clockwise around the mandala.

9 A man snatching fruit out of a tree represents grasping – the response to attachment. This ninth link symbolizes the delusion of strong attachment to the self.

10 The pregnant woman is a symbol of new life. Grasping and attachment strengthen at death and ripen in the mind into seeds of the karma, which are carried into the next existence.

11 A woman in childbirth symbolizes the ripening of the seeds of karma as an individual's elements are reborn.

12 The process of life, growth, development, decay and re-death begins even at conception. In this final link on the Wheel of Life, the individual is represented by a person carrying a heavy bundle, which is symbolic of the burden of karma that the individual created during past lives.

During the process of his enlightenment, which, the scriptures say, took one night, the Buddha unlocked each link in this chain of cause and effect, thus ending samsara. This was an achievement that, it is believed, would normally take three successive lifetimes.

THE FOUR NOBLE TRUTHS

IN HIS FIRST SERMON AFTER ENLIGHTENMENT, THE BUDDHA TAUGHT HIS DISCIPLES THE FOUR NOBLE TRUTHS. THESE TRUTHS ARE THE FOUNDATION OF HIS PHILOSOPHY, THE KERNEL OF DOCTRINE THAT EVERY NEWCOMER TO BUDDHISM MUST KNOW AND ACCEPT.

Above The Scream *by Edvard Munch expresses the tension of existential suffering, the* duhkha *that builds up through life as a result of its inevitable failures, frustrations and disappointments.*

1 TO LIVE IS TO SUFFER

The reality of *duhkha* is the first truth. *Duhkha* (Pali: *dukkha*) is commonly translated as 'suffering', but there are many kinds of suffering, ranging from unease to sorrow. *Duhkha* may be physical pain, illness, bereavement, despair, or psychological pain. It is also the disruption to happiness caused all through life by *anitya*, or impermanence, such as the ending of love. "Birth is suffering", preached the Buddha in the Deer Park at Isipatana, "illness is suffering, ageing is suffering, death is suffering.

Below The Buddha chose to remain on Earth after enlightenment to teach the Four Noble Truths to humanity. This 8th-century Japanese sutra (scripture) shows the incarnation of the Buddha burning after his bodily death.

To be united with the unpleasant is suffering, separation from the pleasant is suffering. Desire that remains unsatisfied is suffering."

2 ATTACHMENT IS THE CAUSE OF SUFFERING

All suffering is caused by craving and greed. The Sanskrit word for suffering is *trishna* (Pali: *tanha*). Its literal meaning is 'thirst', but it is commonly translated as 'desire' or 'attachment'. There is attachment to sensual pleasures, craving for material possessions, and greed for personal gain in terms of wealth, influence, power, or fame. Some people crave eternal youth and immortality; others desire an end to life.

All these cravings distort thinking and perception, shielding the mind from reality, and may result in lying, theft, degradation, oppression of others, hatred and even murder. These actions cause others to suffer, but experiencing craving is itself suffering. Unfulfilled cravings are painful, but the satisfaction or exhilaration of fulfilled cravings is usually short-lived and is replaced by a sense of loss, a form of suffering that causes renewed desire. In his

SANSKRIT TERMS

In Buddhism, the three marks of existence are:

anatman non-self, no soul – the doctrine that there is no immortal spirit at the core of any living being.

anitya impermanence, the view that nothing lasts and that all phenomena will eventually pass away.

duhkha suffering of every type, ranging from unease and lack of satisfaction with life to physical and mental pain.

ATTACHMENT

Craving chocolate, cigarettes, alcohol or tranquillizers; the urge to consume; clinging to people; wanting to make more money than anyone else, or to have the coolest car or the latest fashions – these things ultimately cause suffering. The Middle Way prevails in all the Buddha's teachings, so normal wanting and needing are not the root cause of suffering. Desiring to make new friends, buy a winter coat, or spend time with family and friends are not examples of craving. Never wanting to be alone, shopping till you drop, pursuing power for the sake of it and being irrationally jealous are what the Buddha called "Burning with the fire of desire...the fire of delusion". Behaviour driven by burning desire is suffering because it stifles empathy and compassion, warps the mind and can never really be satisfied. In the 21st-century world, *trishna*, magnified by advertising and marketing campaigns, has a magnetic hold on people.

Above Following the Middle Way brings detachment from craving and opens the mind to reality and an understanding of oneself and the world.

teachings, the Buddha counselled against gratifying the senses and giving free reign to the passions.

3 THERE CAN BE AN END TO SUFFERING

In the Buddha's teaching, there is a message of hope: that suffering can be brought to an end. If attachment, selfish desires and cravings are ultimately the cause of all suffering, then it follows that eradicating them will cause suffering to cease. However, this means going back to their roots and eradicating ignorance – of oneself, of how things are, of the Four Noble Truths. Ignorance is symbolized by the pig that chases the cock (symbol of attachment) and the snake (symbol of aversion) at the centre of the Wheel of Life, so keeping it turning.

The Buddha taught that the disciple who sees things as they are becomes dispassionate toward them. "Being dispassionate, this disciple becomes detached and, through detachment, is liberated."

Attaining nirvana – extinguishing the flame of repeated births and deaths – is the end of all suffering.

4 A PATH LEADS TO THE CESSATION OF SUFFERING

The way to end suffering is, as Siddhartha Gautama learned during his years as a *shramana*, the Middle Way between heedless self-indulgence and extreme self-denial. It is the way along the Noble Eightfold Path that leads the seeker to nirvana. These eight steps to enlightenment were taught by the Buddha in his First Sermon in the Deer Park at Isipatana.

THE NOBLE EIGHTFOLD PATH

TO FOLLOW THE NOBLE EIGHTFOLD PATH IS HARD, BUT AS THE MIDDLE WAY, IT REQUIRES RENUNCIATION AND SELF-DISCIPLINE, NOT SELF-TORTURE. THE WAY OFFERS CALM AND INNER PEACE, INSIGHT AND WISDOM, AND LEADS EVENTUALLY TO NIRVANA.

As he set the Wheel of the Dharma in motion, the Buddha turned to his followers: "And what, monks, is this middle course fully awakened to by the Truthfinder", he asked them, "making for vision, making for knowledge, which conduces to calming, to superknowledge, to awakening, to nirvana? It is the… eightfold way itself."

Part of the initiation into Buddhism is a declaration of faith in the Four Noble Truths and the Noble Eightfold Path, which form the essence of Buddhist doctrine.

Below The Dharmachakra *is the Wheel of the Law. It has eight spokes, each representing a step on the Noble Eightfold Path to enlightenment.*

The first two steps along the Eightfold Path develop wisdom; steps three to five teach moral living; and six to eight train the mind for meditation.

1 RIGHT VIEW

Recognizing the truth of the Buddha's teachings and accepting them is the first stage on the path to enlightenment. That means understanding and accepting the Four Noble Truths, of which the last is the Noble Eightfold Path. What is asked is not blind faith – the Buddha advised the Sangha to question everything – but an acceptance that the Dharma is worth personal commitment. Each Truth is expressed concisely, yet understanding all four involves

Above Meditation is central to Buddhist practice. It helps to deepen understanding of the Four Noble Truths and the Noble Eightfold Path.

mental effort. Buddhist monks spend a lifetime deepening their understanding of the Four Truths and the Eightfold Path through discourse, reading and meditation. The right view is the right understanding or knowledge. In time, the practitioner begins to see the world as it truly is, undistorted by illusion.

2 RIGHT RESOLVE

The essence of Buddhist doctrine is that people can and must change, for the right change can end samsara. Right resolve is a commitment to a process of change, which begins with developing right attitudes, such as an intention to free oneself from attachment to worldly pleasures, to eradicate selfishness and to replace them with sensitivity, empathy and compassion.

3 RIGHT SPEECH

This step means telling the truth. Part of learning to see things as they really are is to recognize the

truth as it is, undistorted by ego, and to cease embroidering it or presenting it in a way that furthers one's interests.

Right speech is thoughtful. It means weighing up one's words so they are not frivolous, insensitive, angry or sarcastic. Speaking ill of others harms them, so silence is better than gossip. The scriptures recount the divisive talk of Devadatta, the Buddha's cousin, who, from jealousy and frustrated ambition, tried to turn members of the Sangha against the Buddha.

4 RIGHT ACTION

Buddhists strive to do nothing that could harm other living beings. Such wrong actions range from killing, stealing ("do not take what is not given") and committing sexual acts that could have harmful consequences, to smaller acts of injury, dishonesty and the abuse of sensual pleasures. The injunction not to kill living beings is interpreted by many Buddhists as a ban on eating meat.

Right action is pivotal in training the mind in right thinking, in the sense that right view, right effort and right mindfulness are bound up with it. "One tries to abandon wrong action and enter into right action: This is one's right effort. One is mindful to abandon wrong action and to enter and remain in right action: This is one's right mindfulness", read the scriptures.

5 RIGHT LIVELIHOOD

This, the third of the steps that teach moral living, rules out work that harms others or hampers one's spiritual progress. A Buddhist's occupation should not infringe right speech and right action.

Some ancient texts single out the arms trade, slavery, dealing in flesh – for example, the slaughter of animals – and trade in

Above Debating Buddhist scriptures is a way to develop right speech. It forms an important part of the daily training of Tibetan Buddhist monks.

intoxicating drink and poisons, such as illegal drugs. Those trades still flourish and Buddhists today are forbidden from being butchers, hunters or executioners. Life is now more complicated, however, so dealers in stocks and shares issued by companies involved in unethical trades, retailers selling goods produced by unethical labour policies, and anyone engaged in business activities that harm the environment and so threaten the survival of living beings, may be seen as examples of wrongful ways of making a living.

6 RIGHT EFFORT

Effort has to be applied to banish harmful states of mind, such as jealousy, covetousness, greed and melancholy. This means learning to control one's negative thoughts and encouraging and instilling positive thinking, especially qualities such as kindness and empathy.

Right effort supports right action and requires that the mind be prepared for meditation, for right effort requires mental energy. Daily practice purifies the thoughts and so releases mental energy for sustained concentration.

7 RIGHT MINDFULNESS

Mindfulness is presence of mind, attentiveness, being aware of what is going on in the present. This second stage of preparation for meditation involves the cultivation of constant self-awareness – of the body, the mind and thought processes, and the feelings. Practising right mindfulness, one becomes aware of the transient nature of thoughts, bodily sensations, feelings, wants and cravings – the impermanence of all things. Constant vigilance of thought, speech and action strengthens the mind, making it easier to cultivate mindfulness. The aim is to discipline the mind to achieve steady concentration.

8 RIGHT CONCENTRATION

Meditation is the eighth step on the path. Achieving right concentration means reaching the stage of being able to calm the mind and concentrate on one object, subject or theme. This involves practising meditation techniques.

THE FIVE PRECEPTS

ALL BUDDHISTS OBSERVE THE FIVE PRECEPTS. THESE ARE NOT LAWS
LAID DOWN BY ANY GOD, NOR A VOW TO ANY SUPERNATURAL BEING,
BUT A PROMISE TO ONESELF TO OBSERVE EACH RULE, THE AIM
BEING TO DIMINISH ATTACHMENT TO HARMFUL PRACTICES.

*Above A respect for living creatures is
enshrined in the First Precept. Buddhists
are prohibited from professions that
involve the intentional killing of animals.*

An important part of the
Noble Eightfold Path,
implicit in right action, right
speech and right livelihood, is the
need to live a moral, virtuous life.
Dishonesty and immorality hurt
others and have a harmful effect
on those who commit them in
that they leave a negative imprint
on the consciousness. This inhibits
the attainment of wisdom and
insight and hence the ability to
achieve enlightenment.

*Below Monks dress statues at
Borobudur in saffron robes. The first
Buddhist monks adopted saffron robes
because they were worn by the poor.*

Committing acts that transgress
the law of Dharma, which
governs the universe, results in
the continuation of the cycle of
death and rebirth, and hence suffering, through the accumulation
of 'bad' karma.

RULES FOR LIVING

The Buddha established a number
of basic rules of conduct for his
followers. The most important of
these have been preserved as the
Pancasila, the Five Precepts that all
lay followers must accept on
becoming Buddhists. By making a
solemn commitment to observe
the Five Precepts and follow the

Eightfold Path, one reduces the
danger of committing acts that
will increase negative karma.

1 TO REFRAIN FROM INJURING LIVING BEINGS

"Whosoever strives only for his
own happiness, and in so doing
hurts or kills living creatures

which also seek for happiness, he shall find no happiness after death", states the *Dharmapada*, a text of the Pali canon.

This first precept requires that Buddhists treat other creatures with compassion and kindness informed by an understanding of the relationship between all living things. The extension of this injunction to all forms of life, including vermin and harmful creatures, can pose ethical conundrums for Buddhists.

2 TO REFRAIN FROM STEALING

Literally "to refrain from taking what is not given", this involves all forms of stealing, including stealing time from one's employer and engaging in dubious business practices, to coveting someone else's boyfriend or wife. Tied in with this precept is the idea that those who acquire wealth should not cling to it but use it for the benefit of humanity.

3 TO REFRAIN FROM SEXUAL IMMORALITY

All Buddhists are urged not to cause harm to others or themselves through enslavement to sexual indulgence. The attraction of the body is transient and training oneself to manage the powerful sexual urge – to deflect it in the direction of creativity, perhaps – is to make an important advance in banishing the second of the 'Three Poisons' that keep the cycle of samsara in motion.

4 TO REFRAIN FROM LYING

To follow the way of the Truth necessarily demands the truth in thought, word and deed. The Fourth Precept requires that one brings tendencies to exaggeration and inaccuracy under control, together with the habit of speaking ill of other people.

5 TO REFRAIN FROM INTOXICANTS

'Intoxicants' include alcohol and recreational drugs, and indeed anything that clouds the mind and prevents one from living in the present and seeing things as they really are, however painful that may be. Most schools and teachers take the Fifth Precept very seriously, but some commentators consider it to be less important than the other four because some texts omit it.

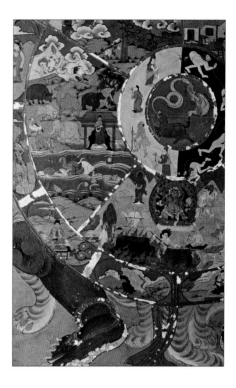

Above A detail of a wheel of life, showing the 'Three Poisons' in the middle keeping the wheel turning. The foot of Yama, the personification of Death, can be seen protruding at the bottom of the wheel.

By making a solemn commitment to observe the Five Precepts and follow the Noble Eightfold Path, one reduces the danger of committing acts that will increase negative karma.

MERIT

Rebirth into a higher realm of the Buddhist universe and the duration of an individual's stay there before rebirth depend on the balance of 'good' and 'bad' karma accumulated during life. Right actions, such as charity, moral conduct and meditation, hearing Dharma talks, attending religious events and making pilgrimages to holy sights, all earn *punya*, or merit, which increases one's balance of 'good' karma. Anything that helps overcome the 'Three Poisons' (ignorance, delusion and hatred), including observing the Five Precepts, acquires merit. Actions taken with good intentions sometimes cause harm, but if the intention was genuine, the consequences of the action do not produce 'bad' karma. However, actions carried out with the intention of earning karma points, rather than a genuine desire to help the afflicted and attain enlightenment, are unlikely to earn 'good' karma.

Right Monks go out each morning to collect food. This is not begging, but rather allowing lay people the opportunity to earn karmic merit by giving.

THE TRIPLE REFUGE

RECITING THREE SIMPLE STATEMENTS CALLED THE 'TRIPLE REFUGE' CONFIRMS A PERSON'S CONVERSION TO BUDDHISM, AND IT IS ALSO A DECLARATION OF CONTINUING COMMITMENT: BUDDHISTS RECITE THE TRIPLE REFUGE ON HOLY DAYS AND BEFORE DAILY MEDITATION.

Above Mañjushri is the Bodhisattva of Wisdom. His right hand wields a flaming sword, symbolizing wisdom cutting through ignorance and wrong views. In his left hand, he holds a scripture, symbolic of enlightenment.

Each Buddhist tradition has its own ceremonies for receiving new members. Some are complex. In Tibetan Buddhism, for example, newcomers must undergo specific initiation to be able to take part in certain introductory practices. But all traditions will at some stage require new members to make these statements:

> *I take refuge in the Buddha.*
> ~
> *I take refuge in the Dharma.*
> ~
> *I take refuge in the Sangha.*

Reciting these declarations, called the Triple Refuge, is the minimum required to become a Buddhist. They may simply be spoken three times by an individual, who should also read and understand the Four Noble Truths, follow the Noble Eightfold Path and observe the Five Precepts (not to harm living creatures, not to steal, to refrain from sexual immorality, not to lie and not to take intoxicants). But it is better to recite or chant the Triple Refuge in the presence of a member of the Sangha, or as part of a group. Becoming a Buddhist – a renunciant – is a solemn commitment, and it is appropriate to celebrate it with some ceremony.

TAKING REFUGE

After his enlightenment, the scriptures recount how the Buddha accepted food offered to him by two foreign merchants.

In return, the Buddha granted them refuge in himself and his teachings. Soon afterward, the five ascetics to whom he preached his First Sermon became the nucleus of the first Buddhist community. This marked the formation of the first Sangha, and some weeks later, the father of Yashas, a young bhikkhu (monk), became the first lay follower to take the Triple Refuge.

To 'take refuge' means to renounce one's former dependence on worldly possessions and achievements for happiness – dependence on social position, for example, earning power, career, or even friends and family – and to trust one's spiritual welfare and future progress and happiness to the 'Three Treasures' (another term for the Triple Refuge, which is also called the Triple Gem).

Left The triratna is the symbol of the Triple Refuge, also called the Three Treasures, the Three Jewels, and the Triple Gem. This Gandharan frieze shows the triratna beneath the Dharma Wheel on the Buddha's footprints.

THREE PRECIOUS THINGS

The Buddha, the Dharma and the Sangha are so precious that they are often represented in Buddhist art as jewels. Each one is invested with many layers of meaning.

1 THE BUDDHA

Having experienced life's comforts and sensual excitements, yet renounced them in order to seek the untrodden path to *bodhi*, the Buddha is a spiritual ideal to follow. To 'take refuge in the Buddha' is to find peace of mind in his example and to learn from his understanding of the nature of reality at times when life ceases to satisfy or becomes painful.

2 THE DHARMA

The ancient law of the universe and morality was the Truth the Buddha rediscovered during his enlightenment. His awakening enabled him to see things as they really are. To 'take refuge in the Dharma' is to accept the Buddha's teachings as a guide for how to live. It offers counsel to those who seek advice, and knowledge of the nature of reality for those in a quest for guidance on the path to nirvana.

Right The Triple Refuge is depicted as three 'baskets', symbolizing stores of knowledge, in this thangka *in the Pemayangtse monastery, India.*

3 THE SANGHA

It is difficult to make steady spiritual progress alone. Concentration is difficult to achieve and all individuals have shortcomings that impede their advancement. The experienced leaders of the Sangha help individuals find the path to enlightenment. To take refuge in the Sangha is to accept support, criticism, help and advice from a community of people who share the same goal.

The true qualities of Buddha, Dharma and Sangha are called 'the Mirror of the Dharma', and reflecting on them is a practice aimed at attaining a 'mind like a mirror'. This helps the meditator develop those qualities and so attain the first stage of enlightenment, or become a 'stream-enterer'.

LAY FOLLOWERS

The Buddhist Sangha consists of bhikkhus and bhikkhunis (monks and nuns), who are forbidden to work for money, and lay people who commit themselves to the Triple Refuge. Lay followers do not aspire to attain nirvana through monastic discipline and meditation, but earn merit through *dana*, or giving. They support the monastic community materially, not only by putting food into the bowls of bhikkhus and bhikkhunis each morning but also by donating tea, cotton cloth for robes, flowers, incense and other items, and money for the monks to build and maintain monasteries and carry out charitable works. (In Cambodia, Thailand and other Buddhist countries, religious communities care for people with AIDS and their orphaned children, for example.) The laity also observe the Five Precepts and make pilgrimages to holy sites, an action that earns merit. Monks and nuns practise *dana* by giving talks on the Dharma to lay members on the twice-monthly holy days.

Right In some countries Buddhist parents send their boys from the age of seven to spend the rainy season at a temple. They take part in ceremonies and receive religious education and moral and spiritual training.

THE GOURMET BUDDHIST

AS AN ASCETIC SEARCHING FOR THE PATH TO ENLIGHTENMENT,
SIDDHARTHA GAUTAMA LEARNED THAT EXTREME SELF-DENIAL
COULD NOT HELP HIM REACH HIS GOAL. IT WAS THE MIDDLE WAY
BETWEEN ASCETICISM AND INDULGENCE THAT LED HIM TO NIRVANA.

*Above Some scriptures of the
Mahayana tradition advocate
vegetarianism. Indeed, many Buddhists
become vegetarians so that they do not
develop a callous attitude toward other
creatures and also to cultivate
compassion and loving kindness.*

The Buddha learned from experience that he needed a healthy body to achieve enlightenment. He therefore taught his followers not to starve themselves and, likewise, not to overindulge. The sixth of the ten moral precepts to which Buddhist monks and nuns still adhere is: eat one simple meal a day, before noon, and only liquids after midday.

VEGETARIANISM

The first of the Pancasila – the Five Precepts all Buddhists must observe – is to avoid killing or harming any living thing. This precept has always been the source of much controversy among Buddhists as to whether they should eat meat. Scriptures record that the Buddha ate meat and he did not make vegetarianism a rule for his disciples to follow. Indeed, the rule was that they should eat whatever they were offered by the public, whether or not they approved of it or liked it. The Middle Way also counselled that rather than starve, Buddhists should eat meat, but in the *Vanijja Sutta*, a Pali scripture, dealing in flesh is listed as one of the livelihoods proscribed by the Buddha in the Noble Eightfold Path.

Monastic rules state that monks and nuns of the Theravada tradition should eat meat placed in their begging bowls, as long as the animal was not killed for them. Buddhists of the Mahayana tradition argue that animals suffer in the production of meat, so that vegetarianism must be seen as the only compassionate solution.

*Left "Let him neither kill, nor cause to
be killed any living being…", states
the* Sutta Nipata, *part of the Pali
canon. No compassionate person, it is
felt, could condone killing simply for
enjoyment, as in blood sports. This
image of a hare hunt is from a French
15th-century manuscript.*

loss of control, which can be dangerous. Dealing in intoxicants is one of the 'wrong livelihoods' specified by the Buddha, according to the *Vanijja Sutta*.

'Drugs' is usually deemed to mean nicotine as well as narcotics and the non-narcotics, such as marijuana and psychedelic drugs. Some commentators also include the caffeine in foods and drinks, such as chocolate, tea and coffee.

Several scriptures omit the Fifth Precept, while others emphasize the need to prevent the slothfulness drugs cause. No one needs alcohol to stay healthy, but sick people may need drugs to combat illness. The ideal is perfect mental, moral and physical control.

Below Monks and nuns traditionally eat food donated by lay Buddhists. They must eat what they are given, whether or not they like it. They eat no solid food after noon.

Buddhists today must consider these same arguments. Some might be equally concerned not to consume eggs or the milk of animals that have been reared inhumanely, fruit and vegetables produced by exploiting farmers in developing countries, or grain and pulses grown to the detriment of the environment.

Healthy food is a further consideration. Modern Buddhists need to weigh up the health effects of convenience foods high in sugar, fats, additives and stimulants.

INTOXICANTS

The Fifth Precept says, "I undertake to refrain from intoxicants, which lead to heedlessness." This is common sense, state the commentators, because the path to enlightenment requires clarity and presence of mind. Alcoholic drink and recreational drugs cloud the mind and, in excess, they cause

THE THREE CARDINAL VIRTUES

MANY VIRTUOUS CHARACTER TRAITS AND THEIR OPPOSITES, VICES, ARE MENTIONED IN THE BUDDHIST TEXTS. TO OVERCOME THE THREE POISONS – IGNORANCE, HATRED AND DELUSION – IT IS NECESSARY TO CULTIVATE THEIR OPPOSITES, THE THREE CARDINAL VIRTUES.

Virtue is the first step on the path to nirvana. As well as abstaining from evil and immoral deeds, Buddhists must train themselves to banish thoughts that are cruel, malevolent or unkind, dishonest or covetous, lustful or immoral. These bad habits of thought can obscure the perception of reality and in turn engender 'bad' karma. Eliminating negative character traits involves training the mind to replace them with more positive habits of thought and behaviour, such as giving and generosity. The most important Buddhist virtues are divided into three groups, which

Above A stone statue of Guanyin, the Buddhist goddess of compassion and mercy, from the Northern Wei dynasty, China, 552CE.

are known as the Three Cardinal Virtues. Buddhists believe that all other virtues emanate from these three.

1 NON-ATTACHMENT
This is the virtue of unselfishness. Buddhists strive to replace the desire to make one's own physical and psychological needs a priority with an impulse to think of others first. Part of this involves not looking to others to provide recognition of one's good intentions, actions or achievements.

2 BENEVOLENCE OR LOVING KINDNESS
This is goodwill toward all living beings. Early in meditation practice, Buddhists are asked to contemplate the consequences of the opposite of this virtue: anger, ill will and hatred. They then contrast those with the fruits of

Left In this Tibetan thangka, seven Medicine Buddhas represent the Buddha's power to heal suffering, using compassion and loving kindness.

COMPASSION

Karuna, or compassion, is the 'Law of Laws, eternal harmony'. Compassion is identification with and empathy toward life's many forms. All Buddhist traditions reject the notion that it is right for people to strive only for their own interests. This produces suffering. To embrace the concerns of other people and other forms of life is to work for the benefit of all life.

The Buddha delayed his passing into the bliss of nirvana out of compassion for humans who were struggling in ignorance, unaware of nirvana. The Mahayana tradition considered it wrong for monks to work for their own salvation and ignore the suffering of others, and elevated to the highest ideal the principle of service to the wellbeing of the world. An important aspect of seeing things as they are is recognizing and accepting one's own mortality and empathizing with the mortality of others.

Right Tara, an emanation of Avalokiteshvara, the Bodhisattva of Compassion, is depicted in this Sri Lankan temple painting. The 3 eyes in her head and those on the palms of her 12 hands enable her to see all human pain.

goodwill and its associated virtues: patience and forbearance. The next step is to shut out negative attitudes, from antipathy to ill will and anger, and replace them with benevolence, first to oneself, then outward to one's family, friends and colleagues, then to rivals and enemies, and finally to humankind and all life.

3 UNDERSTANDING

This is an awareness and comprehension of human suffering, as set out in the Four Noble Truths. The Buddha's recognition that all living beings suffer as a result of samsara is evidence of his extraordinary understanding. The second step on the Noble Eightfold Path, right resolve, promotes understanding of human nature and how it develops and changes, and of human good. The purpose of meditating on understanding is to bring oneself to desire the welfare and happiness of all beings.

FOUR HEAVENLY ABODES

The qualities of compassion, kindness, joy and equanimity, or peace of mind, are highly valued in Buddhism and carefully cultivated. These virtues are called the 'Heavenly Abodes' or the 'Four Immeasurables' (Pali: *Brahmavihara*).

Compassion is the partner of wisdom; it emanates from seeing reality and understanding life as a unity, changeable but indivisible, and oneself as subject to the same suffering as all other humans and other forms of life. Loving kindness is the natural response and it is cultivated by active concern for other people's problems and difficulties through everyday acts of generosity and by kindness.

The word 'charity' may bring to mind patronizing attitudes and assumptions of social and moral superiority. When compassion emanates from wisdom and is expressed through loving kindness, however, charity is offered with unconditional sympathy.

Bodhicitta is the name given in the Mahayana tradition to the compassionate motivation to attain enlightenment not for one's own salvation but solely to benefit others, whatever they might have done to cause them to remain trapped in samsara.

Below Phra Alongkot Tikhapanyo has founded a hospice in Thailand for HIV-positive children. Many Buddhist viharas help children orphaned by AIDS.

MEDITATION

AN ESSENTIAL PART OF BUDDHIST PRACTICE, MEDITATION CAN BRING ABOUT A TRANSFORMATION FROM NEGATIVE TO POSITIVE MENTAL STATES. IT PROMOTES THE PENETRATING INSIGHT AND UNDERSTANDING NEEDED TO ATTAIN ENLIGHTENMENT.

Meditation, or *bhavana*, which was a common practice among ascetics, was the tool the Buddha used to search for enlightenment, and it was during prolonged meditation that he achieved it. Meditation is therefore a central practice of all Buddhist schools and traditions.

To meditate is to bring about an altered state of consciousness in controlled ways that are conducive to liberation. Learning therefore involves becoming adept at a number of mind control techniques, starting with right mindfulness and right concentration – steps 6, 7 and 8 of

Below Monks spend much of their time alone in meditation, traditionally at dawn, midday and in the evening. This monk is at Sarnath, where the Buddha gave his First Sermon.

the Noble Eightfold Path. It is difficult for a beginner simply to concentrate – the mind wanders and extraneous thoughts grab the attention. For this reason, meditation is a serious discipline that requires daily practice. Until fairly recently in the Theravada tradition – an embodiment of the oldest Buddhist traditions – only monks practised meditation.

CALMING THE MIND

A commitment to regular practice brings rich rewards, nevertheless. To achieve right concentration, beginners might focus on the breathing, on repeating a mantra – a sacred word or saying – or they might observe in minute detail an object, such as a coloured disc or a flower, placed a few feet away. This was the meditative stage, *samadhi*, or trance meditation,

Above A buddha in walking meditation, radiating peace and serenity. His right hand, raised in the abhaya *mudra, symbolizes fearlessness; his left is extended in the gesture of giving, the* vadara *mudra.*

that the Buddha reached with his teachers. Trance meditation techniques achieve steady concentration on the object, and eventually absorption in it, so that the difference between 'I' and 'it' dissolves. This induces an exhilarated mental state, or dhyana. Trance meditation calms the mind to a state of deep inner stillness that can be blissful. These states of mind affect the personality generally, so that concentration, calmness and attention are heightened in everyday life.

INSIGHT

From calming meditation techniques, students may move on to *vipassana*, or insight meditation, following the steps of the Buddha, who left his teachers to work on meditation techniques that would

Above The Buddha sits in meditation in the full lotus position in this relief from the Gangarama temple, Sri Lanka. His hands rest on his lap in the dhyana mudra, a gesture that in Buddhist iconography is reserved for buddhas.

Above The dhyana mudra is a commonly used gesture of meditation. It symbolizes perfect balance of thought, peace and tranquillity, and concentration on the Dharma. It is also a comfortable position for the hands during seated meditation.

lead to enlightenment. Many Buddhist schools now teach only *vipassana*. This achieves knowledge derived from insight – not from flashes of insight but from a steady state of deep intuitive perception.

The meditator directs awareness first to the body, beginning with 'one-pointed' focus on the breathing, then going on to notice during meditation, but without making any response, every aspect of the anatomy and the sensations. This stage is called 'bare attention'. Later, the meditator will contemplate death and decay, attending cremations as well as meditating on corpses.

The second stage is to apply the same technique to the mind – its thoughts, moods, feelings. Person and personality are considered from the point of view of the 'three marks of existence' – impermanence (*anitya*), suffering (*duhkha*) and non-self (*anatman*). Under this critical scrutiny thought patterns, such as desire, hatred and ignorance, reveal themselves and the thought processes that give rise to them become clear. To achieve this final stage, called 'clear comprehension', involves mastering a complexity of techniques and can take many years.

Following the Noble Eightfold Path never stops being a prerequisite of meditation. Ceasing to strive for the right view or right resolve, or abandoning right action and right effort, affects the quality of meditation, no matter how advanced the meditator, and imposes an obstruction on the path to enlightenment for the disciple.

THE DHYANAS

Dhyanas are mental states or trance levels reached during meditation that correspond to the realms of the Buddhist universe, illustrated in the Wheel of Life.

The first level is a rapture that stems from success in calming and concentrating the mind to achieve 'one-pointed' meditation. The second-level meditator is adept at 'one-pointed' meditation, and elation is tempered by serenity and trust in the teaching. The third level is characterized by 'one-pointed' meditation and tranquil happiness. At the fourth level, happiness has subsided into equanimity, feeling is blanked out, and sharper mindfulness begins to break down the sense of self. Psychic powers appear, such as retrocognition – memory of past lives.

The Buddha transcended these levels, which are characterized by bodily awareness, and moved into the Sphere of Formlessness. From the fifth level, Infinite Space, and the sixth, Infinite Consciousness, he dissolved into Nothingness at the seventh, and passed from the eighth, the temporary end of consciousness and sensation, into nirvana.

ENLIGHTENMENT

BUDDHA MEANS 'AWAKENED', SO A BUDDHA IS A BEING WHO HAS
ACHIEVED SPIRITUAL AWAKENING (*BODHI*). THIS STATE OF AWAKENING,
USUALLY CALLED ENLIGHTENMENT — OR BY ITS SANSKRIT NAME,
NIRVANA — IS THE GOAL OF BUDDHISTS OF ALL TRADITIONS.

Some people who have claimed to have entered nirvana have attempted to describe their experiences, and their efforts have always supported the truism that the experience of nirvana is ineffable: "I was the cosmos"; "I have forgotten the dread of birth and death". Nirvana is commonly defined as a state of perfect peace, bliss and heightened awareness. The Buddhist scriptures describe it as "the liberated mind that no longer clings", "the great, perfect mirror wisdom", or as the absence of anxiety, fear and doubt, a state

Below Parinirvana, from The Life of Buddha Sakyamuni. *Buddhists see parinirvana neither as death nor as an afterlife, but rather as the ultimate state of non-existence, from which there is no rebirth.*

of non-existence. The *Udana*, a book of the Pali canon, famously describes nirvana as the "Unborn, Unoriginated, Uncreated, Unformed."

'Nirvana' means 'extinction', in the sense of quenching thirst or blowing out a flame. What is extinguished is *trishna*, or desire. The implicit promise of the Third Noble Truth is that liberation will follow the complete cessation of desire: "the withdrawal from it, the renouncing of it, the rejection of it, liberation from it, non-attachment to it". What is also extinguished is samsara, the cycle of birth-death-rebirth. This occurs because the enlightened individual has gained full wisdom and succeeded in overcoming the *kleshas* — ignorance, hatred and delusion — replacing them with compassion and loving kindness, and is able to see existence as it is.

Above In Tantric rituals, a bell, symbol of wisdom, is held in the left hand. The bell is topped by the five spokes of a vajra (thunderbolt), symbolizing the five forms of mystical wisdom.

Above For two weeks after his enlightenment, the Buddha stood staring, unblinking, at the Bodhi tree, as depicted in this monumental rock carving in Polonnaruwa, Sri Lanka.

It was compassion and loving kindness that inspired the Buddha to remain on Earth after his awakening, to show others the path to enlightenment – a state called 'nirvana-in-this-life'. At the end of his life, he entered parinirvana – 'complete nirvana'. Neither death, nor the afterlife, parinirvana is considered to be a state of non-existence, from which the Buddha would never be reborn.

FOUR STAGES TO NIRVANA

'Enlightenment' suggests sudden insight – 'seeing the light' – but in fact reaching nirvana often takes many years. It involves cultivating prajna, or wisdom. This is achieved through meditation, which may act as a catalyst to enlightenment in bringing about sudden flashes of insight.

The Buddha named four stages on the path to nirvana, each of which is marked by release from some of the 'ten fetters' – obstacles to enlightenment. These stages are as follows:

1 **'Stream-enterer'** This first, often momentary and powerful experience of selflessness is a sign that one has overcome the first three fetters. These impediments to enlightenment are the belief that the self is permanent and unchanging; residual doubt in the Buddha's teachings; and the clinging to pointless practices and rituals. Rapture and relief follow when the disciple has understood the nature of 'non-self'.

2 **'Once-returner'** Renewed efforts to weaken the fetters of sensual desire and overcome ill will, aided by the practice of advanced meditation techniques, result in a second, clearer experience of selflessness. At this stage, there is only one rebirth to endure before a disciple attains nirvana.

Above Miroku Bosatsu is the Japanese Maitreya, the future Buddha. Some believe that far into the future he will appear on Earth to save those who have been unable to achieve enlightenment.

3 **'Never-returner'** Complete removal of the first five fetters brings about contentment and loss of desire and a third experience of 'non-self'. 'Never-returners' are reborn into the highest planes of the Sphere of Form.

4 **Arhat** Those who release the last five fetters – craving for material and non-material existence, conceit, restlessness and ignorance – understand the Four Noble Truths and attain enlightenment.

SANSKRIT WORDS

bodhi wisdom, intuition, enlightenment, awakening.

buddha meaning 'awakened', a buddha is any being who has achieved enlightenment (*bodhi*).

mantra a word or phrase with a powerful meaning used as an aid to meditation and as an incantation.

nirvana 'extinction', liberation from the cyclical existence in samsara, or death and rebirth, enlightenment.

parinirvana 'complete nirvana', the nirvana that takes place after death, the complete extinction of the individual, characterized by freedom from the effects of karma.

samadhi a practice in meditation in which one becomes absorbed in the object of meditation, leading to 'one-pointed' concentration.

satori a usually sudden spiritual awakening, an intuitive understanding of the nature of reality, achieved in Zen Buddhism.

vipassana literally 'inward vision' (the Sanskrit term is *vipashyana*), meditation techniques to promote a clear understanding of the nature of reality through insight.

DEVOTION

THE BUDDHA'S DISCIPLES ELEVATED MEDITATION AND OBSERVANCE OF THE RULES ABOVE RITES AND WORSHIP, BUT LATER SCHOOLS ENCOURAGED DEVOTION TO BUDDHAS AND ARHATS. TODAY, RITUAL AND DEVOTION ARE A VALUED PART OF BUDDHIST PRACTICE.

Above A lay follower washes a statue of the Bodhisattva Jizo at a temple in Japan. Buddhist devotion includes cleaning and caring for public and private shrines and sacred objects.

The Buddha warned his first followers against starting a personality cult when he was no longer with them. Their task was to seek out and follow the path that led to spiritual awakening, and his role was to guide them along this path. It was his teaching that was important, not his personality. His life was relevant, but only inasmuch as it acted as an inspiration to others and exemplified the route that everyone's life must take if they are to succeed in achieving spiritual transformation and enlightenment.

Below Circumambulation is an important part of Buddhist devotion. Followers walk around a stupa, statue or shrine reciting mantras or sutras, or meditating.

A FIGURE OF WORSHIP

Despite his wishes to the contrary, within 100 years of his pari-nirvana, the Buddha was being glorified, not as the one god, creator of the world, as in other religions, but as a superhuman. In addition, Buddhism had adopted a complex pantheon of supernatural beings, and had become more of a religion than a philosophy.

This change was due partly to the popularity of the Mahayana tradition, which emerged during the 1st century CE, and held that faith in the compassion of bodhisattvas, rather than personal effort through meditation and careful observance of the rules of the Sangha, was the key to salvation. However, the Buddha never rejected the beliefs and practices of older religions, and neither did the Buddhism that followed him. Further, as the early, more intellectually rigorous Buddhism began to reach out to a wider public, the enthusiasm of that public naturally embraced its spirituality.

The early Sangha laid great emphasis on remembrance of the Buddha and on his 'living presence' in stupas that contained his relics. Disciples reported that when they approached these stupas, they observed magical light rays or even the form of the Buddha himself emanating from the stupas. Visions like these inspired followers to make images and venerate them – as representations of the Buddha, not as deities. To invoke the Buddha's 'living presence', images were engraved with sacred words, and small relics, or mandalas, were secreted inside or beneath them.

BUDDHIST PRAYER

In the Theravada tradition, which claims to follow the Buddha's original teachings, prayer was

PROSTRATION

Lay Buddhists and monks perform prostrations as an act of veneration to the Buddha, his teachings and the Sangha, which are collectively called the Three Treasures or the Triple Gem. Prostrations are believed to cleanse the spirit of pride, suppress desire, and clear the mind of *kleshas* – poisonous emotions such as hatred, desires such as lust, and negative attitudes such as laziness – which impede concentration, so Buddhists prostrate themselves before and after meditation. The prostration practices of the different traditions and schools vary: Zen Buddhists often make half-prostrations; in Theravada Buddhism, three 'five-point prostrations' may be performed at the start of puja (worship): palms, elbows, toes, knees and forehead all touch the floor; Vajrayana Buddhists prostrate themselves fully, usually on a mat placed on the floor, with the arms held out in front. Beads may be used to count 108 full-length prostrations made while reciting prayers or mantras.

Right A Thai monk makes a five-point prostration before a statue of the Buddha at Wat Phra Si Ratana Mahathat, a temple in Phitsanulok, Thailand. In the Theravada tradition, prostration is the most respectful form of worship.

secondary to meditation and studying or chanting the scriptures. The role of all these practices was to concentrate the mind, and prayer involved repeating expressions of universal hope – 'May all beings have happiness and the causes of happiness...' – or of veneration for the Buddha. However, Mahayana monks introduced the practice of praying to bodhisattvas and other deities for personal help. Some schools promoted the chanting of mantras, mystical sayings such as *Om mani padme hum* ('Praise to the jewel in the lotus'), as a prayer-like practice to aid concentration.

All traditions consider it meritorious to worship anything that recalls the Buddha or Dharma, to keep a shrine clean and to decorate it with coverings, artworks and lights, and to pay respect to an image that recalls the Buddha or a bodhisattva by reverential gestures and prostrations.

At home, Buddhists set aside a corner for a household shrine, furnished with a statue of the Buddha, or a painting or mandala, where they can retire to study sacred texts, meditate and pray.

Above Buddhists leave offerings of water and even food at a shrine, as well as incense and candles. Placing her hands together in anjali *mudra, the gesture of offering, this woman recites a mantra to aid concentration, or says a prayer.*

BUDDHIST ETHICS

THE DHARMA, THE UNIVERSAL LAW THAT GOVERNS THE MORAL ORDER OF THE UNIVERSE, IS THE WELLSPRING OF BUDDHISM'S ETHICAL TEACHINGS. TODAY, SCRIPTURES THAT TOUCH ON ETHICS ARE BEING RE-EXAMINED TO FIND STANDPOINTS ON NEW MORAL DILEMMAS.

In light of samsara, the doctrine of rebirth, and *ahimsa*, the doctrine of non-violence, where does Buddhism stand on issues such as abortion, embryo research, war and euthanasia?

There is no Buddhist pope, no central authority to rule on ethical issues, so different traditions, schools and individuals have opposing standpoints on many important questions. Few ethical issues are clear-cut. Buddhists are enjoined to cause no harm to living beings, so it would seem that all would oppose animal experiments. However, in the absence of a ruling body, there is no all-encompassing 'Buddhist policy' on such matters.

Above Buddhist monks march for peace in Russia in front of the State Duma in Moscow. Buddhists oppose war and all forms of violence but are having to rethink their stance on such issues as pacifism and the use of force.

CONCEPTION AND BIRTH

Ancient texts clearly conclude that life begins at conception. The general view among Buddhists is that fertilization is the start of life. In countries where Buddhism is the state religion, abortion is banned; where Buddhism predominates but is not the state religion, the practice is permitted. In Japan, the custom has arisen of invoking the Bodhisattva Jizo, protector of children and expectant mothers, in *mizuko kuyo* memorial services for aborted (as well as for miscarried) children.

Stem cell extraction and human embryo cloning for therapeutic purposes are generally supported in countries where Buddhists are a majority or where Buddhism is the state religion. Individuals have expressed the view that these do not infringe the First Precept, which prohibits the taking of life, and are in keeping with the doctrine of samsara.

Left The Bodhisattva Jizo, patron of the oppressed or dying, the Japanese version of the Bodhisattva Ksitigarbha. The statues are sometimes given adornments, and this figure has been adapted to represent pregnant women and unborn children.

THE ENVIRONMENT

The Buddha opposed animal sacrifice and refrained from killing animals and even from harming plants and seeds. He enshrined non-violence toward all living things in the First Precept and banned his followers from professions that harm animals. He recognized the value of the wilderness by retreating to the forest to meditate. Furthermore, Buddhist cosmology suggests that the fate of the physical universe depends on its inhabitants, so that a world occupied by people who failed to protect it would not last as long as one that was cared for by those who lived there.

However, writers on Buddhist ethics conclude that Buddhism's main concern is human progress toward nirvana, not the protection of animals or the ecosystem. Although individuals may be actively involved in such concerns, and they accord with the requirements of the Noble Eightfold Path, Buddhism does not directly address these issues.

Above The Buddhist teachings do not promote environmental protection, but emphasize simple living, non-violence, compassion and loving kindness, and so indirectly encourage environmental concern.

SUICIDE AND EUTHANASIA

The 1960s' incidents of self-immolation by Buddhist monks in protest against religious suppression have left the impression that suicide is sanctioned by Buddhists. At the time, however, there were strong disagreements about the 1960s' incidents, and the current controversy about suicide and euthanasia extends to the Buddhist community.

Many Buddhists regard suicide as contrary to the Dharma teachings on non-violence and a squandering of the opportunity for enlightenment offered by human existence. Academics who have studied the origins of self-immolation and suicide in Eastern societies have discovered that these practices pre-date the introduction there of Buddhism. The Buddhist canon reveals little evidence that the Buddha sanctioned or condoned suicide. Furthermore, the Buddha prohibited suicide or the assisting of suicide by members of the Sangha in a monastic rule, the Third *Parajika*.

This rule applies equally to euthanasia: causing death intentionally, even out of compassion at the request of someone you love, infringes Buddhist moral teachings.

PEACE

Buddhists and Buddhist organizations have been active in opposing war and terrorism. Yet research has unearthed numerous instances in history when Buddhists have turned to fighting and insurrection.

Damien Keown, a writer on Buddhist ethics, distinguishes between warfare, implying aggression and the intention to kill, and force, which might be applied without aggression – for example, by oppressed Buddhists demanding the right to practise their religion. Warfare changed radically during the 20th century and Keown suggests that, while opposing warfare accords with Dharma teachings, Buddhist thinkers could review their religious stance on pacificism, self-defence, terrorism and concepts such as 'just war'.

Right Tibetans practise prostrations in the presence of the Chinese authorities at the Jokhang temple in Lhasa.

BUDDHISM AND PACIFICISM

THROUGHOUT BUDDHISM'S LONG HISTORY, BUDDHISTS HAVE HAD TO FIND WAYS OF RESISTING LAWS THAT WOULD SUPPRESS THEIR RELIGION AND DESTROY THE SANGHA. PACIFISM HAS BEEN THE ROUTE FOR SOME, PASSIVE RESISTANCE THE WAY FOR OTHERS.

Buddhist doctrine firmly opposes violence. The Dharma teaches that aggression stems partly from a misguided belief that the self is real and needs protection from others. Patience and forbearance are thought to be the correct responses to threat, and compassionate analysis of the situation the only rational response to aggression.

Below In September 2007, monks all over Burma (Myanmar) marched in passive protest against the people's oppression and poverty, brought about by the policies of the military junta.

During the 3rd century BCE, there arose in India a Mauryan ruler who became an icon of pacifism. In 268BCE, Emperor Ashoka of the Mauryan dynasty fought his brothers for the dynastic throne, then set out to conquer what became a vast empire. A bloody war to overthrow Kalinga (modern Orissa), caused a watershed in Ashoka's life. Stricken with remorse at the destruction he had caused, he became a devout lay Buddhist and adopted a policy of complete non-violence. He then dedicated his life to spreading Buddhism throughout his empire.

Above A fragment of an inscription of one of the edicts of the 3rd-century BCE Mauryan emperor Ashoka, who proclaimed his support of the Dharma and a change of policy to peaceful co-existence with neighbouring states.

MODERN CONFLICTS

In modern times, many Buddhists have chosen passive resistance as their response to threat and aggression. This is peaceable action to achieve aims through, for example, non-violent protest, acts of non-co-operation and disobedience, lobbying, or media publicity.

The stance of Tibetan exiles in 1951 against the Chinese occupation of their country is the outstanding example of Buddhist passive resistance to religious repression. The resistance is led by the 14th Dalai Lama, who was strongly influenced by Mahatma Gandhi's *satyagraha* movement of non-violent opposition to colonial rule in India, and he has formed a Tibetan government-in-exile. Inside Tibet, monks, nuns and lay followers have often used permitted religious activities, such as circumambulating a temple, as occasions for demonstrations against the Chinese authorities.

The shocking suicides of six Vietnamese monks and a nun during the 1960s may be seen as an extreme and highly controversial

Right Press photographer Malcolm Browne captured the self-immolation of 73-year-old Vietnamese monk Thich Quang Duc in 1963, in the latter's protest against the anti-Buddhist policies of the Vietnamese premier.

form of passive resistance. Their objective was to make a stand against, and draw the world's attention to, the anti-Buddhist policies of the dictator Ngo Dinh Diem, and to request religious equality. The deaths by self-immolation of the first two, older, monks, Thich Quang Duc and Thich Tieu Dieu, were sanctioned by their religious authorities. These acts had a spectacular impact on world opinion, but they were later condemned by many Buddhists as contrary to Buddhist teachings.

DOES IT WORK?

The effectiveness of non-violent protest is questionable. Some people argue, for example, that despite almost half a century of passive resistance by the Dalai Lama and his followers, the Tibetan people are no nearer independence, and although the right to practise their religion has ostensibly been restored, it is nevertheless heavily restricted.

Faced with persistent economic decline and political repression, Buddhists living under repressive regimes feel there may be no alternative to passive resistance – or at least little to lose by it.

Non-violent protests by Buddhists took place in Burma (Myanmar) during 2007. Small-scale, non-religious protests against the removal of fuel subsidies evolved into what has been called the 'saffron revolution', as some 20,000 monks all over the country led protests against the economic distress of the population. Monks, supported by the people, marched, carrying the Buddhist flag, while chanting the words of the Buddha. They refused to administer religious services to the military. Within days, many had been arrested, to face possible torture and death at the hands of government agents.

CONSCIENTIOUS OBJECTORS

The Buddha is said to have warned that warriors who are intent on killing at the moment of their death go to a special hell. The 4th-century scholar-monk Vasubandhu warned that all killing is wrong, even in self-defence, and even for conscripted soldiers. In recent years, many South Korean Buddhists have been imprisoned for declaring themselves conscientious objectors and refusing to report for military service when they were conscripted.

The experiences of Aidan Delgado, an American who enrolled in the army on 9/11, are more widely known. After enlistment, Delgado became a Buddhist. In 2003, his unit was sent to Iraq, and his experiences there motivated him to apply for discharge from the military as a conscientious objector. Meanwhile, his unit was transferred to the notorious Abu Ghraib prison in Baghdad, where he witnessed horrifying cruelty and abuse. After his discharge, he published a book about his experiences and became an anti-war activist.

Right Since conscription began in South Korea, some 10,000 Buddhists have declared themselves conscientious objectors. This is a criminal offence for which the penalty is imprisonment. Military police arrested Private Kang Chol-min, a conscript, in November 2003, for staging a protest against government plans to send troops to Iraq.

CHAPTER 3

EARLY BUDDHISM

During the first centuries after the Buddha passed away, Buddhism grew from a minor sect into a major religion. Within a year of the Buddha's death, his disciples convened a council to review his words and establish a body of doctrine, then travelled across the Indian subcontinent spreading his teachings. The Buddha had been a pioneer of religious organization, founding the first monastic order, the Sangha, which admitted followers of all castes, and permitting the formation of a women's Sangha.

By the 3rd century BCE, schisms appeared and the Sangha split into two traditions. Those who adhered to the Buddha's original teachings were known as the 'elders'. Today, their tradition is called Theravada, or the 'way of the elders'. Another competing tradition elevated the Buddha to the status of a deity, and emphasized the potential of all beings to attain buddhahood. It is known as Mahayana, or the 'great vehicle', meaning that its adherents view their belief as the way to salvation. Later, a third tradition, Vajrayana, or Tantric, Buddhism, which emphasized the attainment of buddhahood in one lifetime, emerged from Mahayana Buddhism. Today, this tradition, which developed in Tibet after the 7th century, is often called Tibetan Buddhism.

Opposite An 8th-century Chinese silk painting of the Buddha preaching. At the beginning of the first millennium, monks and scholars began to translate Buddhist texts into Chinese, facilitating the transmission of Buddhism to China.

Above A contemporaneous statue of Kanishka, the 2nd-century ruler of the Kushan empire, which extended from Afghanistan into India. Kanishka embraced Buddhism and encouraged its spread into Central Asia.

THE FIRST BUDDHISTS

THE WORK OF PRESERVING THE BUDDHA'S TEACHINGS THROUGH THE ORAL TRADITION GAINED MOMENTUM AFTER THE FIRST BUDDHIST COUNCIL. THE LEADING ARHATS TRANSMITTED THE DHARMA TO THE SANGHA, WHO DISSEMINATED IT WIDELY ACROSS INDIA.

Mahakashyapa, ascetic and disciple, was the force behind the preservation of the Dharma at the First Buddhist Council. Without him, Buddhism might have remained just another minor sect among many. He was the unofficial patriarch, the 'father of the Sangha', for some years until, before passing into nirvana, he handed over the role to another arhat, Ananda.

Below This Tibetan rock painting depicts the Buddha with the 16 arhats. According to Mahayana texts, at the First Buddhist Council they renounced nirvana to devote themselves to relieving suffering by teaching the Dharma.

Ananda, whose ability to memorize was awe-inspiring, was charged with relaying the Buddha's long discourses, including the *Digha Nikaya*, a collection of 34 sutras, or suttas. It is said that he also taught thousands of monks.

THE WOMEN'S ORDER

The Buddha had exhorted his monks to teach "for the welfare of the many". After the First Buddhist Council, the Sangha carried his teachings all over the sub-continent. Among these first disciples were many bhikkhunis, or nuns.

While in Vaishali during the fifth year after his awakening, the Buddha was approached by a

Above Since the time of the Buddha, bhikkhus and bhikkhunis have met twice a month to chant the sacred texts. These Tibetan monks of the Geluk sect chant rhythmically to the accompaniment of cymbals.

party of Sakya women led by his aunt, Mahaprajapati, who asked to join the Sangha. The Buddha refused. The women persisted with their request to found an order of bhikkhunis. Eventually, Ananda, whose gift for resolving disputes the Buddha himself had recognized, intervened. He asked

Right This Chinese Tang dynasty tympanum shows Mahakashyapa and Ananda at the Buddha's side. Each led the Sangha after the Buddha's parinirvana, and both ensured the preservation of the Dharma teachings.

the Buddha whether women could attain nirvana. The Buddha affirmed that they could.

The Buddha is said to have feared that the Sangha would not last if women were admitted. (As many contemporary writers point out, such attitudes may be regarded in the context of strong taboos against women in 3rd millennium BCE India.) The Buddha agreed that a women's Sangha could be founded, but on the condition that the women be subject to extra rules, mainly governing chastity and their subordination to the authority of the monks.

Ananda supported these female disciples, helped them with problems of isolation, rejection and discrimination, taught them the rules of practice, preached the Dharma to them, and encouraged the Buddha to grant them ordination. In time, the women's Sangha flourished.

THE GROWING SANGHA

From the perspective of the 21st century, it can be difficult to appreciate the impact during the 3rd millennium BCE of the Sangha, with its women members, on Indian society and its rigid hierarchy of castes. Monasticism was a form of religious organization pioneered by the Buddha, who imposed certain restrictions on membership – criminals, debtors and runaway slaves were excluded, while any bhikkhus or bhikkhunis guilty of a serious offence, such as violence, sexual misconduct or

theft, were expelled. However, he admitted people from all castes, as well as women, believing that all had the potential to attain nirvana.

Clad in the poorest garb and possessing little, bhikkhus and bhikkhunis travelled the country in pairs or small groups, sleeping and meditating in the forests, approaching villages in the mornings to beg alms. Inspiring respect for their calm friendliness toward people of all castes, they were granted many opportunities to teach the Dharma and gained converts. Thus, the Sangha grew.

CAVE VIHARAS

Caves were natural shelters for the homeless poor in India in the late 3rd millennium BCE, including the bhikkhus and bhikkhunis of the early Sangha. The hills around Rajgir, the ancient capital of Maghada, are studded with caves once used by the Buddha and his followers for meditation or as communal dwellings during rainy seasons. Caves were also used for devotion and for meetings and councils. As converts joined the Sangha, cave settlements were extended to establish more permanent viharas. Where the rock was soft, monks would burrow into cliffs and mountainsides to excavate cave complexes with dwellings, shrines and assembly halls, or build meeting halls and temples in wood. No wooden structures remain, but some 12,000 excavated caves have been discovered on the Indian subcontinent, of which perhaps about 8,000 were created by Buddhists, and the remainder by Jains and adherents of the Brahmanic religions.

Above India's magnificent Ajanta cave temples began as a row of four or five monks' cells cut into an escarpment of the Indhyadri hills in Maharashtra by Buddhist monks during the 2nd century BCE.

THE FIRST BUDDHIST SCRIPTURES

THE TEACHINGS OF THE BUDDHA WERE TRANSMITTED BY WORD OF MOUTH FOR SOME 300 YEARS. ACCORDING TO TRADITION, THEY WERE FIRST WRITTEN DOWN DURING THE 1ST CENTURY BCE BY MONKS WORKING IN A CAVE VIHARA, OR TEMPLE, IN SRI LANKA.

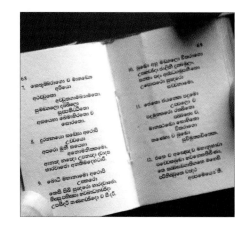

Above Pali, a literary and liturgical language, is written in a number of different scripts. The entire Tripitaka is printed in the Sinhala script, which originated 2,000 years ago, in this modern miniature book.

What language did the Buddha speak? A man of his social status in northern India would have known Sanskrit, the language of the elite, and Magadhi Prakrit, an ancient form of a language that is still spoken today around Bihar. But Buddhism has no official language, because the Buddha directed that the Dharma should be taught in the languages and dialects the people spoke.

Writing was known in India by the 3rd millennium BCE, but not widely, and the Buddha and his followers would have been illiterate. The Buddha's teachings were summarized in short verses called sutras, which were memorized by chanting. Writing spread across India from about the 3rd century BCE, but was used mainly in commerce. As the written word became more widespread, parts of the canon may have been written down by monks in northern India, but there is no historical evidence to determine when the sutras, which for centuries had been spread through the oral tradition, first appeared in written form.

THE PALI SCRIPTURES

The earliest surviving complete version of the Buddhist scriptures was written in Pali, a language that some scholars believe may be

Below This wall in the 11th-century Ananda temple in Bagan, Burma (Myanmar), was painted to teach one of the Jataka Tales, or stories of the Buddha's past lives, from the Khuddaka Nikaya, a section of the Sutta Pitaka.

THE FIRST BUDDHIST BOOKS

Scholars have been unable to date the texts of the Pali canon because they were written on *ola*, the dried young leaves of the talipot, or fan palm, or the Asian Palmyra palm. The leaves were boiled in salt water, to which turmeric may have been added to preserve them, then dried and polished with a pumice stone. They were cut to a regular size, holes were punched in them, and they were bound with cord.

In a tropical climate, palm-leaf manuscripts were vulnerable to attack by damp and insects, so the text had to be repeatedly copied on to new leaves. The oldest surviving palm-leaf texts date from the 11th century CE, but most were made in the 15th century. In cold mountain regions, Buddhists preserved the texts on strips of birch bark, which they rolled up into scrolls. The oldest of these dates from before the 8th century.

related to old Magadhi. Pali was a literary language used for the writing of Buddhist texts.

Buddhism had reached Sri Lanka during the 3rd century BCE through the oral tradition, and it was strengthened during the reign of the Buddhist King Vattagamani (89-77BCE). Under his patronage, a group of monks at the Aluvihara, a cave vihara near Kandy, embarked on a project to write down the Tripitaka (Pali: Tipitaka), the 'three baskets' of teachings that had been established more than a century earlier at the First Buddhist Council and had subsequently spread across the subcontinent.

Transcribing the Tripitaka would have been carried out by the monks as an act of devotion to earn merit, but scholars query why the task was not undertaken in the Buddhist heartlands in north-eastern India, and why it was carried out by monks in a distant cave vihara and not under the supervision of King Vatta-gamani in one of the great monasteries in his capital, Anuradhapura. It is hoped that in time archaeologists may be able to shed light on such questions.

COMMENTARIES

The Pali canon includes commentaries on the core texts, the original Tripitaka. Accompanying the first part, the *Vinaya Pitaka*, or rules for monks and nuns, are supplementary rules, a commentary on the rules and a detailed analysis. The second part is the *Sutta Pitaka*, a collection of discourses attributed to the Buddha and to his leading disciples, while the third is the *Abhidharma Pitaka*, a compilation of texts on Buddhist philosophy. After the 1st century BCE, there were several revisions of the Tripitaka, of which the last part,

Above A monk in the Haeinsa temple library in South Korea holds a volume of the Korean translation of the Tripitaka printed from original 13th-century woodblocks.

the *Abhidharma Pitaka*, reveals some of the biggest changes, with the inclusion of new works.

Despite the difficulty of dating and authenticating the Tripitaka, it remains respected as a work of authority, a trustworthy account of the Buddha's teachings. Since the 1st century CE, it has been copied and translated, modified and supplemented. However, although the various versions differ in their details, all agree on the essentials of the Dharma.

Below A 19th-century illustration of stories from the life of the Buddha as recorded in the Tripitaka. Here, Siddhartha Gautama is engaged in a sumptuous procession with his retinue.

THE GREAT SCHISM

VAJJI, IN INDIA'S FAR NORTH-EAST, WAS THE WORLD'S FIRST KNOWN REPUBLIC, FORMED BY A CONFEDERATION OF CLANS. AMONG ITS CITIZENS WERE THE BHIKKHUS OF THE MAHAVANA MONASTERY IN THE CAPITAL, VAISHALI, WHO RESISTED THE EARLY SANGHA'S STRICT RULES.

There is a legend that the Buddha first visited Vaishali, the beautiful capital of the prosperous Vajji confederation, during the fifth year after his enlightenment. He did this out of compassion, because the city had been visited by drought and a terrible plague. Torrential rains fell after his arrival, washing away the pestilence. The Buddha then delivered the *Ratana Sutta*, the Discourse on Precious Jewels (Buddha, Dharma and Sangha), to the townspeople, and thousands were converted. He also gave other discourses in Vaishali and established several important rules for the Sangha there.

THE SECOND COUNCIL

Much of our understanding of how early Buddhism developed comes from texts written centuries after the Buddha's death, and they often disagree. However, it is generally accepted that about 100 years after the First Buddhist Council met at Rajagriha in order to review and memorize the Buddha's teachings following his death, another council was held, this time at Vaishali.

It is recorded that 700 arhats attended this Second Council to consider ten practices being followed by bhikkhus from the Mahavana vihara in Vaishali. These monks were accused of accepting gold and silver from lay followers, something the Buddha had denounced. They had also broken the rules on eating and drinking, by consuming palm wine, going on two alms rounds in order to eat twice, drinking buttermilk after meals, eating after midday and 'carrying salt in a horn', which was thought to infringe an

Below The Dhamekh stupa at Sarnath is said to mark the spot where the Buddha first revealed the Dharma. It has deep foundations and has endured for more than 2,000 years.

Above In the mid-3rd century BCE, the emperor Ashoka sponsored this pillar surmounted by a lion sculpture at Vaishali. Although it is sinking into soft ground, the pillar still stands at over 11m (36ft) tall.

injunction against storing food. Minor infringements included using the wrong type of mat, and breaking rules governing relationships with other viharas.

The Council leaders found against the Vajjiputtaka bhikkhus and declared their support for strict observance of the rules established by the Buddha. However, the matter did not end there.

NEW SCHOOLS

The Vajjiputtaka bhikkhus did not accept the censure. They may have regarded themselves as progressive, moving on from what they saw as over-rigorous asceticism. To the *sthavira*, or elders of the Council, the conduct of the Sangha was paramount, and to disobey rules and refuse to atone and conform

was heresy. The Vajjiputtaka bhikkhus are believed to have left the Council and, sometime in the months or possibly years that followed, to have convened their own council, perhaps to discuss new ideas that disagreed with accepted doctrine.

The Buddha had taught that the pinnacle of spiritual achievement is to attain nirvana by following his path and becoming an arhat. A buddha himself does not have a path to follow. He achieves nirvana by his own spiritual efforts at a time when the world has forgotten the Dharma. Around this time, another group of bhikkhus cast doubts on the spiritual perfection of the arhat, suggesting that a bhikkhu might aspire to become a buddha. They called themselves the Mahasamghika, or the 'Great Community'. They remained members of the Sangha, but they set off a wave of new thinking. The group that supported the original teachings became adherents of the Sthaviravada, or 'Teachings of the Elders'.

Below Arhats are ordinary humans who have achieved enlightenment with the help of a buddha. They may reside on Earth to teach the Dharma, but they are not buddhas.

EIGHTEEN SCHOOLS

More and more members of the growing Sangha abandoned the peripatetic life to settle in viharas. Communities developed in isolation, and this, added to the Mahasamghika/ Sthaviravada split and the absence of a central authority, resulted in a sectarian phase of Buddhism, with the emergence of many new schools and sects. Eighteen schools are said to have issued from the orthodox tradition, led by the Sthaviravada school, but in fact there were many more.

One was the Sarvastivada school, which emerged during the 3rd century BCE from the Sthaviravada. Similar to the Mahasamghikas, its adherents doubted the perfection of arhats, but they developed sophisticated theories about *sarvasti*, 'the existence of all things through time'. They believed that the smallest elements of existence, called dharmas, do exist, though they may have a momentary existence; and that they exist in the past and future, as well as the present. These ideas challenge the concept of *anatman*, the idea that there is no self.

Indeed, it has been argued that the Sarvastivadins anticipated some of the findings of modern physics. They believed that nothing we experience is as it appears, and that the universe consists of basic elements of existence. Sarvastivadins thought that such phenomena consisted of combinations of 75 impermanent, interchangeable dharmas – elements such as light, heat, colour, sound, breath, even birth and death.

THE FIRST BUDDHIST STATE

IN THE EIGHTH YEAR OF HIS REIGN, THE EMPEROR ASHOKA TOOK REFUGE IN THE THREE JEWELS, AND SO BECAME THE FIRST BUDDHIST EMPEROR. UNDER HIS COMPASSIONATE RULE, BUDDHISM BECAME THE STATE RELIGION OF INDIA'S MAURYAN EMPIRE.

India's first empire arose during the 4th century BCE, when an obscure prince, Chandragupta Maurya, led a conquering Maghada army westward, beyond the Indus, to overthrow the remnants of Alexander the Great's Greek armies there. His grandson, Ashoka, won the imperial throne in a war against his older brothers in 268BCE and went on to conquer the eastern coastland of Kalinga (southern Orissa) at a staggering cost in resources, lives lost and people displaced. The slaughter is said to have brought Ashoka to a spiritual crisis and, encouraged by a charismatic monk, he embraced Buddhism. Although he kept his armies at combat readiness, and a dictatorial hold on Kalinga, Ashoka pursued peaceful policies.

A BUDDHIST EMPEROR

Ashoka established a state based on practical morality. He issued edicts explaining his understanding of the Dharma – 'Few faults, many good deeds, compassion, giving, truth, purity' – and undertaking that he and his officials would govern and administer justice according to his interpretation of it. He promoted religious tolerance, undertook to protect his people and further their happiness, and used the spoils of his wars to build them dispensaries and reservoirs. He had

Above *This engraving shows the emperor Ashoka as an arhat, or enlightened being. He is depicted sitting in the lotus position on a lotus flower, hands in the dhyana mudra. His elongated earlobes and elaborate headdress signify his wisdom and spiritual advancement.*

Below *The emperor Ashoka's inscription in Brahmi script on this polished stone pillar at Sarnath directs bhikkhus and bhikkhunis not to cause dissension in the Sangha. The upper part of the pillar broke away during a lightning strike.*

Below *Ashoka's patronage ensured that Indian stone carving continued to evolve after his reign. The four entrance gates, or* torana, *to the Sanchi stupa, with their beautiful relief carvings, were added in the 1st century* BCE.

roads built, along which trees were planted and wells dug. He became a vegetarian, discouraged the sacrifice of animals and prohibited animal slaughter on certain days.

ASHOKA'S PILGRIMAGES

Furthermore, Ashoka became an *upasaka*, a lay member of the Sangha, and issued edicts throughout his realm providing moral guidance, rules of conduct and summaries of Buddhist principles. The fact that these edicts did not explain beliefs or philosophy has led to suggestions that political strategy rather than Buddhist morality was behind his policies of religious tolerance, but his long pilgrimages to places associated with the Buddha's life belie this. At Bodhgaya, where the Buddha achieved nirvana, Ashoka had a shrine built, and he erected a stupa over the spot at Kushinara where the Buddha's funeral pyre had burned.

After the Buddha's death, his relics had been divided into eight portions and given to princes who had a claim to them. Each portion was enshrined in a stupa, or burial mound. Ashoka had each set of relics unearthed and split into tiny portions, which were sent all over his empire. Tradition recounts that he had 84,000 stupas built to enshrine them.

PILLAR EDICTS

The emperor's proclamations were inscribed on the bases of soaring stone pillars, which he had erected at pilgrimage sites. Others were engraved on rocks and cave walls across his empire. These edicts, which expounded the

Right The Great Stupa at Sanchi, Madhya Pradesh, originally built during Ashoka's reign, was 7.5m (25ft) high and 18m (59ft) across, but 100 years later it was rebuilt, twice as large.

IMPERIAL ART

Ashoka's patronage of decoration on religious monuments made stone sculpture the preferred medium of Indian artists. Earlier works of art and architecture had been made in wood, and none survive. The polished stone pillars he had erected at holy sites and along pilgrimage routes were surmounted by carved animals, such as lions and bulls, and these represent the pinnacle of this early Indian art form. The famous 2.1m (7ft) high lion capital at Sarnath may be the work of artists trained in the influential Persian sculpture tradition. The four alert lions face the four cardinal directions and once supported a huge carved *Dharmachakra*, or Wheel of the Law. Their feet rest on an abacus bearing images of an elephant, a horse, a bull and a lion, symbolizing the four quarters of the world, interspersed with thousand-spoke wheels. The capital symbolizes Ashoka's role as the *chakravartin*, or Universal King.

Right India's national emblem is the sandstone lion capital that once topped Ashoka's inscribed pillar at Isipatana (now Sarnath). Lightning shattered the pillar, but the lion capital fell 14m (46ft) to the ground unbroken.

Dharma, explained Ashoka's policies, and commemorated his visits to holy places, furthered Buddhism's spread during the 3rd century BCE.

Knowledge of Ashoka's reign faded and was lost until, in the 19th century, archaeologists rediscovered and deciphered Ashoka's rock and pillar edicts. They were inscribed perhaps two centuries before the Buddhist scriptures were written down, so they are the earliest independent evidence for the events and ideas of early Buddhism.

THERAVADA BUDDHISM

THE THERAVADA IS CALLED THE 'SOUTHERN SCHOOL' BECAUSE IT IS THE MAIN BUDDHIST TRADITION IN MANY SOUTH-EAST ASIAN COUNTRIES. IT IS THE OLDEST BRANCH OF BUDDHISM AND CLAIMS TO TRANSMIT THE BUDDHA'S ORIGINAL TEACHINGS.

Ideas and practices that had been condemned as heretical by the Second Buddhist Council in the 4th century BCE flourished in the years that followed, for although the Council headed off major challenges, it failed to calm the intellectual ferment that lay behind them. The Mahasamghika school, for example, went on to develop its idea that bhikkhus and bhikkhunis should aspire to become buddhas, and it spawned many sects, including the Lokottaravada, which taught that buddhas are celestial beings whose appearances and actions on Earth are illusory.

Below Theravada devotees circumambulate the Ruwanveliseya Dagoba in Anuradhapura. Theravada Buddhism emerged in Sri Lanka during the 2nd century BCE, after the emperor Ashoka sent monks of the Vibhajjavada tradition there to teach the Dharma.

NIKAYA BUDDHISM

The Sthaviravada, or 'School of the Elders', held to the teachings of the Buddha, but also spawned sects such as the Dharmaguptaka, which flourished in north-western India around the 1st century CE. Its followers believed that the teachings of a buddha are superior to those of arhats. The Gandharan scriptures, a collection of birch-bark texts that were discovered in Afghanistan and are thought to be part of the Dharmaguptaka canon, are the earliest known Buddhist manuscripts.

The many schools and sects that supported the authority of the Pali canon are known collectively as Nikaya Buddhism. Some were short-lived while others endured for centuries. Some flourished outside India – the Dharmaguptaka, for example, influenced the development of

Above When archaeologists excavated Pataliputra near Patna, the Mauryan capital under Ashoka, they exposed 80 black polished-stone pillars that once supported a great hall – perhaps part of Ashoka's palace, or the vihara where the Third Buddhist Council was held.

Chinese Buddhism. Only one Nikaya Buddhist school remains today, however: the Theravada, or 'Way of the Elders'. The Theravada tradition is believed to have evolved from an orthodox branch of the Sthaviravada called the Vibhajjavada.

THE THIRD COUNCIL

It is thought that a council of arhats may have been held around 250BCE. Theravada sources mention a Third Buddhist Council held at Pataliputra, capital of the Mauryan empire under the emperor Ashoka. Its purpose was to examine unorthodox practices. This was necessary because the emperor's patronage of Buddhist viharas attracted novices for financial rather than vocational reasons. Many falsely claimed to have been ordained, they did not observe the rules and practices of the Sangha, and some were corrupt.

The Council also reviewed unorthodox beliefs, such as the doctrine of *pudgala-vada*, held by

Right The stupa of Sariputra, an arhat considered by the Theravada to be one of the Buddha's leading disciples, rises from the ruins of the later university of Nalanda near Rajagriha. Sariputra was born in a village nearby and entered nirvana at Nalanda.

the Sammitiya sect. Contrary to the Buddha's teaching that there is no soul, no individuality to be reborn, the Sammitiya taught that there must be a 'self' (*pudgala*), an entity capable of accumulating karma and of being reborn. The Buddha taught that the personality is composed of five skandhas, or groups of mental and physical elements. After death, the mental skandhas, freed from physical constraints, are reborn in a new body.

The Council expelled unordained monks and confirmed the Buddha's teachings, declaring unorthodox beliefs, such as *pudgala-vada,* heretical.

THE THERAVADA TODAY

Theravada Buddhists uphold the authority of the Pali canon and believe that they transmit the original teachings and practices of the Buddha and the early Sangha. They revere the historical Buddha, not as an omniscient god but as a man with extraordinary insight and wisdom. They believe that at the end of his life, he passed into final nirvana, beyond the reach of human communication. His life and enlightenment remain as the model for other beings to follow. Those who achieve enlightenment become arhats, but can never be buddhas.

The tradition recognizes the pantheon of past and future buddhas, of whom the Buddha Shakyamuni was one, but not the semi-divine bodhisattvas of the Mahayana schools that arose during the 1st century BCE, nor the idea that beings may be saved

by such celestial beings. Buddhas and arhats teach that beings must save themselves by achieving enlightenment through self-discipline and meditation. This path may take many years and many rebirths.

The Theravada tradition is a strongly monastic one. Working toward enlightenment through strict adherence to rules, studying sacred texts and spending long hours in meditation demands a dedication that only members of a monastic community can afford.

Their support comes from lay followers, who hope to accumulate merit and achieve enlightenment in a future life. Meditation was reserved for monks until the 20th century, when the Theravada reached out to Westerners, who had different expectations.

Below The Theravada Buddhist tradition emphasizes monastic discipline and meditation, rather than faith and prayer to a pantheon of deities, as the path to nirvana. These Theravadan monks are at worship in England.

SPREADING THE DHARMA

THE EMPEROR ASHOKA SENT EMISSARIES TO CARRY THE WORDS OF THE BUDDHA TO EVERY PART OF THE KNOWN WORLD, FROM SOUTH-EAST ASIA TO CHINA AND EVEN EGYPT. BY THE END OF HIS REIGN, BUDDHISM HAD GROWN TO THE STATUS OF A WORLD RELIGION.

Ashoka the Great introduced 50 years of peace and economic prosperity to his empire, which extended from the Himalayas to the Deccan Plateau, and from Assam to Afghanistan. As a Buddhist, he continued to expand his frontiers through peaceful policies, which included supporting Buddhist kings, settling disputes peacefully, road-building, protecting merchants and founding Buddhist viharas.

His policies of religious tolerance and protection benefited both Buddhism and Jainism. Merchants supported these egalitarian religions, and expanding trade encouraged pilgrims to follow the caravans, many of whose routes across India were guarded by Ashoka's armies. In this way, Buddhism spread north-west, beyond Mauryan frontiers.

MISSIONS ABROAD

Ashoka despatched missions far and wide. "[His Majesty] considers victory by Dharma to be the foremost victory", reads his 13th Rock Edict, "And moreover [he] has gained this victory on all his frontiers to a distance of six hundred yojanas" (about 2,500 km/1,500 miles). He sent envoys all over the Hellenistic world, to

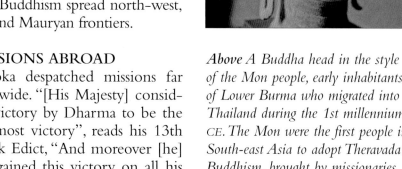

Above A Buddha head in the style of the Mon people, early inhabitants of Lower Burma who migrated into Thailand during the 1st millennium CE. The Mon were the first people in South-east Asia to adopt Theravada Buddhism, brought by missionaries from Sri Lanka perhaps as early as the 2nd century BCE.

Syria, Egypt, Macedonia, Cyrene and Epirus. Buddhist communities may have existed around this time in Egypt – scholars have suggested that the monks of the Therapeutae order of Lake Mareotis (now Lake Mariout), outside Alexandria, could have been bhikkhus of the Theravada tradition. Ashoka also sent emissaries to Central Asia and China.

The *Mahavamsa*, an account in the Pali literary language of the kings of Sri Lanka from 543 BCE to 361 CE, tells the story of Ashoka's first and most successful mission – to Sri Lanka. At its head was his son, Mahinda, a bhikkhu, who converted King Devanampiya Tissa to Buddhism on the Mihintale peak. The king supported Ashoka's emissaries in their work of spreading Buddhism in Sri Lanka, and he commissioned the building of the Mahavira monastery for them outside his capital, Anuradhapura. Later,

Below The Dambulla cave vihara in central Sri Lanka was first inhabited by Buddhist monks as early as the 3rd century BCE, when the emperor Ashoka sent his son Mahinda there to teach the Dharma.

Ashoka's daughter, Sanghamitta, brought to Anuradhapura a cutting of the Bodhi tree under the branches of which the Buddha achieved enlightenment. She remained in Sri Lanka, and established a bhikkhuni community.

SPREAD OF THERAVADA

Ashoka's son, Mahinda, belonged to the Vibhajjavada school, a branch of the Sthaviravada school, which recognized the authority of the Pali canon. The Vibhajjavadins rejected the devotional ideas and practices of the new, progressive Buddhist sects. Instead, they emphasized insight based on experience, reasoning and critical analysis. They believed that they transmitted the Buddha's original teachings and referred to themselves as 'the elders' (*thera* in Pali).

By the mid-3rd century BCE, when Mahinda's mission reached Sri Lanka, Vibhajjavada was already beginning to evolve into sub-sects. Mahinda and his missionaries formed a new group, called the Tamraparniya, or 'Sri

Below Ananda temple in Bagan was built by the Mon people in the 11th century CE. One of the best surviving examples of the Mon architectural style, it is covered in stone sculptures depicting events in the life of the Buddha.

Above Pha That Luang, a Buddhist stupa in Vanchang, Laos, and a symbol of the Lao people, is believed to stand on the site of a temple built by Ashoka's emissaries, who arrived bearing relics of the Buddha during the 3rd century BCE.

Lanka Branch'. This was the school that eventually evolved into the Theravada.

Ashoka sent missionaries beyond Sri Lanka, south-east to a land called Suvarnabhumi. Scholars believe that this was part of South-east Asia, close to Sri Lanka, most probably Burma (Myanmar), where the Mon people may have been Buddhist since the 2nd century BCE. They were the link through which Buddhism

was transmitted to the Khmer peoples, who inhabited the lands that are now Thailand, Cambodia and Laos. From Sri Lanka, Buddhism also spread to Vietnam and Indonesia.

Below The Kashmir Valley was part of the Mauryan empire, and after Buddhist missions reached Srinagar, the capital, during the reign of the emperor Ashoka, the region became a centre of Buddhism.

THE VIHARA

SIMPLE SHELTERS FOR WANDERING BHIKKHUS AND BHIKKHUNIS SOON DEVELOPED INTO COMPLEX TEMPLE PRECINCTS WITH MAGNIFICENT MEETING HALLS, SHRINES AND STUPAS. UNIQUE STYLES OF TEMPLE ARCHITECTURE EVOLVED WHEREVER BUDDHISM SPREAD.

Early Buddhist monks lived in huts made of sticks and leaves. In time these evolved into brick and stone structures built around a courtyard, which was used for meetings and teaching. By the 3rd century BCE, some of the larger communities had replaced the open courtyard with a meeting hall. Shrines, image halls and buildings for special purposes, such as bath houses, soon followed, and the term 'vihara' ('dwelling'), expanded its original meaning to embrace the monastery complex.

THE FIRST VIHARA

Only the stone foundations remain at the site of Jetavana, the first Buddhist vihara, which was built in a grove near the large city of Shravasti by a rich merchant, Anathapindika, as a rainy season retreat for the Buddha and his followers. By the 7th century CE, Jetavana had grown into a large community with separate cells and courtyards for bhikkhus and bhikkhunis, refectories, wells, washhouses, a dispensary and a library, as well as meeting halls and shrines.

Missionary bhikkhus and bhikkhunis established viharas outside towns on trade routes near people, who would give material support, but remote enough to allow peace and solitude for meditation. Jetavana provided the model for these and for the later viharas established outside India. Like Jetavana, many were financed by wealthy business people and supported by local rulers.

Ideally, a vihara occupied a pleasant spot on a hill, sheltered or shaded by trees and near an abundant water supply. It had properly constructed buildings for different uses, and separate dwellings for bhikkhus and bhikkhunis. From early in the 1st millennium CE, viharas were built

Above *Distinctive architectural styles appeared in the Buddhist regions surrounding India. Wat Arun in Bangkok, Thailand, has a tall prang, or tower, a feature adopted from buildings of the Khmer, who once ruled Siam.*

on hills and mountains across Asia, from Persia in the west to China, Korea and Japan in the east.

TEMPLES OF THE EAST

The decorative temples of the Mahayana sects of East Asia, with their curving roofs and overhanging eaves supported on rows of columns and complex bracketing, seem almost to epitomize Buddhist architecture. In fact, they were derived from the Chinese tradition of palace-building, and the pagoda – the East Asian form of the Indian stupa – derives from the traditional palace gatehouse. Few remain in China today, but the

Left *Tibet's Ganden Namgyeling was built on a mountain top outside Lhasa in 1409 by Tsongkhapa, one of the most learned commentators on the scriptures. Ganden became a notable Tibetan Buddhist university.*

Right Wat Naung Khan, Kengtung, built in brick and stucco and heavily gilded, has the stepped roofs that are characteristic of Burmese architecture. The distinctive stupa evolved from the Sri Lankan dagoba.

style was faithfully copied in Japan, where some of the early temples are among the world's oldest wooden buildings.

In China, Korea and Japan, a vihara is traditionally a walled compound surrounding a number of separate buildings, all of which face south, the direction of light and growth. In addition to the monks' residences, a library and hall for lectures and meditation, there are traditionally several shrine halls devoted to the Buddha and to deities, such as Guanyin, the Bodhisattva of Compassion, where offerings are made. Inside, images are arrayed on a platform, like emperors enthroned in their audience halls. There may be a pagoda in the centre of the complex, enshrining relics and other sacred objects.

Below A belfry is traditionally sited on the north side of a temple compound. The bell is struck before ceremonies, to ward off evil spirits. This ancient bronze bell is in the Hwagyesa temple in Seoul.

Many storeys symbolize the sacred status of the pagoda, for at this time only the palaces of emperors had multiple roofs. There may also be a belfry and a drum for summoning practitioners for devotion.

Viharas became increasingly large and powerful, housing thousands of monks, owning vast areas of land and possessing art treasures. Some, such as Nalanda, India's great Buddhist university, became respected teaching institutions.

CHAITYAGRIHAS

Caves that served as temporary accommodation for wandering bhikkhus were expanded into cave viharas as the Sangha grew into more settled communities. A shrine hall was soon added, often with a stupa built into one end. In western India, these Buddhist stupa halls, or *chaityagrihas,* were carved out of rocky cliffs and hillsides on a monumental scale. Those at Bhaja and Karla in Maharashtra were excavated during the 1st century BCE.

The *chaityagriha* evolved into the great Indian architectural tradition of rock-cut temples, of which Ellora in Maharashtra is the outstanding example. The first 12 of Ellora's 34 cave temples were excavated by Buddhists and the remainder by Hindus and Jains. In a spirit of co-operation, followers of different religions in ancient India would often occupy the same temple site.

Right Cave 10 at Ellora is called the Carpenter's Cave because its roof is carved to simulate the curved wooden ribs of an early Buddhist temple. The Buddha statue sits before a 10m (33ft)-high stupa. This magnificent chaityagriha dates from 600–800CE.

THE MONASTIC COMMUNITY

THERAVADA BHIKKHUS AND BHIKKHUNIS MUST MEDITATE AT DAWN, NOON AND SUNSET, AND DEPEND ON DONATIONS FOR FOOD AND CLOTHING. MORE THAN 200 RULES GOVERN EVERY ASPECT OF THEIR DAILY LIFE, FROM EATING TIMES TO BEHAVIOUR AND ETIQUETTE.

Theravada Buddhists accept that to attain nirvana requires rigorous discipline to improve self-awareness and long hours spent in meditation. Traditionally, lay devotees, especially those with families, accept that they may not achieve enlightenment in their current life. Instead, they make it their goal to be reborn into a state of existence from which they may attain nirvana in the next life. They try to accumulate merit by cultivating virtues and by obeying the Five Precepts: not to take life, not to steal or lie, not to take part in inappropriate sexual activity,

Below Monks and nuns gain wisdom and understanding from modern technology as well as from ancient texts. Many log on to the Journal of Buddhist Ethics, *a website offering articles and discussion groups.*

and not to use intoxicants. They study the Dharma and support the Sangha by donating food, robes and even medicines.

PRECEPTS AND RULES

All bhikkhus and bhikkhunis, from novices to vihara leaders, must obey ten precepts. In addition to the basic five observed by all Buddhists, they must not eat after midday, attend public entertainments, ornament themselves or use perfumes, sleep in a 'high' (luxurious) bed, or handle 'gold or silver' (money).

When they join a vihara, they must shave their heads as a mark of renunciation, and wear monastic dress. They cannot earn money to support themselves, but must depend on lay followers to provide the necessities of life. That means eating whatever they are

Above Bhikkhus accept robes donated by the laity on Kathina Day after the rainy season retreat. All must follow special rules governing their daily lives.

given (including meat, as long as it was not killed especially for them), and wearing robes made from fabric donated by the laity.

CODE OF CONDUCT

Lay devotees may also observe more precepts on holy days, when they visit a vihara to meditate and hear talks on the Dharma. Teaching is an important part of the relationship between monks, nuns and lay followers.

OBSERVANCE DAYS

Buddhist monks and nuns have always gathered on new and full moon days – and some also on quarter moon days – to recite the *Pratimoksa*. During this ceremony, called the *posadha* (Pali: *uposatha*), bhikkhus and bhikkhunis confess to each other their infringements of the rules. Any item or privilege gained by breaking a rule must be forfeited.

Monks teach the Dharma on *posadha* days to lay devotees, who attend the viharas to hear talks, join in the meditation and sometimes also in the recitation of the rules.

Five of the year's 12 full-moon days are occasions for special celebration. New Year is one and another is Vesak, or Buddha Day, which takes place on the first full-moon day in May or June, and is held to celebrate the Buddha's birth, enlightenment and parinirvana. Magha Puja, or Sangha Day, in March commemorates the Buddha's delivery of rules for the Sangha, the *Ovada Patimokkha*.

Bhikkhus and bhikkhunis must also follow the sets of rules laid down in the *Vinaya Pitaka*, the first part of the Pali canon. The *Vinaya* begins with the code of conduct, or *Pratimoksa* (Pali: *Pratimokkha*), and it usefully provides a case study on how and why each rule in the code came to be adopted. Many of these rules, which cover dress and comportment toward other members of the Sangha, in addition to rules governing serious moral issues, are obsolete, but the *Parajika* dharmas, or offences that merit expulsion, are enforced. They prohibit killing or inciting others to kill, stealing, all sexual activity, and falsely claiming to have attained superior states of consciousness. Any bhikkhu or bhikkhuni who commits one of these offences is considered 'defeated', and will be expelled from the Sangha.

The *Pratimoksa* has changed since it was written down in the 1st century BCE. In the versions of different traditions and schools, the number of rules ranges from 218 to 263 for bhikkhus and 279 to 380 for bhikkhunis.

Every minute in the life of every bhikkhu and bhikkhuni is structured by rules. They must rise

Above The Buddha taught his followers to probe and question the teachings. This picture shows Tibetan monks debating points of doctrine in the meditation hall of the Kopan vihara in Kathmandu, Nepal.

before dawn, meditate before making their alms round and eat before noon. They must study and teach, observe the twice-monthly holy days and make a retreat for three months every year. Through these rules, their life becomes a preparation and training for attaining enlightenment.

Below Theravada monks meditate in Luang Prabang, Laos. Monks and nuns spend several hours a day meditating as part of their monastic discipline.

BUDDHIST TERMS

Cosmic Buddha In Mahayana Buddhism, the compassionate buddha who is eternally omnipresent and a fount of spiritual sustenance. In esoteric Buddhism, the Cosmic Buddha is represented as Vairocana, the personification of the truth of the universe and of wisdom.

Pitaka A Pali word meaning, literally, 'basket'. The canon of Buddhist scriptures, which consist of the Tripitaka ('three baskets'): the *Vinaya Pitaka*, the *Sutta Pitaka* and the *Abhidharma Pitaka*.

Pratimoksa (Pali: *Pratimokkha*) Part of the Pali canon that lays out rules of conduct both for Buddhist monks and nuns as well as for lay followers.

Sunyata The concept that all phenomena are empty of any unchanging reality.

Sutra (Pali: 'sutta') Short verses that summarize the Buddha's teaching, and that are memorized by chanting.

HOLY DAYS AND HOLIDAYS

FULL MOONS ARE THE OCCASIONS FOR MANY RELIGIOUS FESTIVALS TO CELEBRATE EVENTS IN THE LIFE OF THE BUDDHA. THERE ARE PROCESSIONS AND DANCING, BUT THEY ARE ALSO HOLY DAYS, WHEN MANY LAY PEOPLE VISIT A VIHARA FOR A FEW HOURS OF DEVOTION.

Above A Hawaiian child pours tea over a Buddha statue at the Hana Matsuri flower festival. This festival, called Wesak in other countries, is traditionally held to celebrate the Buddha's birthday.

Nothing in Buddhism is centrally controlled, least of all the calendar. Most Buddhists use a lunisolar calendar, which is based on the Moon's phases. To keep the lunar year in time with the normal calendar year of 365¼ days, intercalary, or leap, days and months are inserted. The Buddhist lunisolar calendar is based on a 3rd-century CE Indian treatise on astronomy, the *Surya Siddhanta*. However, not all Buddhist countries use this calendar – Japan does not, while most South-east Asian countries do, but they do not all use the same version. As a result holy days fall on different dates in the various Buddhist countries. The three main Buddhist traditions, the Theravada (Southern), the Mahayana (Eastern), and the Vajrayana (Tibetan), also hold them at different times.

BUDDHIST FESTIVALS

The full-moon night of the 12th lunar month is the time of a national celebration in Thailand, when tiny wooden rafts bearing leaves, flowers, candles and incense are floated on rivers in homage to a footprint of the Buddha left on the beach of the Narmada River in India. In Sri Lanka during the full moon in late July or early August, a ten-day torch-lit parade, the Esala Perahera, happens in Kandy, with elephants, drummers and dancers. The parade escorts a casket believed to contain a tooth of the Buddha. On the tenth day, the casket is returned to the Temple of the Tooth.

Many festivals in countries where the Mahayana prevails celebrate the lives of bodhisattvas. These include the birthday of Avalokiteshvara in March, and, in China, that of Guanyin, the Bodhisattva of Compassion.

A DAY OF REFLECTION

Festivals are full of colour, dancing and music, but most lay devotees start the day by taking food offerings to a monastic community. They reaffirm their commitment to the Five Precepts (not to kill, steal, lie, participate in immoral sexual acts, or imbibe intoxicants), and many also observe three of the monastic precepts: not to eat after noon, adorn themselves or take part in public entertainments.

Below The August Obon festival in Japan recalls the legend of the arhat Moggellana, who rescued his mother from hell. This image shows women and children participating in the traditional Obon festival dance.

They attend a talk on the Dharma at a vihara and may also join in meditation or chanting. As well as consuming only liquids after mid-day, and giving food and aid to the poor, they may perform a circumambulation – walk clock-wise round a Buddha image, shrine or stupa three times in homage first to the Buddha, then to the Dharma and finally to the Sangha.

Above These Indian bhikkhus in Bangalore chant on Bodhi Day, which is celebrated on the anniversary of the Buddha's enlightenment in May.

Below Every winter thousands of pilgrims and monks converge on the huge Boudhanath stupa outside Kathmandu for Losar, the New Year. They celebrate by throwing tsampa (roasted barley flour) into the air.

MAJOR HOLY DAYS

New Year In the Mahayana tradition, the new year starts on the first full-moon day in January, but in China, Korea and Vietnam its date accords with the lunar calendar. Tibet follows about a month later with Losar, a major three-day festival. In Theravada countries – Sri Lanka, Cambodia, Burma (Myanmar), Laos and Thailand – the new year begins three days after the first full-moon day in April.

Nirvana Day In the Mahayana tradition, the Buddha's death, or parinirvana, is celebrated in February.

Buddha Day Vesak, or Wesak, on the first full-moon day in May or June, is traditionally the Buddha's birthday festival. Many Buddhists now celebrate the Buddha's birth, enlighten-ment and parinirvana on the same day, 'Buddha Day'.

Dharma Day On the full-moon day of the 8th lunar month, usually July, Buddhists pay homage to the Buddha for turning the Wheel of the Dharma with his First Sermon. They celebrate with readings from the Buddhist scriptures.

Bodhi Day Many Buddhists still celebrate Bodhi Day, when Siddhartha Gautama attained enlightenment under the Bodhi tree at Bodhgaya.

Magha Puja Day This holy day, also called Sangha Day, takes place on the full-moon day of the third lunar month (March) to commemorate the miraculous assembling of 1,250 arhats at Rajagriha, shortly before the Buddha arrived there and delivered the *Ovada Patimokkha*, a summary of rules for the Sangha.

THE MAHAYANA

NEW INTERPRETATIONS OF THE BUDDHA'S TEACHINGS EMERGED
FROM THE MANY SCHOOLS AND SECTS THAT AROSE DURING
THE CENTURIES FOLLOWING HIS DEATH. THEY CRYSTALLIZED IN THE
TEACHINGS OF THE MAHAYANA TRADITION, WHICH SURVIVES TODAY.

By the 3rd century BCE, the events of the Buddha's life had become interwoven with myth, and he seemed almost divine. The arhats whom he had guided to enlightenment taught that on his death, he passed into parinirvana, a realm out of reach of human contact. However, later generations challenged this teaching, and bold new philosophical ideas developed, including the belief that the Buddha is everywhere and ever-present.

Above In Mathura, south of Delhi, the Mahayana tradition influenced a style of delicate and realistic art and sculpture. It reached its apogee in the Gupta school around the 5th century CE, which was when this pink sandstone head was carved.

THE 'COSMIC' BUDDHA

One of these schools was the Mahayana, which emerged in the 1st century BCE. Its adherents saw the Buddha as supremely powerful, omniscient and omni-present – that is all-seeing and eternally present to give spiritual help to his devotees.

This conception of the 'cosmic' Buddha owes something to the ideas of early schools, such as the Mahasamghika, which believed that the Buddha lived and died as a man, but was in fact a celestial being who had suffered rebirth to teach earthly beings the way to enlightenment. However, modern scholars do not accept that the Mahayana school evolved from any single school. Some experts think it developed as an intellectual tradition within the Sangha over several centuries.

During the 1st millennium CE, the Mahayana, with its radical ideas about buddhahood, grew to rival the Theravada in the size of its following. It came to be called the Eastern tradition, because pilgrims carried it to Central Asia, China, Korea, Japan, Tibet and Mongolia, where it took root,

Left This detail from a 13th-century Japanese hanging scroll mandala, made of silk and gold, shows Vairocana surrounded by mythical buddhas of the four cardinal directions and the four greatest bodhisattvas.

THE 'GREAT VEHICLE'

So central to Mahayana teachings was the bodhisattva ideal that for many years the school was known as the Bodhisattvayana, or 'Bodhisattva Way'.

It called itself 'Mahayana', a Sanskrit word meaning 'great way', or 'great vehicle', because its founders believed they had understood the truth of the Buddha's message – that personal enlightenment attained without the enlightenment of others was not true enlightenment – and discovered the only way to salvation from samsara. They disparaged the schools that preceded them, led by the Theravada, as 'Hinayana', meaning 'lesser way', or 'lesser vehicle' – implying that their adherents could see only part of the picture, so their ideas were imperfect.

Theravada and Mahayana evolved as separate traditions within the Sangha, but both acknowledged as their foundation the Buddha's teachings preserved in the Pali canon. They also shared universities and even viharas, and some modern scholars believe that certain bhikkhus and bhikkhunis may have accepted teachings of both traditions. The Mahayana, however, went on to develop its own canon. Today, the doctrinal differences between the Mahayana and Theravada traditions continue to exist.

Above The early caves at Ajanta were carved by bhikkhus of the Sravakayana, who depicted the Buddha's past lives in wall paintings. Centuries later, Mahayana communities enlarged the site and painted more images.

merged with local beliefs, myths, deities and religious practices, and eventually flourished.

In fact, the strongest appeal of the Mahayana was as the devotional branch of Buddhism, and to the laity, rather than to Sangha intellectuals. By making offerings of flowers (symbols of impermanence), candles (symbols of enlightenment) and incense (symbol of the spread of the Dharma) at shrines, while chanting sutras or making prostrations or circumambulations, lay followers could invoke the intercession of a buddha or a bodhisattva for salvation. Significantly, however, Mahayana Buddhists supplicate buddhas and bodhisattvas not for personal enlightenment and release from samsara, but rather for the salvation of all beings.

THE BODHISATTVA IDEAL

The traditional belief had been that the Buddha was a bodhisattva until his awakening: a being destined to become a buddha, but who, on enlightenment, did not enter parinirvana, but instead remained on Earth to show others the path to salvation. But both the Buddha and the Elders who led the Sangha after his death taught that few beings are destined to become buddhas. The goal of human existence is to achieve enlightenment and so become an arhat and enter nirvana.

The Mahayana regarded this ideal of the Elders as fundamentally selfish. Arhats, they argued, turn their backs on suffering humanity in order to achieve personal salvation. Mahayana intellectuals considered arhats inferior to bodhisattvas, whose role they exalted as that of saviour of beings trapped in samsara.

The ideal is the bodhisattva: one who works compassionately through many rebirths for the enlightenment of all beings. Mahayana Buddhists believe that everyone can and should aspire to become a bodhisattva and to eventually attain buddhahood.

Above Mahayana bhikkhus spread Buddhism into Central Asia from the 1st century CE – at around the time when the halo may have first appeared in Buddhist art of the region. This 8th-century silk banner was found in the caves at Dunhuang, in modern Gansu province, China.

BODHISATTVAS

MAHAYANA TEACHES THAT EVERY SENTIENT BEING HAS THE POTENTIAL TO BECOME A BUDDHA AND SHOULD STRIVE TO REALIZE IT BY SEEKING SELF-PERFECTION AND FOLLOWING THE PATH TO BUDDHAHOOD. THE FIRST STEP ON THIS PATH IS TO BECOME A BODHISATTVA.

When the Buddha told tales of himself as a young man, he described himself as 'an unenlightened bodhisatta', according to the Pali scriptures. Bodhisatta, or 'bodhisattva' in Sanskrit, literally means 'enlightenment being', and was originally a term reserved for the Buddha who, out of compassion for suffering humanity, remained in the world after his awakening to teach the Dharma.

According to the scriptures, the Buddha lived through many lives and deaths, and before his last appearance on Earth had advanced along the path to enlightenment. He might have attained samsara as an arhat, but as a buddha he could pass on knowledge of the way to enlightenment to others. It is believed that eons earlier, he had taken a vow in the presence of a buddha who had lived on Earth in another age to seek perfect wisdom and attain buddhahood.

Below Wenshu, China's Mañjushri, lives on the sacred Mount Wutai in Shanxi, where he first appeared in China. Pilgrims to the Pusading temple on one of the mountain's five peaks have included two Qing emperors.

During its most formative years, between 100BCE and 100CE, the Mahayana reinterpreted the concept of the bodhisattva and elevated it to an ideal. In Mahayana Buddhism, any being may consciously set out on the path to buddhahood. At some point, a bodhisattva attains a mental state called *bodhicitta* ('enlightenment mind'). This is the motivation or decision to become enlightened – but not for personal salvation.

The 'enlightenment mind' possesses infinite compassion and seeks salvation for all other sentient beings. To this end, a bodhisattva takes a vow to help others along the path to enlightenment through as many lifetimes as it takes. Bodhisattvas can alleviate suffering, teach the Dharma and help other beings to progress along the path to nirvana. They vow to attain enlightenment and pass into nirvana only when all beings have been saved from the burden of samsara.

THE BODHISATTVA PATH

To progress along the path to buddhahood, bodhisattvas must cultivate compassion (*karuna*) and the six *paramitas*, or perfections: generosity (*dana*), morality (*sila*), patience (*kshanti*), diligence (*virya*), concentration (dhyana) and insight (prajna). *Upaya*, or 'skilful means' – the crucial ability to teach in a way that is perfectly adapted for those who receive the knowledge – is a later addition to the list, along with *pranidhana*, or

Above The Laughing Buddha is the 6th-century CE Chinese monk Budai, believed to have been an incarnation of the Bodhisattva Maitreya.

conviction of the rightness of the path, *bala paramita*, or spiritual strength, and *jñana paramita*, or perfect knowledge.

CELESTIAL BUDDHAS AND BODHISATTVAS

On reaching the seventh stage, or *bhumi*, along this path, bodhisattvas attain supernatural powers. They can instantly appear anywhere, for example. However, of the many bodhisattvas, only four have reached this stage. They are the celestial bodhisattvas, who have the powers of spirits and the insights of fully enlightened beings, so they have miraculous abilities to help beings lost in suffering.

The supreme bodhisattva of compassion, and foremost of the bodhisattvas, Avalokiteshvara, protects followers from the Four Great Perils – shipwrecks, wrongful imprisonment, theft and fire – and from lions, poisonous snakes, wild elephants and disease. He is depicted in many different forms – holding a lotus, bearing water, descending from heaven on a lotus, with 11 heads symbolizing the 11 virtues with which he conquers the 11 desires that impede enlightenment, and multiple arms, signifying the many powers that he uses to help the suffering.

Maitreya is the only bodhisattva who waits in the Tushita heaven for the end of the period of the Buddhist Law, when the Buddha Shakyamuni's teachings are forgotten. Then he will descend to Earth as the new buddha, to illuminate the world with the truths about suffering and existence. He is depicted standing, wearing a crown and jewellery, or seated, with one or both feet touching the Earth.

The bodhisattva of wisdom and religious doctrine, Mañjushri is usually shown with a book, the symbol of knowledge, and holding a flaming sword in his right hand, signifying the power of knowledge and wisdom to overcome ignorance. Mañjushri is invoked to improve memory to learn Buddhist

Below Statues of Jizo console the dead in a Tokyo cemetery. Jizo, the Japanese form of Ksitigarbha, protects pilgrims, travellers and children, and is invoked in shrines to commemorate aborted children. Ksitigarbha is also known as Sai-snying-po (in Tibet) and Dizang (in China).

texts. The Chinese believe that the Buddha created Wenshu, their name for Mañjushri, to bring his teachings to them, in order to save them from spiritual ignorance.

The bodhisattva of the dying and the oppressed, and overlord of the ten kings of hell and the six realms of rebirth of the Buddhist universe, Ksitigarbha vowed to release all beings from the torments of hell. He is depicted seated on a lotus, crowned, holding the sacred jewel of Buddhism in his right hand and making the gesture of giving, the *vadara* mudra, with his left, or dressed as a monk descending into the flames of hell to rescue sufferers.

Left Tara is the female form of Avalokiteshvara, foremost of the bodhisattvas. This dynamic Tibetan Drolma, or Green Tara, sits with her right leg extended, indicating her readiness to leap into action to save others. Avalokiteshvara is known as Chenrezi in Tibet, Guanyin (female) in China and Kannon in Japan.

THE TEN *BHUMIS*

Cultivating the *paramitas*, or self-perfection, enables a bodhisattva to progress through ten stages, or *bhumis*, of spiritual growth. Those who reach the final stages may elect to become a buddha. The ten *bhumis* are:

1 **Joy** – accompanies *dana*, giving, or generosity.
2 **Purity** – results from perfecting *sila*, or morality.
3 **Shining light** – is the consequence of mastering *kshanti*, or patience.
4 **Brilliance or radiance** – results from persevering in *virya*, or diligence.
5 **Invincibility, the overcoming of illusions** – the result of attaining the higher stages of dhyana, or concentration.
6 **Supreme wisdom** – follows the attainment of prajna, or insight.
7 **Far-advanced** – the effect of mastering *upaya*, or skilful means.
8 **Immobility** – the effect of *pranidhana*, or conviction in the rightness of the path.
9 **Spiritual intelligence** – accompanies *bala paramita*, or spiritual strength.
10 **Dharma cloud** – the power to end afflictions caused by ignorance is the reward of *jñana paramita*, or perfect knowledge.

THE SANSKRIT SCRIPTURES

AROUND THE 1ST CENTURY BCE, WHEN THERAVADA MONKS IN SRI LANKA WERE WRITING DOWN THE PALI SCRIPTURES, NEW TEXTS APPEARED IN INDIA AMONG MAHAYANA FOLLOWERS. THEY WERE WRITTEN IN SANSKRIT, THE LANGUAGE OF THE ELITE AND EDUCATED.

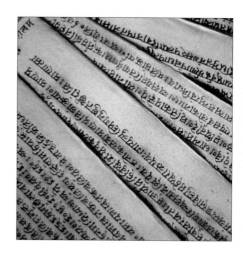

Above Mahayana sutras were written in Sanskrit, which was the language of philosophy and literature in ancient India. Sanskrit brought Buddhist ideas into mainstream Indian thought.

Like the Pali scriptures, the Mahayana texts were written in sutras, or short verses. They were said to represent the words of the Buddha, but they were not the old, familiar teachings that had been learned and chanted by generations of monks. They were new texts, written anonymously, and their origins remain mysterious.

THE PERFECTION OF WISDOM

Among the earliest Mahayana scriptures are the *Prajñaparamita*, or Perfection of Wisdom sutras, which may first have been written as early as 100BCE, but which appeared in revised versions over the following four centuries.

These include the popular short *Diamond Sutra*, which elaborates on ways to cut through the mental attachments and illusions that bind the mind to samsara; and the *Heart Sutra*, which describes the bodhisattva Avalokiteshvara's insight into the fundamental emptiness of all phenomena.

The *Prajñaparamita* literature enlarges on the idea of attaining wisdom (prajna) as a means of release from existence. The texts introduce the ideal of the compassionate bodhisattva and the perfections (*paramitas*) the bodhisattva must achieve in order to attain Perfect Buddhahood. The Mahayana emphasis on the bodhisattva first appears in this literature, which exhorts and inspires Dharma followers to walk the bodhisattva path to the perfection of wisdom for the sake of other beings.

THE LOTUS SUTRA

The term 'Mahayana' first appears in the text of the *Sutra on the White Lotus of the True Law*. This sutra, presented as a discourse the Buddha delivered late in his life to a large assembly at Vulture Peak, outside Rajagriha, introduced many ideas that opposed traditional Buddhist teachings. It portrayed the Buddha as a being who had achieved nirvana eons before his appearance on Earth to teach the Dharma to beings lost in samsara. It also presented the radical idea that the Buddha did not enter a realm out of reach of spiritual communication but remains spiritually present in the world, perhaps even eternal.

Left The Buddha expounds the Diamond Sutra *in the frontispiece to this version, printed from wood blocks on 11 May 868. Found in the Mogao caves, Dunhuang, China, it is the oldest book with a known print date.*

Above The seven-storey Big Wild Goose pagoda of Da Cien temple, Xi'an, was built in the 7th century as a library for texts brought from India by the pilgrim Xuanzang, who spent the rest of his life translating them.

The *Lotus Sutra* is revered in the Far East. Many Sanskrit scriptures did not survive in India after the 1st millennium CE and were preserved in translation in China.

HIDDEN TEACHINGS

Mahayana Buddhists believe the sutras are the Buddha's recorded words. Many Mahayana concepts are reinterpretations of his sayings or actions, and its adherents accept the explanation given in the *Lotus Sutra* that the Buddha had applied 'skilful means' in revealing the Dharma to his followers. He had taught them as much as they could then assimilate, but he had not imparted all of his teachings.

Right Among the treasures of Hemis gompa (vihara) in Ladakh, Tibet, is the Kanjur, the 'Word of the Buddha' Mahayana scriptures in 98 volumes. Wrapped in silk, they are stored on shelves in the library.

THE BUDDHIST TRINITY

The trinity is a common symbol in Buddhist cosmology. For example, there are three types of enlightened being. Arhats (sometimes called *sravakas*) are 'hearers' – they attain enlightenment by following the path shown to them by a buddha. The Buddha Shakyamuni is a *samyaksambuddha* – he attained enlightenment through his own spiritual efforts and remained in the world to teach others. *Pratyekabuddhas* are 'lone buddhas' – they reach enlightenment and enter nirvana without ever teaching the truth to other beings.

The later Mahayana texts describe the Buddha Shakyamuni as having three bodies (*trikaya*), in three dimensions. The *nirmanakaya* is the physical body he inhabited on Earth, which was, nevertheless, capable of miraculous transformations. The *sambhogakaya* is the object of devotion, the heavenly body he inhabits in another plane where he teaches the Dharma to assembled bodhisattvas. The *dharmakaya* is his transcendent body or essence, said to be his 'real' body, which is synonymous with the ultimate truth.

More advanced knowledge had been written down and hidden away – the *Lotus Sutra* had been guarded by the Naga King at the bottom of a lake – until the time, some three centuries later, when the Buddhist community was ready to receive them.

Today neither Theravada Buddhists nor Buddhist scholars accept the Mahayana texts as authentic transcripts of the Buddha's words. During the early centuries CE, however, the ideas set forth in these sutras appealed to the spiritual nature of many in India, inspiring enthusiasm and passion. By contrast, the orthodox texts can seem, as one Indian philosopher commented, "a cold, passionless metaphysics devoid of religious teaching".

MAHAYANA PHILOSOPHY

DURING INSIGHT MEDITATION, MAHAYANA MONKS CONTEMPLATED *ANATMAN*, THE NON-SELF, AND THE IMPERMANENCE OF EXISTENCE. THEIR PHILOSOPHY CENTRED ON THE CONCEPT OF *SUNYATA*, OR EMPTINESS, AND CONCLUDED THAT EVERYTHING IS AN ILLUSION.

The *Abhidharma Pitaka*, the third 'basket' of the Pali scriptures, contains knowledge the Buddha considered too profound for most of his disciples. Only Sariputra, his most advanced arhat, possessed the wisdom to understand it.

The compilers of this remarkable scripture collected and clarified the Buddha's teachings on philosophy, metaphysics and phenomena relating to human experience and psychology, and presented them systematically in seven books. These innovative works explore the nature of reality and the factors that give rise to events, and they had a profound effect on Mahayana thought.

One philosophical conundrum the Buddhists of the ancient world tried to solve was the question of identity. Although they accepted that humans and other beings are empty of *atman*, or self, they questioned the idea that everything is empty of self. Some identifiable aspect of a person must surely endure to be reborn?

DHARMAS

The *Abhidharma* examined experience and classified it in terms of dharmas, the smallest, indivisible components of all phenomena in the universe. It identified 82, all but one of which are said to be conditioned: that is, they come into existence as part of the

Above Nagarjuna (2nd century CE) was one of Buddhism's most influential philosophers. This statue of him is at Kagyu Samye Ling monastery and Buddhist centre in Scotland.

Below The doctrine of dependent arising teaches that phenomena arise together in an interdependent net of cause and effect, an idea often expressed by an image of reflections – and reflections of reflections.

network of cause and effect – according to the doctrine of *pratitya-samutpada*, or dependent arising. Nirvana is different; it arises independently.

Dharmas may be thought of as groups of momentary events, rather like the sub-atomic quarks, leptons and other particles of high-energy physics. They are ever-changing, short-lived and travel only in groups. The skandhas that constitute the physical and mental makeup of living beings – body, feeling, perception, character – comprise groups of dharmas, but the fifth skhandha, consciousness, consists of just one.

The *Abhidharma* found an explanation to the conundrum of non-self in dharmas: these fundamental, irreducible components from which all reality is formed must have an own-identity, an unchanging reality.

EMPTINESS

The *Prajñaparamita*, or Perfection of Wisdom sutras, of the 1st century CE probed emptiness, *sunyata*, more deeply. They examined objects, sensations, beings and, eventually, the 82 dharmas, and concluded that all phenomena are devoid of any unchanging reality.

The great Buddhist philosopher of the 2nd century CE, Nagarjuna, supported their conclusions. Since dharmas are phenomena, he argued, in works inspired by the *Prajñaparamita*, they originate from some cause and cannot, therefore, have a fixed identity. They must be devoid of reality.

Sunyata is a disturbing concept because its implications affect everything. What we think of as the ocean, or a bowl, or the mind has no permanent identity because it is composed of groups of changing, impermanent dharmas, which are themselves devoid of identity or reality. Further, if the

Above Nalanda, near Patna, India, was one of the first great universities and the leading centre of Mahayana learning. At its height, some 10,000 students from all over the Eastern world, adherents of myriad schools and sects, studied there.

world and everything in it is made up of dharmas, and dharmas are not real, the world is an illusion.

Every aspect of existence is affected, right back to the Noble Eightfold Path. Right speech and right action stem from an accepted view of right and wrong, but right and wrong are phenomena composed of dharmas and so empty of any reality. "Even nirvana, I say, is like a magical illusion, is like a dream…", concludes the *Prajñaparamita*.

To the modern mind, these complex ideas seem nihilistic, but scholars speculate that they may have originated among Mahayana intellectuals struggling to interpret the *Abhidharma* in the light of the nothingness, the emptiness they

experienced at the higher stages of insight meditation. Attributing identities and realities to objects, people, opinions and ideas, they realized, puts obstacles in the way of seeing things as they are. Our perception of reality is a construction that enables us to understand the world, but distorts our understanding. Liberation is found at the point where identities, interpretations and opinions disappear.

Below The Abhidharma *preserves the early Buddhists' ideas about time. The* khanavada, *or theory of momentariness, says that a dharma arises, exists for a moment, then passes away before the next one arises.*

MAHAYANA SCHOOLS

THE 2ND CENTURY CE INDIAN PHILOSOPHER NAGARJUNA WAS
SO INFLUENTIAL THAT HE IS OFTEN CALLED THE 'SECOND BUDDHA'.
HIS IDEAS ARE SAID TO HAVE TURNED THE WHEEL OF THE DHARMA,
AND THEY INSPIRED THE FORMATION OF NEW MAHAYANA SCHOOLS.

Nagarjuna was probably born into a Brahmin family in Andhra Pradesh, southern India, around 150CE. He became a Buddhist monk and is believed to have studied at a vihara at Nalanda, near modern Patna. The writings attributed to him indicate that he may have supported orthodox beliefs – he seems to have known the *Abhidharma* – but he strongly defended Mahayana ideas.

THE TWO TRUTHS

The 2nd century CE was a time of philosophical exploration in India. Not only did new Buddhist schools continue to emerge – such as the Sautrantaka and the Vatsiputriya, which took opposite views on self and non-self and the effects of dharmas – new Brahminical schools had also appeared, including a Vedic school of logic, which engaged Buddhists in stimulating debate.

Above Mahayana bhikkhus made long and dangerous journeys into the Himalayan kingdoms to spread the teachings. These young monks are learning the scriptures in Bumthang, Bhutan, in viharas that were founded during the 7th century CE.

As he responded to these challenges, Nagarjuna formulated ideas that furthered the development of Buddhist thought. He called himself a *sunyatavadin*, 'a person who holds to the position of emptiness'. His position on emptiness was to demonstrate through logic that no phenomenon has an eternal, fixed 'self-nature' (*svabhava*), or identity, and that it is precisely this emptiness (*sunyata*), this lack of a fixed identity, that enables change to take place – night to merge into day, life into death, ignorance into enlightenment. Change cannot bring itself about. There is no ultimate cause for anything that exists, and phenomena come into being not by their own volition

Left Nagarjuna's ideas on the emptiness of the physical and mental worlds were significant not just for Buddhism, but also for the evolution of philosophy. Generations of philosophers have studied his writings.

Right The goal of a bodhisattva is to attain the ability to see things in a non-dualistic way; to realize, for example, that good and bad are not entirely opposed. This is a higher perception of the world.

or power but by externally interacting conditions. He applied these arguments equally to nirvana, once famously stating that "there is, on the part of samsara, no difference at all from nirvana".

Nagarjuna asserted that reality is a mental construct, an illusion. To address such dualities, implicit in all thinking about *sunyata*, he posited a doctrine of 'two truths'. There is conventional truth, in the sense of apparent and measurable reality (for example, things and beings seem independent, possessed of an enduring self); and there is ultimate truth, in the sense of higher understandings (for example, the perception that everything lacks a core essence, or permanent selfhood). To understand this is to become aware of how our perception of the world is conditioned by assumptions and attitudes, and to liberate the mind from clinging to accepted truths.

THE MIDDLE WAY

After Nagarjuna's death a new school, the Madhyamaka, arose among commentators on his writings, particularly those on emptiness and his *Mulamadhyamakakarika*, or *Fundamental Verses on the Middle Way*. Followers of the Madhyamaka school adhere

Right Meditating monks who reached high trance states experienced the mind as pure and separate from worldly experience. This may have inspired the Yogacara idea that consciousness is the only reality.

to Nagarjuna's interpretations of reality. They see this position as midway between opposing views: the belief that phenomena, including human beings, possess a core eternal, unchanging self; and the Indian view of nihilism – the idea that all phenomena have been annihilated and cease to exist.

Madhyamakas believe that *sunyata* is not nihilism (in the ancient Indian or modern Western interpretation of the word). To grasp the interdependence of all phenomena is to abandon the dualistic view of the universe, good/bad, samsara/nirvana, and to see things as they really are. This is a step on the way to enlightenment.

THE CONSCIOUSNESS SCHOOL

Around the 4th century CE, a new school emerged in India that took Nagarjuna's thinking in a different direction. Its name, Yogacara, stems from its emphasis on yoga and meditation, which its followers saw as the key to enlightenment. Yogacara sought to avoid nihilism and instead developed a philosophy known as *cittamatra*, or mind only – the idea that the world of objects does not exist, and that consciousness is the only reality.

The Yogacara introduced a new concept that they called 'storehouse consciousness', in which the effects of willed actions are stored in the consciousness as seeds. These seeds take root and ultimately transform the individual's consciousness.

CAVE TEMPLES

THE WALL PAINTINGS, SCULPTURES AND CARVED RELIEFS THAT ADORN BUDDHIST CAVE TEMPLES WERE EXECUTED AS RELIGIOUS ACTS TO EARN MERIT AND FOR TEACHING. IN THE PROCESS, DISTINCTIVE BUDDHIST ART AND ARCHITECTURAL TRADITIONS EVOLVED.

It was the huge arch of Cave 10 on a hillside at Ajanta, still just visible behind heavy undergrowth, that caught the eye of John Smith, one of a party of British army officers out on a tiger hunt in April 1819. Cave 10 is the earliest of the magnificent Ajanta cave temples in the Indhyadri hills of Maharashtra. The soldiers, guided across the ravine by a local boy who led them into it, cleared the undergrowth blocking the entrance and found themselves inside an early *chaityagriha*, an ancient assembly hall with a barrel-vaulted roof supported on beams and pillars and a stupa at one end. All had been carved out of solid rock by Buddhist monks more than 2,000 years earlier, in imitation of their traditional wooden temples. Fragments of some of India's oldest known wall-paintings could still be seen on the walls.

The Ajanta caves are said to have been founded by an arhat, Arcala, during the 2nd century BCE, but 24 of the 29 caves were excavated centuries later, around 450CE, by Mahayana monks. The monks had used some caves as dwellings and carved others into shrines and temples, which they filled with religious sculptures. They covered the walls with colourful paintings. The pigments

Above These stupas in one of 18 caves at Bhaja in the Western Ghats were carved from rock. The oldest cave dates from the 2nd century BCE and is one of the earliest chaityagrihas in India.

were applied to a wet plaster made of clay, lime, hay and dung. When the paint and plaster dried, the paintings were varnished with a mixture of lime and powdered seashell. Not long after the 5th century CE, Ajanta was abandoned, unfinished. Today, it tells the story of the evolution of Indian Buddhist art and architecture.

THE SILK ROUTE

From the early centuries CE, Buddhist monks from India began to follow the trading caravans northward into Central Asia and north-east into China to spread the Dharma, establishing cave viharas in cliffs and hillsides along the way. Monks' cells honeycombed the mountains overlooking the fertile Bamiyan Valley in the Hindu Kush, where monks had carved two colossal figures of

Below The stupa hall at Karli in southern Maharashtra, India's largest cave at 37 x 13m (121 x 43ft), dates from the early centuries CE and contains a stupa carved from the rock. Fifteen of the 37 octagonal pillars have exquisite relief carvings.

the Buddha that dominated the landscape. Hidden in a gorge on the edge of the Taklamakan Desert, the Bezeklik cave community flourished from the 8th to the 9th century CE. Its 77 caves are known as the 'Bezeklik Thousand Buddha Caves' because their ceilings are covered with multiple paintings of the Buddha.

CAVE TEMPLES OF CHINA

The richly decorated Yungang grottoes in Shanxi were excavated under an imperial edict from 460CE. Set high in a cliff-face, the caves are reached by a stone staircase. Chinese sculpture was undeveloped before the 5th century, and Yungang, where one of the earliest Chinese groups of stone figures was identified, was a nursery of the art. The development of a Chinese sculptural style, influenced by the artistic traditions of South and Central Asia, is represented by thousands of reliefs and free-standing sculptures.

Luoyang, in Henan, became the capital of the Northern Wei dynasty in 493CE, when its famous grottoes were begun in

Above Tiers of statuettes in niches are cut into the walls around this colossal Buddha figure in the Yungang caves in China. Brilliant colour still adheres to the sculptures and decorates the cave walls and ceiling.

mountains on either side of the Feng River. More than 1,000 caves have withstood the region's earthquakes. The figure sculptures in these caves are more mature than those of Yungang, with rounder faces and heavier, more imposing bodies. Artist monks filled the caves with sculptures, some tiny, others colossal, and covered their walls and ceilings in decorative carvings and reliefs.

OASIS VIHARAS

Dunhuang, an oasis settlement and border town on the Silk Route between Central and East Asia, was a flourishing settlement for missionary monks from India from the 3rd century CE. They built viharas, temples and libraries, where they translated Buddhist texts. Of the three main groups of cave temples, collectively known as the 'Thousand Buddha Caves', Mogao, the largest, contains 492 caves cut in three storeys into a cliff above a river valley. Here artist monks created figures in stucco, set against walls of a soft stone on which they depicted the Jataka Tales of the Buddha's past lives in innovative horizontal narrative strips. The early works, in earth colours, are light and full of action; the later works depict still, meditative bodhisattvas in brighter hues. Dunhuang remained a Buddhist centre until the 14th century. Today it is China's largest and longest-surviving cave-temple complex.

Above Stucco sculptures in their niches look upon walls covered in painted narrative strips depicting the Jataka Tales in Cave 285 at Dunhuang, Gansu province, China. The ceiling, too, displays a profusion of painted decoration.

BUDDHISM CROSSES BORDERS

DURING THE FIRST MILLENIUM CE, BUDDHISM SPREAD NORTHWARD FROM INDIA TO CENTRAL ASIA. MONKS FROM INDIA'S GREAT SEATS OF LEARNING TOOK NEW BUDDHIST IDEAS INTO TIBET, AND BY 1000CE, BUDDHISM HAD BECOME AN INTERNATIONAL RELIGION.

Taxila, ancient India's respected centre of Vedic learning, was at the confluence of trade routes linking India with Kashmir, Bactria (Balkh) and Central Asia. People of all religions from across the known world enrolled to learn Sanskrit grammar, medicine, law, military science and ayurvedic medicine, as well as the Veda.

The first Buddhist monasteries were founded at Taxila during the 3rd century CE, and Buddhist monks, confronted by sceptical enquiry into their beliefs, participated in debates on religious issues. By about the 1st century CE, Mahayana viharas there had become famous for advances in logic and philosophical analysis.

Buddhism continued to develop in Taxila, even when its fortifications were overridden by waves of invaders – kings from Greece,

Parthia (an Iranian empire) and, during the 2nd and 3rd centuries, the Kushan empire. During times of peace, monks carried Buddhism to centres along the trade routes, to Bactria, Samarkand – the capital of neighbouring Sogdiana – Parthia, Sassanid Persia, and even Merv (modern Mary, Turkmenistan).

THE EMPEROR KANISHKA

The Kushans were originally Yuezhi tribal people from the Mongolian steppe, and their empire, which was bordered by the Himalayas, extended from Central Asia to northern India. The mid-2nd-century Kushan emperor, Kanishka I, became a Buddhist and spread Buddhism into what is now Afghanistan, into Central Asia and thence to China. By the 7th century, Buddhism was flourishing in the oasis towns of the Tarim Basin.

Above A small tiered stupa stands in what was once a monk's cell at the Mohra Moradu vihara on the archaeological site of Taxila, Pakistan.

NALANDA

Before the 4th century CE, Chinese pilgrims were journeying to northern India in search of Buddhist scriptures for translation. Many texts were copied and translated into Sanskrit at Nalanda. Mahayana doctrine took shape at this seat of Buddhist learning, and its libraries became the main repository of Mahayana sutras. Students travelled from all over the Buddhist world to sit at the feet of its many outstanding teachers, such as renowned logician Dharmakirti, and Shantideva, a philosopher of the Madhyamaka school.

From Nalanda, monks spread Buddhism widely through China, from where it reached Korea and Japan, and to parts of South-east Asia. By the 7th century, Nalanda had become a famous international Buddhist university.

Left The high passes of the Pamir Mountains were a through route for the spread of Buddhism into Central and East Asia and for merchants and scholars entering India from the Silk Route.

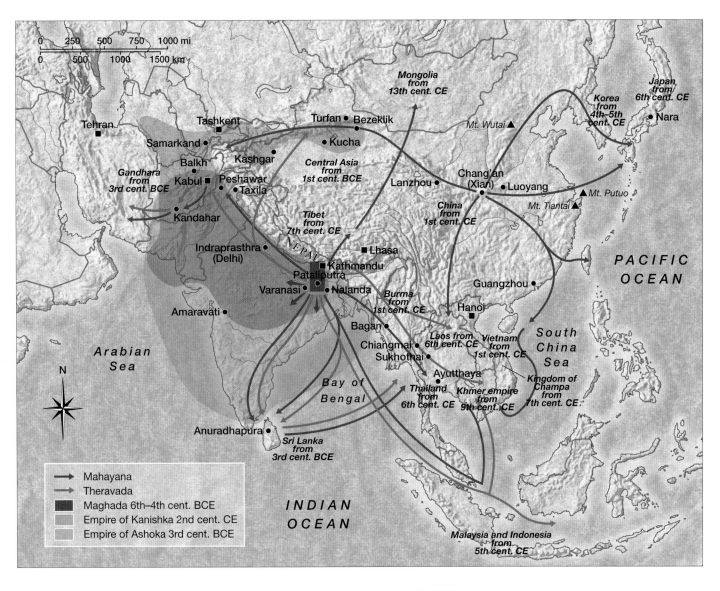

THE ORIGINS OF TIBETAN BUDDHISM

From the 10th century, Tibetans travelled to Nalanda, whose libraries held copies of the *Prajñaparamita,* or Perfection of Wisdom sutras, and many tantras. The university became the focus for the development of Vajrayana, a strand of Mahayana Buddhism based on belief in the potential buddhahood of every being, and on practices such as the recitation of mantras.

Vikramashila, a new university of advanced learning (in what is now Bihar), overtook Nalanda in size and reputation during the 10th century, and became the established centre in India for Tantric Buddhism. Students from

THE SPREAD OF BUDDHISM

This map shows the spread of Buddhism, from its roots in India across the Asian continent, between the 5th century BCE and the end of the 1st millennium CE.

Tibet and elsewhere flocked to study under famed teachers, such as Dipankara Srijnana, called Atisha. During the mid-11th century, Atisha travelled to Tibet, where he was instrumental in revivifying Buddhism, which was

at that time in decline there. He resided at the Samye monastery in central Tibet, where he translated texts from Sanskrit into Tibetan.

During the 12th century, Buddhism declined in India, but as the map above shows, it continued to spread northward and eastward during succeeding centuries.

Left The spread of Buddhism was encouraged by Emperor Kanishka, the 2nd century CE ruler of the Kushan empire, which extended from Central Asia to Afghanistan, where the remains of Buddhist temples, such as this one at Takht-i-Rustam, can still be seen.

TIBETAN BUDDHISM

TIBETAN BUDDHISM IS THE NAME BY WHICH THE WEST KNOWS THE
NEW BUDDHIST TRADITION THAT EMERGED IN INDIA IN THE 7TH
CENTURY CE, AND WHICH, BY THE END OF THE 1ST MILLENNIUM, WAS
FLOURISHING IN TIBET AND SURROUNDING REGIONS.

The third major tradition of Buddhism emerged from the Mahayana in the 7th century CE. It was at first called Tantrayana ('Tantra Vehicle'), or Tantric Buddhism, because many of its beliefs and practices were based on scriptures called tantras. It was also known as Mantrayana ('Mantra Vehicle'), because the recitation of mantras – sacred words or sounds – was central to its practice. Tantric Buddhism is often described as 'esoteric', or 'secret', mainly because tantric techniques were open only to the initiated. To maintain secrecy, tantras were kept hidden and some were written in code.

Below Monks at the Jokhang temple in Lhasa chant tantras, marking their progress by ringing hand bells. Ritual practices such as these are important features of Tibetan Buddhist devotions.

A variation of the new tradition, which emerged during the 8th century CE, was Vajrayana. *Vajra* means 'diamond' and also 'thunderbolt' – Vajrayana saw the tantric way as cutting through and destroying ignorance and other fetters that tie beings to samsara. Vajrayana Buddhism originated from ideas of the Madhyamaka and the meditational focus of the 4th-century Yogacara school.

Both forms of Buddhism use techniques to enable devotees to reach enlightenment instantly. They use mantras and mandalas, for example, to deepen concentration, with the aim of accelerating the loss of self and so bringing about instant liberation and attainment of the state of buddhahood.

Because the new tradition spread northward, into Tibet, the surrounding Himalayan kingdoms,

Above Mani are rocks traditionally inscribed with the mantra Om mani padme hum ('Hail to the jewel in the heart of the lotus'). Mantras are sacred chants to clear the mind for meditation or to express devotion.

Mongolia and into parts of Russia, it is also known as Northern Buddhism.

TANTRIC TECHNIQUES
The Northern tradition may have begun as early as the 5th century CE in north-western and north-eastern India as part of a wider movement that also influenced Hinduism and Jainism with its

Below This Tibetan painting depicts Vajrasattva, Bodhisattva of the Diamond Light. His right hand holds a vajra ('diamond sceptre'), symbolizing the destruction of ignorance, against his heart.

Above Kalmyk followers of Tibetan Buddhism wait outside the Khurul Datsan (monastery) north-east of their capital, Elista, in the northern Caucasus, to greet the Dalai Lama during his 2004 visit to their region.

tantric techniques. These include meditation and yoga; the reciting of mantras; mysticism and mudras. As it spread, Buddhism adapted to local religions, absorbing popular beliefs in magic and ritual.

The *Guhya-samaja-tantra*, or 'Tantra of the Secret Society', an early text, introduces the idea of multiple buddhas – the five Dhyani Buddhas. Each may appear during trance meditation as one of five bodhisattvas. The Adi-buddha, or Primordial Buddha, who existed in time before anything else, is said to have given rise to the Dhyani Buddhas.

MANTRAS AND MANDALAS

All schools of Tibetan Buddhism emphasize reliance on a spiritual guru, who can transmit not only texts and teachings but also spiritual energy to the acolyte. All are strongly devotional – as well as prostrations, prayers and practices such as the recitation of mantras for spiritual purification, visualization techniques using mandalas are important.

A mandala is a sacred representation of the Buddhist universe. Through meditation, devotees visualize themselves entering the mandala, passing through its outer circles, which represent the

external world, and following the path through the gateways leading to the bodhisattva or buddha at the centre. They visualize losing their sense of self and actually becoming the deity. Chanting, ringing bells and other ritual practices, many of them esoteric, or secret, feature in devotions. They are believed to invoke the help of deities for protection from danger or ensure personal salvation.

By the 8th century CE, tantric techniques dominated Indian Buddhism. Their appeal for Mahayana monks was that they seemed an effective, even powerful medium for achieving enlightenment and buddhahood.

NEW DIRECTIONS

The tradition became established in Tibet after the 7th century CE, spreading from there to surrounding kingdoms and northward to Mongolia and eastward to China, Korea and Japan, where it still

Above The Samye gompa *near Lhasa was Tibet's first Buddhist vihara, founded in the 8th century by Padmasambhava. It is designed as a sacred mandala, with a central temple symbolizing Mount Meru, the centre of the Buddhist universe.*

flourishes as Shingon Buddhism. Intertwined with the beliefs of native religions, Tibetan Buddhism took tantrism in new directions, searching for meditation and other techniques that would lead to enlightenment in one lifetime.

Many centuries earlier, texts such as the *Guhyasamaja-tantra* had posited the gratification of desire as a path to liberation. Later, Tantric Buddhists developed this idea and sought to achieve transcendence of the self through techniques involving ritual sexual intercourse.

Tibetan Buddhism continues to evolve. Suppressed in its homeland, it has migrated to the West, where it has flourished.

MANDALAS

MANDALAS ARE SACRED DIAGRAMS, USUALLY CIRCULAR AND FULL OF COMPLEX, COLOURFUL SYMBOLS AND IMAGES THAT REPRESENT THE UNIVERSE. VISUALIZING THE HIGHER SPIRITUAL REALMS DEPICTED IN A MANDALA HELPS DEEPEN CONCENTRATION DURING MEDITATION.

Mandala is the Sanskrit word for circle, and mandalas are called 'cosmic' or 'sacred' circles. They were originally symbols used by Brahmans and are a part of Hindu worship. They may have originated with the practice of chanting the verses of the *Rigveda*, which is divided into ten 'mandalas', from whose verses the universe was believed to originate, or from the ancient ritual of circumambulating stupas. In Tibetan Buddhism, mandalas are

Below The Gyantse Kumbum, in Tibet, is a perfect mandala. The stepped tiers symbolize the Sangha, the square upper tier the Dharma and the topmost sphere the Buddha.

often used for meditation. They are also used during initiation rituals for monks, when they represent the universe with the Buddha at the very centre.

Simple drawings of mandalas dating from the 9th century BCE have been found on cave walls along pilgrimage routes between India and the East – close to the oasis town of Dunhuang in China, for example. Mandalas were also painted on temple walls, including on those of the Mystic Mandala temple of the Tabo monastery in Himachal Pradesh, which may date from the late 10th century.

Temporary mandalas are made from paper, or painted in coloured sand or chalk for Tibetan Buddhist

Above Mandalas were originally simple circular diagrams like those drawn on the walls of caves by Buddhists in ancient times. This more elaborate example, engraved on stone, was found in the Rupshu region of Ladakh.

initiation rites. When the rites are over, the mandalas are destroyed and the sand is swept up and deposited in a river or a lake to emphasize the transitory nature of all things.

Permanent mandalas are painted on textiles or wood, usually to invoke buddhas or bodhisattvas. They may look square rather than circular, but their complex designs, which often incorporate hundreds of elements, such as

Below Monks at the Thiksay gompa in Ladakh paint a mandala to celebrate a festival, using sand and the dust of precious stones. After the festival, the mandala will be destroyed as a reminder of the impermanence of visible things.

deities and supernatural beings, have features that are common to all 'sacred circles'.

LORD OF THE CIRCLE

The mandala is envisaged as a lord's domain, with the residence of the deity enthroned at its centre. The deity resides in a temple in a square, walled court-yard with a gateway on each side. The central courtyard may be surrounded by others, each with four gateways. The east gateway is usually white, the west gateway red, and the north and south ones green and yellow, respectively. All have elaborate roofs. The temple is enclosed in a protective circle in which the central deity may rest on a lotus surrounded by guardian beings, such as gatekeepers, goddesses and bodhisattvas.

Devotees visualize themselves crossing the mandala's outer circles, which represent the external world, and following the path to the internal gateways to approach the deity. They meditate on each guardian figure and bodhisattva, then on the central buddha or bodhisattva.

Tantric Buddhist devotees may invoke the deity and proceed to visualize it emitting luminosity, for example, or may strive to lose the sense of self and imagine becoming the deity.

Right Five buddhas are commonly depicted in mandalas: the Buddha Shakyamuni is at the centre, with buddhas from the world systems constructed by Mahayana Buddhism inhabiting east, west, north and south.

THREE-DIMENSIONAL MANDALAS

Some Buddhist temples were also constructed as mandalas, allowing the ideal of entering a mandala to become a reality. These include the Kumbum (100,000 buddha images) chorten (stupa) at Gyantse, Tibet, and the oldest and most magnificent example, Borobudur in Java. Pilgrims can enter the gates and follow the ascending path to the centre, meditating on the wall paintings at Gyantse and stone reliefs at Borobudur along the interior walls.

TIBETAN SCRIPTURES

ALL THE EXTRAVAGANT COMPLEXITY OF TIBETAN BUDDHISM – THE
RICH COSMOLOGY AND SYMBOLISM, DEITIES AND DEMONS,
MANDALAS, MANTRAS AND MYSTICISM – CAN BE FOUND IN THE
SUTRAS AND TANTRAS ON WHICH IT IS BASED.

Above *Sacred texts, or tantras, were written in a script that was specially devised for them, and were sometimes embellished with inks made from precious metals and stones.*

Tantric beliefs and practices were first transmitted by word of mouth before the 3rd century CE, when tantras were first written down by monks who may have wanted to revive spirituality in Buddhism at a time when it had become dry and academic. Tantras appeared up to the 12th century, by which time, Buddhism had almost disappeared from India, though it was flourishing in the surrounding regions where it had spread.

THE TIBETAN COLLECTIONS

Tibetan Buddhism's sacred scriptures form two major collections. The *Kanjur* (Translated Word of the Buddha) consists of 108 volumes and more than 1,000 texts of the Buddha's teachings. The *Tenjur* (Treatises) contains more than 3,000 commentaries on the *Kanjur* texts in 225 volumes, plus poems and songs of praise, manuals on meditation and mandalas, rituals for consecrating monasteries and commentaries on doctrine.

Most of the texts of the *Kanjur* and *Tenjur* were written in Indian languages and were subsequently translated into Tibetan. No Tibetan script existed until the 7th century, when a king, Songtsen Gampo, instructed a learned courtier to devise one so that the Dharma could be translated from Sanskrit and read to his people. The period of feverish translation that followed ensured the preservation in Tibetan of Sanskrit texts that might have been lost. The work of identifying, classifying, recording and translating this voluminous literature still continues today.

Left *Monks in the sacred Jokhang temple in Lhasa print religious texts from carved wood blocks on both sides of long, thin paper sheets, called* pechas, *made from root fibres.*

THE TANTRAS

The sutras and tantras of Tibetan Buddhism purport to be the word of the Buddha, which was kept secret for centuries until Buddhists were ready to understand the texts. Thus, the arcane and esoteric nature of much of Tibetan Buddhism stems directly from its scriptures. There are some 450 tantras in the *Kanjur* and more than 2,400 in the *Tenjur*. These deal with the esoteric aspects of Buddhist teaching – tantra originally meant 'loom' or 'weaving' and symbolized the harmony of body and mind – but it later became associated with occult teachings. Many tantras were written in a 'twilight language' or *Sandhabhasya* so that only an initiate – a lama (or guru) – could read them and impart the teachings to selected students.

The tantras are classified into four or five major groups. The largest and earliest is the Kriya group, written between the 5th and 7th century. It is concerned with cultivating the magical powers of mantras and meditation to achieve worldly goals such as control of illness and weather.

Later groups were concerned with achieving buddhahood – but not gradually, over many disciplined lives. They sought instant transformation into buddhas. The most important of the eight Carya tantras focuses on identification with the Buddha Vairocana, a symbol of ultimate reality, while the principal Yoga tantra of the 8th century centres on Mañjushri, who symbolized wisdom.

Ritual sexual practices featured in the later tantras – the male symbolizing compassionate action

Right A lama studies the Tibetan scriptures. Lamas ministering to a dead or dying person recite passages from the Bardo Thodrol.

Above An image of the revered Tibetan yogin Milarepa (1040–1123) carved into rock. Milarepa is most famous for his poems, The Hundred Thousand Songs of Milarepa, *in which he extols the Dharma. These poems are part of the Tibetan canon.*

and the female wisdom – as did the consumption of forbidden substances, such as alcohol and meat. One objective of such practices was to liberate the mind from dualistic thinking (bad/good). A result of this phase of Tantric Buddhism was the importance attributed to female bodhisattvas. Female deities figure prominently in 9th–10th-century Yogini tantras.

THE TIBETAN BOOK OF THE DEAD

The *Bardo Thodrol*, known in English as *The Tibetan Book of the Dead*, is a scripture on the theme of death, life after death and rebirth. It describes the world called 'Bardo' that lies between death and rebirth.

One of the duties of Tibetan lamas is to read 'The Great Liberation by Hearing' from the *Bardo Thodrol* to the dying. This is part of the rite of passage for the dying person.

The work is a spiritual treasure that Padmasambhava, the sage said to have brought Tantric Buddhism to Tibet, is believed to have hidden in the wilds of the Himalayas. It was later found by the Tibetan religious *terton*, or 'treasure hunter', Karma Lingpa.

The Tibetan Book of the Dead has been lauded as a great contribution to world literature on the states of dying and death, but Padmasambhava offers wise guidance on transforming everyday living, as well as addressing one's own experience of dying and how to help dying people.

CHAPTER 4

WORLD BUDDHISM

Buddhism began to spread beyond the Indian subcontinent as early as the 3rd century BCE, when the great Mauryan emperor Ashoka sent emissaries all over the known world. During the 1st millennium CE, monks from India and Central Asia made the journey east to China, from which Buddhism was then carried to Korea and Japan. Merchants trading between India and Sri Lanka and the Malay peninsula, Sumatra, Java and Cambodia, transported Buddhist passengers along with their cargoes. Buddhism reached Tibet during the 7th century, where it evolved and spread to surrounding Himalayan kingdoms and Mongolia.

By the 13th century, Muslim invaders had conquered most of the Indian subcontinent, but Buddhism survived. Today, Burma (Myanmar), Thailand, Cambodia and Laos preserve the Theravada tradition. Mahayana schools have survived Communist suppression in Vietnam and China, and they flourish in South Korea and Japan.

During the 19th century, scholars from Western colonizing countries discovered Buddhism and initiated a revival in India, the place of its birth. Beginning in the 20th century, masters of Eastern Buddhist traditions established monasteries and meditation centres in the West.

Opposite This exquisite painting of Padmapani holding a blue lotus adorns the wall of Cave 1 at Ajanta in Maharashtra, western India. Padmapani is a form of Avalokiteshvara, the Bodhisattva of Compassion.

Above The Boudhanath stupa in the Kathmandu Valley, Nepal. It is one of the largest monuments of its kind in the world, and is believed to have been built in the 5th century CE.

THE SPREAD OF BUDDHISM

FOR MORE THAN A MILLENNIUM, BUDDHISM RIPPLED OUT ACROSS ASIA FROM ITS HEARTLAND IN NORTH-EASTERN INDIA. THE 20TH CENTURY SAW IT CROSS NEW FRONTIERS INTO THE WESTERN HEMISPHERE TO BECOME A WORLD RELIGION.

The first missionaries to leave the Buddha's homeland of Maghada in north-eastern India to teach the Dharma were the first arhats, those disciples who had achieved enlightenment. Buddhism remained a local religion, however, until Ashoka, Mauryan emperor of India during the 3rd century BCE, made it his state religion.

Above Xuanzang, depicted in this early 20th-century book on the myths of China, was one of many Chinese monks who made long and dangerous pilgrimages across Asia in search of Buddhist scriptures.

Ashoka spread the Buddha's teachings throughout his empire, which extended over most of the Indian subcontinent and into Gandhara (modern Afghanistan).

Ashoka sent a group of monks, headed by his son, Mahinda, to Sri Lanka. This first wave of missionaries carried the Theravada Buddhist tradition to Sri Lanka, where it became the state religion and a staging post for the spread of Theravada south-eastward, to Burma (Myanmar), Thailand, Laos, Cambodia, Malaysia and Indonesia.

Merchants were among the strongest supporters of the Sangha (the Buddhist monastic

Left The monk Mahinda, who brought Buddhism to Sri Lanka, is represented as the Buddha in this statue at Mihintale near Anuradhapura. While Buddhism declined in India, its teachings were preserved in Sri Lanka.

Right Buddhism flourished in Indonesia until the 1300s. These statues guard a Buddhist monastery on the island of Bali.

community) during the first centuries after the Buddha. In the hierarchical society of ancient India, these were lower-caste people who were attracted to Buddhism's egalitarian beliefs. Monks and nuns followed the trading caravans north, across the high passes into Central Asia, where they formed large communities in the desert oases.

From about the 1st century CE, merchants forged trade routes between the Hellenistic world and China. Monks also followed these routes, later called the 'Silk Route', eastward. In China, they won imperial patronage, which furthered the spread of Buddhism across China to Korea during the 4th century, from which it reached Japan by the 6th century.

NEW TRADITIONS

Monks of the Theravada and Mahayana schools lived in harmony and travelled together, so that Buddhist monks of both traditions carried the Dharma to new peoples. However, during the early centuries CE, the Mahayana tradition, which challenged the orthodox Theravada teachings with new philosophies, rose to prominence in northern India.

The monastics who ventured eastward into China, and later Korea and Japan, belonged mainly to the Mahayana schools, and it was the Mahayana – often called the Eastern tradition – that dominated in the Far East. From there, it penetrated into Vietnam, Laos and Cambodia.

The Himalayan kingdoms were among the last regions of Asia to embrace Buddhism. Monks of the Mahayana tradition

first reached Tibet during the early centuries CE, but they seem to have had limited success. During the 700s, however, Padmasambhava, a monk from the north-west of the Indian sub-continent, introduced Tantric Buddhism to Tibet.

This branch of the Mahayana emphasized the use of aids such as meditation, mantras and mandalas to attain enlightenment in one lifetime. Buddhism became the state religion of Tibet and spread to the surrounding Himalayan kingdoms of Nepal, Bhutan, Ladakh and Kashmir, and north-ward into Mongolia.

WESTERN FRONTIERS

By the dawn of the second millennium, Buddhism, under attack from Hinduism and Islam, was in decline in India. Yet regions outside India where

Right This bronze head of the Buddha, from the 3rd–4th century CE, is from the oasis town of Khotan (modern Hotan, Xinjiang, China), which was once the site of a large Buddhist community in Central Asia.

Buddhism had taken root – such as Sri Lanka, Burma, Tibet and China – preserved its three main traditions and their texts and teachings. The energy that had driven the early waves of expansion dissipated, and in some regions it was suppressed. Muslim armies invaded most of Central Asia, for example, and Buddhism began to decline in Indonesia after Islam arrived there in the 13th century.

Not until the mid-20th century and the spread of Buddhism to the West was the decline arrested. Despite the suppression of Buddhism in many countries by some colonial powers and communist regimes, Buddhist ideas, brought to the West by colonialists and explorers, managed to gain a foothold. During the 20th century, Western countries have provided a haven for many Buddhist refugees from oppression and persecution in the East.

THE DECLINE OF BUDDHISM IN INDIA

WITH THE PATRONAGE OF EMPERORS AND KINGS, BUDDHISM BECAME A MAJOR RELIGION ACROSS MOST OF THE INDIAN SUBCONTINENT DURING THE EARLY CENTURIES OF THE COMMON ERA. NEVERTHELESS, BY THE 19TH CENTURY, IT HAD ALMOST DISAPPEARED.

The Chinese pilgrim Faxian, who travelled to India during the 5th century CE to search for texts of the Vinaya, or monastic rules, to copy, found many in a library at Pataliputra, capital of the Gupta empire. He described two large monasteries, each of 600–700 monks. Yet only two centuries later, another pilgrim, Xuanzang, found the city long-deserted, with stupas and temples by the hundred lying in ruins among its foundations.

Above The Buddha attained enlightenment beneath a Bodhi tree at Bodhgaya in India. According to tradition, the tree has been cut down and damaged many times but has always miraculously regenerated.

THE WHITE HUNS

Pataliputra had been sacked by White Huns, nomads from the Mongolian steppe. They had gained power in the Oxus Basin, and in the mid-5th century, overthrew Sogdiana and Bactria in Central Asia, and Gandhara in the north-west. In 440CE, they invaded northern India and conquered the Gupta empire, razing cities, burning monasteries and killing monks.

THE DECLINE OF BUDDHISM

Buddhism survived in the north, even under the White Huns, and continued to flourish in other regions. In 5th-century Mathura, for example, Faxian found 20 viharas, supporting perhaps 3,000 monks, while Xuanzang,

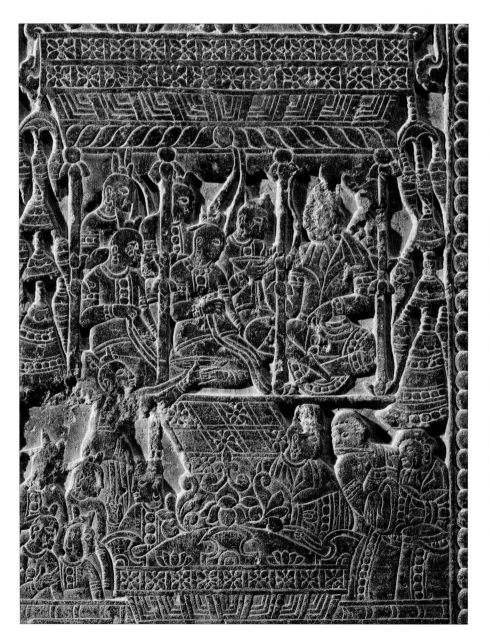

Left Sogdiana, like north-western India, was overthrown by the nomadic White Huns. This 6th-century grey limestone funerary stone from the Northern Qi dynasty depicts the Sogdian New Year festival.

writing in 634CE, found a Buddhist state there, with 20 monasteries and 2,000 monks. Yet the invasions of the White Huns seem to mark the start of a slow decline in Buddhism from around the 5th century. Xuanzang's accounts of his 7th-century journey around the subcontinent describe many ruined Buddhist teaching centres and abandoned viharas.

BUDDHISM AND HINDUISM

Some historians view the fading demarcation between Buddhism and Hinduism as a factor in this decline. Buddhism had always co-existed with Hindu and Jain sects, with which it shares many similarities. In temples of, for example, the 7th-century ruler Harsha and kings of the later Pala dynasty, whose empires spanned northern India, the Buddha was worshipped as a Hindu deity. Later Hindu scriptures even identified him as an incarnation of the Hindu god Vishnu. Hinduism declined during the early 800s, but was revived by the 9th-century Advaita Vedanta philosophical movement. During this resurgence, some Hindu rulers may have withdrawn their support from Buddhist institutions.

To ordinary, uneducated people, Buddhism may also have seemed inaccessible. Over the centuries many viharas had become enriched by donations from supporters. While Hindu religious leaders had regularly visited villages to minister to people, historians surmise that many Buddhist monks may have neglected their teaching role and devoted their time to philosophy and meditation.

MUSLIM INVASIONS

From the 8th century, Muslim Turks made raids into the north-west and advanced into

the Buddhist heartland of the north-east. In 1192, Muslim armies established their rule over northern India. Buddhist institutions, with their libraries, paintings and sculptures of buddhas and bodhisattvas, which were considered idolatrous by the Muslims, were a target. They were razed and burned.

Neverthless, Buddhism survived for a number of centuries in Orissa, Andhra Pradesh and

Left The side of the Dhamekh stupa at Sarnath is decorated with Gupta reliefs. The Gupta dynasty ruled northern India and parts of central and western India from the 4th to 6th century CE, until it was overtaken by the White Huns and also, in all likelihood, collapsed due to internal factors.

southern India. The Mulavesa vihara, founded on the Kerala coast in the 9th century by a king of the Varadu dynasty, flourished until it was eventually inundated by rising seas, beneath which it remained hidden until, according to legend, it reappeared briefly during a tsunami, a poignant reminder of the impermanence of all things.

However, by the 19th century, Buddhism had become virtually extinct in India to the south and west of the Himalayas.

Below Around 460 the White Huns from Central Asia crossed the Khyber Pass and raided Gandhara. They destroyed Buddhist monasteries, stupas and temples at Taxila, a great centre of religious teaching, which never recovered. Today it is a UNESCO World Heritage site in Pakistan.

BUDDHISM IN SRI LANKA

AROUND 250BCE, THE MONK MAHINDA, SON OF THE FIRST BUDDHIST EMPEROR, ASHOKA, TOOK THE FIRST BUDDHIST MISSION BEYOND THE INDIAN MAINLAND TO SRI LANKA. TODAY, SRI LANKA IS THE WORLD'S OLDEST CONTINUALLY BUDDHIST COUNTRY.

It was in Sri Lanka, during the 1st century CE, that Buddhist monks first wrote down the Buddha's teachings, the Tripitaka. Today, this is the only complete canon of an early Buddhist school to have survived in the language (Pali) in which it was written.

Early in the 1st millennium BCE, Sri Lanka cradled the developing Theravada, the only early Buddhist school that still exists. The lineage (the line of ordination of Sri Lankan Theravada bhikkhus) has passed from generation to generation, rarely broken since the 3rd century BCE. However, the bhikkhuni lineage died out.

ANURADHAPURA

Devanampiya Tissa, who was king of Anuradhapura during the late 3rd century BCE, was Mahinda's first convert. His capital became a centre of the Vibhajjavada school to which Mahinda adhered and that closely followed the Buddha's teachings. The king

founded a Mahavihara, or 'Great Monastery', at Anuradhapura, which became a major Theravada centre, and he also built a dagoba, the Thuparama, to enshrine relics of the Buddha. Later kings built the Ruwanvali Mahaseya and the huge Jetavana stupa, 88m (289ft) in diameter and about 91m (299ft) high. Stupas were also built at Mihintale, the hill where Mahinda is said to have converted King Devanampiya Tissa.

Close relationships between kings and the Sangha continued for two millennia and Buddhist monks are still influential in Sri Lanka, although today the constitution bars them from holding any political office.

Below The Theravada art of Sri Lanka focuses on events in the life of the Buddha. This colossal image of the Buddha in parinirvana in the Isurumuniya temple at Anuradhapura dates from the reign of the first Buddhist king of Anuradhapura, Devanampiya Tissa.

Above The colossal standing Buddha at Maligawila, Sri Lanka, dates from around the 7th century CE and is carved from crystalline limestone.

During the 1st century CE, King Valagamba lost his throne to forces raised by Brahmans who had lost political authority to bhikkhus and were supported by Hindu Tamil armies. Valagamba defeated the Tamils in 89CE, and to mark his victory, he constructed the Abhayagiri monastery and the great Abhayagiri dagoba, which still stands.

The Abhayagiri threatened Theravada dominance from the 3rd century CE, when many monks turned to Mahayana traditions. Mahayana flourished in Sri Lanka for 1,000 years until King Parakramabahu (1153–86) restored the Mahavihara and the Theravada tradition to prominence.

Anuradhapura was sacked by armies from southern India at the end of the 10th century and abandoned to the jungle. Explorers in the 19th century rediscovered it and found the sacred Bodhi tree. It was believed to have grown

from a shoot of the Bodhi tree at Bodhgaya that had been brought to Sri Lanka by Ashoka's daughter, the nun Sanghamitta, more than 2,000 years earlier.

DECLINE AND RESURGENCE

From the 16th century, the Portuguese, the Dutch and, in the late 1700s, the British, established their influence and Christianity in Sri Lanka. About 20 per cent of the population became Christian, and after decades of neglect and official opposition, Buddhism and the Sangha declined.

Independence groups emerged among Sinhalese Buddhists in the late 19th century, when the patriot Anagarika Dharmapala cited the *Mahavamsa*, a 5th-century chronicle of Sri Lankan Buddhism, to support the Sinhalese claim for political rights to the island and Buddhism as its main religion. However, the Tamil Hindu ethnic minority also used historical sources to claim rights to political control and oppose government protection of Buddhism.

Above The sacred Ruwanveliseya Mahaseya stupa in Anuradhapura dates from the 2nd century BCE. It is the classic bubble shape of Sri Lankan dagobas, symbolizing impermanence.

After independence in 1948, Christianity declined and the population is now officially 69 per cent Buddhist. In 1972, Buddhism was enshrined in the constitution as 'foremost' among the island's religions. Since 1983, the Tamil Tigers have fought a civil war to establish an independent state in the traditionally Hindu north and east of Sri Lanka.

BUDDHAGHOSA

During the 5th century an Indian scholar, Buddhaghosa, travelled to Sri Lanka to study commentaries on the Buddhist scriptures written in Sinhalese. He was born a Brahman, possibly in Bodhgaya, but became a Buddhist monk.

Buddhaghosa studied in a monastery in Anuradhapura, where he wrote the summary of Theravada doctrine for which he is best remembered, the *Visuddhimagga* ('Path of Purity'). He also examined Buddhist commentaries, which he edited and translated into Pali. He studied and translated in Anuradhapura for many years before returning to India.

Buddhaghosa was a prolific writer of commentaries on the Tripitaka and canon law. As many of the original Pali commentaries on the scriptures are lost, his works provide a valuable insight into the thought and traditions of the Indian Theravada community during the 1st millennium.

Below The festival of Esala Perahera is held in July or August in Kandy. A casket containing a tooth relic of the Buddha is carried around the city.

INDIA'S BUDDHIST RESURGENCE

IN INDIA IN THE 19TH CENTURY, A PROTEST MOVEMENT GAINED
FORCE AGAINST THE RIGID BRAHMAN UPPER-CASTE HEGEMONY.
IN THEIR QUEST FOR EQUALITY, INDIAN SOCIAL REFORMERS TOOK
REFUGE IN THE EGALITARIAN TENETS OF BUDDHISM.

By the 1800s, Buddhism had disappeared from mainstream Indian society, but it had not died out from the national consciousness. It survived in places among the Newar peoples of the Kathmandu Valley, in Ladakh, Sikkim and Bhutan, among the tribal peoples of Bengal (modern Bangladesh) and among the lower castes in Maharashtra and bordering states.

REAWAKENING

The colonial upheaval in India in the 19th century aroused not only nationalist sentiment but also a surge of protest against caste inequality. In 1862, a Hindu in Orissa, Mahima Gosain, founded a new monastic sect that reflected Buddhist ideas, such as the rejection of violence and the caste system. His ideas appealed to the lower castes and were popularized by Bhima Bhoi, a poet from an Orissa tribal group. In 1885, another Hindu, Jotiba Phule, raged against Brahman elitism in *Gulamgiri* ('Slavery'). A middle-caste social reformer, Phule worked among low-caste people in Maharashtra and established India's first school for girls.

RECLAIMING BODHGAYA

In 1891, a young Buddhist lay follower, Anagarika Dharmapala, made a pilgrimage from Sri Lanka

Above The Mahabodhi temple at Bodhgaya was built c. late 6th century CE on the spot where the Buddha attained enlightenment. The temple was restored by the British in 1880.

to the sacred Mahabodhi temple at Bodhgaya, where the Buddha had attained enlightenment. He found the temple, recently restored by the British, in use by a Hindu priest, the great Buddha image inside transformed into a Hindu icon. Buddhists could not worship there. Horrified, Dharmapala founded a Buddhist protest movement.

Educated as a Christian in British Ceylon, David Hewavitarne encountered Buddhism while working in Colombo for the Theosophists Madame Blavatsky and Colonel Olcott, who were Buddhist converts. He became a celibate Buddhist lay follower, or *anagarika,* and launched a lawsuit against the Hindus who had charge of the temple, to reclaim the site for Buddhists. In 1949, after Hewavitarne's death, the government granted

Below This 20th-century relief on the Japanese Buddhist Peace pagoda in Darjeeling, West Bengal, shows the Buddha teaching his disciples.

management of the temple to a committee of four Buddhists and four Hindus.

THE UNTOUCHABLES

As early as the 1860s, a scholar from Tamil Nadu, Iyothee Thass, who had been born a low-caste untouchable (known as Dalits), began a campaign to raise public awareness of the cruel treatment of his people. At the 1891 census, he urged Tamil untouchables to register as casteless Dravidians. Another social reformer who turned to Buddhism as a solution for caste inequalities, Thass established the Sakya Buddhist Society in Tamil Nadu.

Iyothee Thass foreshadowed the extraordinary achievements of Bhimrao Ramji Ambedkar. Born an untouchable in Maharashtra in 1891, Ambedkar became one of the first untouchables to gain an education. He earned degrees at

Above Bhimrao Ramji Ambedkar, India's law minister (1947–51), championed the rights of Dalits ('the Suppressed') – low-caste Hindus known as 'untouchables'. Ambedkar renounced Hinduism and took refuge in Buddhism's egalitarian teachings.

the universities of Bombay, Columbia in the USA (in 1916) and the London School of Economics by 1923. In London he was called to the Bar. As a lawyer in India, he advocated political rights for untouchables and led campaigns to allow them to use public drinking-water facilities and to worship in Hindu temples. He embarked on a long and distinguished career as a legislator, politician, writer and social reformer. In 1936 he founded India's Independent Labour Party and he became an architect of the Constitution (1947–9).

Ambedkar studied Buddhism and enshrined some of its principles in the Constitution. In 1956, he famously made a public conversion to Buddhism and converted 380,000 of his supporters. Today, Ambedkar Buddhists number around four million, the largest Buddhist group in India.

DHARAMSALA

In 1959, Tibet's spiritual and politial leader, His Holiness, the 14th Dalai Lama, Tenzin Gyatso, escaped from the Potala Palace in Lhasa to India. The following year Indian Prime Minister, Jawaharlal Nehru, granted him permission to establish a government-in-exile at the hill town of Dharamsala in the state of Himachal Pradesh.

From Dharamsala the Dalai Lama appealed for international help in his struggle for Tibetan independence, and, since his exile, he has built the framework for an independent, democratic Tibetan state founded on Buddhist values and modern political ideas of freedom and human rights. In 1963, he enshrined these ideas in a draft constitution for a new Tibet, and in 1989 he was awarded

the Nobel Peace Prize for his "consistent resistance to the use of violence in his people's struggle to regain their liberty".

The Dalai Lama has made India the centre of a worldwide Buddhist revival. In monasteries around Dharamsala and the beautiful Kangra Valley, overlooked by the Himalayas, live

Above Tibetan Buddhist monks perform a fire puja (purification ceremony) at Dharamsala. After the fire has burnt out they circumambulate the ashes.

more than 20,000 Tibetan Buddhist monks and nuns from all sects. It is one of the largest Buddhist communities in India.

THE BAMIYAN BUDDHAS

THE WORLD'S LARGEST STANDING BUDDHA IMAGES WERE THE COLOSSAL ROCK-CUT BUDDHAS AT BAMIYAN IN AFGHANISTAN. THEY DATED FROM THE 5TH CENTURY CE AND TOOK 100 YEARS TO CARVE FROM THE SHEER FACE OF A SANDSTONE CLIFF.

Lying between the Hindu Kush and the Koh-i-Baba mountain ranges is the long, broad, fertile Bamiyan Valley in present-day Afghanistan. In the 1st century CE, this valley was a crossroads for caravans trading along the Silk Route between southern and Central Asia, China and the Roman empire. Visitors to Bamiyan were met by the sight of two gigantic painted and gilded statues of the Buddha, carved out of a sheer cliff-face.

Below Buddhist monks of many different schools and sects cut thousands of caves in the sandstone sides of the Bamiyan Valley, and hewed the great Vairocana, symbol of the universe, out of the cliff-face. Today, visitors are greeted by the poignant sight of an empty niche.

BAMIYAN

The city of Bamiyan, capital of a small kingdom, was part of the Kushan empire from the 1st century CE, a hub of religions, languages and peoples. As trade expanded under the 2nd-century ruler Kanishka I, who was a follower of Buddhism, Bamiyan grew in commercial importance.

Itinerant Buddhist monks settled in caves excavated from the cliffs that flanked the valley. There are more than 20,000 such caves, from monks' cells to large meeting halls, indicating that by the 5th century CE, the valley had become a major centre of Buddhism. Wall paintings decorate many caves and some of those painted between the late 600s and the 900s have recently been identified as the world's oldest-known oil paintings.

Above This beautiful 6th-century wall painting, once brilliantly coloured, is one of many that adorned the niches of the Bamiyan Buddhas and the walls and ceilings of many surrounding caves. The Taliban destroyed much of this art.

THE BUDDHAS

The earliest and smallest of the Bamiyan Buddhas, at the western end of the cliff-face, was about 35m (115ft) tall; the largest, at the eastern end, was 53m (174ft).

Above The great Maitreya, the Buddha of the future, at the Bingling temple, near the Liujiaxia Reservoir and Yongjing, Gansu province, China, has stylistic similarities to the Bamiyan Buddhas and gives an impression of how they may have looked.

Bamiyan was part of the Gandhara region, whose innovative sculptors produced the first Buddha statues, and the smaller of the two colossi was in the Gandharan style, showing Greek influence in the drapery, while the larger Buddha represented the Mathura style of India, with more natural physical proportions.

The large buddha was painted red, the smaller one predominantly blue, and their hands were gilded. Their faces were missing, and while some historians attribute this to destruction by Muslim invaders in earlier centuries, others think the faceless heads may once have been covered with gilded masks. The statues were hung with ornaments and jewels.

The two buddhas were cut in deep relief from the cliff rock, with the details, such as hands and drapery, crafted from mud mixed with straw and coated with stucco. Conservationists have discovered that the folds of drapery on the large buddha were fashioned from ropes hung from pegs driven into the statues, then coated with stucco. The holes in the surface of the statues were made by pegs driven into the rock to support the plaster.

Art historians have identified both statues as being representations of the Buddha Vairocana, the Adi-Buddha – first among the five Dhyani Buddhas, who, in Tantric Buddhism, are believed to be generated by meditators in a state of trance, and who represent the teachings of the Buddha Shakyamuni.

Right The great Buddha of Bamiyan had stood for more than 1,500 years before its destruction in 2001. Its plastered and gilded limbs had fallen away and its paintwork had faded, but protected by its stone niche, the Buddha remained largely intact.

The artists treated the statues and niches as a composition reminiscent of a mandala. The niches surrounding the central sculptures are painted with buddhas, bodhisattvas and celestial deities, and the niche roofs represent the dome of heaven. Cut into the cliff walls between the two niches are caves, once used as shrines, the walls and ceilings of which are also covered with the remains of colourful wall paintings.

DESTRUCTION

In March 2001, the Taliban regime destroyed the ancient Buddhas of Bamiyan. The site has since been put under the protection of UNESCO (the United Nations Educational, Scientific and Cultural Organization), which is funding a long-term project to sort and preserve the thousands of fragments of the giant Buddhas, with the aim of eventually reconstructing them.

BUDDHISM IN THE HIMALAYAN KINGDOMS

GOMPAS AND CHORTENS FLUTTERING WITH PRAYER FLAGS, WHIRLING PRAYER WHEELS AND WALLS FORMED FROM ROCKS AND STONES, EXQUISITELY INSCRIBED WITH MANTRAS, SPEAK OF CENTURIES OF BUDDHISM AMONG THE PEOPLE OF THE HIMALAYAN VALLEYS.

Above Padmasambhava, also called Guru Rinpoche, who brought Tantric Buddhism to Tibet, is revered in all Himalayan countries. Here a pilgrim worships at the world's tallest statue of the tantric master, at Namchi, Sikkim.

Below Buddhist and Hindu practices merge in the Kathmandu Valley. Adherents of both Hindu and Buddhist tantric sects take part in the Rato Machhendranath festival, which is held in Patan, Nepal, in January, to ensure a good rainfall.

The Buddha was born in the Terai, the narrow, humid plain of Nepal at the foot of the Himalayas, where some of Buddhism's most sacred pilgrimage sites, including Kapilavastu and Lumbini, are found.

Buddhism flourished among the tribal peoples of that region from its earliest days. Some historians believe Buddhist monks from Maghada may also have migrated north-west and established viharas in the beautiful wetlands of the Kashmir Valley before the 3rd century BCE.

Around 250BCE, the Buddhist emperor Ashoka extended the Maurya empire into Nepal. According to tradition, he sent the Buddhist scholar Madhyantika to spread the Dharma in Gandhara, founded Pandrethan, a Buddhist city in the Kashmir Valley, and sent missions eastward across the high passes into Ladakh and Zanskar.

TIBETAN BUDDHISM

From Nepal, Buddhism was transmitted to its northern neighbour, Tibet, but it did not gain a foothold there until the 7th century CE. By then, all three of the great Buddhist movements – Theravada, Mahayana and tantric forms – had developed in India.

Mahayana and tantric forms had the greatest success in Tibet, where syntheses of their teachings developed. The tantric master Padmasambhava was one of the most prominent figures involved in establishing Buddhism in Tibet, and he is said to have introduced

THE KATHMANDU VALLEY

Eyes of wisdom and compassion gaze in four directions across the Kathmandu Valley, Nepal's historic cultural centre, from the *harmikas* of the richly carved and ornamented Swayambhunath and Boudhanath stupas. The eyes are thought to represent the all-seeing gaze of Vairocana, the Buddha of Wisdom and embodiment of *sunyata*, or emptiness. Built during the 5th century, Swayambhunath is the oldest stupa in Nepal, while the 7th-century Boudhanath is the largest.

The Boudhanath stupa, believed to contain relics of previous buddhas, is sacred to followers of Tibetan Buddhism. During the 1st millennium CE, Nepal's golden age of Buddhist art, artists created exquisite sculptures and statuettes depicting Mahamaya giving birth to the Buddha, and later, bodhisattvas such as Tara, the female Bodhisattva of Compassion, who is a manifestation of the tantric branch of Buddhism.

The first capital of the Kathmandu Valley was Patan, where the remains of five great stupas built by the emperor Ashoka still mark the cardinal points around the city's ancient centre.

tantric forms into the surrounding kingdoms of Nepal, Sikkim and the tiny kingdom of Mustang. During the 10th century, when Buddhists were severely persecuted in Tibet, Ladakh and Zanskar became sanctuaries for Tibetan Buddhists, who built temples and chortens on their mountainsides.

The 11th- and 12th-century Muslim invasions that devastated Buddhism in north-western India and turned Kashmir into a Muslim state did not reach the remote eastern mountain kingdoms. Tibet became, and has remained, the traditional centre of Tantric Buddhism.

BUDDHISM IN THE HIMALAYAS TODAY

Tibetan Buddhists put up strong resistance to the suppression of their religion after the Chinese invasion of Tibet in 1950–1. Severe suppression followed their 1959 uprising against the Chinese, and thousands of Tibetans fled to surrounding countries. Since the 1980s, Tibet has had somewhat greater religious freedom.

Tibetan Buddhism is the state religion of the Kingdom of Bhutan. Since the 1950s, thousands of refugees from Tibet have swelled the numbers of Buddhists living there and in neighbouring Sikkim, which has been an Indian state since 1975. Hinduism is the religion of 60 per cent of the population of Sikkim, while 28 per cent are Buddhists.

Nepal is officially a Hindu state, with about 80 per cent Hindus, 10 per cent Buddhists and 4 per cent Muslims. Many ethnic minorities, such as the Sherpas and about 15 per cent of the Newars, the original inhabitants of the Kathmandu Valley, practise Buddhism. In modern Nepal, however, Hindu and Buddhist beliefs and practices often merge.

Pockets of Tibetan Buddhism survive among the mountain tribes of Himachal Pradesh. The people of the spectacularly beautiful Kinnaur, Lahaul and Spiti valleys are mostly Buddhist. There are ancient wall paintings in the Tabo *gompa* in Spiti and the Kardang *gompa* in Lahaul, and statues of Padmasambhava in the

Above A Tibetan monk of the Black Hat sect (Kagyu) commemorates the assassination in 842 of Langdarma, a Tibetan king who persecuted Buddhists, by performing the Black Hat Dance.

Guru Ghantal in Lahaul, all founded in the 10th–12th centuries. Medieval Buddhist monasteries survive in the tiny Buddhist kingdom of Mustang on Nepal's north-eastern border.

Above Prayer wheels containing printed mantras or fragments of sutras are everywhere in the Himalayas. Turning one is an offering made not to the Buddha, but to turn negativity into a positive attitude and action.

BUDDHISM IN KASHMIR AND LADAKH

ALTHOUGH BESET BY BORDER DISPUTES AND CONFLICT, BUDDHISM FLOURISHES IN THE WESTERN PROVINCES OF JAMMU AND KASHMIR, AS IT HAS FOR 2,300 YEARS. LADAKH, A FORMER BUDDHIST KINGDOM, PRESERVES ITS CENTURIES-OLD TRADITIONS OF TIBETAN BUDDHISM.

Above Buddhism in Ladakh is alive, despite the region's political pressures. This is the message conveyed by the Shanti stupa founded outside Leh in 1985 by the Nipponzan Myohoji Japanese Buddhist organization, promoters of world peace.

Srinagar, the summer capital of Jammu and Kashmir, lies just north of Pandrethan, the city founded in the Kashmir Valley by the Buddhist emperor Ashoka. Stupas and a vihara excavated there indicate that Pandrethan was an important 3rd-century BCE Buddhist centre. At Harwan, near Srinagar's Shalimar Gardens, archaeologists have excavated the site of the Sadarhadvana vihara, a centre of Buddhist learning, where Nagarjuna, the influential Indian philosopher who founded the Madhyamaka school, is believed to have resided for a time during the 2nd century CE.

Below 'The Word of the Buddha', sacred Tibetan Buddhist scriptures and commentaries translated from Sanskrit after the 8th century CE, are housed at the Karsha monastery in the Zanskar Valley, Ladakh.

THE FOURTH BUDDHIST COUNCIL

The rise of the Mahayana tradition took place during the 2nd century, when there is evidence that Kanishka I, the 5th Kushan emperor, may have convened the Fourth Buddhist Council in Kashmir. Mahayana texts relate that 500 bhikkhus gathered there to examine the Sarvastivada school's version of the *Abhidharma* scriptures, which discuss existential phenomena and psychology. Afterward, they summarized their conclusions in a commentary, the *Mahavibhasa*.

The philosophy of the Sarvastivada school may be summarized as the belief that dharmas, the smallest, indivisible components of the universe, exist in three time spheres: the past, present and future. The school is closely associated with Kashmir, where, under Kanishka's policy of religious toleration, Sarvastivadins were free to develop and disseminate their ideas.

SCHOLARSHIP

Kashmir's reputation as a centre of Buddhist learning persisted for a millennium, reviving even after the destruction of Buddhist monasteries *c.*440 by the White Huns.

During the 4th century, Vasubandhu, founder of the Yogacara school, wrote a critical commentary on the Sarvastivadin *Abhidharma* in Kashmir. The scholars Dharmottara and Vinitadeva established the school of logic founded by Dignaga, a disciple of Vasubandhu, in Kashmir during the 8th century, and Kashmiri bhikkhus helped transmit this school of Buddhist logic to Tibet. Ratnavajra, a

Right At the Hemis festival, monks of the Kagyu school celebrate the birthday of Padmasambhava, who brought Tantric Buddhism to Tibet, with ritual masked 'cham dances. The festival is held in July at the Hemis gompa, Ladakh's largest monastery.

Kashmiri, became the first Central Pillar of Vikramasila University and later translated Mantrayana texts in Tibet.

From the 12th century, as Muslim armies attacked northern India, Kashmiri scholars fled into Tibet, and Buddhism in Kashmir fell into decline.

LADAKH

Mountainous and remote, Ladakh has preserved the Buddhist beliefs first brought there 23 centuries ago by the emperor Ashoka's missions – the Mon hill peoples have been Theravada Buddhists since time immemorial.

During the 10th century, political turmoil in Tibet sent monks fleeing eastward into Ladakh, where they established Tibetan Buddhism. Today, Ladakh is again a sanctuary for Tibetan monks, this time seeking refuge from Chinese religious suppression. Mountaintop monasteries in Ladakh have preserved not only priceless paintings, sculptures and Tibetan texts but also the ancient traditions and rituals of Tibetan Buddhism.

JAMMU AND KASHMIR

Kashmir and Ladakh are part of the northern Indian state of Jammu and Kashmir, territory that has been disputed by India

Right This wall painting is one of the treasures of the isolated Rangdum gompa of the Geluk sect, in the remote Suru Valley. It depicts Buddhist warriors of the Shambhala mystical kingdom.

and Pakistan since 1947. The population of the Kashmir Valley is 95 per cent Muslim and 4 per cent Hindu, while Jammu, in the state's south-eastern corner, records more than 66 per cent Hindus and 30 per cent Muslims.

Buddhists account for 46 per cent of Ladakh's population. Most inhabit the district surrounding the capital, Leh, while the 47 per cent of mainly Shi'a Muslims live mainly in the western Kargil district.

However, there is also a large Sunni minority in Leh district, and Buddhist communities in Kargil.

For centuries in Ladakh, native Buddhists and Muslim migrants from India and Kashmir have co-existed peacefully and even intermarried. However, recently, militant Buddhist groups demanding separate constitutional status in Muslim-dominated Jammu and Kashmir have clashed violently with Muslims in Leh and Kargil.

BUDDHISM IN TIBET

BUDDHISM BECAME TIBET'S OFFICIAL RELIGION IN THE 8TH CENTURY,
WHEN THE SCHOLAR-MONK SHANTARAKSHITA GUIDED THE FOUNDING
OF THE FIRST TIBETAN MONASTERY NEAR LHASA. TODAY, BUDDHISM
IS REVIVING IN TIBET, DESPITE SUPPRESSION BY THE RULING CHINESE.

Shantarakshita, who came from Nalanda University in India, taught the philosophical strand of the Mahayana – the Yogacara and Madhyamaka – to the first Tibetan monks at Samye. They adopted the vinaya, or monastic rules, of the Mulasarvastivada school, an off-shoot of the orthodox Vaibhasika. The rigorous Mulasarvastivadin vinaya listed 253 precepts, including 112 personal faults, and all Tibetan monks embraced it as the basic monastic code, though with varying degrees of strictness – for instance, some orders required monks to be celibate, others did not. This consensus around the rules meant that the divisions into

Below The Jowo Rinpoche in Lhasa's ancient Jokhang temple represents the Buddha Shakyamuni, aged 12. It was a gift of Chinese Princess Wenchen, who married Songtsen Gampo, the first king of the Tibetan empire, in 641CE.

separate schools (*nikaya*) that split the early Sangha in India never took hold in Tibet, and the Tibetan schools were able to retain their distinctive characters.

BUDDHIST DIFFUSIONS

Padmasambhava, the legendary Indian Buddhist mystic, is reputed to have travelled throughout Tibet during the 8th century, working wonders and initiating Tibetans in tantric rituals. There is, however, little concrete evidence of his actions.

In this first period of diffusion, the monarchy began to regulate the development of Buddhism. From the mid-9th century, Tibet underwent political fragmentation. When stability returned after 1000CE, widespread support for Buddhism inspired what is often called the 'second diffusion' of the teachings. During the second diffusion, characteristic Tibetan schools emerged. The first was the

Above A late 14th-century bronze statue of Tsongkhapa, who founded the Ganden university monastery of the Geluk order near Lhasa. Geluk monks are known for their celibacy, discipline and scholarship.

Kadam, established by Dromdon, a Tibetan disciple of the highly revered Indian teacher Atisha (982–1054). Its teaching, which set the pattern for many later developments in Tibetan Buddhism, combined the philosophical perspective of the Mahayana with the meditational ritualism of tantra.

After travels in India, collecting texts and initiations and compiling them into several traditions, the Tibetan monk Drokmi established a monastery at Sakya, which became the headquarters of the Sakya school.

One of Drokmi's students, Marpa Lotsawa (1012–96), followed his teacher's example and went to India to acquire tantric initiations. Marpa's most famous disciple, Milarepa (*c.*1040–*c.*1123) taught tantric *mahamudra* rituals. *Mahamudra* is meditation on one's own mind to achieve enlightenment. It utilizes calming and insight techniques to bring about

the experience of emptiness. This experience of emptiness is invoked repeatedly to attain enlightenment.

Milarepa's disciple Gampopa (1079–1153) combined *mahamudra* with the Kadam discipline to found another new Tibetan Buddhist order, the Kagyu.

The last major Tibetan order to be created was the Geluk, which traces its origins to the 14th-century scholar Tsongkhapa. He arranged the various Buddhist teachings and schools into a hierarchy. He also developed a scheme of study for monks that took them through a progressive examination of Mahayana texts and, in a masterly synthesis, a graded progression of tantric practices. The Geluk order, founded on this novel scheme, became the dominant political force in Tibet under the 5th Dalai Lama in the 17th century.

LINEAGE TRADITIONS

The transmission of teachings through master–pupil lineages was often conducted within monastery-based orders, but monks from one monastery could study at another, and, like Marpa, individuals sometimes acquired initiations in India that allowed them to establish new lineages in Tibet. The lineage traditions thus acted as types of schools.

Many Buddhists, particularly lay followers, claimed to hold initiations and texts deriving from the first period of dissemination. They called themselves Nyingma ('The Old School') and traced their origins back to Padmasambhava.

Right The Potala Palace, Lhasa, was home to Tibet's head of state, the Dalai Lama, until 1959. Its construction was initiated by the 5th Dalai Lama (1617–82), who fought a civil war to unite Tibet under the Geluk school.

THE TIBET–MONGOLIA LINK

Tibet and Mongolia have strong historical links. The Tibetan empire reached as far as Mongolia in the 9th century under King Ralpacan, but Tibetan Buddhism took root in Mongolia from the 13th century, when the Great Khans incorporated Tibet into the Mongol empire. In 1244, Godan, grandson of Genghis Khan, encountered Kunga Gyeltsen, head of the Sakya school of Tibetan Buddhism, and appointed him spiritual adviser, thus establishing a 'priest-patron' relationship: the Khans allowed Tibet protection from military invasion in return for religious sanction from the lamas. In 1253, Kublai Khan made Buddhism his court religion and made Drogon Chogyal Phagpa, a nephew of Kunga Gyeltsen, ruler of three provinces of Tibet. After the overthrow of the Mongol (Yuan) dynasty in China in 1368, Altan Khan, a descendant of Kublai Khan, gained power in Mongolia and initiated a Buddhist revival by persuading Sonam Gyatso, subsequently the 3rd Dalai Lama, to attend his court.

The Communist regime that ruled Mongolia from 1921 dismantled much of the Buddhist establishment. After a peaceful democratic revolution in 1990, however, Mongolia has seen a resurgence of Buddhism.

Right The Erdene Zuu monastery was built in 1586. It marks the adoption of Buddhism as Mongolia's state religion under Altan Khan, a descendant of Kublai Khan.

Monks and nuns from different orders could thus place themselves within a number of different lineages, each authenticated with a recognized line of master–pupil transmissions. The schools of Tibetan Buddhism were therefore much less self-contained than their Indian counterparts.

BUDDHISM IN THE EASTERN HIMALAYAS

BUDDHISM REACHED THE SCATTERED HILL TRIBES OF THE EASTERN HIMALAYAS DURING THE 7TH CENTURY. TODAY, BUDDHISM IS STILL THE OFFICIAL RELIGION OF BHUTAN AND HAS A STRONG FOLLOWING AMONG THE HILL PEOPLES OF ARUNACHAL PRADESH AND SIKKIM.

According to tradition, the 8th-century tantric master Padmasambhava – Guru Rinpoche, revered by Tibetan Buddhists as a second Buddha – introduced Buddhism to the regions that are now Bhutan and Sikkim. Scholars have found little evidence for many of the activities attributed to him, however, and the region's oldest religious buildings predate him.

Many of Bhutan's *gompas* (monasteries) and *lakhangs* (temples) date from the mid-7th century. The two oldest of these, Kyichu *gompa* in the Paro Valley and Kurjey lakhang in Bumthang, were established by Songtsen Gampo, who reigned in Tibet from 618, during a period of Tibetan imperial expansion. By the 10th century, many local hill tribes practised Buddhism alongside their traditional animism.

BHUTAN
In 1616, Shabdrung Ngawang Namgyal, a former abbot of the Drukpa lineage of the Kagyu order of Tibetan Buddhism, fled from the ruling Geluk sect, then dominant in Tibet. He went to Druk Yul ('land of the thunder dragon') – or Bhutan – where he united clan leaders under his rule.

For defence against successive retaliatory armies sent by the Tibetans and, after 1630, by the Mongols, who had seized power in Tibet, he extended the network of *dzongs*, or fortified monasteries,

begun earlier by another powerful lama. At the head of the Thimphu Valley, for example, he built the Simtokha *dzong*, from where he could control the passage along two valleys. He adopted the title *shabdrung* (literally, 'at whose feet one submits') and established an independent theocratic government and legal system, with himself as head of state, an elected abbot, the Je Khenpo, as monastic head, and an elected civil governor, the Druk Sesi. His death in 1651 was kept secret for 54 years to forestall political uprisings and his remains still rest in a secret chamber in Punakha *dzong*.

Bhutan, now a monarchy in transition to a constitutional system, still supports Buddhist institutions, and about 75 per cent

Above Kyichu gompa *is one of Bhutan's oldest temples. It was built in the 7th century by Songtsen Gampo, the first king of the Tibetan empire, who was believed to be the first of Tibet's three Dharma Kings – literally 'rulers of the Dharma'.*

Below Elaborately dressed and masked monks and lay followers perform a ritual dance accompanied by cymbals, horns and tambourines, at a tsechu held in April in Bhutan's Paro Valley.*

of the population is Buddhist. Isolated for centuries, Bhutan has only recently allowed limited, controlled tourism to its *gompas*, *lakhangs*, *dzongs* and *tsechus*. The latter are religious festivals, held annually over three to five days to extol the Guru Rinpoche. Monks, masked and dressed in colourful costumes, re-enact legendary events. On the last day, *thangkas* (paintings) may be displayed. The sight of one is believed to deliver the viewer from samsara.

SIKKIM

Colourful festivals are also part of the culture of neighbouring Sikkim. The first *chogyal*, or temporal and religious ruler of Sikkim, Phuntsog Namgyal, was a Tibetan, who, according to tradition, was consecrated in 1642 by three virtuous lamas. Sikkim remained a Buddhist monarchy until 1975, when it became India's northernmost state.

Below The Taktshang ('Tiger's Lair') gompa in Bhutan was built in 1692 on a sacred site, a cave where the 8th-century tantric master Padmasambhava is said to have meditated.

EASTERN HILL TRIBES

The 17th-century inhabitants of Sikkim were the Lepchas, a people whose folklore is founded on harmony with the Himalayan landscape. The Lepchas also inhabit parts of Bhutan, Nepal and West Bengal. Most practise Tibetan Buddhism alongside their traditional shamanism, but many have converted to Christianity.

The Bhutia migrated from Tibet into Bhutan and Sikkim from the 14th century. They now make up half the population of Bhutan and inhabit the northern regions of Nepal and West Bengal. Most follow the Nyingma or Kagyu Tibetan Buddhist traditions, although many have become Hindus. Bhutias once practised polyandry and today the women have considerable independence and equality.

Among other Buddhist hill tribes are the Sherpas of Nepal, who may be descended from intermarriage between Lepchas and Bhutias. Sixty-three per cent of the people of Arunachal Pradesh belong to 105 tribal groups, of which 40 per cent are Buddhists. Most practise Tibetan Buddhism, but groups close to the Burmese border practise the Theravada.

Migrations of Hindus from Nepal, Christian missionarizing, and the withdrawal of state support for Buddhism have reduced Buddhists to about 28 per cent of the population of Sikkim today.

Some 200 monasteries of the Nyingma and Kagyu Buddhist sects remain in Sikkim. Of these, the Sangha Choeling, which was built in the 17th century, perched 2,000m (6,562ft) above a valley, is one of the oldest. The Pemayangtse, which is Sikkim's leading Nyingma monastery, overlooks Mount Kangchenjunga and contains treasured wall paintings, sculptures and *thangkas*.

Below The Rumtek gompa, Sikkim's largest monastery, is the seat of the Karma Kagyu (Black Hat) Tibetan Buddhist tradition. It became a refuge for the tradition's spiritual head, the 16th Karmapa, after the Chinese invasion of Tibet in 1959.

PRAYER FLAGS, WHEELS AND WALLS

STREAMING IN THE WIND ON THE MOUNTAIN PEAKS AND ROOFTOPS OF TIBET, BRIGHTLY COLOURED FLAGS CARRY PRAYERS AND MANTRAS HEAVENWARD, WHILE EACH TURN OF A PRAYER WHEEL COUNTS AS A PRAYER SAID AND MERIT GAINED.

Until the late 8th century, when Buddhism became established in Tibet, most Tibetans followed the Bon religion, a shamanistic tradition that, it is thought, used primary-coloured plain flags in healing ceremonies. As Buddhism blended with Bon, sacred mantras were painted on to the flags, thus creating what are known today as Tibetan prayer flags. When the great Indian monk-scholar Atisha arrived in India in 1042, he taught his disciples how to print sacred texts and mantras on to the flags.

PRAYER FLAGS

There are two kinds of prayer flags: horizontal ones, called *lung ta* (Tibetan for 'wind horse'), and vertical *darcho* (*dar* means 'to increase life, fortune, health and wealth'; *cho* means 'all sentient beings'). The horizontal flags are either square or rectangular in shape and are usually attached to a cord, which is then suspended between a high place, such as the top of a stupa or mountain, and a lower one. Vertical prayer flags are generally planted in the ground, in cairns, or on rooftops.

Traditionally, the flags come in sets of five colours: red, blue, green, white and yellow. The colours represent the Five Buddha Families and the five elements, and are arranged from left to right in a specific order. Skilled craftsmen, mainly monks or lamas, carve the woodblocks, from which texts and images are printed on to the flags.

The central image is usually the *lung ta*, or wind horse, a symbol of speed and the transformation of bad fortune into good fortune. On its back are the three flaming jewels, which symbolize the Buddha, the Dharma and the Sangha. Surrounding the central image are a variety of sacred mantras. The names or images of the four supernatural animals – the dragon, the garuda (a wise eagle-like bird), the tiger and the snow lion – often adorn the four corners of the flag.

Exposed to the elements, the flag's images and mantras fade in time, becoming a permanent part of the universe. Tibetans symbolically renew their hopes for the world by replacing the old flags with new ones. This act signifies a welcoming of life's changes and an acknowledgment that all beings are part of a greater cycle.

Above Tethered by strong cords, hundreds of brilliantly coloured prayer flags, each one inscribed with images and mantras, flutter and dance in the strong winds that blow ceaselessly across the Tibetan plateau.

Left These Tibetan women, seated together in a courtyard of the Jokhang temple, Lhasa, rotate their prayer wheels clockwise while reciting the mantras. The whirr of the turning wheels and the softly repeated mantras are familiar sounds in Tibet.

Right Not all prayer wheels are hand held. Many monasteries have large cylindrical drums set side by side in a row. Here, pilgrims at Tibet's Sakya monastery turn the wheels simply by sliding their hands along the surface.

Tibetans believe that the word, spoken or written, forms one of the Three Supports (the three elements that comprise the quintessence of every being) and is therefore sacred. Merely to read or write prayers, or extracts from the scriptures, are acts of spiritual advancement. Flags are hung in high places so that the wind will carry the blessings and mantras to people throughout the world and thus will bring benefits to those who hang them and to their families and loved ones.

During the Chinese Cultural Revolution, prayer flags were discouraged, though not entirely eliminated, by the Communist government. Today most of the traditional flags are made in Nepal and India by Tibetan refugees or Nepali Buddhists.

PRAYER WHEELS

Turning the prayer wheel is part of the daily life of a Tibetan. The wheels fulfill the same purpose as the flags: to spread compassion and spiritual blessings and to accumulate merit. A hand-held wheel is a hollow wooden, leather or metal cylinder attached to a handle. A chain attached to the wheel helps it to spin. The long roll of paper inside the wheel has the invocation to Avalokiteshvara – *Om mani padme hum* – printed

on it many times. Tibetans believe that every rotation of the wheel equals one utterance of the mantra. The wheel must be turned clockwise, as that is the direction in which the mantras are written. Before and after turning the wheel, the mantra is repeated.

Some wheels are large drums turned by hand, some are turned by flowing water, some by the heat of a candle, others simply by the wind. Today, there are even prayer wheels powered by electric motors. Not only do they contain a thousand copies of the mantra of

Avalokiteshvara, but the turning of the wheel can be accompanied by lights and music.

PRAYER WALLS

Throughout Tibet and Tibetan-inhabited areas, carved stones (called manis) can be found piled on to walls or cairns on mountain passes, outside temples, or at a busy crossroads. For Tibetans, every stone on the plateau has a soul and, when carved with Buddhist scriptures or the eyes of the Buddha, becomes a divine object, bestowed with supernatural power.

Right Elements of ancient folk religion, including the worship of stones, merged with Buddhism in all of the Himalayan kingdoms. A mantra – a sacred sound or syllable – is engraved on the mani stones that make up this prayer wall in Ladakh.

BUDDHISM IN CENTRAL ASIA

THROUGH THE KHYBER PASS HIGH IN THE HINDU KUSH, BUDDHISM SPREAD FROM THE MAURYAN EMPIRE TO THE GRAECO-BACTRIAN KINGDOM, FROM PRESENT-DAY PAKISTAN INTO AFGHANISTAN, AND EASTWARD, ACROSS THE VASTNESS OF CENTRAL ASIA INTO CHINA.

Above Buddhist monks may have excavated these spartan cells for solitary retreats in natural caves near Haibak (ancient Samangan), north-west of Kabul in Afghanistan. Nearby is the large stupa known locally as Rustam's Throne (Takht-i-Rustam).

From the 3rd century BCE, monks crossed the Khyber Pass and spread across what is now Afghanistan. The remains of stupas and viharas around the Muslim city of Jalalabad mark the sites of Nagarahara, a centre of the Sarvastivada sect during the 1st century BCE, and Hadda, where a treasure trove of Gandharan sculpture and the oldest known Buddhist manuscripts, dating from the 1st–2nd century CE, were

Below The Silk Route from Balkh, Samarkand, Aksu and Khotan passed through the Kashgar oasis at the foot of the Tian mountains. In Kashi, its modern descendant on China's western frontier, a textile market recalls its ancient days of glory.

found. On his pilgrimage in the 7th century, the Chinese monk Xuanzang noted 100 viharas with 6,000 Mahayana monks at Kapisa (modern Bagram), 3,000 Lokottaravada monks at Bamiyan, and at Balkh (on the border with Uzbekistan), 3,000 Theravada monks teaching and practising alongside Zoroastrians.

ROUTES WEST

The Kushans, horse-riding archers from what is now Tajikistan, forged an empire during the 2nd century BCE, north to the borders of Sogdiana, west as far as Iran and eastward across the Khyber Pass to Varanasi. The Kushans traded as far west as Egypt, as is evidenced

by Roman statuettes and glassware found at Bagram and Kapisa, and they protected their trade routes, enabling Mahayana and Sarvastivadin monks to follow the caravans north-west to Merv (Mary, Turkmenistan) and into territories of the former Persian empire.

SERINDIA

In the 1920s, the archaeologist Marc Aurel Stein named eastern Central Asia around the Tarim Basin 'Serindia' (from the Greek *sere*, meaning 'silkworm'). The Silk Route traversed this vast region of deserts and mountains, which, during the first millennium CE, was a complex of kingdoms and tribal territories peopled by diverse ethnic groups. An Shigao, a nobleman from Parthia, an empire that arose in ancient Iran, may have been one of the first Buddhist monks to cross Central Asia into China around 150CE. An Shigao travelled the Silk Route to Luoyang, China's capital dating from the Later Han dynasty (25–220CE), where he led the translation of Buddhist texts into Chinese.

EXCAVATING THE SILK ROUTE

A Hungarian-born British archaeologist, Marc Aurel Stein (1862–1943), developed a childhood fascination for the travels of the Buddhist monk Xuanzang along the Silk Route. In 1900, he became one of the first archaeologists to excavate in the oasis towns of the Taklamakan Desert, and found Buddhist texts, paintings and sculptures. On a second expedition in 1907, he explored the spectacular Mogao caves at Dunhuang, in modern Gansu Province, China, and discovered thousands of Buddhist paintings and manuscripts, including the *Diamond Sutra*, the world's oldest printed text. He also made important discoveries at Loulan and Turfan.

Stein's lifetime ambition was to excavate for Graeco-Buddhist remains in the ancient city of Balkh, Afghanistan, but, though he received official permission, he died, aged 80, when he reached Kabul. Despite his rediscovery of the Silk Route, Stein is a controversial figure, because he removed many treasures from Asia and presented them to museums in Britain and India.

Left This colourful Tang dynasty seated monk was part of a terracotta frieze in the Mogao caves at Dunhuang, the Silk Route gateway into China, which is now in China's western Gansu province.

The Kizil caves, near Kucha on the Taklamakan Desert's northern rim, are resplendent with the wall paintings of Buddhist monks. They arrived at the oasis before the end of the 1st century CE and established a major centre of the Shravakayana, which was an off-shoot of the Theravada school.

Kumarajiva, a monk from a noble Kuchean family, travelled to China's capital, Chang'an (modern Xian), in 401, and there translated Sanskrit texts into Chinese. A Sarvastivadin at first, he became a Mahayana adherent.

Another early Theravada site was Miran, once a booming oasis town on the edge of the Lop Nur Desert. In 1907, Marc Aurel Stein found many treasures of Gandharan art and a cache of early Tibetan manuscripts there.

The wall paintings of the Bezeklik caves, near Turfan, exemplify mature Mahayana art. The Vajrayana tradition may have first appeared in Central Asia in Khotan (modern Hotan), a city-state in the Kushana empire on the Taklamakan's southern edge.

It was a thriving trading centre, the first place outside China where silk was cultivated, and also a major centre of Mahayana Buddhism.

MUSLIM INVASIONS

Arab armies advanced east during the 7th century, invading Bactria and Gandhara. Some of the thousands of Buddhist monasteries in Central Asia survived until the 15th century, but by then most had been abandoned or razed and Islam had replaced Buddhism as the dominant religion of Central Asia.

Below These earthen stupas overlook the modern Karakoram Highway, once part of the Silk Route between China and north-western India.

SILK ROUTE PILGRIMS

THE SILK ROUTE WAS THE PATH ALONG WHICH BUDDHISM SPREAD NORTH, WEST AND EAST FROM INDIA. FROM THE 3RD CENTURY BCE, CHINESE PILGRIMS TRAVELLED TO INDIA IN SEARCH OF NEW IDEAS, SACRED RELICS, ARTEFACTS AND BOOKS OF THE BUDDHIST CANON.

By the 5th century BCE, northern India, where the Buddha had lived, preached and died, had become a holy land to Buddhists of East and South-east Asia. Buddhism reached China as early as the 1st century CE, but centuries of political conflict and fragmentation prevented Buddhist ideas from spreading through the empire. Early Chinese Buddhists possessed only a fragment of the Buddhist canon, and of that, much was poorly copied and translated. From the 3rd century, pilgrims made the dangerous journey across Central Asia to India in search of sacred texts.

The first of these pilgrims to leave an account of his travels was Faxian (Fa-hsien; *c.*337–*c.*422CE), a 65-year-old monk who set out in 399CE from China's ancient capital, Chang'an (modern Xian) for north-eastern India.

FAXIAN'S JOURNEY

In his *A Record of Buddhistic Kingdoms*, Faxian recounted, on silk, his journey – mainly on foot, sometimes by camel train – across Central Asia along the Silk Route. He describes his camel trek from Dunhuang at the end of China's Great Wall, across the Taklamakan Desert to the oasis of Lop Nor, and every monastery he visited, noting the numbers of monks, their history and religious practices.

In northern India, Faxian visited Kapilavastu and the temple at Bodhgaya, and recounts with emotion his visits to the Jetavana vihara, where the Buddha gave

Above This map at Taiwan's Wenwu temple shows the route of the pilgrim Xuanzang on his epic journey from China to India in the 7th century.

many lectures. He recorded the legends of the Buddha's life and every Buddhist relic he saw.

Faxian returned in 413 by ship to Nanjing via Sri Lanka and Java. He had visited almost 30 kingdoms and collected many sacred texts, including the full *Vinaya* (rules for monastics).

TRAVELS OF XUANZANG

Monkey, the English version of the 16th-century Chinese novel *Journey to the West* by Wu Cheng'en, is the story of Tripitaka, aka Xuanzang (Hsuan-tsang; 600–664CE), the most famous of all the Chinese pilgrims who travelled to India. In 629CE, the monk left Chang'an for India in search of Buddhist texts and teachings. He embarked on a spiritual odyssey to find truth among the Indian Buddhist schools and sects.

Left Sand dunes threaten to engulf Dunhuang, once a garrison trading town at the point where the Silk Route from Chang'an forked to follow the northern and southern edges of the Taklamakan Desert.

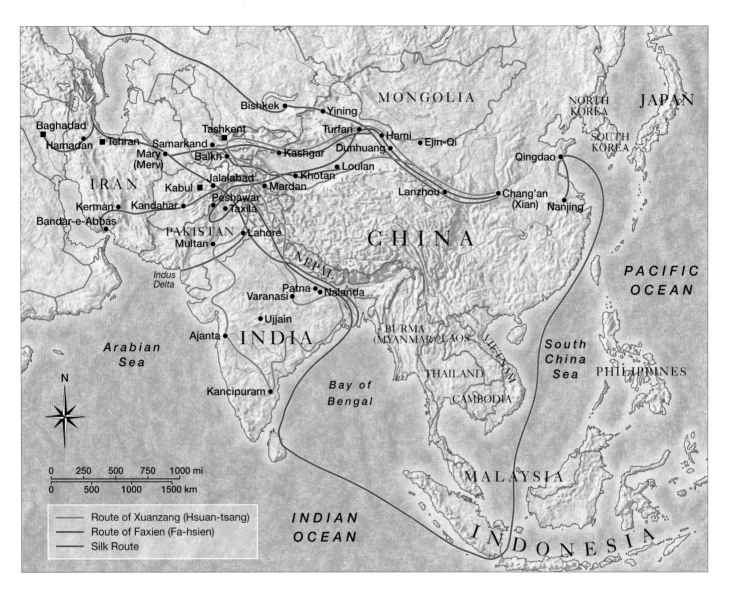

PILGRIMS ON THE SILK ROUTE

The map shows the routes followed by Chinese Buddhist pilgrims Faxian, in the 5th century, and Xuanzang, in the 7th century, in search of Buddhist scriptures.

Above Tajik farmers and traders, descendants of the Parthians, Sogdians and Bactrians, still tread the Silk Route on their Bactrian camels, although the glory days of the trading caravans faded long ago.

Xuanzang described the fabled Samarkand and the high frontiers of India's north-west. Travelling from monastery to monastery, he reached Taxila, ancient India's greatest centre of learning, where the Buddhist scriptures were debated alongside the Vedas and the tenets of Jainism. Xuanzang followed the Mahayana tradition of Buddhism, the 'great vehicle', which was said to have originated at Taxila.

Xuanzang's journey took him to the Hindu holy sites such as Mathura – Krishna's birthplace, also famed for images of the Buddha – Ujjain and Varanasi.

Xuanzang also visited the cave viharas of Ajanta so that he could see the masterpieces of Buddhist painting and sculpture.

For years he studied, taught and debated at the great Buddhist university of Nalanda, from which he visited the holy pilgrimage places of the north-east.

In 645CE, after 16 years of pilgrimage, Xuanzang returned to China with a cache of Buddhist texts and commentaries that were unknown there. He retired to the Da Cien temple, Chang'an, where he spent his remaining years making copies and translations.

SYMBOLIC OBJECTS

AN EMPTY THRONE SYMBOLIZES THE BUDDHA IN ANCIENT BUDDHIST ART, AND A LION SCULPTURE ON THE ASHOKA PILLAR AT SARNATH PROCLAIMS THE POWER OF HIS TEACHINGS. THE SYMBOLS OF BUDDHISM CARRY THE SAME WORDLESS MESSAGES TO PEOPLES OF ALL CULTURES.

Above Following the Buddha's example, Theravada monks wear plain saffron robes draped over the body. They symbolize detachment from the world of material things.

The Buddha taught his disciples, by his own example, to live the simplest of lives, owning minimal possessions. The most basic of robes with a cloth belt, a needle and thread, a begging bowl for the daily meal, and a water filter so that tiny creatures would not be swallowed in their drinking water, were all the objects a monk was permitted to own.

SYMBOLS OF POVERTY
In time, as Buddhism developed and adapted to the religious practices of diverse new cultures, these basic objects acquired symbolic meanings. On leaving home, the Buddha is said to have exchanged his princely dress for a beggar's rags. His disciples adopted the same dress to indicate that they too had given up riches and comfort for poverty. They wore robes they had sewn together from rags and stained with earth or dyed with cheap colourants. These are traditionally yellow, a colour that can be produced cheaply from turmeric, an abundant plant in India. Tibetan monks wear red robes, perhaps dyed with inexpensive logwood. Korean monks stain their robes grey with charcoal as a reminder that the body will eventually become ash. Monks cut up fabric donated by lay followers and wear robes made of pieces sewn together to accord with tradition.

Similarly, begging bowls became symbolic of the Buddha soon after his death. He is often depicted in ancient wall paintings throwing a golden bowl, in which he had been offered food, into a river rather than keeping gold as a possession.

Below A vajra (a ritual implement) may have one, three or five prongs at both ends. Made of metal and ornately decorated, the vajra is invested with many layers of symbolism.

SYMBOLS OF THE BUDDHA
The devices adopted in early Buddhist art to represent the Buddha – footprints, parasols, trees – continued to be used as Buddhist symbols, even after artists began to depict figures of the Buddha and bodhisattvas. Footprints are commonly used as symbols of the presence of the Buddha, who is said to have left his print in many places as he travelled around India teaching the Dharma. Some of the Eight Auspicious Symbols usually cover the footprint. There is often a *Dharmachakra*, or Wheel of the Law, indicative of

Buddhist teachings; a parasol, which symbolizes the dome of the sky and casts the shadow of protection from the harmful effects of craving, lust and other vices; and two golden fish, which denote the salvation that results from freedom from attachment.

THE JEWEL IN THE LOTUS
The lotus grows up from the slimy mud on the lake bottom to bud on the underwater stem and burst into fragrant bloom on the surface. In Buddhism, the lotus represents the ability of the mind to transcend human desires through the Buddha's teachings to attain enlightenment. On the great pillar erected at

Left Vessels such as this 12th–13th-century Korean ritual water vase are used in Buddhist ceremonies of all traditions to sprinkle cleansing water over images of deities, officiating monks and lay followers. The water symbolically washes away obstacles to enlightenment.

Sarnath by the emperor Ashoka, the lion, signifying the power of the Buddha's teachings, is seated on a lotus. In later, figurative art, the Buddha is often depicted walking on lotuses, and deities are portrayed seated on a flowering lotus.

Avalokiteshvara, the compassionate bodhisattva, is shown holding a lotus. The White Tara, a female form of Avalokiteshvara, who symbolizes purity of the mind and transcendant knowledge, holds an eight-petalled white lotus in her left hand, a reminder of the Noble Eightfold Path. Padmapani, a male manifestation of Avalokiteshvara,

Above This porcelain Buddha is seated in meditation on a cushion of lotus leaves, which, like lotus flowers, grow from mud but remain unstained. In fact, lotus leaves are now known to have a marvellous self-cleaning property not found in any other plant.

holds a blue lotus, a symbol of the perfection of wisdom and knowledge.

Akashagarbha, a guardian of the Buddha Vairocana, is often depicted holding a lotus in one hand and a jewel in the other. The jewel represents enlightenment, the ability of the Buddha to see and understand all things. A jewel, the diamond, the principal symbol of Vajrayana Buddhism, cuts through ignorance, but is not itself destroyed. *Vajra* is a Sanskrit word that also means 'thunderbolt', and in Tibetan Buddhism the *vajra*, or *dorje*, is an object used extensively in ritual. It denotes the indestructible and indivisible nature of enlightenment. In Tibetan Buddhist ceremonies, a lama may hold a *vajra* in the right hand, and a bell in the left. A *vajra* bell is a ritual object with a bell at one end and a *vajra* at the other. The sound of a bell recalls the aim of attaining enlightenment.

STUPA SYMBOLISM

The stupa was one of the earliest ritual objects of Buddhism and it is imbued with symbolism. The square base on which the stupa rests represents the Earth. Its dome shape may originally have represented Mount Meru, the cosmic mountain, which, like the pole that passes through the structure of a pagoda (as a stupa is called in China and Japan), from the relics buried beneath it to the stylized *chattra*, or parasol, above it, forms the axis of the Buddhist universe and links heaven and Earth. Its spire is tipped with a diamond or other jewel. Small stupas of wood or bronze are made to be carried in Buddhist countries as objects of devotion.

Below Monks and the laity use malas, or prayer beads, to count the number of mantras or prayers they recite. Malas, used in the esoteric schools of Japan and Tibet, usually have 108 beads. Each bead represents a human passion that impedes enlightenment.

BUDDHISM IN EAST ASIA

BUDDHISM ENTERED THE EAST THROUGH THE SILK ROUTE, VIA MISSIONARIES AND TRADERS OF BUDDHIST OBJECTS AND ARTEFACTS. HAVING TAKEN ROOT IN CHINA, IT SPREAD INTO KOREA, AND FROM BOTH KOREA AND CHINA, FINALLY REACHED JAPAN.

East Asia encompasses China, Japan and Korea. Each country has its own history and its own local cultures, and therefore each has seen a different development of Buddhism. However, just as some cultural features are common to the three countries – for instance the adoption of Chinese characters and the spread of Confucian values – so too, aspects of Buddhism are shared by the three nations. The most important shared aspects are the practice of Mahayana, the adoption of the Chinese Tripitaka and the large number of fully ordained Buddhist nuns. Another important feature of East Asian Buddhism is devotion to the *Lotus Sutra*, which became the main Buddhist scripture in the region.

Below Built in Luoyang in 68BC, commissioned by the Han emperor Ming, the White Horse temple is the oldest Buddhist temple in China. Next to the temple is the Qiyun pagoda, China's oldest pagoda.

MAHAYANA AND THE BODHISATTVA PRECEPTS

The Mahayana tradition is characterized by the emphasis on bodhisattvas. Mahayana laity and monastics follow the bodhisattva path, which is based on the bodhisattva precepts. The *Brahma Net Sutra* is a Mahayana text on ethics that lists 10 major and 48 minor vows that are the guidelines for behaving as a bodhisattva. These vows are taken in a ceremony that involves a symbolic offering of the body of the practitioner. This ceremony, which is peculiar to the East Asian tradition of Buddhism, is still performed regularly in China and Taiwan.

When lay Buddhists take the bodhisattva precepts, three dots of incense are burned on their left forearm, leaving permanent scars. Transmission of the bodhisattva precepts also forms an important part of the full ordination ceremony for Buddhist monks and nuns. This consists of three stages. The first is the transmission

Above Ksitigarbha (Chinese: Dizang; Japanese: Jizo; Korean: Jijang) is the bodhisattva who made the vow to empty the hells. Ksitigarbha is usually associated with the Scripture on the Ten Kings, as seen in this painting on silk from Dunhuang.

of the Ten Precepts, as a result of which they become novices. The second part of the ceremony involves the transmission of the vows for monks and nuns. Finally, the new bhikkhus and bhikkhunis have their tonsured heads burned with three dots of incense, take the vows listed in the *Brahma Net Sutra* and make the commitment to serve as bodhisattvas.

BRIDGING EAST ASIA

Student monks played an important role in the spread and exchange of Buddhist scholarship throughout East Asia. There is historical evidence that student monks travelled from both Japan and Korea to China as early as the beginning of the 7th century CE.

Such exchange was not limited to the pre-modern period: at the beginning of the 20th century, monks and nuns from Taiwan, helped politically by the Japanese occupation, moved to Japan to enrol in Buddhist academies and made the exchange of scholarship possible. Later, after the end of World War II and in the tense post-colonial years, Taiwanese scholar-monks continued moving to Japan to study, thus maintaining a dialogue between the two regions.

Above The 80,000 carved wooden blocks of the Tripitaka Koreana, *which are preserved in Haeinsa, are venerated in a festival every spring. Both monastics and laity participate in this festival, which involves ritual dances and lighting candles and lanterns.*

THE CHINESE BUDDHIST CANON

Today, three collections of canonized text are recognized by Buddhists: the Pali canon, the Tibetan Buddhist canon (the first edition of which is dated to the early 15th century CE) and the Chinese Buddhist canon. The first edition of the Chinese canon, or Tripitaka, (1,076 scriptures in 480 boxes), was completed in 983CE. Several other editions were printed later, during the reign of Buddhist emperors. These sponsoring rulers selected which scriptures were to be included and which texts were to be omitted. Most of the texts that were excluded thus fell into oblivion and disappeared from the history of Buddhism.

The Chinese Tripitaka that is commonly used today is called the *Taisho Tripitaka* (because it was completed in Japan during the Taisho period). It comprises 55 volumes (with a total of 2,184 texts), to which a further 45 volumes of complementary scriptures have been added.

Right The Lotus Sutra *has been considered the bible of East Asian Buddhism. Parables from the scriptures were often painted on material objects, such as this Japanese fan, which dates from the late Fujiwara period (1069–1155).*

OTHER EAST ASIAN BELIEF SYSTEMS

When Buddhism arrived in East Asia, it had to confront a number of other religions and systems of thought, the principal ones of which were:

Confucianism: A Chinese school of thought rooted in the teachings of Kong Fuzi (Confucius) (551–479BCE), Confucianism lists Mencius (372–289BCE), Zhu Xi (1130–1200) and Wang Yangming (1472–1529) as later eminent figures. The philosophy emphasized personal and governmental morality and became popular in all East Asian countries, especially China, Korea and Vietnam.

Shamanism: Centred on the figure of a medium and communication with the spirit world, Shamanism is common to different cultures all over the world. Korean Shamanism is inherent to the local culture and is the most important form existing in East Asia.

Shinto: Usually translated as 'the Way of the Gods', Shinto is the native belief system of Japan, which focuses on the worship of spirits. According to Shinto, everything has a spirit and deserves respect, and the natural elements are especially venerated.

Daoism: A Chinese school of thought that is based on the teachings of Laozi (6th century BCE), and that was later developed by Zhuangzi (370–301BCE). Daoism, which promotes non-action (*wu wei*), retirement from social responsibilities and a return to spontaneity, spread throughout East Asia, where schools still survive.

BUDDHISM IN CHINA

FOR ALMOST TWO MILLENNIA, BUDDHISM HAS PLAYED AN ACTIVE ROLE IN CHINESE CULTURE. PILGRIMAGES TO THE FOUR SACRED MOUNTAINS, VEGETARIANISM AND SCHOLASTIC TRADITION ARE SOME OF THE FACETS THAT CHARACTERIZE BUDDHISM IN CHINA.

China's first encounter with Buddhism dates back to the 1st century CE, during the Han dynasty. The trade along the Silk Route facilitated the arrival of Buddhist missionaries and scriptures as well as material artefacts into China. From the 2nd century CE, teams led by figures such as An Shigao and Lokaksema, and later

Below This Qing dynasty painting shows Kong Fuzi (Confucius) introducing a very young Buddha Shakyamuni to Laozi, founder of Daoism. These figures symbolize the three main religions in China: Confucianism, Daoism and Buddhism.

Dharmaraksa and Kumarajiva, produced the first translations of Buddhist texts into Chinese, thus beginning the spread of Buddhist terminology and literature in the region. The first Buddhist monasteries were established a century later, while the end of the 4th century saw the rise of sectarianism among Chinese Buddhists and the formation of the first Chinese schools, the major of which are Chan, Pure Land and Tiantai.

The Pure Land school emphasized vocal recitation of the name of Amitabha Buddha and visualization of the Western Paradise. It became the tradition of easy practice, the counterpart of the difficult practice based on meditation that Chan was promoting. The Tiantai school focused on the study of the *Lotus Sutra*.

RESHAPING BUDDHISM

Confucian and Daoist China accepted and reshaped 'foreign' Buddhism, which resulted in the forging of a new Chinese religion. In order to abide by essential Confucian (and Chinese) values, Mahayana Buddhism, which entails the participation of monastics in social duties, became the most popular tradition.

Because of the cultural importance of ancestor worship in China, prospective monks first needed to guarantee descendants of the family to maintain the lineage and ensure that the practice of ancestor worship would continue. Only then could they apply to 'leave the house' (*chu jia*, a

Above The transmission of Buddhism into China resulted in the formation of teams of scholars who dedicated their lives to the translation of Sanskrit texts into Chinese. This painting on silk depicts the emperor Xian Di (Han dynasty) and a group of translators.

Chinese expression that means to become a monastic) and become members of the ordained Sangha.

The Chinese showed a preference for the meditative Chan and the recitative Pure Land schools, which have a greater focus on personal spiritual development and meditation, and neglected schools, such as Madhyamaka and Yogacara, neither of which flourished in China.

TRANSFORMING CULTURE

The Chinese domestication of Buddhism occurred in parallel to a Buddhist transformation of Chinese culture. For instance, the establishment of Buddhist-style monasteries and monastic life within Daoism (8th century CE), as well as the adoption of Chan-style meditation by the Chinese philosopher Zhu Xi (1130–1200) in his Neo-Confucianism, are signs of the Buddhist reshaping of Chinese local religious traditions.

Right Mount Emei is devoted to the worship of the Chinese bodhisattva Puxian (Sanskrit: Samantabhadra; Japanese: Fugen; Korean: Pohyun). Samantabhadra is usually represented riding an elephant with six tusks, standing on a lotus flower.

Even the daily life of Chinese people was affected by the spread of Buddhism. For example, the Chinese used to sit on the floor, but the arrival of Buddhist statues depicting the Buddha sitting on a throne inspired the use of chairs in houses, while references to sugar in Buddhist scriptures led to the Chinese adoption of sugar as a sweetener.

IMPERIAL INFLUENCE

The emperors of the various dynasties of China decided the fate of Buddhism, which at times was enshrined as the state religion, but at others underwent harsh persecution (the worst of which took place in 845CE). The favour of rulers toward Buddhism took various forms: in the 6th century CE, for instance, Buddhist monks were appointed to political posts. The empress Wu Zetian (625–705CE) became well known for claiming to be a *chakravartin* (Universal Sovereign) and therefore fostered an unprecedented dissemination of Buddhism. In addition, the many editions of the Chinese Tripitaka depended on imperial sponsorship, which allowed the survival of Buddhist texts, and therefore defined the scriptural identity of Buddhist China.

BODHISATTVAS

Chinese Buddhists are devoted to four main bodhisattvas, each of which is rooted in the original Indian Mahayana tradition of Buddhism, embodies a Buddhist virtue and is sacred to a local mountain. They are Wenshushili (Sanskrit: Mañjushri), who symbolizes Wisdom and whose pilgrimage takes place on Mount Wutai; Dizang (Ksitigarbha), who embodies the Vow and is related to Mount Jiuhua; Samantabhadra (Puxian), who represents Practice and is linked to Mount Emei; and finally Guanyin (Avalokiteshvara), the Bodhisattva of Compassion, whose sacred site is Mount Putuo.

GUANYIN, BODHISATTVA OF COMPASSION

Guanyin is the best case of Chinese domestication of a bodhisattva. Avalokiteshvara is male, but in China, this bodhisattva has become female, as compassion is seen as being primarily a female virtue. Chinese Daoists also venerate Guanyin as an immortal.

Various rituals and legends are related to Guanyin, who has also appeared in different iconographical forms. The most popular are the white-robed Guanyin holding a bottle of water and a twig, and Guanyin with a thousand eyes (to see the suffering of all human beings) and a thousand arms (to bring relief to that suffering).

Right Guanyin (Japanese: Kannon; Korean: Gwan-eum) is the Chinese female transformation of the bodhisattva Avalokiteshvara. This wooden statue of Guanyin dates from the Song dynasty (960–1279).

CHINESE INTERPRETATIONS

AFTER A FEW CENTURIES, BUDDHISM IN CHINA FOUND A NATIONAL IDENTITY, CHARACTERIZED BY CHAN AND PURE LAND PRACTICES, THE ARRIVAL OF TIBETAN BUDDHISM, THE DEVELOPMENT OF BUDDHIST SECRET SOCIETIES AND THE IMPORTANCE OF THE LAITY.

During the Medieval period, Chan and Pure Land schools became combined into a single form of spiritual development. Even today, most of the monasteries in mainland China, Hong Kong and Taiwan retain the joint practice of Chan meditation and Pure Land recitation.

The Tang (618–907CE) and Song (960–1279CE) dynasties, which are regarded as the 'golden age' of Chinese Buddhism, were followed by the Yuan (1271–1368), which saw the spread of Tibetan Buddhism, the Ming (1368–1644), when a strong lay Buddhist movement was formed, and finally the Qing dynasty (1644–1911), which experienced the renewed patronage of Tibetan Buddhism.

MONGOLS AND LAMAS

Kublai Khan, the Mongol emperor, conquered China in 1271. The new foreign rulers of China preferred to support the 'foreign' religion of Buddhism rather than native Daoism or Confucianism. In particular, they favoured the Lamaist school. Introduced into China during the Tang dynasty, Tibetan Buddhism spread out only during the Yuan period.

Above This limestone artefact dating from the Northern Wei dynasty (386–534BCE) depicts the descent of the future Buddha Maitreya.

Below The White Tower of the Miaoying temple in Beijing was the largest tower built in China during the Yuan dynasty (1271–1368) by the Lamaist Buddhist school.

Besides its esoteric teachings and form of spirituality, Tibetan Buddhism became a mark of the Yuan dynasty in the several peculiar bottle-shaped pagodas that were built in China during this time. The most famous of these is the White Tower of the Miaoying temple, which was built in the capital of the empire and still stands in Fuchengmen, Beijing. The pagoda, which stands 51m (167ft) high, is divided into three sections and covered with Tibetan paintings, was the work of Nepalese artist Ahnigethe Miaoying.

ZHU YUANZHANG AND THE WHITE LOTUS SOCIETY

Originally a secret society in rebellion against the Yuan rulers in the 13th century CE, the White Lotus Society found a leader in the figure of Zhu Yuanzhang, who conquered the capital Beijing in 1368 and was enthroned as the first emperor of the new Ming dynasty with the name of Hongwu. However, in order to become emperor, Zhu Yuanzhang had to transfer his interest in Buddhism to an affiliation to Confucianism, an act that Chinese Buddhists never accepted or forgave.

Organized as a Buddhist heterodox sect, and very popular, especially among the needy, the White Lotus Society was a millenarian movement whose militants fought the existing government and were awaiting the descent of the future Buddha Maitreya, which would provoke the start of a new Buddhist era as well as a new secular world.

Other rebellions led by the White Lotus Society continued throughout the Qing dynasty (1644–1911) until the end of the 18th century.

Left This famous portrait of Zhu Yuanzhang, the founder and first emperor of the Ming dynasty, is preserved in the National Palace Museum of Taipei, in Taiwan.

YANG WENHUI AND THE BUDDHIST LAITY

From the mid-19th century, the Buddhist laity began to play an increasingly important role within Buddhism, modernizing the religion and travelling internationally.

Yang Wenhui (1837–1911) was a lay reformer who helped to promote Buddhist culture and renew Buddhist education. In 1866, Yang established the Jinlin Scriptural Press with the aim of publishing new editions of scriptures that had disappeared in China. During a trip to England (1878–86), he met the Japanese scholar Nanjio Bunyu, who helped him to reintroduce into China hundreds of Buddhist texts that had been missing. In 1910, Yang founded the Buddhist Research Society, which provided teaching for the laity as well as monks. His students included the early 20th-century reformer of Chinese Buddhism, Ouyang Jingwu, and the monk Taixu.

THE JADE BUDDHA TEMPLE

Built in 1882, the Jade Buddha temple has become both a pilgrimage site and a tourist attraction in Shanghai. The temple was originally a monastery following the traditional Chinese joint practice of Chan and Pure Land schools. The two jade Buddha statues were imported from Burma. It is said that the Chinese monk Huigen travelled to the Wutai and Emei mountains in China, then to Tibet and finally reached Burma. Impressed by the beauty of the local jade, Huigen ordered five jade Buddha statues to bring back to China. He gave two of those (a big standing Buddha and a smaller reclining Buddha) to a group of Buddhist followers in Shanghai, who eventually built a temple to host the precious jade artefacts. Huigen was appointed abbot of the temple after the construction of the religious site was completed.

Right Monks wearing the monastic robes for important Buddhist ceremonies sit in front of the Buddha statues in the main hall of the Jade Buddha temple.

WOMEN IN BUDDHISM

ANANDA APPROACHED THE BUDDHA THREE TIMES BEFORE WOMEN WERE ALLOWED TO JOIN THE SANGHA. TODAY, ONLY MAHAYANIST EAST ASIA COUNTS BHIKKHUNIS; IN THERAVADA COUNTRIES AND TIBET, WOMEN STILL FIGHT FOR THE RIGHT TO BE FULLY ORDAINED.

Mahaprajapati, the Buddha's step-mother, was the first nun in the history of Buddhism, but according to some Buddhist interpretations, the admission of women into the Sangha was a misfortune for Buddhism. Women were considered to be impure and inferior because of their different body-build and biological factors, such as menstruation and pregnancy. It was therefore generally believed that women could not achieve enlightenment; only rebirth in a male body could enable them to attain buddhahood. Women in many regions were therefore denied the opportunity of being ordained as nuns and following a monastic life.

Where women are allowed to receive full monastic ordination, they wear the same robes as their male counterparts, but live in separate nunneries and have to follow more precepts than monks.

From the inception of the bhikkhunis in ancient India, Buddhist nuns were discriminated against by monks, reflecting the low status of women in Indian society at that time. The main doctrinal support for the thesis of the inferiority of nuns were the *asta gurudharma*, the eight chief rules governing relationships between nuns and monks. According to these, for example, even a senior nun must bow in front of a novice monk, and nuns must always walk and sit behind monks.

Below Buddhist women at the Taktsang gompa, *Bhutan, in 1904. It is said that Guru Rinpoche flew there from Tibet and began the spread of Buddhism in Bhutan.*

Above A Tibetan novice standing among prayer flags in Tagong, China. Prayer flags, a distinctive feature of Tibetan Buddhism, symbolize compassion, peace and wisdom.

WOMEN IN THE THERAVADA TRADITION

In most countries where Theravada Buddhism is prevalent, including Laos, Cambodia, Burma (Myanmar) and Thailand, the Order of Buddhist Nuns has never been established. Women practise Buddhism as lay followers or gather in groups that have become distinct to the region.

In Thailand, for instance, *mae-chi* are Buddhist women who take the Eight Precepts, wear white robes and shave their heads. They live and study in special *mae-chi* institutions, but are not fully ordained bhikkhunis. (Recently, a few Thai women have been fully ordained elsewhere, but according to a non-Theravada discipline, and they therefore remain unrecognized by the male Sangha.)

Similar groups of female Buddhist followers exist in other countries. These include the *thila shin* in Burma, who wear a pink and brown uniform, the Laotian *maekhao* and the Cambodian *donchee*, who wear white clothing, and the Sri Lankan *dasasilmata*, who wear brown or yellow robes. All these groups follow the Ten Precepts. (There are also some fully ordained Buddhist nuns in Sri Lanka.)

In the West, an increasing number of women have joined the Theravada Buddhist tradition.

THE FIGHT FOR ORDINATION IN TIBET

It is known that Buddhist nuns were active in Tibet until the 17th century. These fully ordained nuns later disappeared, but there are still a large number of female novices in Tibet, living in miserable conditions with no education.

In recent decades, an increasing number of Western women have become interested in Tibetan Buddhism. Many have been ordained in Taiwan or Korea, but according to a vinaya that is not the Mulasarvastivada followed in Tibet, and they are consequently not recognized by the Tibetan monks. Nevertheless, these Western women now fight in defence of the right of Buddhist women in Tibet to be ordained, and thanks to the generous support of an international network, they have founded nunneries and institutes for nuns near Dharamsala.

MAHAYANIST NUNS

The first Buddhist women to take the Ten Precepts and become novices were fully ordained by monks in 357CE. In 434CE, a delegation of 19 Sri Lankan Buddhist nuns visited China, where they organized the first monastic ordination for Chinese women, led by both monks and nuns who belonged to unbroken lineages. This was the first monastic ordination for Chinese women to be recognized as being in accordance with the monastic discipline (vinaya).

Right Nuns of the Drukpa lineage of Tibetan Buddhism recite scriptures for the long life of their spiritual leader Gyalwang Drukpa, believed to be the 12th reincarnation of the sect's founder.

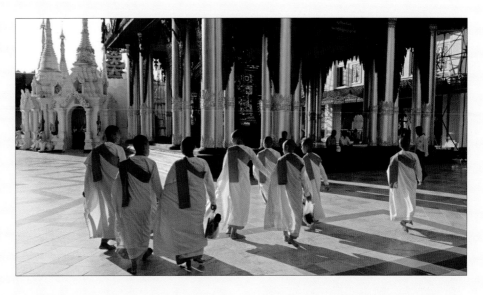

The lineage of Chinese Buddhist nuns has survived since then, despite ruptures and persecutions, and today there are also socially engaged nuns active in Taiwan, and Tibetan female followers in south-western China.

The Order of Buddhist Nuns in Korea has likewise survived since the inception of Buddhism in Korea in the 4th century CE. Nuns studying at the major Korean temple of Unmun-sa and female speakers on Buddhist music radio programmes reflect something of the current high status of Buddhist women in Korea.

Above Burmese Buddhist women wearing the traditional pink robe and brown stole, at the Shwedagon pagoda in Rangoon, Burma (Myanmar).

Buddhist nuns have existed in Japan since the spread of Buddhism from Korea in the late 6th century. Indeed, according to imperial records, the first ordained Japanese Buddhist was a woman, Shima, who received the Buddhist name Zenshin. The performing nuns at Kumano, courtesan nuns and the wives of Buddhist priests are only some of the Buddhist women who can be seen today in Japan.

BUDDHISM IN KOREA

DESPITE PRESSURE FROM CHRISTIANITY AND PERSECUTION BY CONFUCIANISM, BUDDHISM SURVIVED AS A VITAL PART OF KOREAN CULTURE. BUDDHIST CEREMONIES ARE NOW CELEBRATED NATIONALLY, AND EXAMPLES OF BUDDHIST ARCHITECTURE ARE STATE TREASURES.

Above Tongdo-sa is the largest Buddhist temple in Korea; it is located in Jeolla province. Its 65 buildings are said to have been built on the relics of Buddha Shakyamuni, which its founder, Chajang, received in China from the bodhisattva Mañjushri.

In 372CE, Chinese missionary monks arrived in the northern kingdom of Koguryo with scriptures and statues. Buddhism thus started its spread throughout the Korean peninsula, entering the south-western kingdom of Paekje in 384CE, Karak in the 5th century CE and Shilla in the following century. Famous Buddhist temples, such as Songmun-sa and Ibulran-sa, were built during these first centuries of Buddhism's diffusion throughout the peninsula.

Below Songgwang-sa temple is known as a site for Son meditation. Built in the 12th century, the temple was destroyed during the Hideyoshi invasion in the late 16th century. It was restored to glory in the 1980s.

Buddhism experienced phases of strong development during the Unified Silla period (668–935, when the peninsula was united under a single reign), and during the Koryo dynasty (935–1392), but it later suffered persecution during the Confucian Choseon dynasty (1392–1910). It was revived during the Japanese occupation of the country from 1910 to 1945, and afterward.

A FUSION OF RELIGIONS

When Buddhism entered Korea, it had to confront the animistic beliefs of Shamanism. Interaction between the two religions was evident from the beginning. For instance, mountains that were believed to host gods venerated by Shamanism later became sites of Buddhist temples. The three main gods of Korean Shamanism – San-shin (the Mountain God), Toksong (the Recluse) and Ch'ilsong (the Big Dipper) – were embraced by Buddhism, and even painted and enshrined in Buddhist temples. Traces of Korean Shamanism are still visible in the arts and architecture of local Buddhist temples.

Above The celebration of the Buddha's birthday in Korea is characterized by lotus lanterns hung outside temples. Long processions of big Buddha- and bodhisattva-shaped lanterns weave through the main cities of the country.

Above Seokgatap is the Shakyamuni pagoda in Bulguk-sa. The three-storey structure and simple style are characteristic of Buddhist art during the Silla period. Built to represent the Buddha, this pagoda became Korea's National Treasure No. 21.

KOREAN TEMPLES

Buddhist temples in Korea provide places of worship, lodgings for devoted practitioners and space for monastic education. They are thus more than merely residences; indeed, in their architecture, layout and symbolism, they have become important icons of Korean identity.

The temples are usually compounds of buildings that are built on mountains and close to water. The main halls are preceded by three gates: the 'One Pillar' gate; the 'Four Guardians' gate, which depicts the four protectors of Buddhism; and the 'Non-duality' gate, which represents the passage from the mundane to the sacred. The rite of purification that such a passage demands is associated with crossing a river or pond located between the third gate and the main hall. The compounds also include stone or wooden pagodas and pillars, called *pudo*, which are built on the ashes of famous monks and flanked by a stele with a turtle-shaped base.

BUDDHISM AND CONFUCIANISM

At the beginning of the Choseon dynasty, whose rulers supported Confucian thought at the expense of other beliefs, Buddhism became subject to harsh persecutions. Buddhist monks lost their involvement and influence in politics, the establishment of new Buddhist temples was banned, and monastics were forbidden from entering the capital.

However, in the 16th century, thousands of Korean Buddhist monks participated in an attack against Japanese invaders and eventually won the fight, which led to a greater degree of tolerance from the Confucian Choseon. In another attempt to find a solution to the Confucian attacks, Korean Buddhists proposed a close and combined development of both these systems of thought. Following this line of reasoning, one of the most important Buddhist leaders in Korea, Hyujong (1520–1604), supported the syncretism of the three doctrines – namely Buddhism, Daoism and Confucianism – as the only path to the realization of the one Truth.

Above San-shin, the Korean Shamanist Mountain God, was assimilated into Buddhism and transformed into a bodhisattva. The tiger in this 16th-century depiction symbolizes strength.

THE THREE JEWELS TEMPLES

Three monasteries have been regarded as representing the 'three jewels' (*triratna*) of Buddhism: Tongdo-sa is the 'temple of the Buddha' (the Buddha is the first jewel), Haein-sa is the 'temple of the Dharma' (the Buddha's teachings are the second jewel), and Songgwang-sa is the 'temple of the Sangha' (the community of the Buddha's followers is the third jewel). Tongdo-sa was built in Jeolla province in 646CE. Its uniqueness lies in its symbolization of the Buddha: there are no statues of the Buddha in the main hall; instead his relics are preserved, and venerated, in a pagoda on its Diamond Precepts platform. Haein-sa, in Gyeongsang province, was first founded in 802CE and contains the *Tripitaka Koreana* wooden printing blocks (National Treasure No.32, UNESCO World Heritage Site) with carved Buddhist scriptures. Songgwang-sa (Gyeongsang province) dates back to the 12th century, and became well-known for the number of remarkable monks who lived there, including Chinul (1158–1210).

THE PAGODA

PAGODAS ARE STUPAS – SHRINES CONTAINING SACRED RELICS.
PORTUGUESE TRADERS IN INDIA FIRST CALLED THEM 'PAGODAS',
FROM A PERSIAN WORD MEANING 'TEMPLE OF IDOLS'. AS BUDDHISM
SPREAD, DECORATIVE STYLES OF PAGODA ARCHITECTURE DEVELOPED.

The simple hemispherical stupas that were erected over the Buddha's relics at the eight holy places associated with his life rapidly evolved elsewhere into more elaborate bell shapes, such as the stupas of Borobudur in Java, and tall pyramids, including the 127m (417ft) high Phra Pathom Chedi in Thailand. As Buddhism advanced, stupas became the religious centres of temples, and as it spread through Asia, temple complexes encircled pagodas built to house relics brought from India. One of Burma's oldest pagodas, the beautiful Shwezigon Paya in Bagan, was erected in the 11th century as a reliquary for a tooth of the Buddha. Others were built to house the remains of revered monks and teachers or ancient Buddhist manuscripts.

THE PAGODAS OF CHINA

In the Western mind, pagodas are inextricably linked with the multi-storeyed towers the Chinese call *ta*, their word for stupa. These had as many as 15 superimposed storeys to indicate prestige – only the rulers lived in multi-storey buildings. Each storey had an upward-curving roof, decorated with brilliantly coloured, glazed ceramic tiles, carvings and other decorations. They were curved to ward off evil spirits, which were believed to travel in straight lines.

Above The 13-storey Qiyun pagoda in the White Horse temple, Luoyang, was constructed in brick in the shape of a parabola. It was built in 1175 to replace an earlier one that burned down.

Below Kyoto's To-ji temple pagoda is Japan's tallest wooden tower at 57m (187ft) high. Japanese pagodas are square, exquisitely carved structures that were built to survive earthquakes, so are only three to five storeys high.

The first Chinese pagodas were built of stone or wood, but later they were built of brick, often faced with colourful ceramics. At different periods in history they have been square, hexagonal, octagonal, and even tetragonal. The height of each storey decreased regularly between the base storey and the summit, which was surmounted by the traditional parasol. With so many roofs, the structure was heavy, and its weight was carried by a central pillar, or by rows of colonnades on the ground. Inside, the relics were laid in a shrine on the ground floor, or in an underground vault. The interiors were often brightly painted.

JAPANESE PAGODAS

Some of the oldest wooden buildings in the world survive in Japan in the form of Buddhist temples and pagodas. Near Nara, the capital during the Asuka period, is the Horyu-ji complex, built in the early 600s as a private royal temple for Prince Shotoku, an important early proponent of Buddhism in Japan.

The construction of Japan's ancient wooden pagodas, using a type of bracket called a *tokyo*, have enabled them to survive earthquakes. The bracket is assembled from component pieces and friction causes these to heat, converting the movement of the earthquake into thermal energy.

CHINOISERIE

Pagodas are found in most countries of East and South-east Asia where Buddhism is or has been influential. During the 18th century, when chinoiserie became fashionable, imitation pagodas were built in many grand gardens across Europe – Louis XIV had one built at Versailles, for example.

In 1762, a pagoda was built at Kew, then a royal residence, by William Chambers. It was octagonal, almost 50m (164ft) high, and decorated in Chinese fashion with coloured roofs, gilding and carved dragons. However, its ten storeys broke an important rule of Eastern architecture: Chinese pagodas always have an uneven number of storeys, because this is considered lucky.

Above Elaborately carved and painted woodwork in the traditional Korean dancheong *('red and blue') style under the eaves of the Bulguksa temple in Gyeongju.*

Below The temples and stupas of Bagan rise above the jungle. The distinctive bell shape of pagodas in Burma, with their towering spires, was established in Bagan, capital of the first Burmese empire.

BUDDHISM IN JAPAN

BUDDHISM IN JAPAN IS CHARACTERIZED BY TRADITIONAL ZEN MEDITATION RETREATS, THE RECITED VISUALIZATION OF *NAMO MYOHO RENGE KYO*, ESOTERIC ASCETICISM AND TANTRIC PRACTICE. MONKS AND NUNS MAY BE NEITHER CELIBATE NOR VEGETARIAN.

Buddhism was transmitted from Korea to Japan in 538CE and was enshrined as the state religion by Prince Shotoku only a few decades later. The main schools of Japanese Buddhism came into existence during the Nara period (710–94). Later, during the Heian period (794–1185), Japan became familiar with the Tendai school of Saicho and the Shingon school founded by Kukai.

In the medieval Kamakura period (1185–1333), Nichiren Buddhism, the esoteric reading of the *Lotus Sutra*, and the eschatological view of the dark age (*mappo*), as

Below A painting of the sohei *Saito Musashibo Benkei (1155–89) during a fight. This famous figure, who was a symbol of strength and loyalty, became the subject of folkloric tales and of plots for Kabuki and Noh traditional theatre.*

well as what would become the two main sects of Japanese Zen – Soto and Rinzai – spread throughout the empire. Substantial changes occurred in the Buddhist world of Japan during the Meiji period (1868–1912) with the move toward secularization and the appeal for nationalism.

SHINTO

Buddhism also interacted with Shinto, the local Japanese religion. An animistic and polytheistic belief system, Shinto involves the worship of *kami*, the spirits of natural phenomena. One of the most important *kami* is Amaterasu, the Goddess of the Sun, from whom the Japanese imperial family is said to descend.

Kami and buddhas were included together inside the same shrine or other form of sacred

Above Prince Shotoku Taishi (574–622CE) and his sons Yamashiro Oe and Ekuri. The Yamato ruler is known as the Japanese Ashoka for his elevation of Buddhism to the level of a state religion in Japan.

space, and both received worship from the Japanese. During the Heian Period, Amaterasu became linked to the Buddhist Dainichi Nyorai (the Japanese version of Vairocana, also called the 'Cosmic Buddha'). The Japanese syncretism of Shinto and Buddhism, known as Shinbutsu-shugo, survived until the Meiji restoration, which declared the separation of the two belief systems in 1868.

THE WARRIOR MONKS

Enryaku-ji on Mount Hiei, close to Kyoto, is the famous mountain monastery residence of the *sohei*. Popular in medieval Japan, *sohei* were ascetic monks organized into armies that lived hidden up in the mountains. They emerged in the 10th century during the feudal medieval era, and ended up influencing the structure of Buddhist religious institutions.

Warrior monks of different monasteries fought in defence of their own monastery's rights and

Right This 11th-century Japanese silk painting shows a royal minister and a court lady mourning the death of the Buddha.

for political appointments. *Sohei* wore robes, used different sorts of armaments and fought on horseback. These warrior monks were in existence until the beginning of the 17th century. Like the Shaolin monks in China, they have also been depicted in fiction.

MUMMIFIED BUDDHAS

Sokushinbutsu were Japanese Buddhist monks whose goal was to 'become Buddhas in their own body', believing that they could reach eternal life through the self-mummification of their bodies. Though no one has been able to explain fully how the monks became mummified, it is thought that a special diet, meditation and the right environment may be able to prevent the body from decaying. Through the practice of austerities, a strict diet – which began with abstention from cereals, then gradually reduced until the monks did not even drink water – and the practice of deep meditation and Shugendo, these Buddhists showed how the physical body and not only the mind could be an instrument of religious practice.

The school found inspiration in the example and writings of the monk Kukai (774–835CE), and there are now more than 20 cases of mummified monks, the most famous of these being Tetsumonkai (18th century, now enshrined at Churen-ji). This practice was declared a form of suicide, and therefore illegal, at the end of the 19th century, but it is known that *Sokushinbutsu miras* (mummies 'in the making') were in existence even in the 20th century.

CULTURAL OBJECTS

The *ema*, a small wooden plaque, is often found at Japanese Buddhist temples. One side is decorated with Buddhist symbols or images relating to the temple from which it is sold. The other side is left blank to give space for the believer to write his or her name, age, address and personal wish. The *ema* is usually left in the temple until the wish is fulfilled, after which, according to tradition, it should be burned.

Right Ema *hung outside a temple. These tablets are used in both the Shinto and Buddhist religions, and are a common souvenir in Japan.*

Buddhist Art in East Asia

DURING THE EARLY CENTURIES OF THE COMMON ERA, BUDDHIST ART OF INDIA SPREAD GRADUALLY EASTWARD TO CHINA, KOREA AND JAPAN. AS IT TRAVELLED, IT MINGLED WITH NATIVE ARTS AND TRADITIONS AND TRANSMOGRIFIED INTO NEW ART FORMS.

Above Ogata Korin (1658–1716), an artist of the Japanese Edo period, drew Bodhidharma in ink on silk in his own interpretation of the humour and caricature with which Chinese artists often depicted the founder of Chan and Zen Buddhism.

Along with the merchants and monks, artistic ideas and techniques flowed along the early trade routes out of India. The first Buddhist art of East Asia was an interpretation of Indian painting and sculpture, the result of contacts between China's westward-expanding Han dynasty and Buddhist traders and pilgrims travelling north from the Indian subcontinent. Their meeting place was Central Asia, the crossroads of India, China and the Western, Hellenistic civilizations of Asia. From the 1st century CE, Buddhist communities formed around the desert oases and grew to dominate the region. Caravans set out from Taxila in modern Pakistan to Bamiyan in Afghanistan, Kizil (Kucha), Turfan (Turpan) and Dunhuang in modern Gansu province, carrying artistic ideas and techniques from Gandhara, Byzantium, Persia and, by the 6th century, from the Middle East.

EARLY SCULPTURE

Buddhism arrived in China around the 1st century CE and made its way slowly across the country, bringing with it new art forms, such as more mature forms of sculpture. The imperial court of the Northern Wei dynasty (386–534) embraced Buddhism and established the Longmen caves near their capital, Luoyang.

Left Many exquisite images of Amida Buddha, the Buddha of Infinite Light, were carved from the 12th century, the Heian period, when Amida Buddhism was introduced to Japan.

During the first half of the Tang dynasty (618–907), Xuanzang and other monks made long and dangerous pilgrimages to India in search of Buddhist scriptures. On their return, they reintroduced China to artistic influences from the Gupta empire, which then ruled in the northern Indian subcontinent. Tang artists transformed the stolid and solemn sculpture of earlier dynasties into lighter, more lifelike and dynamic figures.

Pure Land Buddhism came into prominence in China during the 400s, and the Tiantai sect emerged during the 500s. Both inspired monumental, colourful paintings. However, it was the Chan sect, brought to China around 500 by the Indian monk Bodhidharma, that had the deepest impact on Chinese art. The first artists to be inspired by Chan were Tang monochrome landscape painters, who attempted to capture the essence of a landscape in painting. They also explored calligraphy, so influencing the evolution of ink painting.

Under the later Tang, Buddhism was persecuted. But from the Tang capital, Xian, which became an important centre for Buddhism, the Dharma spread to Korea and Japan.

THE INFLUENCE OF CHAN

As a result of Buddhist influence, silk and paper scrolls had become the format for Chinese painting. The artists of the Song dynasty (960–1279), a period of relative peace in which the arts flourished, developed this medium, exploring

Right The Longmen caves were founded by the Wei dynasty rulers in 494CE, when they changed their capital to Luoyang. The relief sculpture with which the artist-monks covered the limestone grottoes represents the zenith of Chinese stone-carving.

ink painting on large hanging scrolls. The Song period saw a flowering of landscape painting and paintings of nature – birds, bamboo and flowers. The artists may not all have been Buddhists, but their paintings reflect the Chan emphasis on direct expression and personal experience as a key to sudden, intuitive enlightenment. They explored direct expression through the artistic use of calligraphy, with which they could capture the essence, the 'buddha nature', of their subject.

ZEN

Arriving in Japan late in the 9th century, Zen Buddhism flourished until the 1600s. It spread the ideas and techniques of Chinese Song art throughout Japan. Calligraphy, ink painting and also sand-, rock- and moss-gardening, flower arranging, the tea ceremony, architecture and literature all flourished. The Zen art of Japan was austere – simple ink paintings and stark calligraphy.

Through art, the individual sought personal enlightenment. Chan and Zen Buddhism teaches

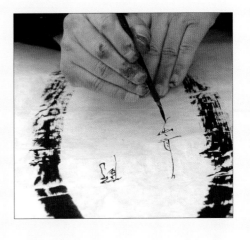

Above A monk at a temple in Seoul, South Korea, practises calligraphy. Since the Chinese Han dynasty, calligraphy has been considered a serious art form. Its ability to express more than words was especially important to artists influenced by the Chan, Son and Zen traditions.

that enlightenment comes through the realization that one is already enlightened, and that realization may be a gradual or an instant process. Zen artists sought to awaken that realization, to spark off in the mind of the beholder the flash of insight that can trigger the transformation from human being to bodhisattva.

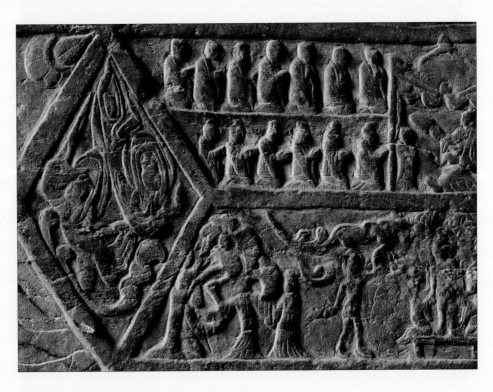

NEW BUDDHIST SCHOOLS IN JAPAN

AFTER AN INITIAL PERIOD OF INTEGRATION, BUDDHISM FLOURISHED IN JAPAN, WITH THE FORMATION OF NEW SCHOOLS, SUCH AS ZEN AND JODO, THE RISE OF EMINENT FIGURES, INCLUDING NICHIREN, AND ITS OWN SOCIO-POLITICAL INSTITUTIONS, SUCH AS THE *DANKA* SYSTEM.

Japan was the last East Asian country to welcome Buddhism, but the first one to modernize and secularize the religion, and it did so in ways that were sometimes almost extreme.

The abandonment of celibacy and vegetarianism among Buddhist monks and nuns made Japan unique within Mahayanist East Asia. This was but the last step of a historical development that had seen the medieval Nichiren's emphasis on the *Lotus Sutra* to the threat of Christianity under the Tokugawa. These elements are still seen today: the *Lotus Sutra* remains the scriptural reference for the lay associations of Soka

Gakkai and Rissho Koseikai, and the temple Buddhism that derives from the *danka* system.

ZEN AND *MAPPO*

The two main schools of Zen that dominate the scene of Japanese Buddhism even today, namely Rinzai and Soto, made their appearance in Japan during the Kamakura period (1185–1333). The monk Eisai (1141–1215) began Rinzai Zen in Japan after a trip to China (1191). Soto Zen was brought to Japan from China by Dogen (1200–53) following his travels there in 1227. Rinzai is characterized by the mental meditation over the abstruse

Above A wooden statue of a seated Dainichi Nyorai, the Japanese version of Vairocana. Dainichi Nyorai is usually, as here, represented in a seated position and making the Dharmachakra mudra.

questions called *koans* (*gong-ans* in Chinese), considering the answers of those enquiries as key to reaching enlightenment. Soto Zen, on the other hand, proposes the apparently easier method of practice, the sitting meditation, known in Japanese as *Zazen*.

Developments in the Jodo (Pure Land) school during the Kamakura period, as well as Nichiren's interpretations of the *Lotus Sutra*, shed new light on the concept of *mappo*. Originally conceived as 'the final period of Dharma', the word *mappo* came to indicate not only the time when Dharma would be corrupted, but also, and especially, the end of the world.

Left A detail from a hanging scroll from the Kamakura period showing the mandala of the Kasuga Grand Shrine at Nara, in Japan. As capital of Japan during the 8th century, Nara witnessed a flowering of Buddhist temples and Shinto shrines.

THE *DANKA* SYSTEM

During the Edo period (1600–1868), Buddhism was threatened in China as Spanish and Portuguese missionaries began to spread Christianity throughout Japan. With the aim of turning the Japanese away from Christianity and strengthening Buddhism, the imperial family established a system of affiliation to local Buddhist temples for the population.

This system was called *danka*, a name that was meant to translate as *dana*, the Sanskrit word for 'perfection of giving'. In Mahayana Buddhism, practitioners should cultivate Six Perfections, the first of which is *dana*, or generosity.

In the *danka* system, the concept of giving was concretized in the giving-based relationship between the temple patron and parishioners. The parishioners supported the temple financially – indeed, they were obliged to do so – and took part in temple rituals and prayers, while the temple patron could benefit the local population through blessings and the performance of funeral services. As a result, Buddhism under the Tokugawa also became known as 'funerary Buddhism'.

MODERNIZATION

The Meiji Restoration of 1868 signalled the beginning of modernity in Japan. This process of modernization, which was an emulation of Western civilization and thought, affected religion too. Shinto was separated from Buddhism, and Buddhism, which

Right A Buddhist monk performing a fire ritual at Enryaku-ji on Mount Hiei. Playing a fundamental role in esoteric Buddhism in Japan, fire rituals are performed as a purification ceremony and are celebrated by monastics and laity together.

Right A 17th-century figure of Kannon Bosatsu, the Japanese version of the Chinese bodhisattva Guanyin and the Indian bodhisattva Avalokiteshvara. Venerated as the 'Goddess of Mercy', Kannon is most often represented in a female form, although there are male depictions.

was seen as a foreign religion with plenty of superstitious elements, lost its imperial support.

This did not signal the end of Buddhism, however, but rather the beginning of a transformed Buddhism, which was characterized by the establishment of academies, erudite monks and married priests. Vegetarianism and celibacy, two essential features of East Asian Mahayana Buddhism, became neglected in Meiji Japan, and monks were allowed to marry and eat meat, thanks to the new law called *Nikujiki saitai* (literally translated as 'getting married and eating meat').

This process of secularization was condemned by the Chinese and Korean Sangha. An interesting aspect of this new Buddhist environment was the appearance of the figure of the priest's wife and the hereditary temple run by the family.

Another essential feature of the Meiji period was the blossoming of modern Japanese nationalism, which provoked a revision of Zen. This eventually led to Zen Buddhism becoming enshrined as a key aspect of Japanese national identity.

ZEN GARDENS

WHEN ZEN BUDDHISM ARRIVED IN JAPAN IN THE LATE 9TH CENTURY, IT HAD A PROFOUND IMPACT ON NEARLY EVERY ASPECT OF LIFE, FROM DRINKING TEA TO CALLIGRAPHY AND PAINTING. ITS INFLUENCE WAS PARTICULARLY PERVASIVE IN THE ZEN GARDEN.

The ancient tradition of Daoist landscapes, introduced to Japan via Korea in the 7th century CE, established the basic design criteria of early Zen gardens. However, it was probably not until the prosperous Muromachi period in the 14th century, that the true Zen garden appeared. Skilled craftsmen began to create in temple courtyards havens of calm and solitude where priests, scholars and warriors could retreat from the stresses of their daily lives.

Characterized by their extreme abstraction of form and simplicity, these gardens provided an ideal setting for the quiet contemplation

Below A monk performs part of the daily ritual of a Zen temple. The white sand or gravel is raked into various patterns, some resembling waves, others the ripples or currents of a river.

and meditation so essential in Zen Buddhism. The Zen tradition of meditation takes two main forms: the Soto tradition, in which the meditator practices just sitting (*Zazen*), and the Rinzai tradition, which combines sitting meditation with the use of *koans* (Chinese: *gong-ans*) – enigmatic riddles to which there are no answers. The goal is to attain spiritual enlightenment, and the Zen garden, with its aura of peace and tranquillity, is an ideal environment in which to pursue it.

SAND, STONE AND WATER

Although Zen gardens come in many forms, those most associated with Zen are the dry rock type called *karesansui*, literally meaning 'dry-mountain-and-water gardens'. Rocks of various sizes are grouped in a seemingly random

Above Autumn maples are reflected in the large pond that lies at the heart of the exquisite moss garden at Saiho-ji in Kyoto. The garden is carpeted with some 120 varieties of moss.

pattern on a ground of small white pebbles or sand. The rocks represent mountains or waterfalls, the sand or gravel signifies water, which is carefully raked to look like the rippling currents of a river.

The regular maintenance of the garden and the raking of the sand are seen as part of the daily life of the temple. These tasks require great skill and concentration and represent yet another step down the road to enlightenment.

There have been many attempts to explain the layout of the Zen garden. One suggestion is that the gravel represents the ocean while the rocks represent the islands of Japan. A recent theory claims that the rocks form the subliminal image of a tree: while this image cannot actually be seen, the subconscious mind is able to perceive a subtle association between the rocks.

Perhaps the best known example of a Zen dry garden is at Ryoan-ji in Kyoto. Constructed in *karesansui* style, it has 15 rocks of varying sizes – some surrounded by moss – arranged on a bed of white gravel. The rocks are so placed that visitors, no matter where they stand, can see only 14 rocks at a time. According to tradition, it is not until someone achieves spiritual enlightenment

that he can see the invisible 15th rock in his mind's eye. The power and beauty of the garden lies in the grouping of the rocks and the spatial relationship between them.

BONSAI

Another element in the design of *karesansui* gardens is the miniature 'tray' landscape, imported from China and known in the West as bonsai. To the sand and rocks are added dwarf plants set in flat containers made of stone or bronze. These gardens, which create the impression of a vast landscape, echo the ink-wash Daoist landscape paintings of the earlier Song dynasty, which were brought back from China by travelling Zen monks. The technique of compressing a great outdoor space into a minute area became known

as 'the great within the small'. This type of garden influenced the design of Japanese gardens from the Muromachi period onward.

MOSS GARDENS

A temple precinct often contains not only a dry rock garden but a lush green one, as at Saiho-ji in Kyoto, perhaps the most famous of the Buddhist moss gardens. Often called the Moss temple, or Koke-dera, this is a park-style 'stroll garden' that creates in the mind of the stroller the illusion that he has taken a long journey, albeit in a limited space. At every turn he encounters a special object or symbol that helps to focus his mind on spiritual matters. In Kyoto's humid climate, the moss flourishes, remaining fresh and green throughout the year.

Above An elevated view of the garden at Tofuku-ji in Kyoto clearly shows the patterns created by the raked sand. The effect is of powerful ripples spreading out from a rock thrown into the water.

Below Ryoan-ji, or the temple of the Peaceful Dragon, in Kyoto is the most famous example of a Zen dry garden. The garden is often referred to as 'a sermon in stone' because it embodies many of the beliefs of Zen Buddhism.

BUDDHISM IN SOUTH-EAST ASIA

MORE THAN 90 PER CENT OF THE PEOPLE OF BURMA (MYANMAR), THAILAND AND CAMBODIA FOLLOW THERAVADA BUDDHISM, AND IT IS THE MAIN RELIGION IN LAOS. IN VIETNAM, 10 PER CENT FOLLOW MAHAYANA, WHILE INDONESIA IS ALMOST 90 PER CENT MUSLIM.

Buddhism reached South-east Asia by land and sea from India and what is now Sri Lanka perhaps as early as the 3rd century BCE. The *Mahavamsa*, the ancient Sri Lankan chronicle, records that the emperor Ashoka sent missions into what are now Burma (Myanmar), Thailand and Cambodia.

Buddhist stupas, shrines and viharas, dating from the 6th century, have been excavated at the site of the former city-state of Sri Ksetra beside the Irrawaddy River near Prome, in Burma. Sri Ksetra was the capital of a civilization

Below Ancient stupas crowd the shore of Inle Lake in Burma. The lakeside dwellers are called the Intha, Buddhists descended from the Mon, who spread across northern Burma and Thailand.

known as the Pyu, and these are among the oldest known architectural structures on mainland South-east Asia. The earliest, at a settlement called Beikthano, date from the 4th century, but similar structures in wood may predate them, so Buddhism may have been established in the region by the 1st or 2nd century CE.

BUDDHIST KINGDOMS

During the 1st millennium, South-east Asia was peopled largely by migrating tribal groups. Like the Pyu, many had moved southward from China and settled to form city-states and kingdoms. The kingdoms of Dvaravati and Haripunchai extended across modern Thailand into Burma and Laos. They were founded during

Above The Emerald Buddha in Wat Phra Kaew, in Bangkok, is Thailand's most sacred work of art, but in the past it belonged to the Cambodians and the Burmese, who still claim it today.

the 6th and 7th centuries by the Mon, who may have been indigenous to the region and who had practised Theravada from early in their history. These ancient kingdoms influenced the development of South-east Asian art – the stupas of the Pyu and the Mon were the models for the Shwedagon pagoda in Rangoon.

The Tai-speaking peoples of modern Burma, Thailand and Laos trace their origins to the kingdom of Nanzhao, which was founded in the 8th century by an association of tribes in Yunnan, in southern China. Nanzhao expanded southward, sacking Pyu city-states in the region that became Burma in 849. Pyu declined during the 9th century, forcing its population into a slow migration southward into Burma, Thailand and Laos, where their form of Mahayana Buddhism flourished.

The Shan people of these countries are believed to be descendants of the early Buddhist tribal groups. During the 14th century, they founded powerful kingdoms, including Ava in Burma, Lanna and Ayutthaya in Thailand, and Lan Xang in Laos. Today many Shan people live in the Shan state in Burma (Myanmar), and in the adjoining mountainous province of Mae Hong Son in Thailand.

ANGKOR

The Khmer are thought to have migrated from southern China more than 3,000 years ago. During the 1st century CE, they founded Funan, a trading nation, on the Mekong delta, and expanded into southern Vietnam, Laos, Thailand, Burma and, during the 3rd century, Malaysia. The Funanese absorbed Hinduism and Buddhism from India. Influenced by Indian sculpture and reliefs, they pro duced masterpieces of Buddhist art to decorate the temples of their god-kings. The artists of Chenla, an inland state that rose to prominence and overran Funan in the 6th century, developed this artistic tradition, carving regal statues of Hindu and Buddhist deities.

The rise of the prosperous states of Srivijaya, and later dynasties in Malaysia and on the island of Java,

Above This Shan boy, whose head has been shaved as a mark of renunciation, is dressed in traditional Poi Sang Long costume. The festival to celebrate the ordination of novice monks is held in Mae Hong Son on Thailand's border with Burma.

in Indonesia, whose peoples built the monumental stupa of Borobudur, may have contributed to the demise of Chenla during the late 8th century. In its wake, a new Khmer kingdom arose in Cambodia. Khmer kings practised a form of Hinduism strongly influenced by Buddhism and ancient animistic religion. The 5th-century King Kondanna is said to have been a devout Buddhist, but Buddhism did not become firmly established in the Khmer empire until the 12th century.

At Angkor, the Khmer built a magnificent capital with thousands of temples, including Angkor Wat and the Bayon in Angkor Thom nearby. At its zenith, the Khmer empire spread across South-east Asia from southern Thailand and Laos to Vietnam, but it fell to invaders from Thailand in 1431. Angkor was abandoned to the jungle until the 19th century, when it was excavated by colonial archaeologists.

BUDDHISM TODAY

Cambodia, Laos and Vietnam came under 19th-century colonial rule as French Indo-China, and Burma, Malaysia and Singapore became British colonies, and Indonesia Dutch. Thailand escaped colonial domination thanks to the adroit diplomacy of its kings. South-east Asian people traditionally regarded their kings as semi-divine, and they ruled with the support of the sangha. Colonial powers imposed secular government, undermining the king's role and disestablishing the sangha. National sanghas were further weakened by occupation and dislocation during the wars of the 20th century, by military governments and dictatorships, and by communism. In order to survive in modern South-east Asia, Buddhism has had to adapt and to find a new role. This adaptation has taken a different form in each South-east Asian country.

Below Buddhists in Vianchang, Laos, donate food to monks on the morning alms round. Despite colonial rule, challenges from other religions, and communist and military regimes, South-east Asians continue to support the sangha.

MILITANT MONKS

MILITANCY IS NOT NORMALLY ASSOCIATED WITH BUDDHISM, BUT THROUGHOUT HISTORY, THERE HAVE BEEN THOSE FROM FANATICAL RELIGIOUS GROUPS, INCLUDING SECTS OF BUDDHISM, WHO HAVE SOMETIMES RESORTED TO VIOLENCE TO FULFILL THEIR OBJECTIVES.

An early example of militant Buddhism was the Ikko-ikki, a massive group of Buddhist fanatics, consisting of disorganized mobs of peasant farmers, monks and local nobles, whose stated aim was to overthrow Japan's feudalist government and spread the teachings of Jodo Shinshu Buddhism.

The Ikko-ikki believed that only total devotion to the Amida Buddha would bring salvation. In 1488, these fearless warrior monks, lightly armed and carrying banners inscribed with Buddhist slogans, overthrew the samurai rulers of Kaga province, a territory they subsequently held for 100 years. In 1528, they attacked Japan's capital, Kyoto. By 1570, they had become a major force in Japanese politics, posing both an economic and a political threat. Their militancy was finally extinguished by the samurai warlord,

Oda Nobunaga, who destroyed the fortress monastery of Mount Hiei in 1571 and the Ikko-ikki in 1580 after a long and bloody campaign.

THE BURMESE FIGHT FOR INDEPENDENCE

Buddhist monks played an important role in Burma's fight for independence from British colonial rule, which had been established in 1886. By the turn of the century, a nationalist movement began to take shape in the form of the Young Men's Buddhist Association (YMBA).

In the 1920s, two monks, U Ottama and U Seinda, were prominent political activists. U Seinda later led an armed rebellion against the British. U Ottama and another monk, U Wisara, were imprisoned by the British for several years, the latter dying in custody in 1929 after a 166-day hunger strike.

Above The gardens of Enryaku-ji in Japan belie the monastery's turbulent past. In 1571, the warlord Oda Nobunaga, determined to end the threat posed by the warlike Ikko-ikki, destroyed most of its buildings.

In December 1930, an anti-tax protest led by a Buddhist monk, Saya San, escalated into a national insurrection, known as the Galon rebellion. The rebels, armed only with spears and swords, and protected by charms they believed would make them invulnerable to bullets, defied the British for two years. Saya San was tried and executed, but the revolt had revealed the unpopularity of British rule.

A statue of U Wisara, the most prominent political martyr of Burmese Buddhism, stands near the Shwedagon pagoda, the holiest shrine in Burma (Myanmar), and was the rallying point for the huge demonstrations by Buddhist monks against the military dictatorship in the summer of 2007.

MILITANCY IN VIETNAM

In the 1960s, South Vietnamese Buddhist monks were involved in some of the most effective protests

Left Monks in Burma (Myanmar) have been increasingly involved in political protest since the 1920s. Here, Buddhist monks march through Rangoon in September 2007 to protest against the brutal military regime.

Above Monks stage a demonstration in Saigon, South Vietnam, to demand the resignation of President Thieu. Thich Tri Quang (far left), the most powerful Buddhist leader in South Vietnam, is credited with the overthrow of President Diem in November 1963.

against the anti-Buddhist policies of the country's Catholic president, Ngo Dinh Diem. The most extreme protests took place in 1963, when several monks set themselves on fire in Saigon. The horrific images of these self-immolations shocked the world.

From 1963 to 1965, the militant Buddhist movement was the primary cause of political instability in South Vietnam. Eventually, Buddhist opposition to the Saigon regime culminated in the expulsion of large numbers of Buddhist monks from the country.

RELIGIOUS CONFLICTS IN SRI LANKA

Militant Buddhism is now a major factor in Sri Lanka, which has long been plagued by ethnic tension between the minority Tamils and the majority Sinhalese. In 1983, this tension erupted into civil war. The conflict has a religious dimension in that most Sinhalese are Buddhist, while the Tamils are mostly either Muslim or Hindu.

Since the late 19th century, Sri Lanka has experienced the growth of a strand of militant Buddhism that is centred on the belief that the Buddha exhorted the Sinhalese people to make the island a stronghold for 'pure' Theravada Buddhism. This less tolerant type of Buddhism was inspired by the Sinhalese Buddhist activist and nationalist, Anagarika Dharmapala (1864–1933), pioneer in India of the Buddhist Revival Movement and pledged to the revival of Buddhism in Sri Lanka.

Christianity, which has been established in the country since the 16th century and is today followed by only 7 per cent of the population, is seen as an alien religion. It is viewed as 'the enemy within' – and also responsible for corrupting indigenous Sri Lankan culture. Christians are now facing persecution by Buddhists.

Numerous churches have either closed or been destroyed, and in some places Christians are forced to worship in secret. Employing tactics such as 'fasts unto death' and violence, Buddhist extremists have put pressure on the Sri Lankan government to pass laws that would ban religious conversions and establish Buddhism as the official state religion. Thus far, these attempts have not succeeded.

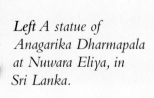

Left A statue of Anagarika Dharmapala at Nuwara Eliya, in Sri Lanka.

BUDDHISM IN BURMA

BUDDHISM HAS ENDURED IN BURMA (MYANMAR) FOR MORE THAN 2,000 YEARS. TODAY, DESPITE COLONIZATION AND REPRESSIVE MILITARY GOVERNMENTS, 90 PER CENT OF THE COUNTRY'S POPULATION FOLLOWS THE THERAVADA BUDDHIST TRADITION.

The Shwedagon pagoda glitters from the Singuttara Hill overlooking Rangoon, where eight hairs of the Buddha and relics of three of his predecessors are believed to be enshrined. The present structure, the latest of many, was built during the 14th–15th centuries, but it has since suffered earthquake damage and been rebuilt, refurbished, replastered and regilded countless times. The Shwedagon represents the graceful, mature form of the Burmese stupa, in which the *anda* (dome), *harmika* (platform) and *chattra* (parasol) curve up to a tall, tapering spire.

BAGAN

During the 800s, the Burman (Bamar) people took over the city-states built by their predecessors, the Pyu, and founded the kingdom of Bagan. The Burmans were influenced by Pyu belief in Ari Buddhism, which combines Mahayana Buddhism, Hinduism and the worship of *nats* – deities of trees, animals and the ghostly spirits of people.

In 1044, King Anawrahta seized the Bagan throne, and in 1057, he conquered Thaton, capital of the Mon kingdom of Dvaravati, which extended across Burma and Thailand. The Mon were Theravada Buddhists and Anawrahta, a Theravada convert, famously transported their king, his retinue of educated monks, the Thaton copy of the Pali Tripitaka and skilled craftsmen to Bagan. He founded monasteries and pagodas, so that Bagan became a centre of Theravada study, attracting Buddhist monks from India, Sri Lanka, Thailand and the Khmer kingdom.

BUDDHIST DYNASTIES

By the 13th century, Bagan's political power extended deep into South-east Asia, but in 1287,

Above Burmese Buddha statues are traditionally depicted with open eyes. This seated Buddha is in the Dharmikarama Burmese temple in Penang, Malaysia.

the Mongols invaded the kingdom, which split into smaller states. The Shan – descendants of migrants from the north who had embraced Buddhism – gained power in the northern regions and, during the 14th century, they founded a capital at Ava, near modern Mandalay. Earthquakes have reduced Ava's palaces and monasteries to ruins, but Burmese literature, which flowered under the Ava kings, survives. Monks composed classic accounts of the Jataka Tales and the history of Buddhism in verse.

Tradition says that Pegu (now Bago), capital of an ancient southern kingdom, was originally founded in the 6th century by two Mon princes from Thaton.

Left The graceful 12th-century Ananda temple (top middle), Burma's architectural masterpiece, dominates Bagan's skyline. The temple buildings rise in a unified composition from their square plinth to a round central dome and spire.

Right The beautiful Shwedagon in Rangoon is the most sacred pagoda in Burma (Myanmar). The dome and 99m (325ft) spire are covered in gold leaf, the parasol is decorated with diamonds and rubies, and the tip of the finial is a huge diamond.

Mon kings endowed Pegu's 8th-century Shwemawdaw pagoda with its soaring, 88m (289ft) spire, and the 10th-century temple where the colossal Shwethalyaung Buddha reclines, open-eyed.

The devout Baña Thau, a queen of a later dynasty, had the Shwedagon pagoda gilded with her own weight in gold leaf. In 1460, she renounced her throne for the religious life, appointing a monk, Dhammazedi, to succeed her. As king, he reformed and unified the sangha.

From 1544, Burman kings reunited Burma and expanded its frontiers, conquering Ayutthaya in 1766 and invading India in 1824. This brought Burma into conflict with the British, who annexed and conquered the country and, in 1886, made it a province of India.

POLITICIZED MONKS

The British took a neutral position on religion, but imposed a secular government on Burma. Since the traditional political role of the sangha had been to support and legitimize the monarch, the result was that the sangha also lost political support and legal protection in turn.

The effect of this policy was effectively to unravel the cohesion of Burmese society and pull apart its sense of what it meant to be Burmese. However, out of the people's struggle to adjust to their loss of nationhood, a foreign cultural presence and precipitous modernization, Buddhism re-emerged in the early 20th century as a unifying force. The British had prohibited nationalist organizations, but the Burmese formed them, under the guise of permitted religious associations.

Independence followed World War II, in 1948, and Burma's first Prime Minister, U Nu, attempted to restore Buddhism and the sangha to their former authoritative position. In 1962, however, the military established a dictatorship, and again cut the sangha out of political affairs.

The regime set up monastic councils through which it succeeded for years in controlling monks and suppressing their political activism, until, on 8 August 1988, decades of political and economic mismanagement culminated in a nationwide uprising. Many monks became victims of the brutal suppression that followed.

Since the '8888 Uprising', an estimated 60 per cent of monks in Burma (Myanmar) have actively supported democratic protest, and

Right King Mindon, who built the royal city of Mandalay in the late 19th century, revived the female sangha. Today there are many nunneries in the north-east, but Burmese nuns do not have full bhikkhuni status.

some scholars interpret their public support for democracy as evidence of a new role for the sangha. Monks are revered in Burma (Myanmar) for their moral strength and wisdom, so their support for democracy lends it legitimacy. Since 1988, they have taken a defiant role in protests against worsening economic conditions, and this is widely seen as a condemnation of the military junta's policies.

It is striking to note, when reviewing the development of Buddhism in Burma, that in a nation that has endured so much strife and hardship in recent history, the practice of Buddhism serves as a strong and uniting force.

BUDDHISM IN THAILAND

THAILAND HAS BEEN A BUDDHIST KINGDOM SINCE ITS FOUNDATION IN THE 13TH CENTURY. TODAY, THAILAND IS A CONSTITUTIONAL MONARCHY AND BUDDHISM IS NO LONGER THE STATE RELIGION, BUT 96 PER CENT OF THAI PEOPLE ARE BUDDHISTS.

The waning of Khmer power during the 13th century was an impetus to Thai-speaking people who, over the previous 200 years, had migrated southward to the north-western fringes of the Angkor empire to settle in the central and southern regions of what is now Thailand. Tradition states 1238 as the date when an alliance of Thai chiefdoms captured the Khmer town of Sukhothai in north-western Thailand and made it the capital of a new kingdom. Further north, a second Thai kingdom, Lanna, was founded at the end of the 13th century, with Chiang Mai as its capital.

SUKHOTHAI

Shamanism had been the main religion of the migrating Thai, who had also assimilated elements of Buddhism from the Chinese,

Above This 14th-century bronze 'Buddha at the moment of Victory' has the elongated features and sinuous hands of the classic Sukhothai style.

the Mon people of Burma and Thailand, and the Khmer. From the late 11th century, Theravada Buddhism spread into Thailand from Burma and was adopted by Indraditya, Sukhothai's first king, who sought to impose unity by making it the state religion.

An informal relationship of mutual support evolved in the Thai city-states between monarch and monks. The kings sponsored the building of stupas and founded and supported monasteries and, in return, gained moral legitimacy through the monks' support. Indraditya sponsored Wat Mahathat in Sukhothai to enshrine relics of the Buddha, and his successors extended the Wat and donated its colossal Buddha images.

A promoter of Buddhism, King Rama Khamheng of Sukhothai (1279–c.1300) is remembered for

Left Wat Phra That Haripunchai in Lamphun, former capital of the Mon kingdom of Haripunchai, was built in 1044 on the ruins of the palace of Chamadevi, a Mon queen. The chattra (parasol) is made of gold.

his benign rule. An inscription records that he installed a bell outside his palace gates for subjects to strike if they needed help. He is credited with designing the Thai alphabet. His reign was an age of expansion of the kingdom of Sukhothai into Burma, Laos and the Malay peninsula, and the beginning of the classic age of Thai culture. During the 14th century, bhikkhus from Sri Lanka were invited to reform Buddhist teaching and practice in Sukhothai and promote the Theravada tradition.

Drawing on influences from India, China, the Mon and the Khmer, Sukhothai architects and artists created a style that became a classic. The dagobas of Sri Lanka inspired the Thai chedi (stupa) with its soaring spire and lotus-bud finial. Sukhothai builders followed the Mon building tradition of brick with stucco decoration. Interior walls were painted with scenes from the Buddha's life, using a limited palette of colours – red, black, white, gold and blue-green pigments. Thai artists mastered large-scale bronze-casting and produced graceful Buddha images, seated and walking, displaying elongated, sinuous hands and a flamelike *ushnisha,* or protruberance, on the crown of the head. They carved stone statues in the round, representing the clothing with a line or fold.

AYUTTHAYA

In the mid-14th century, Sukhothai became a vassal state of the new kingdom of Ayutthaya. Founded in the fertile Chao

Right Buddhists honour the Buddha with light, symbolizing enlightenment, at the Loy Krathong festival in November. These monks launch a paper lantern, using a torch to heat the air, and light firecrackers as it rises.

Above Ayutthaya, capital of an empire founded in 1350, was sacked by the Burmese in 1767. The ruins of its great brick temples, built, Khmer style, with high stupa towers (prangs), were the forerunners of the Thai pagoda.

Phraya basin, it grew prosperous and forged a commercial empire that traded with India, China, Japan, Persia and western nations, such as Portugal, France, Holland and England. Ayutthaya's rulers distanced themselves from their people, governing from behind a screen of ritual, retinue and courtly language. They declared

themselves *dhammaraja* (righteous rulers), who exercised absolute authority over their subjects and imposed a strict social hierarchy, from princes down to slaves, and they maintained tight control over monastic practices.

Ayutthaya flourished until 1767, when it fell to an invading Burmese army. Thailand was reunited under a new dynasty of Chakri kings, who founded a new capital at Bangkok and expelled the Burmese.

MODERNIZING MONKS

The remarkable King Mongkut, who inherited the throne in 1851, had been a Buddhist monk since 1824 and had founded a reformed sect called the Thammayut ('those adhering to the doctrine'). His influence cleared the path for the formation of a sangha, a national body of monks. As king, he deconstructed the monarch's quasi-divine status, discouraged slavery, elevated the status of women and children, introduced public health reforms and established beneficial relations with Western powers, enabling Thailand to avoid colonization. His liberal modernization policies, continued by his successors, paved the way for the later re-organization of government and the successful transition to democracy under a constitutional monarchy after 1973.

Today, Buddhist monks, though banned under the constitution from taking political office, play a vigorous and often controversial part in Thailand's political system, addressing poverty, prostitution, drug addiction, AIDS and environmental damage, and resisting what they see as the erosion of moral and religious values in society. In recent years, there have been efforts to overcome religious and political resistance to the establishment of a women's sangha.

AYUTTHAYA

AT ITS IMPERIAL ZENITH DURING THE 17TH CENTURY, THE ISLAND CITY OF AYUTTHAYA CONTAINED MORE THAN 100 TEMPLES. ITS ART AND ARCHITECTURE EVOLVED INTO NEW FORMS INFLUENCED BY THE HISTORIC CULTURES OF THE KHMER AND THE MON.

Above In 1957, archaeologists found a chamber filled with relics and valuable antiquities secreted in the crypt of Wat Ratchaburana's prong, or stupa tower. Its walls were covered in paintings mainly in red, black and white.

Around 1350, a prince from the city of U Thong, capital of a kingdom on the edge of Thailand's central plain, is said to have fled to a monastery at the confluence of the Chao Phraya, Pasak and Lopburi rivers to escape a plague. There he founded the capital of a new state, naming it Ayutthaya after the Hindu god Rama's legendary city described in the *Ramayana*. His city, which he ruled as Ramathibodhi I, would become the capital of a great sea-trading empire that would endure for four centuries, extend north to China and south to engulf Malaysia, and trade with Europe, whose greatest cities it rivalled in magnificence.

TEMPLE BUILDINGS

In his new capital, King Ramathibodhi ordered the building of a royal palace and a temple, Wat Buddhasawan, with a high *prang*, or stupa tower, in classic Khmer style. On the king's death in 1369, Wat Phra Ram was built as his funerary temple.

A *wat* is a group of temple buildings, enclosed by a wall pierced by gateways. Important buildings were the *bot*, the Thai form of the Indian pillared *chaitya*, or assembly hall, with a Buddha statue on a high pedestal, and the vihara, or image hall. These structures were built in laterite, a clay found underground that hardens on exposure to air, and later restored with brick and stucco. The interiors were whitewashed and decorated with stucco, murals, mosaics and gilding. The 14th-century *bot* of Wat Suwan Dararam has a central dip characteristic of the early style, and its supporting pillars are beautifully carved.

MONUMENTS FOR MONARCHS

Ayutthaya's 33 kings were absolute rulers and semi-divine. Patrons of Buddhism, they founded new palaces, pavilions and temples, which reflected changes in architecture and decoration. Their funerary chedis – stupas they built for themselves – were raised on a cylindrical or bell-shaped shrine, which often contained a relic chamber. The group of three chedis of Wat Phra Sri Samphet, each pierced by a porch and three

Below Wat Ratchaburana's restored prang, or stupa tower, built in 1424 and seen here through the gateway of the temple's chaitya, or assembly hall, is characteristically tall with a domed roof. The tower is embellished with carvings of folded lotus leaves.

niches with Buddha images, is almost a symbol of Ayutthaya. The forerunners of the typical Thai pagoda with its characteristic inward curve and tall, slender *chattra* (parasol) can be seen in these early stupas at Ayutthaya.

To reflect Ayutthaya's expanding empire and foreign influence, its buildings grew tall and monumental in scale. The restored towers of Wat Chai Watthanaram today soar impressively high above the lacustrine landscape. This temple in quincunx (having a central *prang* and four chedis forming an X-shape) was founded in 1630 as a royal monastery for Buddhist ceremonial.

The *prang* is a stupa tower that developed from the corner tower of the Khmer temple. During the Ayutthaya period, it grew taller, its elliptical shape becoming more streamlined, as at Wat Chai Watthanaram. However, the huge main *prang* of the early Wat Mahathat (temple of the Great Relic), built to house relics of the Buddha, has collapsed several times since it was built in 1374, and remains a huge brick ruin.

Above These chedis at Wat Mahathat, built around 1374, have the bell shape, the lotus-bud spire and the brick and stucco structure of the Sukhothai style, which influenced earlier buildings at Ayutthaya.

The architectural innovation that allowed increased height was the redented wall: the corners of the tower are cut back into a series of indented right angles. The indentations strengthen the structure (a cylinder of pleated paper standing on one end is stronger than a cylinder of smooth paper). The redentions buttress the wall so that it can be built higher, and the vertical lines of the redented brickwork carry the eye upward, so emphasizing the tower's height. Hidden chambers found in the domes and vaults of some of these *prangs* have contained sacred relics and treasures.

Conflict with Burma dogged Ayutthaya's kings until, in 1767, the Burmese captured the city after a long siege, deposed the rulers, and looted, burned and destroyed the city, killing and enslaving most of its one million citizens. Ayutthaya never recovered. Today, however, the ruins are a UNESCO World Heritage Site, and are gradually being rebuilt and restored to some of Ayutthaya's former magnificence.

Below Wat Chai Watthanaram was a royal monastery built in 1630 and recently restored. The central prang – *a representation of Mount Meru, the centre of the universe – has the redented (cut-back) corners of the Ayutthaya style, which enhance its height.*

BUDDHISM IN LAOS

MOST OF THE HISTORY OF LANDLOCKED LAOS IS A STORY OF DOMINATION BY NEIGHBOURING POWERS, YET DESPITE INVASION, WAR AND DECADES AS A COMMUNIST STATE, AN ESTIMATED 65 PER CENT OF LAOS'S 6.5 MILLION PEOPLE ARE BUDDHISTS TODAY.

The Lao people settled in the region that is now Laos round the 9th century CE. Like the Thai, they had migrated in small groups from Nanchao in modern Yunnan, China, where they had absorbed Mahayana Buddhism from the Chinese. In Laos, they came into contact with Theravada Buddhist ideas from the Mon people, who had spread east from Burma. Elements of Buddhism also reached the Lao through the Khmer, whose empire extended into what is now southern Laos. Buddhist remains

Below Wat Xieng Thong in Luang Prabang was founded in 1560 by King Setthathirath. The tree of life mosaic on the back of the temple was made by Lao craftsmen in 1960, in coloured glass on a red background.

have been excavated at Wat Phu, an ancient Khmer temple in Champasak province, that predate the civilization of Angkor.

THE KINGDOM OF LAN XANG

Large areas of Laos were part of the kingdom of Sukhothai until the mid-14th century. In 1349, Fa Ngum, a prince of a city in northern Laos, and the son-in-law of a Khmer king, raised an army and conquered territories extending north to China, east to Vietnam and west into the Isan region of north-eastern Thailand. In 1354, he was crowned king of this new realm, which he called Lan Xang, 'Land of 1,000 Elephants'.

Lan Xang was the early kingdom of Laos, and it probably extended south as far as modern

Above Hundreds of ceramic and gilded Buddha statues line the cloister wall of Wat Si Saket in Vianchang. This temple was built in 1818 with ornate roofs and stupas in the Siamese style.

Thakhek. Fa Ngum renamed his capital Luang Prabang, and he made Buddhism the state religion.

Early in the 16th century, King Photisarath I attempted to purify Buddhism in Lan Xang of animistic and Brahmanic elements. His son, Setthathirath, moved the capital to Vianchang in 1563, from where, in 1570, he defended his kingdom against invasions from Burma. Setthathirath built monasteries and temples, notably Wat Phra Keo to house the Emerald Buddha, a gift from the king of Sri Lanka, and That Luang, both in Vianchang, and Wat Xieng Thong in Luang Prabang.

Suriya Vongsa, a 17th-century ruler of Lan Xang, was the kingdom's most devout Buddhist, famous for rejecting luxury and living simply. He embodied the Laotian ideal of kingship: through their moral lives and beneficent actions, kings were believed to accumulate the good karma they required to be reborn into the

royal line. His kingdom became prosperous through international trade, and monks travelled from all over South-east Asia to study at the monasteries of Vianchang.

Suriya Vongsa was Lan Xang's last monarch, and his death presaged a period of almost fatal decline for Buddhism in Laos. He died childless, and his kingdom became a vassal of Thailand. In 1827, in retaliation against a rebellion, Thai armies sacked and destroyed Vianchang, so that little more than the That Luang stupa remained of the city.

DECLINE OF THE SANGHA

In 1893, Laos became a colony of France, whose administrators steadily undermined the authority and role of the sangha. Monks had previously been accorded honour and status and had advised and supported the monarch. Now, French rule aimed to separate sangha and state and replace Laotian law and practice with French law and education.

After World War II, Laos won independence and Buddhism was re-established as the state religion.

Below At the start of the Pha That Luang festival, held in Vianchang each November, monks walk from the sacred That Luang stupa to make offerings at Wat Si Muang, a temple that enshrines the city's foundation pillar.

ISAN

Laos is the least populated South-east Asian country, and about one-third of its people belong to ethnic minorities, many of them hill tribes. There are small Lao communities in neighbouring Cambodia and Vietnam, but the largest Lao population – 20 million people of Lao origin – live in neighbouring Isan, the north-eastern province of Thailand, which borders Laos and Cambodia. Isan was once part of the kingdom of Lan Xang and has been dominated alternately by Thailand and Laos at many points in its history. The people speak a dialect of Lao, which, until recently, they wrote in the Lao script. The people are traditionally Theravada Buddhists, but, as in Laos, many hold animistic beliefs.

Laos and Isan share numerous cultural affinities, including: their dress, characterised by the traditional sarong; their cuisine, which is based around sticky rice and includes insects and grubs as delicacies; their festivals such as Prapheni Bun Bang Fai (a rocket festival); and their architectural and artistic traditions.

However, the newly formed state was beset by rivalry between the Pathet Lao, a communist nationalist political movement, and the USA for domination of the government. This struggle for influence intensified as officially neutral Laos became embroiled in the Vietnam conflict.

Thousands of Buddhist monks fled to Thailand and the West after December 1975, when the Pathet Lao overthrew the monarchy and government and set up the Lao People's Democratic Republic. While those that remained continued to play a role in state ceremonies, the Pathet Lao rigidly controlled their activities. They forced the sangha to promote party policies at a national level and, through education, to the masses.

Yet so strongly is the national identity of the Laotian people invested in Buddhism, that they resisted the regime's efforts to suppress religion, and since the late 1980s, support for the sangha has surged. Party control continues, but it has relaxed. Today, not only the masses but also many communist leaders are Buddhists.

Below Laotian monks offer thanks for donations from lay followers at the beginning of their rainy season retreat. During this time, they retire into their monasteries for a three-month period of meditation and study.

BUDDHISM IN CAMBODIA

OVER THE CENTURIES, BUDDHISM IN CAMBODIA HAS SURVIVED
ATTACK FROM BRAHMANIC KINGS, CHRISTIAN MISSIONARIES AND,
DURING THE 1970s, THE COMMUNIST KHMER ROUGE. TODAY,
THE SANGHA IS STRUGGLING TO RE-ESTABLISH ITSELF.

Most of the kings of Cambodia's Khmer civilization, which arose during the 9th century CE and grew to dominate South-east Asia, worshipped ancestral deities and Hindu gods. The tide of religious belief turned after 1181, when Jayavarman VII took the throne. In 1178, when he was in his 60s, Jayavarman raised an army to defeat invaders from the Vietnamese kingdom of Champa, who had sacked the Khmer capital and assassinated the monarch. After his coronation, he made Buddhism the state religion.

Below The faces carved into the great towers of the Bayon, the temple at the centre of Angkor Thom, are believed to represent King Jayavarman VII, god-king and founder of the temple complex, as a bodhisattva.

Jayavarman VII emulated the Mauryan emperor Ashoka in building and endowing 121 rest houses for pilgrims along the roads of his kingdom, as well as 102 hospitals, and many reservoirs, monasteries and temples. He rebuilt the great temple-city of Angkor Wat and founded a new city, Angkor Thom, nearby. This complex structure is covered in magnificent relief sculptures depicting life in 12th-century Cambodia, and the central shrine was once gilded.

THE DECLINE OF THE KHMER EMPIRE

Many of Jayavarman VII's temples were defaced after 1244 by Jayavarman VIII, a Hindu who destroyed Buddhist temples, or turned them into temples

Above From a boat on a lake near Phnom Penh, Buddhist monks, watched by villagers, make offerings to lok yeay sar (animist spirits) to ask for protection. They perform this ancient ceremony on the day after the annual Pchum Ben festival.

dedicated to Shiva. Many more have suffered from neglect. Yet some of Jayavarman's greatest temple complexes – Angkor Thom and Banteay Chmar in the far north-west – have survived.

The Khmer empire ended after a long siege of the capital, raised in 1430 by the armies of Ayutthaya. The conquering armies removed Buddhist statues to Ayutthaya, and Angkor Wat was abandoned to the jungle.

The Mahayana tradition, which was established in Cambodia as early as the 5th century CE, co-existed with Brahmanic beliefs before the reign of Jayavarman VII, and it continues in Cambodia today. After the demise of Buddhism in India, however, a reformed and dynamic Theravada tradition spread to Cambodia from Sri Lanka and became deeply embedded in Cambodian society from palace to village level.

Above The Buddhist stupa at Choeung Ek was raised on the site of the Killing Fields south of Phnom Penh. The glass-sided stupa contains more than 5,000 human skulls of some of the 17,000 people – monks, as well as lay Buddhists – who were executed by the Khmer Rouge.

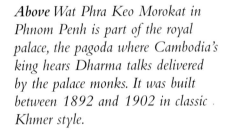

Above Wat Phra Keo Morokat in Phnom Penh is part of the royal palace, the pagoda where Cambodia's king hears Dharma talks delivered by the palace monks. It was built between 1892 and 1902 in classic Khmer style.

From the 15th to the 19th centuries, Cambodia became a pawn in struggles for hegemony between neighbouring Thai and Vietnamese kingdoms. In 1863, in a move to prevent the break-up of his kingdom, King Norodom transferred it to French colonial rule.

The population resisted conversion to foreign religions during the colonial era. King Norodom, who had studied Buddhist scriptures in Bangkok, established a national sangha, headed by the senior monk of the established Mohanikay order. However, in 1863, he established the reformist Thommayut order from Thailand in Cambodia's new capital, Phnom Penh. This division persisted: the Thommayut order, stricter in its observance of the monastic rule, remained small, modernized, patronized by the aristocracy and centred mainly on

the capital, while the larger, traditional Mohanikay order was influential in the villages, where the *wat*, or temple-monastery, traditionally provides primary education, health and social care.

The first king of an independent Cambodia was Sihanouk, who ascended the throne in 1941 and led the country to independence in 1953. However, he abdicated in 1955 to launch a Buddhist socialist party, which promoted Buddhist principles, such as charity toward the poor and the endowment of monasteries as meritorious acts. Monastic education, in particular, benefited from these policies after the party won power in 1955.

Numbers of concerned monks took part in demonstrations against the French during the colonial era and against the occupying Japanese during World War II. In 1970, Sihanouk was deposed in a republican coup. The leaders of the new republic sought to win the sangha's support in combating the growing influence of the communist Khmer Rouge. A few monks responded, speaking out in favour of nationalism and democratic republicanism. The Khmer Rouge, whose influence was

growing, targeted Buddhism, criticized the economically unproductive sangha and began recruiting monks.

THE DARK DAYS OF THE KHMER ROUGE

In 1975, the Khmer Rouge seized control of Cambodia. As part of its attempt to restructure society, it suppressed Buddhism. Monks were defrocked and forced into agriculture and military service, lay support was discouraged, almost all monasteries were closed and many ransacked for building materials, images were defaced and libraries destroyed, their palm-leaf manuscripts used to roll cigarettes. Later calculations suggest that around 20 per cent of an estimated 60,000 monks in Cambodia died or were executed by the regime.

The Khmer Rouge were defeated by the Vietnamese in 1979. Since then, the sangha has struggled to re-establish itself and to minister to the Cambodian people, who retained faith in Buddhism throughout their horrific recent history. Today, 95 per cent of Cambodians declare themselves Buddhists.

ANGKOR THOM

UNKNOWN IN THE WEST UNTIL ITS 'DISCOVERY' IN THE MID-NINETEENTH CENTURY, THE VAST TEMPLE COMPLEX IN NORTH-WESTERN CAMBODIA IS ALL THAT REMAINS OF A VANISHED CIVILIZATION. AT ITS HEART LIES THE GREAT CITY OF ANGKOR THOM.

Rumours of a mythical lost city in Cambodia had filtered through to the outside world for many years before a French naturalist parted the jungle creepers and found himself gazing upon the ruins of Angkor Wat, a magnificent temple of sculptured stone.

Built by the Hindu king Suryavarman II in the early 12th century, Angkor Wat is just one building in a vast complex of structures that constituted the capital of the Khmers of Cambodia, who dominated the Indo-China peninsula from the 9th to the 15th century. Recent research, aided by satellite photographs, has shown that Angkor was once the largest pre-industrial city in the world, with an urban sprawl of nearly 3,000 square kilometres (1,160 square miles).

CULT OF THE GOD-KING

The most characteristic feature of the Khmer civilization was its cult of the god-king, who was seen as the lord of life and the source of all blessings. The temple was both his abode as a god and his shrine as a king. Each Khmer monarch constructed his own temple, resulting in a building programme that lasted some 500 years.

The temples consisted of a complex arrangement of walls, moats and bridges that surrounded a raised platform, usually with five towers to represent the five peaks of Mount Meru, home of the gods. A single sanctuary, housing cult images of deified ancestors, further linked the king and his family with the divine.

The wealth of the Khmers depended above all on water. In a region that suffers from a six-month dry season, successful irrigation was essential for the population's survival, especially one for which rice was the staple diet. Fed by water from the Siem Reap River, an intricate network of canals, reservoirs and irrigation ditches was built. One canal, some

Above From one of the five entrance gateways into Angkor Thom, the giant masks of the god-king Jayavarman VII look toward the four points of the compass. The gates were approached by broad causeways lined with giant figures of the gods.

65km (40 miles) long, is almost perfectly straight, proof of the extraordinary skill of the engineers who built it.

JAYAVARMAN VII AND THE BAYON

Angkor Thom (Khmer for the 'great city') was built by Jayavarman VII, a devout Mahayana Buddhist, who reigned from 1181 to c.1220. It is surrounded by a moat 90m (295ft) wide and 16km (10 miles) long. To the east and west, two vast reservoirs, or *barays*, once held 1 billion gallons of water.

At the exact centre of Angkor Thom stands the Bayon, representing Mount Meru, the only Buddhist temple-mountain in Cambodia. The Bayon's 54 towers are decorated with more than 200 monumental faces. These faces, with their mystical aura and enigmatic smiles, are thought to be idealized portraits of Jayavarman VII himself, depicted as the incarnation of the Avalokiteshvara, the compassionate 'Lord of the Worlds'. The great towers at the entrance gates to Angkor Thom feature these same enormous heads with their silent gaze and haunting expression.

Left The great builder-king, Jayavarman VII, sits with legs crossed and eyes downcast in imitation of the meditating Buddha. Angkor Thom reached its zenith under this Buddhist king's rule.

Along its many galleries and terraces, bas-reliefs record the sacred myths and daily lives of the Khmers. The magnificent Royal Terrace is decorated with a 900m (2,953ft) long frieze of life-size elephants. Another bas-relief, carved with exquisite care and humour, shows a group of Khmers enjoying a cockfight. Many of the rough stone surfaces of the Bayon were once painted and gilded, the wooden doors enriched with elaborate decoration.

Bas-reliefs depicting countless scenes of warfare bear witness to the frequent battles between the Khmers and their enemies. In 1177, the Chams, a maritime nation from the east coast of the Indo-China peninsula, sailed up the Mekong, took the Khmers by surprise and sacked Angkor.

Jayavarman VII finally drove them out. The king not only repulsed the Khmer's enemies but extended his kingdom and its culture throughout the Indo-China peninsula. Temples, reservoirs, roads and hospitals were constructed in the most intensive building programme in Khmer history. The Bayon is the summit and symbol of his achievements.

THE COLLAPSE OF ANGKOR

Around 1431, Angkor was sacked by Thai invaders and abandoned. Factors other than war, such as climate change, bubonic plague, or the rise of Theravada Buddhism, have been suggested for its rapid decline and collapse. Whatever the causes, the city lay dormant for centuries, fighting a losing battle with the encroaching jungle.

Above A superbly carved bas-relief in the Bayon shows a Khmer warrior, armed with a spear and mounted on his war elephant. He is accompanied by foot soldiers; one carries a standard, another a huge ceremonial parasol.

Below A view of Angkor Thom, or the 'great city', shows the many face-towers of the Bayon. The central group of towers was identified with Mount Meru, centre of the Buddhist universe.

BUDDHISM IN VIETNAM

WHILE THERAVADA BUDDHISM IS THE RELIGION OF BURMA (MYANMAR), THAILAND AND CAMBODIA, VIETNAM IS DIFFERENT: ITS NORTHERN BORDER WITH CHINA HAS ENSURED THAT CHINESE MAHAYANA SCHOOLS HAVE HAD THE GREATEST INFLUENCE THERE.

Above State oppression of Buddhism has been a reality of Vietnamese life since 1975. Today, 80 per cent of Vietnamese people do not profess a religion and only about half of the remainder are Buddhists.

In 111BCE, Chinese armies invaded and conquered the Red River delta on the Gulf of Tonkin. For the next 1,000 years, while Indian culture and Theravada Buddhism from Sri Lanka spread across most of South-east Asia, China shaped and dominated the politics and culture of northern Vietnam.

Nevertheless, monks from India reached northern Vietnam early in its history. At the beginning of the 1st century CE, the Han dynasty Chinese founded a vassal state in the Red River delta, which they called Jiaozhi ('South China'). Its capital, Luy Lau, was on a major India–China trade route. Merchants and missionaries, among them Theravada bhikkhus from India and Sri Lanka, took the sea route through the Strait of Melaka to land on the Jiaozhi coast. Before travelling on to Yunnan and Luoyang, the missionaries would reside in the many pagoda-monasteries in Luy Lau, which became a celebrated Buddhist centre for the translation of Pali texts into Chinese.

CHAMPA

From the late 2nd century CE, the Chams, a sea-trading people who were descended from the ancient inhabitants of central Vietnam, founded the kingdom of Champa.

In time, Champa grew to occupy central and southern Vietnam and parts of what are now Laos and Cambodia.

The worship of the Brahmanic god Shiva was the main religion of the Chams, whose temples were influenced by Indian Hindu architecture like that of the Khmers. Buddhist influences are evident, however, in the sculptures on their great temple-towers, which were built as expressions of the divine nature of their god-kings.

In 875, King Indravarman II founded a new dynasty at Indrapura (modern Quang Nam) in the north, and adopted Mahayana Buddhism. There he founded the monastery of Dong Duong, the central temple of which, was dedicated to the bodhisattva Avalokiteshvara. After the 12th century, Champa came increasingly into conflict with the Khmer empire and with the expansionist Dai Viet kingdom in the north and, during the 13th century, with the Mongol (Yuan) rulers of China.

Below Building 'B5', far right, is the storehouse of a Hindu temple built during the 10th century in My Son (Quang Doc province), capital of the kingdom of Champa. Pali inscriptions and Buddhist deities are carved on stelae (funerary monuments) at the site.

THE GOLDEN AGE OF BUDDHISM

The kingdom of Dai Viet ('Great Viet') was founded under the Ly dynasty (1010–1225). The Ly held back the Chinese and wrested territories from Champa. The Tran dynasty, which followed it (1225–1400), resisted invasions by the Mongols and expanded the frontiers of their kingdom.

The Ly rulers made Buddhism their state religion, and appointed monks to political office, while also supporting Confucianism, Daoism and the people's centuries-old animistic beliefs. The One-pillar pagoda in Hanoi, a classic of Vietnamese architecture, is one of many founded during this era of Buddhist ascendance. It was endowed by Emperor Ly Thai Tong in 1049 and built on one pillar (originally of wood, now of concrete) driven into the centre of a lotus pond.

During this period, Chan Buddhism, brought to Dai Viet by Chinese Chan masters, along with the Pure Land sect, was the dominant Buddhist school. Some Tran dynasty kings were ordained as monks. Tran Nhan Tong, a Buddhist scholar, reigned for ten years from 1388, until he abdicated for the monastic life. He founded Truc Lam, the first Vietnamese Chan sect.

DECLINE AND REVIVAL

As Dai Viet expanded southward from the 15th century, annexing parts of Champa and the Khmer empire, Confucianism gained prominence at Court. During the Le dynasty (1428–1788), Confucianism became the state ideology, and Buddhism went into decline – although some later rulers attempted to revive it, renovating pagodas and stupas and building monasteries in newly acquired territories. The

Above Quan Am (Guanyin, Bodhisattva of Compassion and the female form of Avalokiteshvara), is revered by Vietnamese Buddhists. This wood carving of Quan Am was made in 1657 for a pagoda in Bac Ninh province, northern Vietnam.

Theravada tradition penetrated the state's southern territories through contact with the Khmer.

Between 1859 and 1885, the French gradually colonized Vietnam and eventually made it part of French Indochina, along with Cambodia and Laos. Colonial power excluded the sangha from government, but in Vietnam, Buddhist pagodas and monasteries continued to function at a village level, supported by local lay followers and even the ruling elites. Buddhists also led local uprisings against French occupation.

During the early decades of the 20th century, a revival of Buddhism was cut short by prolonged wars and by partition.

Buddhism was suppressed by the communists in North Vietnam, and, in the southern Republic of Vietnam, by the policies of the first president, the Roman Catholic Ngo Dinh Diem. It was in protest against Diem's promotion of Catholicism that six Buddhist monks and one nun publicly burned themselves to death during the 1960s.

Buddhism survives in post-1975, reunified Vietnam, but it has not regained its former prominence. Observers have reported some persecution of monks and nuns – and of members of syncretic movements, such as the Cao Dai, which merge elements of Buddhism with other religious beliefs. However, in 1986, state controls were relaxed and new religious freedoms have permitted a modest resurgence of Buddhism.

Below Thien Mu pagoda in Hué, Vietnam's southern capital during the 18th century, is in classic Chinese style, octagonal with seven storeys. The Thien Mu monastery was founded in 1601, during a period of Buddhist revival, and its pagoda was built in 1844.

BUDDHISM IN MALAYSIA AND INDONESIA

EARLY IN THE 1ST MILLENNIUM, TRADE BROUGHT BUDDHISM TO THE MALAYSIAN PENINSULA AND INDONESIA'S ARCHIPELAGOS. A THOUSAND YEARS LATER, MUSLIM TRADERS ARRIVED IN THE COASTAL REGION. TODAY, ALMOST 90 PER CENT OF INDONESIANS ARE MUSLIMS.

Above Around 500 Buddha statues sit on Borobudur's upper terraces, 72 of them seated inside bell-shaped stone stupas of carved latticework.

By the early centuries of the Common Era, a busy sea-trading network had grown up between India, South-east Asia, China and the myriad islands of what is now Indonesia. Along with their cargoes of rice, spices and rare woods, merchants carried religious ideas and philosophies, and sometimes Hindu priests and Buddhist monks.

In 414, they carried a Chinese pilgrim, Faxian, across the Indian Ocean on his return to China. His ship was wrecked on a small island off the coase of Sumatra and he spent several months in Java, where Buddhist ideas were already becoming established.

Below Indonesian bhikkhus complete a circumambulation of the great monument of Borobudur in a ceremony to celebrate Buddha Day.

SRIVIJAYA

During the 5th century, a state called Srivijaya arose on a wave of new trade passing through the Straits of Melaka situated between the island of Sumatra and the Malay peninsula. Srivijaya, a loose confederacy, may have been the first major state in the Indonesian archipelago. During the 8th century, it ruled Sumatra, the Malay peninsula and western Java.

The Srivijayans were ship-builders and navigators, traders and travellers, and Sumatra became a way-station for Buddhist monks making the long, dangerous sea journey between India and China. Foreigners from Persia, Nalanda, Canton, Angkor and neighbouring islands, many of whom were Buddhist scholars, thronged its cities. A Chinese pilgrim who visited the state in 671, described it as a place of Mahayana learning.

Srivijaya survived for six centuries, but the decline of the China trade was a major factor in its demise.

BOROBUDUR

Indonesia's first states were influenced by Hinduism and Buddhism from India, which merged with local religions. The earliest kings, including the rulers of Srivijaya, were Hindus, but Buddhism eventually predominated. However, Hinduism and Buddhism always co-existed and even intermingled in the region, so that, while one ruler or dynasty favoured one religion, another changed allegiance or supported both equally.

More than one 7th-century Chinese pilgrim describes visiting and making translations of Buddhist texts in a powerful city-state called Ho-ling, five days' sailing from Palembang, Srivijaya's capital. The identity of Ho-ling has never been established, but scholars think it was most probably on the island of Java, where several states grew prosperous on the fertile rice-growing central Kedu plain.

Above The reliefs at Borobudur depict scenes from the life of the Buddha. This one shows him tempted by women sent by the evil Mara.

The Sailendra dynasty arose in central Java during the late 700s. Its rulers were Mahayana Buddhists and god-kings, who built many temples and monasteries. By the 800s, the Sailendras had overtaken Srivijaya and eclipsed rival states on Java.

In building the canals and terraces needed to cultivate paddy rice, the peoples of the Kedu plain had developed formidable engineering skills. In the 8th–9th centuries, they erected the massive Borobudur complex, the world's largest Buddhist monument.

The origins of Borobudur are unclear, but many scholars believe it was founded by the Sailendras, whose prosperous kingdom lasted until 832. It may have been the work of more than one dynasty since it probably took 50 years to build. It must have required huge

Right Borobudur is built on a square plan, with two lower terraces forming a plinth upon which rest five square stepped-out terraces, and three circular terraces surrounding a central stupa.

labour resources and considerable engineering expertise to quarry and cart uphill its one million huge stones.

Borobudur is a three-dimensional mandala. The devotee circumambulates it along an ascending path from the two lowest levels (the earthly realm), through the five middle terraces (the celestial realm) to the three upper levels, which represent the sphere of formlessness, the highest level of the Buddhist universe. At the top is an empty stupa, perhaps intended to symbolize the attainment of the realm of formlessness.

The circumambulating pilgrim progresses along passages whose walls are covered with reliefs that depict the law of cause and effect, events in the Buddha's life, scenes from the Jataka Tales, and the quest for enlightenment.

THE INFLUENCE OF ISLAM

By the 1300s, the states of Malaysia and Indonesia were primarily Buddhist. However, the Majapahit empire, which gained power during the early 1300s, became Indonesia's greatest kingdom and its last Hindu one – although Hindus and Buddhists co-existed peacefully under its rule.

Muslim traders first reached Java late in the 11th century, and in 1292, the Italian voyager Marco Polo wrote about a Muslim state in Sumatra. By the 14th century, most traders visiting Malaysia and Indonesia were Muslims. Under their influence, the region that is modern-day Indonesia rapidly converted to Islam.

Today, most Indonesians are Muslims. Modern Malaysia has a very mixed population, and while most Malays are Muslims, there are also many Chinese, Sinhalese and Thai Buddhists. These mainly immigrant peoples make up 20 per cent of the state's population.

BUDDHISM SUPPRESSED

BUDDHISM HAS SUFFERED FROM PERIODIC SUPPRESSION SINCE ITS INCEPTION, BUT FROM THE BEGINNING OF THE 20TH CENTURY, IT HAS BEEN SUBJECT TO GREATER PERSECUTION THAN AT ANY OTHER TIME THROUGHOUT ITS LONG HISTORY.

By the 8th century, Buddhism had become fully established in China, encompassing every level of society. But from the late 9th century onward, it began to suffer a slow decline. The Tang dynasty, weakened by an internal rebellion and by external threats from its neighbours, lost its cosmopolitanism and self-confidence. Buddhism, which had entered China from India, was now derided for being a foreign religion. The expenditure on Buddhist temples and ceremonies, the perceived laziness of the monks and the tax-exempt status of Buddhist lands were resented. The persecution of Buddhism that followed, from 842 to 845, saw the destruction of 4,600 monasteries and 40,000 shrines, and 260,000 monks and nuns were required to pay taxes.

SUPPRESSION IN KOREA

The suppression of Buddhism in Korea sprang from similar causes. Although initially enjoying wide acceptance during the Koryo period (918-1392), Buddhism had become a serious drain on the national economy, due to corruption and the abuse of its privileges. There were too many temples and too many monks and nuns, a large percentage of whom were in the sangha only as a means of escaping taxation. Buddhism lost its position as the official state religion. The extreme suppression that followed was to last for 500 years, during which time the number of monasteries dropped from several hundred to 36 and the monks and nuns were forced to flee into the mountains. From 1623 to 1895, monastics were even barred from living in the capital. During this period, Neo-Confucian ideology overcame the prior dominance of Buddhism.

Above From the early 10th century, Buddhism occupied a prominent position in Korean society. Its impact on the country's art appears at its best in sculpture in stone and metal. This beautiful iron Buddha Shakyamuni would have stood in a temple hall.

SUPPRESSION IN MONGOLIA

In Mongolia, traditionally a Buddhist country, Buddhists suffered severe repression in the years 1924 to 1989 when the country was a communist state. In a series of violent purges, more than 17,000 monks of middle and high rank were arrested. Virtually none of them was ever heard from again.

Some 700 monasteries were closed, ransacked and burned. Four were preserved as museums, but the only one to survive as a working monastery was Gandan monastery in Ulaanbaatar, which also served as a living museum

Below Gandan monastery, Ulaanbaatar, where these lamas are eating breakfast, was closed in 1938 under communist rule, but reopened in 1944 as the only functioning monastery in Mongolia. Currently, Gandan has more than 400 monks.

and tourist attraction. All religious worship and ceremonies remained forbidden until 1990. Over the past few years, however, there has been a remarkable revival of Buddhism, and monasteries have been reopened.

SUPPRESSION IN TIBET

The most recent, and shocking, suppression of Buddhism was likewise carried out by a communist government. In October 1950, the Chinese army rumbled into Tibet, penetrating as far as Lhasa. A year later, Tibet became a 'national autonomous region' of China, ostensibly under the traditional rule of the Dalai Lama, but actually under the control of the Chinese government.

The suppression of the monastic orders that followed prompted several uprisings, but in 1959, a full-scale revolt erupted. The Chinese responded with fierce reprisals, and the Dalai Lama and 80,000 of his followers fled. Buddhist lands were seized, religious practices were banned, more than 4,000 monasteries were dismantled, and thousands of monks were forced to find other work.

The Cultural Revolution in China brought further misery and suppression to Tibet. In the words of the Dalai Lama: "The truth remains that, since the Chinese invasion, over a million Tibetans have died as a direct result of Peking's policies." In 1965, the United Nations adopted a resolution on Tibet, which declared that China's occupation of the country had been characterized by "acts of murder, rape and arbitrary imprisonment; torture and cruel, inhuman and degrading treatment of Tibetans on a large scale."

Although some monasteries have been in operation since the early 1980s, protests in Tibet in the late 1980s and early 1990s were violently suppressed and martial law was imposed in 1989.

Today, Tibetans are still denied freedom to practice their religion, criticism of the authorities is severely punished, and the country is being swamped by Han Chinese who take the best jobs. Tibetans are treated as second-class citizens in their own land.

Below A Buddhist nun in traditional Mongolian dress prays at a doorway of the Kumbum monastery, one of the most important monasteries of Tibet's predominant Geluk sect.

Above In the brutal suppression of Buddhism that followed the 1959 uprising, some 87,000 members of the Tibetan resistance in Lhasa and surrounding areas were killed by the Chinese army between March and October alone. This photograph shows Tibetans laying down their arms.

BUDDHIST INFLUENCES

BUDDHISM HAS BEEN ONE OF THE FASTEST-GROWING RELIGIONS IN MANY EUROPEAN COUNTRIES SINCE THE MID-20TH CENTURY. IT IS THE FOURTH LARGEST RELIGION IN FRANCE, WITH ABOUT 160,000 ADHERENTS, WHILE IN BRITAIN, THERE ARE ABOUT 150,000.

Above This 10th-century codex, an illustrated Lotus Sutra, is one of many Buddhist manuscripts and scrolls in the British Library. It was discovered in 1910 in the Mogao caves at Dunhuang in Central Asia by the explorer Marc Aurel Stein.

Europe has its own communities of Buddhists who have lived and practised in remote Siberia for some 400 years. Tibetan Buddhists emigrated north from Mongolia to the eastern shores of Lake Baikal in Russia during the 17th century, and Buddhism became the main religion of the republics of Buryatia, Tuva and Kalmykia. A Dutch Moravian missionary, Isaac Jacob Schmidt, worked among the Kalmyks during the early 19th century and produced

Below Khushud Khurul monastery outside Elista, the capital of Kalmykia, Russia, was built around 1912 by a Kalmyk cavalry officer in the style of Leningrad's Kazan Cathedral.

the first grammar and dictionary of Mongolian. Under the Tsars, these Buddhist populations could practise their religion, but from the late 1920s, under Stalin, they were imprisoned and executed and their temples were destroyed. The Soviet authorities had more relaxed policies, and in 1946, Ivolginsk Datsan, Russia's largest Buddhist monastery, near Ulan-Ude, Buryatia's capital, was rebuilt.

The great wars of the 20th century brought soldiers fighting in Asia into contact with Buddhism, whose message of peace and compassion left a lasting impression. They presented Buddhist conscripts with an ethical dilemma. However, Buddhist historian Brian Victoria has researched darker sides of Buddhist reaction to modern warfare. In Japan, where in feudal times warrior monks trained for battle, many Zen and Pure Land schools fully supported Japan's militaristic role in World War II. Soka Gakkai was one that did not. Victoria cites the statements of Zen masters, trusted by thousands of Western followers today, who used arguments from Buddhist philosophy to justify killing.

POPULAR BUDDHISM

Academics in departments of Buddhist studies often deplore the distorted view of Buddhist doctrine and philosophy transmitted by popular writers and movements, from Theosophy to the Beat Generation. Yet all such movements have acted as catalysts in bringing Buddhism to the awareness of thousands of people who might not otherwise have encountered it.

Theosophy had a central role in the spread of Buddhism. It influenced the founding of the Golden Dawn, an occultist organization whose members included Aleister Crowley and Charles Henry Allan Bennett.

THE THEOSOPHIST CONNECTION

The Theosophical Society was founded in New York in 1875 by a Ukrainian, Madame Helena Petrovna Blavatsky, and an American lawyer, Colonel Henry Steel Olcott. Madame Blavatsky's Theosophy Movement incorporated into its beliefs the ideas of reincarnation, universal consciousness, spiritualism and direct experience of the divine through intuition or ecstasy. In 1879, Madame Blavatsky travelled to India with Colonel Olcott, and in 1880, they publicly took the Pancasila vows in Sri Lanka. In 1882, they moved the headquarters of the Society to Madras. Theosophy became fashionable among the middle classes in the late 19th century in Britain and the USA.

In 1879 Edwin Arnold, a journalist, published *The Light of Asia*, an epic poem on the life and teachings of the Buddha written in melodramatic Victorian style but with lines of great beauty. The poem, though criticized today by scholars for its inaccurate portrayal of Buddhism, had immense popular appeal, including among members of the Theosophical Society.

Right *Madame Helena Petrovna Blavatsky, charismatic founder of the Theosophical Society, claimed to have converted to Buddhism in Sri Lanka and to have been initiated in Tibet.*

Later known as Ananda Metteya, Bennett was the first Westerner to be ordained a bhikkhu in the Theravada tradition, in Burma in 1902. He set up the first Buddhist Mission in Britain. Theosophy also influenced Travers Christmas Humphreys, a celebrated barrister and judge, who converted to Buddhism at the age of 23 and founded the Buddhist Society in 1924. He wrote books on Mahayana Buddhism, which, although of questionable authority, inspired many during the 1950s, '60s and '70s.

The German philosopher Arthur Schopenhauer acknowledged his debt to Buddhism in his major work, *The World as Will and Representation* (1819) Theosophy and Schopenhauer both influenced Hermann Hesse, Nobel prizewinner and the author of *Siddhartha*, the story of a

Right *Monks and nuns garden at a branch of the Kagyu Samye Ling Buddhist monastery and Tibetan Centre on Holy Island, off Arran on the west coast of Scotland.*

Brahman and his spiritual journey in India at the time of the Buddha. Hesse had learned about India from his mother, who had lived there, and a journey to Sri Lanka and Indonesia in 1911 inspired him to write *Siddhartha* after he had served in World War I.

Together with the writings of the English philosopher Alan Watts, a Theosophist and Buddhist, who wrote several books on Zen Buddhism, such volumes inspired the baby-boom generation in post-1950s' Europe and North America to explore Buddhism.

ALEXANDRA DAVID-NÉEL

THE FIRST WESTERN WOMAN TO VISIT TIBET, ALEXANDRA DAVID-NÉEL WAS AN OUTSTANDING TRAVELLER, SPIRITUAL SEEKER AND WRITER. SHE SPENT MOST OF HER LIFE TRAVELLING IN ASIA AND WROTE MANY BOOKS ABOUT EASTERN RELIGION AND HER ADVENTURES.

Alexandra David-Néel was born in Paris in 1868 and spent her childhood and youth between France and Belgium. A rebellious spirit from birth, she had a hunger to travel and had visited Switzerland, Italy, England and Spain on her own spiritual quest in her youth.

At the age of 21, she enrolled at the Theosophical Society in Paris and concentrated on Oriental studies, especially at the Sorbonne and at the Musée Guimet. In those years, she developed her love of empty, wide spaces, and, in particular, her interest in Tibet and in its monks, meditation, music and dance.

At the age of 36, Alexandra married a railway engineer, Philippe Néel, whom she met in Tunis. Although they officially separated in 1925, they remained friends and he continued to support her until the end of her life.

Above Alexandra David-Néel reading Tibetan Buddhist scriptures in their classical format of separate foils. This picture was taken in October 1968, when Alexandra was 99 years old.

After years of travelling throughout North, South and East Asia, she moved back to France and settled in Digne-les-Bains, which became her refuge for meditation. Most of her writings date back to these years, with the exception of the ten years between the late 1930s and the late 1940s that she spent travelling in China.

She died in 1969, at the age of 100. In 1973, her ashes were dispersed in the Ganges, and in 1986, the 14th Dalai Lama paid a visit to her hermitage in Digne-les-Bains, as a sign of his esteem and respect for this Western traveller.

TRAVELS AND MEETINGS
Possibly the only person ever to have their passport renewed at the age of 100, Alexandra made her first trip to the East in 1890, when

Left The 13th Dalai Lama, Thubten Gyatso, whom Alexandra met in 1912. She was the first European woman to interview, and study Buddhist doctrines with, a Dalai Lama.

Right Lama Yongden was adopted by Alexandra in 1914 and became one of her mentors and her main guide when she made her several visits to the Himalayan region.

she went to live in India for a year, supported financially by her mother. Having explored India extensively, her spiritual quest took her to Muslim North Africa.

In 1911, some years after her marriage, she travelled to Asia again, this time visiting China as well as Central Asia. A year later, she reached Sikkim, from which she was expelled in 1916. On another trip, beginning in 1917, Alexandra went to Japan, which she found disappointing, Korea, which reminded her of Tibet, and finally China. In the 1920s, she returned to Tibet and finally arrived in Lhasa. In 1937, she went back to China, despite the ongoing Sino-Japanese War and the threat of World War II, then returned to India in 1946.

Alexandra considered her travels not only as spiritual quests but also as opportunities to improve her knowledge of the local culture and language, and she devoted herself especially to the study of Sanskrit and Tibetan.

Three people were particularly influential to Alexandra in her travels, and some accompanied her on her missions: her husband, Philippe Néel, who supported her both during and after their marriage, her adopted son Lama Yongden, and the scholar Ekai Kawaguchi, whom she met in Japan. Lama Yongden, whom she met in 1914, followed and also guided Alexandra on her travels in Tibet until his death in 1955.

WRITINGS

Alexandra's very first writing was an anarchist work dated 1899 and published by her partner Jean Haustont, but thereafter, she focused on Asian culture and philosophy, especially Tibetan Buddhism. Most of her books are reports of her trips to Tibet, studies of Chinese philosophies and Tibetan Buddhism. Although originally written in French, quite a few of her works have been translated into English, Italian, Spanish and German. English translations include the following: *My Journey to Lhasa, Magic and Mystery in Tibet, The Superhuman Life of Gésar of Ling, Tibetan Journey, Mipam: The Lama of the Five Wisdoms, Love Magic and Black Magic, The Secret Oral Teachings in Tibetan Buddhist Sects,* and *Immortality and Reincarnation.*

THE ALEXANDRA DAVID-NÉEL CULTURAL CENTER

In 1977, the Alexandra David-Néel Cultural Center was opened in Alexandra's home town of Digne-les-Bains in southern France. The Center incorporates the Alexandra David-Néel Museum and shops of Tibetan artefacts and hosts an association that sponsors the education of Tibetan children. The main objectives of the Center are circulating Alexandra's writings, promoting Tibetan culture and sponsoring Tibetan Buddhist teachings. The Cultural Center thus continues the missions of this extraordinary woman.

BUDDHISM IN NORTH AMERICA

THE 1849 CALIFORNIA GOLD RUSH BROUGHT CHINESE GOLD-SEEKERS AND THE FIRST WAVE OF BUDDHISTS TO NORTH AMERICA. TODAY, BUDDHISM IS ONE OF THE FASTEST-GROWING RELIGIONS ON THE CONTINENT, WITH AN ESTIMATED 5 MILLION ADHERENTS.

From the mid-19th century, Chinese labourers began working in the mines and on the railways of the USA and Canada. It was for these immigrants that the first Buddhist temple opened in San Francisco in 1853. Temples were also built in Hawaii, San Francisco, Vancouver and other cities for Japanese and Korean immigrants of the 1880s and 1900s.

THE INTELLIGENTSIA

By the mid-19th century, Eastern religions were also beginning to interest American intellectuals. The Transcendentalists read translations of Sanskrit texts and wrote about Buddhism: Henry David Thoreau and Ralph Waldo Emerson published part of the *Lotus Sutra* in English translation in their literary journal, *The Dial*.

Above Temples in New York City represent Buddhist traditions from many Asian countries. Chinese-American Buddhists adhere mainly to the Chan and Pure Land schools.

The Theosophical Society, founded by Helena Blavatsky, a Ukrainian, and Henry Steel Olcott, a US army colonel and Civil War veteran, in 1875 in New York City, resonated with the intelligentsia. Its link with Buddhism was strengthened during the 1880s by the publication of Edwin Arnold's *The Light of Asia*, which became a bestseller in the USA. After 1879, when Blavatsky and Olcott departed for India, their co-founder, William Quan Judge, ran the New York Society.

The World's Parliament of Religions, the first meeting of representatives from Eastern and Western spiritual traditions, took place during the 1893 Chicago World's Fair. Those who addressed the assembly included Colonel Olcott's Sri Lankan protégé, Anagarika Dharmapala, who represented the Theravada

Left This gigantic Buddha outside the Jodo Buddhist mission at Lahaina, Maui, commemorates the arrival of the first of thousands of Japanese immigrants who came to Hawaii to work in the booming sugar industry during the 1870s and '80s.

Buddhist tradition, the Japanese Zen master Soyen Shaku, and Chinese and Thai monks.

Among the Americans who had a pioneering role in advancing knowledge of India and Buddhism in the West was Walter Yeeling Evans-Wentz, an anthropologist and graduate of Stanford and Oxford, who teamed up with a Sikkimese–English translator, Lama Kazi Dawa-Samdup, whom he met in Darjeeling in 1919. Evans-Wentz published Dawa-Samdup's translations of Tibetan Buddhist texts, including a short version of *The Tibetan Book of the Dead* in 1927.

MASS MOVEMENTS

The psychologist Carl Jung wrote a commentary for the 1935 reprint of Evans-Wentz's *The Tibetan Book of the Dead*. Sales spiralled and a 1960 reprint became a long-term bestseller.

The Beat Generation – a group of American writers that included Allen Ginsberg and Jack Kerouac – were an integral part of the surge of interest in Eastern

religions during the post-war era. They read about Eastern philosophy and made Buddhism the subject of some of their writings.

The work of these influential writers and of others, such as Alan Watts, who taught Asian Studies in San Francisco during the 1950s and '60s, was read by a generation of affluent young middle-class Americans searching for alternatives to Western religions. Cheap air travel enabled them to visit the East to pursue their search for spiritual guidance.

At the same time, Eastern teachers were giving talks and classes in the USA. Dr. D.T. Suzuki was a professor at Columbia University during the 1950s, and his books inspired enthusiasm for Zen Buddhism. The Soto Zen monk Shunryu Suzuki gave classes in San Francisco from 1959, and his generally Caucasian followers (Americans not of Asian extraction) opened many Zen centres and temples, mainly in California.

Theravada monks established a vihara in Washington, DC in 1965, but it was Zen Buddhism

Above The Lotus Buddha at the Byodo-In temple on Oahu, Hawaii. Carved out of wood and covered in gold and lacquer, it is 2.7m (9ft) tall.

that took hold in the USA in the 1960s and spread from there into Canada and across the Atlantic.

THE MAN WHO BROUGHT ZEN TO THE WEST

Dr Daisetz Teitaro Suzuki (1870–1966) was a powerful force in the spread of Zen Buddhism to the West. He was born in Japan, raised in Jodo Shinshu Buddhism and trained in Rinzai Zen at the Engaku-ji temple in Kamakura, where he lived as a monk. His Zen master was Soyen Shaku, who became the first Zen master to teach in the USA. Suzuki mastered several languages and, during the 1890s, worked in the USA as a translator of Eastern spiritual literature into English. He joined the American Theosophical Society and married an American Theosophist.

Suzuki dedicated himself to bringing Mahayana Buddhism to the West. He lectured, taught and wrote about Mahayana, Zen and its origins in Chinese Chan Buddhism, and, later on, about Jodo Shinshu Buddhism. He visited Europe, speaking in London, in 1908 and 1936. However, although he became the catalyst for a worldwide revival of Mahayana, Suzuki was neither an ordained Zen monk, nor a recognized historian, and the accuracy of his writing has been questioned by some academics.

Right Suzuki translated important Buddhist works into English, including the Lankavatara Sutra, *and wrote a number of influential books on Zen Buddhism.*

Monks, Nuns and Laity

THE CO-OPERATION, OR SOMETIMES ANTAGONISM, BETWEEN MONKS, NUNS AND LAITY HAS CREATED A VITALITY WITHIN BUDDHISM SINCE ITS INCEPTION. IN RECENT YEARS, MANY SIGNIFICANT LAY FIGURES HAVE ARISEN WHO HAVE CHANGED THE FACE OF BUDDHISM.

In ancient India, monks and nuns lived mostly through the support of the laity, who in return received blessings and religious merits. This situation occurred in early Chinese Buddhism and in medieval Japanese Buddhism, as well as in Tibet and South-East Asia. Even today, this exchange based on Buddhist merits is a key aspect of the relationship between monastics and lay followers.

Another important factor that has defined the fate of Buddhism throughout various regions and historical periods has been the presence of charismatic figures, both from the monastic community and among lay followers.

THE BUDDHIST LAITY

Since the early days of Buddhism, male lay disciples have been called *upasaka* and female ones *upasika*. The Buddhist career for lay disciples begins with taking refuge in the Three Jewels (Buddha, Dharma, Sangha), and is confirmed when they receive the Five Precepts (not killing, not lying, not stealing, not committing sexual misconduct, not taking intoxicants). Both these steps are undertaken in formal ceremonies officiated at by Buddhist monks or nuns. Lay followers may also take further vows and commitments depending on the Buddhist tradition to which they belong.

Above Two mendicant Japanese nuns, dressed in characteristic large straw hats, receive offerings from a samurai dressed in the traditional manner. The image dates from the mid-19th century.

Below Monks and nuns unfold a huge thangka on the slope of a hill during the Monlam Prayer festival at Labrang monastery in China. Lay Buddhists also participate in these celebrations.

Right A young Theravada monk receives an offering from a lay Buddhist outside Wat Benchamabophit in Bangkok. By providing sustenance to the monastic community, lay people can accumulate merit and be blessed.

A few scriptures exist that give details of the disciplines required of Buddhist laity, the most famous of which is the *Upasakasila Sutra* (Sutra on the Discipline of the Laity), which explains the meaning of the commitments taken by the lay community.

Two important aspects of the practice of the laity involve giving offerings to the monastic community and the worship of Buddhist relics and sacred sites through the undertaking of pilgrimages.

BRIDGING THE GAP

According to many early scriptures, laity and monastics are very distant from each other: lay followers are unable to became arhats, although they can hope for better rebirths and the possibility of becoming monastics in future lives.

This strong distinction was undermined later in South-east Asian Theravada countries, where lay followers were able to take temporary ordination as monks. This sharing, even if only for a short period, of monastic austerities helped to unite Buddhist monks and laity.

Although this practice never took place in Mahayana countries, specific doctrinal features of Mahayana helped to bridge the gap in other ways. Firstly, the Mahayana concept of emptiness, which deletes all apparent contradictions, also negates the distinction between monastics and the laity. Secondly, the institution of the bodhisattva precepts and practice, which Mahayana prescribes for all Buddhists, highlights the importance of Dharma practice in the secular world.

In recent times, the movements to reform Buddhism in Theravada and Mahayana countries have been led by laity rather than monastic communities.

A BUDDHIST NUN FROM LONDON

Diane Perry was born in East London in 1943 and even as a teenager showed an interest in Buddhism, which she later developed through attending lectures and working at the library of the School of Oriental and African Studies at the University of London.

In 1964, she moved to India, where she dedicated herself to the study and practice of the Kagyu school of Tibetan Buddhism. In India, she met her guru, the 8th Khamtrul Rinpoche, and became one of the first Westerners to be ordained as a Buddhist nun.

Adopting the Buddhist name of Tenzin Palmo, she underwent a retreat of almost 12 years in a cave in the mountains of Himachal Pradesh. In the early 1990s, she built the Dongyu Gatsal Ling nunnery in India. She has also been an active campaigner for the right of Tibetan women to receive full monastic ordination.

Above A view of the Kangra Valley in Himachal Pradesh, India. The Buddhist nun Tenzin Palmo (Diane Perry) established the Dongyu Gatsal Ling nunnery here, so that young nuns could receive the appropriate education and training.

THE 20TH-CENTURY DIASPORA

THE WEST'S FIRST BUDDHIST ORGANIZATIONS WERE FOUNDED IN THE EARLY 20TH CENTURY BY MONKS AND TEACHERS FROM THE EAST. IN LATER DECADES, THE WEST BECAME A REFUGE FOR MANY BUDDHIST TEACHERS FLEEING POLITICAL UPHEAVAL.

The first Buddhist organization in the West was an American branch of the Maha Bodhi Society, established in 1893. The society's founder, Anagarika Dharmapala from Sri Lanka, opened a London branch in 1926, and a vihara there shortly afterward. He thus ensured that the Theravada was the first Buddhist tradition to gain a foothold in the West.

Theravada monks from Burma arrived in Australia as early as 1910, but Theravada bhikkhus from South-east Asia established a foothold in Europe only after World War II. The King and Queen of Thailand funded the Buddhapadipa temple in Wimbledon, London, in 1966, and expatriate Burmese Buddhists opened viharas in the UK during the 1970s and '80s.

The appeal of Theravada Buddhism in the West has been the opening up of the Vipassana or insight meditation tradition to lay followers. Bhikkhus of the Thai Forest tradition played a central role – Americans such as Joseph Goldstein, Jack Kornfield and Sharon Salzberg studied in Asia during the 1970s under luminaries such as Ajahn Chah of the Thai Forest Tradition, and returned to teach in the

Above The first Buddhists are thought to have arrived in Australia from China during the gold rush of 1851. This pagoda is part of the Nan Tien temple in Wollongong, New South Wales, built in 1995.

USA, where they formed the Insight Meditation Society in Massachusetts. Since the 1980s, when monks of the Thai Forest tradition established the Amaravati Buddhist monastery in England, it has founded branches in other European countries, the USA, Australia and New Zealand.

ZEN SCHOOLS

Distinguished masters, mainly from Japan, oversaw the transmission of Zen Buddhism to Europe, as they did to the USA, after 1945. An Austrian woman, Irmgard Schloegl, trained in Rinzai Zen in Japan and taught in London, becoming one of the first to take the tradition there.

Left Master Xuan Hua brought Chan Buddhism to the West during the 1960s. He taught in Hong Kong and Australia before travelling to San Francisco in 1962, where he gave talks and taught meditation and, in 1968, established the first American sangha.

Most Buddhists in Western countries are from Asian families. In the USA, an estimated 75 per cent of Buddhists were brought up in Buddhist families who have played a major role in the development of Buddhism there. Since the 1950s, and after the Vietnam War, large numbers of people, mainly from China, South Korea and Vietnam, have settled in the USA. Chinese, Vietnamese and Indians also emigrated in large numbers to Australia during the post-war period, and Canada has extensive Chinese and Japanese communities.

With a desire to increase its population, its humane refugee policies and historic links with the region, France has received large numbers of immigrants from South-east Asia since 1945, and an estimated 500,000 French people are Buddhists from Buddhist families. As well as large numbers of Chinese Buddhists, Britain has communities of Buddhists from Sri Lanka, Burma and Thailand.

A Soto Zen association founded in Paris in 1970 by Japanese monk Taisen Deshimaru spread to Germany and Belgium.

The Chinese Chan tradition became established early in the USA when, in 1959, the Chan master Hsuan Hua founded what is now called the Dharma Realm Buddhist Association, the Gold Mountain monastery, and, in 1975, the City of Ten Thousand Buddhas – one of the largest Buddhist communities in the West – in California.

The first Korean Son (Zen) master to live and teach in the West was Seung Sahn, who founded the Providence Zen Center in Cumberland, Rhode Island, USA, where a unique form of Son evolved that was adapted to Western lifestyles. His Kwan Um school has since spread worldwide.

REFUGE IN THE WEST

During the 1960s, political upheaval in the East caused a new stream of Buddhist teachers to emigrate to the West. The invasion of Tibet by the Chinese (1950–1) resulted in an exodus of lamas, led by the nominal head of state and spiritual leader of the Geluk order of Tibetan Buddhism, the Dalai

Above Kagyu Samye Ling monastery in Dumfriesshire, Scotland, was the first Tibetan Buddhist centre in the West. It was founded in 1967 by Chogyam Trungpa Rinpoche and Akong Tulku Rinpoche.

Lama. They went to Bhutan and then India. Many of these refugees later found their way to Western countries and founded schools and sects. The young Chogyam Trungpa Rinpoche, for example, a *tulku* (recognized incarnation of a spiritual master) from the Karma Kagyu tradition, arrived in Britain to study. In 1967, he and Akong Tulku Rinpoche founded the first Tibetan Buddhist centre in Western Europe. In 1970, he went to the USA, where he established Karma Kagyu centres. His teachings evolved into the Shambhala Buddhism sub-school.

From 1975, France gave asylum to thousands of refugees from the conflicts in Vietnam, Cambodia and Laos, many of whom were Buddhists. Germany, Belgium and Switzerland also took in South-east Asian refugees.

By the 21st century, Buddhism had become a recognized and accepted part of cultural life in most countries of the world.

Above Buddhism is the fourth largest religion in France. Here, Parisian Buddhists attend a ceremony in the temple of Fo Guang Shan, a modern Taiwanese monastic order.

CHAPTER 5

BUDDHIST TRADITIONS

During the centuries following the Buddha's death, many schools and sects emerged. The Theravada tradition, which models itself on the original teachings of the Buddha as preserved in the Pali canon, is said to have emerged in the 2nd century BCE. Today, Theravada is the dominant form of Buddhism in South-east Asian countries, such as Burma (Myanmar), Sri Lanka, Cambodia, Laos and Thailand.

The second major Buddhist tradition, the Mahayana, emerged in the 1st century BCE and later led to the development of numerous new schools and sects. The Chinese Tiantai (Tendai in Japan), founded during the 6th century, is a leading devotional school, whose teachings are based on the *Lotus Sutra*. Another devotional school, Pure Land, originated in India, but became more fully developed in China during the 6th century. Chan, a meditation-oriented school, became an established tradition in China by the 7th century and spread to Korea and Japan, where Zen sects developed independently.

The 20th century also witnessed the establishment of new Buddhist offshoots, some of which gained ground in the West. They demonstrate the continued relevance and appeal of Buddhism in the modern world.

Opposite Avalokiteshvara is perhaps the most popular deity in many Mahayana schools. He appears in early Mahayana texts as an infinitely compassionate bodhisattva and became an international figure of devotion.

Above Tibetan novice lamas in Leh, India. Since the Chinese invasion of Tibet in 1951, many Tibetans have had to practice their religion in other countries. Tibetan Buddhism has also become increasingly popular in the West.

BUDDHIST SCHOOLS

THERE HAVE BEEN, AND STILL ARE, MANY DIVISIONS WITHIN THE
BUDDHISM, MOST OF WHICH, AT ONE TIME OR ANOTHER, HAVE BEEN
REFERRED TO AS 'SCHOOLS'. THE MOST GENERAL AND FAR-REACH-
ING OF THESE ARE THE GREAT MOVEMENTS OR *YANAS*.

The terminology of *yanas*, or 'vehicles', was first employed, a century or so before the beginning of the Common Era, by Buddhists wanting to proclaim a revitalized teaching based on new revelations of the Dharma, which they set down in texts that came to be known as the *Mahayana Sutras*. They distinguished their approach from that of more traditional Buddhists by claiming that they were following the bodhisattva path toward buddhahood rather than the traditional path of the disciples toward arhatship.

They called this new path 'Mahayana' (the 'great vehicle'); and named the old path 'Hinayana' (the 'lesser vehicle'). Modern scholars tend to refer to pre-Mahayana Buddhist groups as Shravakayana, rather than the disparaging Hinayana used by their Mahayanist critics.

TANTRIC BUDDHISM

A few centuries after the rise of Mahayana came another wave of new scriptures known as 'tantras'. These texts offered novel, often esoteric, teachings that displayed features of the emerging pan-Indian movement of Saktism, which focused on the worship of the great goddess (*devi* or Sakti). Tantric teachings were sufficiently distinctive for Buddhists of the time to recognize that they constituted a new *yana*. Often referred to as 'Vajrayana' (the 'diamond vehicle'), Tantric Buddhism was also called 'Mantrayana' because magical formulae were commonly employed in its rituals.

Above An Indian relief dating from the 3rd–4th century CE *depicting the Buddha leaving the gods of the Tushita heaven and descending to Earth for his final incarnation.*

SPLITS IN THE SANGHA

Even quite pronounced doctrinal differences do not necessarily prevent Buddhist monks from sharing the same monastery, and Hinayanist and Mahayanist monks lived together according to the same set of vinaya rules. If, however, one group decided to modify the rules – for example, by changing ordination procedures or by relinquishing an optional rule – then communal life became impossible, the community divided, and a new school (*nikaya*) was created.

The splitting of the Sangha is often associated with the great councils that have punctuated Buddhist history. The primary purpose of such gatherings was a communal recitation of the scriptures in order to ensure that all branches of the Sangha were in agreement. Not surprisingly, it was at such councils that differences of both doctrine and discipline came to the fore. Even at the First Buddhist Council, held shortly after the Buddha's death, there is a record of dissent.

Left The Ajanta caves in Maharashtra, India, date from the 2nd century BCE. *During the 5th century* CE, *the caves were used by Mahayanist monks as a centre for religious activity.*

Left A relief sculpture of a small Buddha seated in prayer at the Mohra Moradu monastery, which lies within the archaeological area of Taxila, in Pakistan. The monastery dates from the 3rd–5th century CE.

However, it was after the Second Council that the Sangha experienced its first major split: between the elders (*sthavira*) and those who called themselves the 'Great Community' (*mahasamgha*). The latter were disinclined to accept the decisions made at the Council, which essentially meant that only the texts determined what was legitimate Buddhist teaching and practice. For the Mahasamghika, teachings could also be transmitted outside the scriptures on the basis of personal experience. Mahasamghika sub-groups appear to have been most prevalent in eastern and southern India. Some still existed when Chinese pilgrims visited India in the 7th and 8th centuries CE, but none survived into modern times.

STHAVIRAVADA GROUPS

The Sthaviravada also divided into sub-groups. There were three such major sub groups, each of which sub-divided following later disagreements. These three groups were Vatsiputriyas (also known as

Right A lama meditates in the Zanskar Range in the Himalayas of northern India. Meditation has played a central role in each school of Buddhism from the very beginning.

Pudgalavadins), Vibhajjavadins and Sarvastivadins. Vatsiputriyas taught the existence of a 'person' (*pudgala*) in addition to the five skandhas. The *pudgala*, they claimed, 'carries' the burden of the skandhas. This was a popular view, and these groups survived in India until the 13th century.

The other major division among the *sthavira* was between the Vibhajjavadins (of which the Theravada is a sub-group) and the Sarvastivadins. One of their main points of dispute was regarding the existence of an intermediate realm (*antarabhava*) between one life and the next: Sarvastivadins accepted it; Vibhajjavadins did not. Another concerned the nature of an arhat: Sarvastivadins taught that arhats could 'fall away', whereas for Vibhajjavadins, the arhat's attainment of nirvana was permanent and unshakeable. Yet another concerned the nature of dharmas, the constituents of existence: Sarvastivadins taught that all dharmas had an essential nature that persisted through temporal changes; Vibhajjavadins rejected this notion, claiming that dharmas had merely momentary existence. No Sarvastivada group survived into modern times, although their entire Tripitaka has been preserved in Chinese and parts of it in Tibetan. The only Vibhajjavadin group to survive is the Theravada.

BUDDHIST SCHOOLS IN CHINA AND JAPAN

WITH THE DISSEMINATION OF BUDDHISM OVER TIME, THE PHILOSOPHIES OF THE INDIAN BUDDHIST SCHOOLS EVOLVED AND INCORPORATED LOCAL CULTURES AND HISTORIES, LEADING TO THE PRODUCTION OF NEW BUDDHIST SCHOOLS.

The expansion of Buddhism beyond India was given a major boost in the middle of the 3rd century BCE, when the emperor Ashoka sent missionaries to a number of regions outside his empire. One of Ashoka's rock edicts relates that some of these Buddhist missionaries even went as far as Greek states around the Mediterranean Sea. They made little impact there, but closer to home, in the Greek Bactrian kingdoms of modern Afghanistan, north-western India and the western end of the Silk Route, Buddhism put down firmer roots. Although its fortunes fluctuated during the centuries following Ashoka's initiatives, Buddhism reached its high point between the 1st and 5th centuries CE.

Buddhism made its way into China during the early centuries of the Common Era, and the Silk Route continued to be the major

Above The Amitabha Buddha is the principal buddha of the Pure Land school. This lacquered wooden statue dates from the second phase of the Heian period in Japan.

conduit until it was closed off by the initially anti-Buddhist Tibetans in the 7th century and, later, by its Muslim rulers.

Buddhism's establishment in China was not, however, a matter of transplanting Indian schools into another environment. Geography, history and culture all played their part in creating what became distinctively Chinese versions of Buddhism. The evolution of Buddhism in China can be conveniently divided into four phases: 1st–3rd centuries CE, 3rd–6th centuries, 6th–9th centuries and 9th–20th centuries.

BUDDHISM IN CHINA

In the first phase, Buddhism was largely the religion of foreigners – merchants and diplomats from Central Asian states – though there may also have been some native Chinese converts. The available evidence indicates that there were at least three centres of Buddhism during this period: at Tonkin in southern China; at Pengcheng on the Huai River (where the first Chinese Buddhist temple was built), and at Luoyang on the Yellow River (where the first centre for translating Buddhist texts into Chinese was founded).

Left A 13th-century silk painting of Kukai (774–835CE), also known as Kobo Daishi, as a child. Kukai was the founder of Shingon, a Japanese form of esoteric Buddhism.

Buddhists in China often used Daoist concepts to communicate their ideas in Chinese, and the Daoists began to claim that Buddhism was nothing more than Daoism in Indian guise, and that Daoist master Laozi had gone to the West and converted the barbarians, who were now bringing his teaching back to China in the form of Buddhism.

By the end of the Han dynasty in 220CE, a substantial body of Buddhist texts had been translated into Chinese. This number was increased significantly after an Indian scholar-monk, Kumarajiva, was brought to Chang'an in 401. Study groups formed around either one or a collection of these. These groups are sometimes referred to as 'schools' (*zong*), but their main concern seems to have been identifying the connecting threads that gave the teachings a coherence rather than establishing a lineage of authoritative teachers.

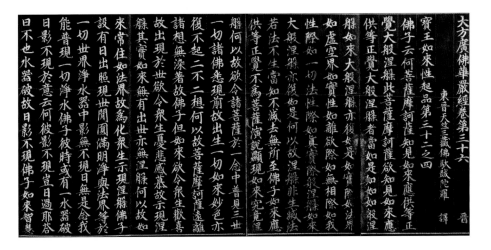

Above The Avatamsaka Sutra, *here in Chinese, is a valuable source of information about the evolution of early Buddhist philosophy into the Mahayana strand.*

After the collapse of the Han dynasty, invaders from the north began to take over much Chinese territory. Many scholars fled to the south, while the invaders established their own dynasties in the north. Buddhism began to flourish in both regions, though in rather different ways. In the north, the Xiongnu rulers converted to Buddhism and gave it their support. Texts were translated and pilgrims travelled west along the Silk Route in search of new ones. In the south, the displaced intelligentsia, disillusioned with the indigenous traditions of Daoism and Confucianism, found solace in Buddhist accounts of impermanence, suffering and the way to transcend them, as well as a congenial lifestyle in the monasteries, which developed into centres of learning and culture.

However, not until the reunification of the empire under the Sui dynasty of Yang Jian in 589CE

Right A Buddhist monk meditates in front of a statue of Kukai, the founder of Shingon Buddhism, at the miniature shrine on the island of Shodoshima, Japan.

did Buddhism acquire a secure footing on Chinese soil. Over the next 400 years, distinctively Chinese schools appeared, and these Buddhist schools were then exported to both Korea and Japan.

TYPES OF SCHOOLS

Three types of Buddhist schools emerged in China, and forms of each were successfully established in Japan. First were those based on the key texts of Indian schools. One notable example was the Zhenyan (tantric or esoteric) school. It thrived briefly in the 8th century, but declined thereafter, in part due to a lack of tantric teachers arriving from India. It did, however, survive and flourish in Japan as Shingon, and its popularity can be gauged from the 10,000 or so Shingon monasteries there.

The second type of school was a product of the fact that the Chinese had translated texts from most of the Indian Buddhist traditions but had discovered that the teachings they contained were not always easy to reconcile with each other. One response to this problem was the creation of a scheme that classified teachings according to hierarchical principles. This schematic approach (called *panjiao*, meaning 'dividing the teaching') was adopted by two of China's most influential schools: Tiantai (Tendai in Japan) and Huayan (Kegon in Japan). Both were established in the 6th century and survived as such until the great persecution of 845CE. However, such schemes bore little resemblance to the relationships between the teachings listed in their arrangements, and they were also embedded in complex philosophies that were incomprehensible to ordinary people.

Lay Buddhists and monks tended to gravitate instead toward the schools of the third type, which simplified the teachings down to a few essential principles. Pure Land devotionalism (Jodo) and meditative Chan (Zen) both survived the persecution of 845 and thus ensured the continued existence of Buddhism in China.

THERAVADA SCHOOLS

THE THERAVADA BUDDHIST TRADITION HAS SURVIVED IN SRI LANKA, BURMA (MYANMAR), THAILAND, CAMBODIA AND LAOS, AND ITS FUNDAMENTAL FORM HAS BEEN RETAINED IN ALL THESE COUNTRIES, DESPITE VARIOUS DISRUPTIONS OVER THE CENTURIES.

The Theravada tradition is defined and has been maintained by a twofold commitment: firstly to the Pali version of canonical Buddhist scriptures, and secondly, to preserving an authentic lineage of monastic ordination.

Doctrinally, the Theravadins established their interpretation of Buddhist teachings through debate with other early schools. Against the Pudgalavadins, for example, they asserted the non-existence of any kind of 'bearer' of the skandhas (the physical and mental components of human beings), while against the Mahasamghika schools, they asserted the spiritual perfection and fully liberated nature of arhats, and against the Sarvastivadins, the momentary nature of all dharmas (elements of existence). All modern Theravada groups maintain these doctrines.

The commitment to the Pali canon also provides Theravada groups with a common vinaya (discipline) with which to regulate monastic life. Differences in optional rules or ordination procedures can easily create disunity in the sangha, however, and this sometimes leads to the formation of new *nikayas* (monastic ordination lineages).

THE INFLUENCE OF KINGS

New Theravada divisions were often instigated by kings who had decided to promote the tradition – not least because its teachings recognized the right of kings to

Above A sculptural representation of the Buddha's head, Cambodia, 12th–13th century. The long earlobes indicate his royal lineage, and the closed eyes and serene expression are typical of the Bayon style. Many such statues were modelled on Jayavarman VII.

rule, so long as they did so according to the principles of the Buddhist Dharma.

In some cases, divisions were caused by kings offering gifts in a manner that was not in keeping with the Dharma. The founding of the Abhayagiri and Jetavana monasteries and their associated *nikayas* in Sri Lanka (in the 1st century BCE and the 4th century CE, respectively) provide notable examples. In other cases, however, the king was attempting to reinstate ordination lineages that had been broken by social upheaval or war, or to restore a commitment

Left The seated Buddha, carved in granite at Gal vihara, Polonnaruwa, Sri Lanka. The ancient garden-city of Polonnaruwa was created in the 12th century by Parakramabahu I, who reformed the Sri Lankan sangha.

to the vinaya. An example of the first is King Vijayabahu's invitation, in 1065, to Burmese monks to restore the ordination lineage that was lost as a result of Sri Lanka's war with the southern Indian Cholas. An example of the second is the 'purification' initiated by the 15th-century Burmese king Dhammaceti. At that time, many monks had virtually abandoned vinaya regulation and had accumulated considerable wealth for themselves. So the king sent monks to Sri Lanka to be re-ordained, and on their return, 'invited' all Burmese monks to undertake the new re-ordination and commit themselves to living within the vinaya framework.

Thus kings have played a significant role in the splittings and reunifications of the Theravada Sangha throughout its history in South and South-east Asia, often according to agendas that were as much political as religious. One thing is clear, however: without their patronage, the Theravada may well not have survived.

THERAVADA TODAY

In modern times, governments of Theravada countries have continued to play an active role in promoting the tradition. In 1954, the Burmese government sponsored what was called the Sixth Buddhist Council (though it was restricted to Theravadins) in order to foster a sense of unity within the Theravadin world. The following year, a group of Burmese meditation teachers was invited to Sri Lanka by the government to promote the practice of *satipatthana* (mindfulness meditations) so as to enrich local religious life.

Today, there are four *nikayas* in Sri Lanka: the Siyam, Amarapura, Ramanna and, most recently, the forest *nikaya*, which resulted from the government's recognition, in

***Above** Burma has followed Buddhism for over a thousand years, and today the Theravada tradition predominates. Here, a monk bows in obeisance in front of a statue of the Buddha at the Shwedagon pagoda in Rangoon.*

1968, that a number of otherwise unaffiliated forest monks constituted an independent branch of the tradition. In Burma there are many, including the Thudhamma, Shwegyin and Dvara; and in Thailand two: Mahanikaya and Thammayut. In Cambodia, the two *nikayas* (Mahanikaya and Thammayut) preceeding Khmer Rouge rule were re-established in 1992. In Laos, the 'unified sangha' (with no *nikayas*) that was established by the Communist government still seems to be in place.

Two other divisions that have a particular prominence in modern times are the divisions between

***Right** This young Buddhist monk wears the distinctive orange robes of the Theravada tradition. He is studying at the Bagaya monastery, which was built in 1593 in the old Burmese capital of Ava.*

traditionalists and modernists, and the divisions between city or village monks and forest dwellers.

Modernists, both monks and nuns and the laity, tend to be sceptical about traditional teachings on cosmology (such as heavens and hells), the existence of gods and the value of rituals. Some even deny the existence of rebirth. Instead, they seek to find connections between Buddhist teachings and modern science. Some have claimed, for example, that the Buddha was the first scientist and that many elements of modern cosmology can be found prefigured in Buddhist scriptures. Modernists also propagate a more active vision of lay Buddhist life than was traditional. Meditation is deemed to be beneficial for lay people as well as monks, and many monasteries have begun to offer meditation classes for lay followers. The laity has also taken the initiative in forming organizations that seek to adapt the tradition to the needs of people living active lives in the modern world.

FOREST SCHOOLS

OVER THE CENTURIES, TWO TYPES OF BUDDHIST MONK EMERGED: THE SCHOLAR, WITH A SETTLED LIFESTYLE AND PERMANENT MONASTIC HOME, AND THE FOREST-DWELLER (*ARANNAVASIN*), WHO, LIKE THE FIRST BUDDHISTS, CONTINUED TO ROAM.

The earliest Buddhist monks were wanderers. The four 'resources' on which they were allowed to rely were alms for food, old rags for clothing, cow's urine for medicine and the shelter of trees for residence. The Indian climate does not, however, support a wandering lifestyle all year round. Moving around is virtually impossible for the three months of the rainy season, so monks tended to settle down together in temporary dwellings during that period. Over time, lay supporters started to provide more permanent accommodation for the resident monks, some of whom began to

Below Ajahn Sumedho (far right) leads an alms round in Thailand. Sumedho, a disciple of Ajahn Chah and abbot of the Amaravati Buddhist Centre, England, has been instrumental in bringing the Thai forest tradition to the West.

take up residence and remain in these proto-monasteries throughout the year.

SCHOLARS AND FOREST-DWELLERS

In Sri Lanka, the separation between scholars and forest-dwelling monks was recognized in the 12th-century reforms of King Parakramabahu I, and persisted through the reforms of 1753 – when the Siyam Nikaya, with its divisions into village-dwellers and forest-dwellers was created. In 1968, unaffiliated forest monks were granted permission to form their own *nikaya*.

In Thailand, the situation was different. When King Rama V (reg 1868–1910) created a national organization for the Thai sangha, he sent representatives out to find a meditation tradition worthy of royal support. They returned

Above A monk walks down the path at Wat Nong Pah Pong Buddhist forest monastery, which was founded by Ajahn Chah in 1954.

empty handed, so he put all his energies into promoting textual study. The texts do, however, preserve information about the *arannavasin* lifestyle, and in the late 19th century, two monks from north-western Thailand, Phra Ajahn Sao Kantasilo and Phra Ajahn Mun Bhuridatto, decided to put this lifestyle into practice.

THE NEW FOREST MONKS

After ordination in 1893, Ajahn Mun went to study meditation with Ajahn Sao, who taught him a mantric form based on repetition of the word *buddho*. They went on pilgrimages together and engaged in ascetic practices known as *thudong*, which were designed to promote detachment and vigour. The Pali texts list 13 of these *thudong*, the most popular of which are living off alms food, eating just one meal per day, living at least half a mile from a village, wearing robes made from rags and sleeping in the sitting position.

Following their pilgrimage to the shrine at Phra That Phanom, Ajahn Mun wandered alone

AJAHN CHAH

Born in rural north-eastern Thailand in 1918, Ajahn Chah requested admission to a monastery at the age of nine. In 1931, he was ordained as a novice, and he took full ordination in 1939.

After a few years of intensive study, he went on pilgrimage to central Thailand, adopting the lifestyle of a forest monk as he travelled. In his search for an effective means of putting the Buddha's teachings into practice, he was led to Ajahn Mun Bhuridatto, who taught him mindfulness meditation. He adopted the lifestyle of a forest monk until 1954, when he was invited back to his home village. He established the meditation centre that would later become Wat Nong Pah Pong nearby. Disciples moved in to learn meditation, and soon branch monasteries were established in other parts of Thailand. From 1969 onward, Wat Nong Pah Pong saw a small but steady stream of Westerners come to study, including Sumedho, who became the first abbot of the International Forest monastery (Wat Pah Nanachat).

Ajahn Chah was invited to England in 1977 and 1979, and then went on to teach in the USA and Canada, leaving Sumedho and others behind in Great Britain. Other monasteries were soon established both in Britain and throughout the English-speaking world. Ajahn Chah died in 1992, leaving a vibrant legacy of Buddhist teaching, practice and lifestyle.

Above Ajahn Chah, whose monasteries have flourished around the world, engages in meditation in the forest, sheltered by a canopy.

around the wilderness of north-eastern Thailand and then, in 1911, walked to Burma (Myanmar) in order to further his studies of meditation. In 1913, while meditating in a cave in Nakhon Nayok province, he attained, according to his disciples, the state of 'non-returner' (*anagami*). The rest of his life was spent wandering the length and breadth of Thailand, often alone, sometimes guiding other monks in the practices of *thudong*, and undertaking meditation retreats.

In the late 1920s, the monastic authorities unsuccessfully attempted to suppress the 'vagrant' forest monks and turn them into 'productive' members of society. Ajahn Mun's disciples recorded his attainment of arhatship in the late 1930s. Ajahn Sao died in 1942, and Ajahn Mun in 1948. By then the Thai forest tradition was firmly established.

Right The classic bell-shaped chedi at Wat Nong Pah Pong contains the relics of Ajahn Chah, and thousands of people pay their respects every year.

The most influential forest monk in modern times has been Ajahn Chah, who opened the tradition to Westerners. They, in turn, have established Thai forest centres across the English-speaking world. The meditation taught at these centres is mainly of the *satipatthana* type, which Ajahn Mun may have brought back from Burma.

Another prominent teacher was Buddhadasa Bhikkhu (1906–93). He practised simple, ethical living combined with extensive meditation. He soon attracted followers with his modernist approach to doctrine and a meditation practice that embraced elements of concentration (dhyana) as well as mindfulness (*sati*).

MEDITATION SCHOOLS

SINCE THE BUDDHA'S OWN ENLIGHTENMENT, MEDITATION HAS BEEN
A CENTRAL PRACTICE OF ALL BUDDHIST SCHOOLS AND TRADITIONS.
SOME SCHOOLS HAVE, HOWEVER, APPROACHED THE PHILOSOPHY OF
MEDITATION AND CONSCIOUSNESS IN DIFFERENT WAYS.

In India, no school of meditation emerged because it tended to be integrated into the regular lives of Buddhist monks and nuns. Meditation is an explicit part of Buddhist practice, with step seven of the Noble Eightfold Path being concerned with mindfulness, and step eight imparting the need for meditation. Perhaps the closest thing to a meditation school in India was the Yogacara (the 'practice of yoga' or 'mind-only' school), which emphasized the role

Below With his eyes shut and sitting in the traditional cross-legged position, this Buddhist practises meditation inside the colourful Shwedagon pagoda in Rangoon, Burma (Myanmar).

of meditation on the spiritual path, though its theoretical and metaphysical teachings were as rich as any to be found among Indian Buddhist communities at the time.

THE YOGACARA SCHOOL

Established in India in the 4th century CE, Yogacara emphasized the twin practices of yoga and meditation. Yogacara masters sought to explain the processes by which we mistake our mental constructs for reality, and set out the meditational strategy for overcoming this tendency. They believed that the fundamental construct a person must uproot, in order to escape from rebirth, is that which divides the world into

Above A seated arhat in a meditation pose, eyes half open and gazing toward the nose, feet in the lotus position and hands resting in the lap.

subject–object and self–other. This uprooting is achieved by a revolution of the 'storehouse consciousness' (*alaya-vijnana*).

The storehouse consciousness contains and preserves all past memories and potential psychic energy, and is the reservoir of all ideas, memories and desires. In this manner, *alaya-vijnana* is believed to perpetuate samsara, the cycle of birth–death–rebirth, as all the 'seeds' *(bija)* stored within it are conditioned by the subject–object distinction.

In the 4th century CE, the Yogacara master Asanga, one of the founders of the Yogacara school, stated in his *Compendium of the Mahayana (Mahayana Samgraha)* that the Buddha preached the Dharma for the destruction of the *alaya*. This view echoes the meanings of a number of terms in the Pali texts that are generally

regarded as synonyms for nirvana: *alaya-samugghata* (the uprooting of the *alaya*) and *analaya* (*no-alaya*). The way to transform the store-house consciousness is to destroy all the seeds contained within it through meditation. The *alaya* will then be 'pure', unaffected by subject–object distinctions, and the world will be seen without distortion. This is awakening.

INSTANT OR GRADUAL AWAKENING?

The early Buddhist philosophers also grappled with the question of whether a follower could become enlightened by degrees, or only instantaneously. On the one hand, there is the example of the Buddha himself. He became enlightened through a single night of striving (though tradition also claims that he had been working toward this for many lifetimes). There are also accounts of early arhats, some of whom attained awakening simply by hearing the Buddha preach the Dharma.

On the other hand, there is the Buddha's teaching on the Four Noble Truths, the fourth of which is the path to awakening with its eight (sometimes ten) stages. There are also Mahayana teachings on the cultivation of the perfections and the stages of the bodhisattva path.

The early Buddhists solved this issue with teachings on the four levels of attainment. Some people, on hearing the Dharma and seeing nirvana, become 'stream-enterers'. Guaranteed liberation within seven lives, they have to follow the path with diligence in order to achieve full awakening. Others become 'once-returners', guaranteed liberation within one further birth and have to follow the path to full awakening. Yet others become 'non-returners', who are guaranteed no more rebirths in this world and will

Above A 16th-century ink drawing of Ge Changgeng, the fifth patriarch of the southern sect of Chan Buddhism, sitting on a three-legged toad.

complete their journey along the path in a heavenly realm. Finally, there are the worthy ones, arhats, who have achieved full awakening and will be born no more.

MEDITATION IN CHINA

This concept of the four levels of attainment never became popular in China. For many Chinese Buddhists, the complexity of this theory and the vast amounts of time that the bodhisattva's path seemed to require appeared alien to the spirit of simplicity at the heart of the Buddha's Dharma. The Chinese thus turned away from this scriptural heritage and sought a direct teaching based on meditative experience, leading to the establishment of the Chan ('meditation') school, which in time developed in Korea as Son Buddhism, and was transmitted to Japan to become Zen Buddhism.

BODHIDHARMA

Believed to be the first patriarch of the Chan school in China, Bodhidharma is a figure of Buddhist legend. Some accounts suggest that he was a Persian, others an Indian ex-Brahman. He is reputed to have meditated for nine years and lost the use of his legs, to have foiled six attempts to poison him, to have had many riddling conversations with his disciples, and to have returned to India or Central Asia to die.

The evidence available suggests that Bodhidharma taught a form of Mahayana doctrine based on the Perfection of Wisdom sutras (*Prajñaparamita*) and the *Vimalakirti-nirdesa Sutra*.

Bodhidharma spent years gazing at a blank wall, and as such symbolizes the absolute commitment needed if a meditator is to nudge the mind back into its original nature. In this manner, he is a good example of the dedication to meditation that underpins the Chan and Zen traditions.

Above Daruma, the Japanese version of Bodhidharma, as depicted on a votive tablet and sold at Buddhist temples. Daruma allegedly introduced Zen into Japan at the same time as he spread Chan in China.

CHAN BUDDHISM

'CHAN' IS THE CHINESE EQUIVALENT OF THE SANSKRIT WORD 'DHYANA', COMMONLY TRANSLATED AS 'MEDITATION'. THE SCHOOL'S ORIGINS ARE SHROUDED IN LEGEND AND RECORDED IN TEXTS THAT WERE COMPOSED LONG AFTER THE EVENTS THEY DESCRIBE.

In all likelihood, the Chan movement originated with wandering monks in the 4th and 5th centuries CE, who blended Buddhist teachings with Daoist ideas. One of the most notable of these is that the nature of things cannot be captured in words. A famous Chan story that illustrates this tells of how one of the Buddha's most eminent disciples, Mahakasyapa, asked the master to

Above This red-lacquer figure from China, which dates from the 13th–14th centuries, depicts the Buddha as an ascetic emerging from the mountains.

teach him about the nature of awakening. The Buddha held up a flower, and Mahakasyapa awoke.

CHAN AND DAOISM

Another influential idea that is found in both traditions is the universality of the truth that disciples seek. In Daoism, this is expressed through the teaching that the unnameable Dao is everywhere, in animals, plants, soil and even in excrement. In Buddhism, it is expressed as the ultimate identity of samsara and nirvana.

Such views enabled the Chan masters to introduce the belief that monks should engage in productive labour, for Buddha-nature (the pure *alaya-vijnana*) could be experienced as easily in the field as in the meditation hall. One effect of

Left Bodhidharma (right), the first Chan patriarch, and Huike, the second Chan patriarch, in an ink painting attributed to Sesshu, a 15th-century Rinzai Zen Buddhist priest famous for his Chinese-style ink paintings.

Right This marble votive stele, which depicts the Buddha Shakyamuni and his assembly, dates from the Northern Qi dynasty, 550–77CE, the period in which Chan Buddhism was introduced to China.

this was that Chan monks could no longer be criticized by Chinese traditionalists for being parasitic. This also helped them – as did the remote location of many Chan monasteries – to survive the great persecution of 845.

CHAN PATRIARCHS

Because Chan teachers sought awakening through direct experience, rather than through scriptural study, it became imperative for them to show that their meditation practices were authentically Buddhist. To this end, they claimed that Chan was a special transmission outside the scriptures with no dependence on words or letters. The conduits for this transmission were the patriarchs, who passed the teaching on to their disciples.

The first of these, according to the legends, was Bodhidharma, a wandering monk from the West. His chief disciple, and the second Chan patriarch, was Huike (487–593CE), who passed the mantle of patriarch to Sengcan (d. 606CE). From him it went to Taoxin (580–651CE) and then to Hongren (601–674CE). This was a significant period in the development of Chan, for the sixth patriarch that followed gave Chan a distinctive character that would come to define its essence.

THE SIXTH PATRIARCH

Hongren spent most of his later life at the monastery of the Eastern Mountain. Many of his disciples became abbots of other monasteries across China, but the Eastern Mountain monastery seems to have passed into the keeping of an elderly meditation master with imperial connections called Shenxiu. His claim to the patriarchate was challenged, however. One of Hongren's disciples, Huineng (638–713CE), was abbot of a regional monastery in what is now Guangdong province. His disciple, Shenhui, started a debate about whether Shenxiu had really been designated as Hongren's successor and whether his teachings

on meditation were authentic. Some of what Shenhui said (and the anecdotes and stories he told) must have had an impact, for the Chan community was led to create its first sutra text in response. This is the famous *Platform Sutra of the Sixth Patriarch*, a composite work that presents Huineng as the unorthodox, brilliant and true sixth patriarch. He taught a doctrine of sudden awakening that is contrasted with Shenxiu's supposed gradualist approach.

From then on, the Chan approach to awakening (*wu*), while it retained the formal meditational techniques of concentration and mindfulness, would always embrace elements designed to jolt the mind out of its everyday patterns and propel meditators into an instantaneous understanding of their true nature. Some schools took this idea much further than others.

Right The Chinese Chan master Hsu Yun, died in Jiangxi, China, in 1959 at the age of 120. He is recognized as the successor to all five houses of Chan Buddhism.

CHAN TEXTS

ALTHOUGH THE CHAN SCHOOL OF BUDDHISM CHARACTERIZED ITSELF AS A TRANSMISSION OF THE DHARMA OUTSIDE THE SCRIPTURES, ITS PATRIARCHS AND TEACHERS CAN BE SEEN TO HAVE DRAWN INSPIRATION FROM A NUMBER OF INFLUENTIAL TEXTS.

The texts that shaped Chan can be divided into two broad groups. The first is formed of original Indian Buddhist texts, the most significant of which were the 'Perfection of Wisdom' sutras (*Prajñaparamita*), the *Instruction of Vimalakirti Sutra* (*Vimalakirti-nirdesa*), the *Descent on Lanka Sutra* (*Lankavatara*) and the *Flower Garland Sutra* (*Avatamsaka*). The second comprises texts that were composed within the Chan tradition itself, the most notable of which is the *Platform Sutra of the Sixth Patriarch* (*Tanjing*).

KEY BUDDHIST TEXTS

The Perfection of Wisdom sutras included the *Perfection of Wisdom in 100,000 Lines*, the *Perfection of Wisdom in 25,000 Lines*, the *Perfection of Wisdom in 8,000 Lines* and the *Diamond Cutter Sutra* (*Vajracchedika*). A copy of the latter, held in the British Library, London, is the oldest dated printed book in the world, produced with carved wooden blocks *c.*868CE. These texts offer early Mahayana expressions of the Buddha's teachings, along with shifts in perspective between conventional truth and supreme truth, which was a favourite device of the Chan masters.

The *Instruction of Vimalakirti Sutra* is a teaching that was delivered by a layman bodhisattva called Vimalakirti on how to attain the 'perfection of wisdom'. One of its attractions to the Chan masters was its argument that being active in the world (in other words, working) was no obstacle to spiritual progress.

The *Descent on Lanka Sutra* identifies Buddha-nature (the reality behind all phenomena)

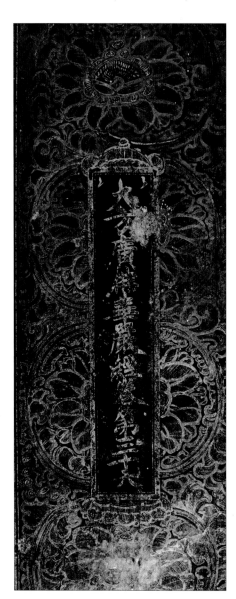

Left A panel from the Flower Garland Sutra, *one of the most influential scriptures in East Asian Buddhism and a foundation of the Huayan school of Chinese Buddhism.*

Above A Shinto painting of Yuima (Vimalakirti). The Instruction of Vimalakirti Sutra *is an important Indian Buddhist text and one that was influential in shaping Chan.*

with the 'storehouse' consciousness, which is inherently pure but can be tainted by the misguided subject–object distinction. This is transformed by meditation, which can be gradual (as in traditional dhyana practice) or sudden, because it is only the distinction that has to be eradicated for all other experiences to be transformed as well.

FLOWER GARLAND SUTRA

The two most important sutras within the *Flower Garland Sutra* are the *Ten Stages Sutra* (*Dasabhumika*) and the *Array of Ornaments Sutra* (*Gandavyuha*). The first of these describes the ten stages on the path of a bodhisattva toward buddhahood. The second presents a cosmology from the perspective of an awakened being. This is an essentially idealist vision (called *dharmadhatu*, or 'realm of truth') in which all phenomena, while remaining distinct, are revealed to be holographic in nature – each is interdependent and 'reflects' all other phenomena. This is because they are all facets of the Buddha-mind, and therefore empty of self-existence.

The image of a net draped over the palace of the god Indra is used to convey this idea. At every intersection of the net is a jewel that reflects not only all the other jewels but also the reflections from them. This vision provided the foundation for the philosophy of the Huayan school, which was one of the three foundations of Korean Chan (Son) established by Chinul (1158-1210), the other two being the *Platform Sutra* and

gongan practice. The holographic doctrine of the *Flower Garland Sutra* offers the possibility of awakening at any time and in any place, for everything contains the essential mystery and can be the occasion for the realization of the Buddha-mind.

TEXTS BY CHAN AUTHORS

The *Platform Sutra* (*Tanjing*) is the most important and influential of the texts composed by Chan authors. The work, which probably took something like its present form around 820CE, has two clear sections. The first is a sermon attributed to Huineng, the sixth partriarch, which has a biography of him inserted into it. This sermon communicates a number of basic Mahayana teachings, most prominently those concerning the 'perfection of wisdom', which Hongren expounded to Huineng on the night he passed on the patriarchate. It explains that while meditation does not

cause awakening, it prepares the mind for it. It criticizes the practice of seeking merit through activities such as temple building, and Pure Land teachings, which it deems to be for people of low intelligence. The second part is a miscellaneous collection of verses and stories on various Chan teachings, criticisms of those deemed to be 'gradualist', verses on the transmission of Chan teachings by the patriarchs and praise for Huineng's teaching.

Other influential Chan compositions include the *gongan* collections known as the *Blue Cliff Record* (*Bi yen lu*) and the *Gateless Barrier* (*Wu men guan*), as well as the various 'lamp records', which established the lineages, and hence legitimacy, of the Chan masters.

Below *An illustration from the* Sutra of the Ten Kings *(early 10th century), one of many Buddhist manuscripts excavated from the Mogao caves at Dunhuang, Gansu province, China.*

CHAN SCHOOLS

DURING THE 10TH AND 11TH CENTURIES THE FLOURISHING CHAN
TRADITION EVOLVED INTO FIVE 'HOUSES' OR SCHOOLS: THE GUIYANG,
LINJI, CAODONG, YUNMEN AND FAYAN SCHOOLS. EACH SCHOOL WAS
LED BY CHARISMATIC MONKS WITH DISTINCTIVE TEACHING STYLES.

The great Buddhist persecution of 845CE, initiated by the Emperor Wucong, affected Buddhism throughout the empire. Chan and Pure Land survived and became the two faces of Chinese Buddhism in the ensuing centuries. In the post-persecution years of the late Tang and early Song dynasties, the Chan tradition consolidated itself around five groups of monasteries or 'houses'.

GUIYANG
The notable feature of Guiyang is that the founders developed a method wherein the master would ask a question to which the disciple would reply with an action rather than words.

Below Some gongan *focused upon everyday activities and the need to bring awareness to the simple tasks of daily life, such as eating and resting.*

LINJI
This school, named after its founder, is known for its teaching through highly metaphorical images. During the Song dynasty (960–1279), Linji's disciples introduced the technique of *gongan*, a kind of riddle to which there is no rational answer. Instead of a rational answer, the master looks for a response in the disciple that indicates an understanding that transcends the rational. Often, this will be in the form of a poem, a short enigmatic retort, an action (as in the Guiyang technique), or even another riddle. Collections of *gongan* began to circulate in Chan communities from around the beginning of the 12th century.

CAODONG
The Caodong tradition adopted the use of *gongan* – in fact, one of its masters, Hongzhi Zhengjue,

Above A gilt bronze statuette of the Buddha in meditation from the Tang dynasty, 618–907CE. This period witnessed a flourishing of art, sculpture, poetry and Buddhism in China, and Chan schools in particular benefited from new translations of key Buddhist scriptures and the transmission of ideas.

compiled an influential collection of them – and developed its own variant of the Madhyamaka dialectic called the 'five ranks formula', but was best known for its technique of silent illumination (*mozhao*) – essentially a form of mindfulness meditation.

YUNMEN AND FAYAN
The Yunmen and Fayan traditions, although short-lived, also contributed distinctive techniques to Chan Buddhism in general. When questioned by disciples, master Yunmen would offer short, enigmatic replies – often just a single word. Like *gongan*, these were designed to jolt

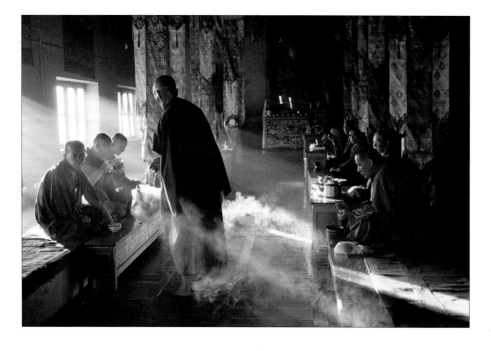

the hearer into non-conceptual, more intuitive modes of thought. Many examples of his methods are preserved in *gongan* collections. Fayan's most distinctive technique was simply to repeat a word or phrase to a disciple until an appropriate response was forthcoming.

Of these five Chan houses, only the Linji and Caodong survived as separate schools. Chan history was rewritten so that the entire tradition became one that had always advocated the sudden method of awakening. Chan masters began to explore the arts as a means of conveying and expressing their teachings. They also engaged in dialogues with Daoist and Confucian masters, thereby underlining the Chinese identity of Chan that was so crucial for its continued survival.

Right A 16th-century depiction of Laozi, the famous Chinese philosopher who lived in the 6th century BCE and established Daoism. Buddhist schools in China, and Chan schools such as Linji and Caodong in particular, were influenced by Daoist thought and philosophy.

Above 'Five-coloured Parakeet on a Blossoming Apricot Tree' by the emperor Huizong. During the Song dynasty more rarefied forms of art were devised, including gong-an, calligraphy and the painting of birds and flowers.

GONGAN

Collections of *gongan* started to appear at the beginning of the 12th century. Of these, the earliest known is the *Bi yen lu*, which was first published in 1128. Influential collections also include the *Wu men guan* and the *Cong rong lu*. The following are some famous *gongan*:

If a man seeks the Buddha, he will lose the Buddha; if he seeks the path, he will lose the path; if he seeks the patriarchs, he will lose the patriarchs.
(*attributed to Linji*)

Followers of the way, as to the Buddha's teaching no effort is necessary. Be ordinary with nothing to do: shitting, pissing, donning clothes, eating food and lying down when tired. Fools laugh at me but the wise understand.
(*attributed to Linji*)

Q: Where do all the Buddhas and patriarchs come from?
A: Eastern Mountain walks on water.
(*attributed to Yunmen*)

A man hangs from a tree branch by his mouth. His hands cannot grasp a bough, his feet cannot touch the trunk. Another man stands below and asks the meaning of Bodhidharma coming from the West. If no answer is forthcoming, the man's need is not met; if an answer is offered, the hanging man will fall to his death. How should he respond?
(*from the* Wu men guan)

CHAN MASTER XUAN HUA

A CHAN MASTER IN THE GUIYANG TRADITION, THOUGHT BY MANY
TO HAVE DIED OUT DURING THE SONG DYNASTY, XUAN HUA
FOUNDED THE DHARMA REALM BUDDHIST ASSOCIATION AND
BECAME AN IMPORTANT FIGURE IN WESTERN BUDDHISM.

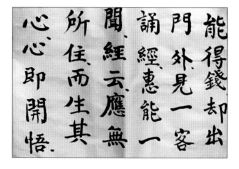

Above Calligraphy by Xuan Hua of part of the Platform Sutra of the Sixth Patriarch, *the most notable of Chan texts. In a dream, Xuan Hua was instructed by the 6th patriarch to take Chan Buddhism to the West.*

Xuan Hua (1918-95) received full ordination in 1947 and Dharma transmission from master Xunyun the following year. (Dharma transmission is a formal acknowledgement by a master of a pupil's awakening and status as a master in his or her own right.) He then went to Hong Kong, where he developed a version of Buddhist teaching that wove the different strands of Chinese Buddhism together.

INFLUENCING THE WEST

As a youth Xuan Hua had a dream that Huineng (the sixth Chan patriarch) had told him to take Buddhism to the West. So, in 1961, he went on tour in Australia, and the following year, turned his energies toward the USA, where his disciples had founded the Sino-American Buddhist Association, which was later renamed the Dharma Realm Buddhist Association (DRBA).

Once Xuan Hua had become established in the USA, his reputation grew steadily. Then, in 1968, five young Americans, three men and two women, approached him requesting ordination as novices. The first full ordination ceremonies were held in 1972 at the Gold Mountain Dhyana monastery in San Francisco (founded in 1970). Regular ordinations were conducted in following years at the City of Ten Thousand Buddhas at Ukiah, California. Theravada bhikkhus were invited to participate in these ordinations as a way of promoting greater understanding and co-operation between Buddhist traditions.

In 1973, the Institute for the Translation of Buddhist Texts was created in San Francisco, and in 1976, the DRBA acquired the 448-acre site for what was to become the City of Ten Thousand Buddhas retreat centre. This now houses the Dharma Realm Buddhist University. The Dharma Realm Buddhist Association currently has a dozen centres in the

Left Xuan Hua engaging in meditation in San Francisco in 1978. The City of Ten Thousand Buddhas had been established by him in the city two years earlier.

USA, two in Canada, five in Malaysia, two in Hong Kong, three in Taiwan and one in Australia.

BUDDHIST CO-OPERATION

Xuan Hua took a further step in the direction of Buddhist co-operation when, in 1987, he held a grand ceremony at the City of Ten Thousand Buddhas and invited more than 70 members of the sangha from mainland China to attend. Three years later, his disciples went to Beijing to collect an edition of the Chinese *Tripitaka*. Reciprocal arrangements were extended when American nuns were invited to stay at the Mingru monastery in Jilin and address the nuns there. In 1995, the year of Xuan Hua's death, two of his disciples were invited to Shanghai to participate in ceremonies at the Long-hua monastery.

Xuan Hua was also active in promoting inter-faith dialogue and understanding, a mission that has been embraced by the DRBA. He was a special presidential guest of George Bush in 1989.

Below The huge Avatamsaka monastery in Calgary, Alberta, Canada, founded in 1985, is one of two Dharma Buddhist Realm Association centres in Canada, and among many others around the world.

THE CITY OF TEN THOUSAND BUDDHAS

One of the first Chinese Zen Buddhist temples in the USA, the City of Ten Thousand Buddhas is one of the largest Buddhist communities in the West. It is situated about 3km (2 miles) east of Ukiah and 177km (110 miles) north of San Francisco. The 488-acre site, formerly belonging to the Mendocino State Hospital, was purchased in 1976. More than 80 per cent of the grounds are made up of meadows, forests and orchards, and the remainder comprises well-equipped buildings, including the Dharma Realm Buddhist University, the Jewelled Hall of 10,000 Buddhas, elementary and secondary schools and a vegetarian restaurant.

Right The gateway of the City of Ten Thousand Buddhas in California, one of the largest Buddhist communities in the West.

All residents live under six guiding principles – not to fight, not to be greedy, not to seek, not to be selfish, not to pursue personal advantage and not to lie – and commit to eating a pure vegetarian diet. Monks and nuns also commit to living under full vinaya regulations. Training programmes are in place for lay Buddhists as well as those wishing to be ordained as monks or nuns. Fully ordained monks live according to 250 bhikkhu precepts plus 10 major and 48 minor bodhisattva precepts. Nuns take the same bodhisattva precepts and 348 bhikkhuni precepts. Visitors are welcome and a virtual tour of the city is available on the official website: www.cttbusa.org.

SON BUDDHISM

THE KOREAN VERSION OF THE CHINESE BUDDHIST MEDITATION SCHOOL CHAN, SON ARRIVED IN KOREA DURING THE UNIFIED SILLA PERIOD (688–918CE). IT IS A DISTINCTLY KOREAN SYNTHESIS OF MATERIAL FROM VARIOUS BUDDHIST SOURCES.

Pomnang, the monk who first took Chan to Korea, combined two Chinese traditions of Chan with the idealist teachings of the *Awakening of Faith in the Mahayana*, a text composed in China that is attributed to the Indian Buddhist Ashvaghosa. During the 8th and 9th centuries, nine schools of Son emerged. The oldest of these was the Huiyang-san, which was founded by a disciple of Pomnang. The others were formed by various Korean masters after they returned from China. Each school

had its headquarters on a mountain, and they came to be known as the Nine Mountain schools.

THE CHOGYE CHONG

In the late 12th century, the Son master Chinul (1158–1210) developed a distinctively Korean version of Son: the Chogye Chong. This was a synthesis of the practices of the Nine Mountain schools with *kongan* (Chinese: *gongan*; Japanese: *koan*) techniques for cultivating sudden enlightenment, along with the teachings of various schools,

Above A gold lacquer figure of the seated Buddha, 18th century. Korean art absorbed influences from many sources, from the Mahayana and Theravada schools, and Tantric Buddhism, as well as Shamanism and Confucianism.

particularly the Huayan (Korean: *Hwaom*). He did not repudiate textual study but rather combined it with meditation practice, placing particular emphasis on the *Platform Sutra of the Sixth Patriarch* and the *Avatamsaka Sutra*. Son practice, Chinul came to realize, led to the experience of *dharmadhatu* (the realm of truth, the holographic Buddha-mind) as described in the *Avatamsaka*.

From 1424 until the Japanese annexation of Korea in 1910, the Chogye Chong was merged with two Chinese-derived schools to form a unified Son school, the

Left A bronze figure of the Buddha surrounded by two bodhisattvas from the Koryo period (918–1392). It was during this period that the Chogye Chong form of Son was established as Korea's main Buddhist tradition.

Son Chong. Throughout this period, the Son was one of just two Buddhist schools in Korea, the other being the Doctrine school (Kyo Chong). In 1935, these two were amalgamated and named, somewhat confusingly, Chogye Chong.

MODERNIZATIONS

Under the Japanese, Buddhist monks were encouraged to marry, and by 1935, almost all of the senior incumbents in monasteries were married. This was anathema to traditionalists, and after World War II, the Korean Buddhist community split into the T'aego Chong, a faction representing married monks, and the Chogye Chong, representing the traditionalists. In 1954, the South Korean government supported the Chogye Chong in its attempt to regain control of the monasteries, and now only celibate monks are allowed to become abbots.

Today, around half of the 50,000 or so Korean monks and nuns are married. They serve the needs of more than six million Korean Buddhists. In an effort to adapt traditional Korean Buddhism to the modern world, Son leaders emphasize education and social welfare, run retreats for the laity, operate a number of newspapers and, at Donnguk University, are sponsoring a systematic translation of Buddhist texts into Korean. Korean Buddhism has also gone international: the Kwan Um school, founded in 1983 by the Chogye monk Seung Sahn, now has around 60 branches across Europe and the Americas.

Right A Buddhist monk beats a ceremonial bell at Bulguksa temple in South Korea. The temple was first built in 774CE, during the Silla dynasty, and many buildings were reconstructed during the 20th century.

THE KWAN UM SCHOOL

The Kwan Um School of Zen was founded in 1983 by Seung Sahn (1927–2004), a Korean Son monk who emigrated to the USA in 1974. Shortly after his arrival in Rhode Island, he started teaching Western students a Korean version of Rinzai Zen practice based on *kongan* (Chinese: *gongan*; Japanese: *koan*). The popularity of this, especially with students from nearby Brown University, gave him the confidence to open more centres: one in Los Angeles (1974), one in New York (1975) and one in Berkeley (1977). He then travelled extensively and established more centres in Israel, Russia and South Africa. There are now some 60 centres across the world, most of them located in Europe and the USA. The present headquarters is in Cumberland, Rhode Island.

Seung Sahn's approach to Son was both eclectic and modernist. He combined traditional Son ritual with Rinzai *kongan* practice and Pure Land chanting and prostration. (One thousand bows per day is a typical practice for helping to loosen the grip of the ego.) The *kongan* material was a mixture of the traditional and *kongans* that Seung Sahn had created himself. He later incorporated *Zazen* ('just sitting') practice, as many of his students had been introduced to Zen through *Zazen* training. He also employed 'Dharma combat', a technique not dissimilar in spirit to the debate traditions of Tibetan Buddhism, in which a disciple's knowledge of Buddhism is tested by a teacher.

Right Seung Sahn, the 78th patriarch in the Chogye order of Korean Buddhism and founder of the Kwan Um school of Zen.

ZEN BUDDHISM

ALTHOUGH BUDDHISM HAD BEEN THE STATE RELIGION SINCE THE MID-6TH CENTURY, IT WAS NOT UNTIL THE HEIAN PERIOD (794–1185) THAT ZEN BUDDHISM, A SCHOOL OF MAHAYANA BUDDHISM, WAS INTRODUCED TO JAPAN FROM CHINA.

State support for Buddhism led to corruption in the monasteries and a corresponding desire on the part of some monks to seek out the original purity of Buddhist teaching. One such was Saicho (767–822), who founded a strict monastery on Mount Hiei (north-east of Kyoto) in 788 and then spent a year in China (804–5). On his return, he introduced the Tendai school into Japan. This was not, however, a direct transplant of the Chinese school into Japan, but rather the creation of a distinctive synthesis of Buddhist traditions with native Japanese Shinto. One element of this synthesis was Zen (the Japanese word for the Chinese 'Chan', which means meditation).

EARLY ZEN

The two 'founding fathers' of Japanese Zen, Eisai and Dogen, both studied on Mount Hiei.

Above Kinkaku-ji, also known as the Golden Pavilion, in Kyoto, Japan. An important Zen temple, built in 1397, it is covered in gold and houses relics of the Buddha.

Eisai (1141–1215) made two visits to China, a brief one in 1168, and a more extended stay from 1187 to 1191, during which he practised *Zazen* (seated meditation) and *koan* (the contemplation of key questions) and experienced an awakening. On his return, he established what is often regarded as the first Zen temple on the southern island of Kyushu.

Even there, however, Zen was not completely disentangled from the other components of the Tendai synthesis. This was eventually achieved in the next generation by four Chinese masters, who introduced Soto (called *Caodong* in Chinese). The Soto form of Zen involves sitting meditation.

The 14th century saw an improvement in the fortunes of Zen, particularly its Rinzai version, where devotees meditate using breath and *koan* practice. Its ability to accommodate neo-Confucian ideas made it popular

Left The tea ceremony is central to Japanese ritual and culture, and has its roots in Zen Buddhist philosophy and practice. This woman is wearing the traditionally elaborate court dress.

with the new generation of warrior aristocrats, as did its association with the Japanese tradition of martial arts (Bushido).

STATE PATRONAGE AND CONTROL

Once again, state patronage of Zen led to a loss of vitality. Answers to *koans* and certificates for the achievement of awakening (*satori*) became available for purchase, and monks started to spend much of their time on pursuits such as poetry, flower arranging, calligraphy, painting, garden design, the tea ceremony and Noh drama. (According to the most eminent proponent of the Noh theatre, Zeami Motokiyo, 1363–1443, the training of Zen monks and Noh actors was rooted in the same fundamental principles.)

There were reactions to this perceived decadence. Reformist monks wrote verses criticizing the hypocrisy of the establishment temples, while others challenged social mores through the obvious flouting of monastic rules, seeking to promote outrage, discussion and a return to earlier standards.

Toward the end of the Kamakura dynasty (1185–1333), Japanese society was fractured by incessant wars between rival clan chiefs. This was brought to an end with the decisive victory of Oda Nobunaga. As part of his reunification plans, he destroyed the great temple power bases of the militarized monks who had fought in the wars. From 1571 to 1603, Nobunaga and his successor, Toyotomi Hideyoshi, destroyed or brought under state control all the fortified monasteries in Japan. The Zen monasteries escaped most of this destruction as their monks had declined to take up arms, and thus they were able to flourish in the highly regulated conditions created by the Tokugawa shogunate.

Above A bodhisattva by the Japanese Buddhist sculptor Kaikei (1183–1236). During the Kamakura period, Zen Buddhism had a pronounced influence on Japanese art.

A NEW ZEN TRADITION

Obaku Zen, a blend of Zen and Pure Land teachings, was brought from China in 1654 to become the third, though always the smallest, Zen tradition in Japan.

Hakuin Ekaku (1685–1769), one of the foremost Zen masters, also lived around this time. He is noted for arranging the collected *koans* into five grades. Success at the first level brought an awakening (*satori*) that had then to be deepened by *koan* meditation at the higher ones. He discouraged monks from becoming too involved in the arts and was highly critical of the 'silent illumination' approach advocated by the rival Soto tradition. All modern Rinzai masters trace their lineage back through Hakuin.

MODERN ZEN

In the modern period, Zen, and in particular Rinzai, reinvented itself as representing the spirit of the Japanese people, with their combination of aesthetic sensitivity and military discipline. Links with Bushido, which had been rather tenuous for many of the earlier Zen masters, were emphasized as monks were called upon to train the laity in Zen discipline while Japan prepared for war.

After World War II, Zen monks adapted to the new democratic and capitalist environment by teaching meditation and Zen philosophy to corporate workers in search of economic success and intellectuals seeking a distinctively Japanese approach to philosophy. They also began exporting Zen to the West.

Below These monks practising Zazen meditation at the Eihei-ji Zen temple in Japan focus on careful breathing and concentrated awareness in order to attain enlightenment.

ZEN SCHOOLS

THE THREE MAIN ZEN SCHOOLS IN JAPAN – RINZAI, SOTO AND OBAKU – WERE ALL IMPORTED FROM CHINA. ALL THREE WERE ADAPTED TO JAPANESE CULTURE AND CIRCUMSTANCES, BUT STILL RETAINED THEIR DISTINCTIVE CHARACTERISTICS.

Above Tenryu-ji in Kyoto is the head temple of the Rinzai school. Founded in 1339, it occupies the site of Danrin-ji, the first Zen temple in Japan, built in the 9th century CE.

In modern Japan, Zen remains of great importance. The three main schools, Rinzai, Soto and Obaku, have the most adherents, but there are also five independent Japanese Zen organizations that claim no affiliation with any of the main Zen schools. These are the Ichibata Yakushi Kyodan, the Senshin Kyodan, the Nyoraikyo, the Isson Kyodan and the Sanbo Kyodan. All of these schools have their roots in Buddhist history.

RINZAI ZEN
Practitioners of the Rinzai school use breathing and *koans* (questions aimed at producing awakening) to seek enlightenment. The introduction of this school to Japan is usually attributed to Myoan Eisai (1141–1215), who brought it from China. However, the pure Rinzai tradition did not arrive until the beginning of the 13th century, when it was introduced by Chinese monks.

Among this school's most prominent exponents during the following centuries were Nampo Jomyo (1235–1308), Bankei Yotaku (1622–92) and Hakuin Ekaku (1685–1769). Nampo Jomyo founded the Otokan sub-school, which was dedicated to maintaining a 'pure' form of Rinzai, uncontaminated by teachings from other schools, within or outside Buddhism. Otokan still survives in modern Japan.

Bankei Yotaku based his instruction on the Mahayana teaching of the unborn Buddha-mind in all sentient beings. For him, to practise *Zazen* (seated meditation) was to be in the Buddha-mind, which meant to be awakened. He believed that a person could be in the Buddha-mind at any time and in any situation. He kept his guidance clear and simple, attracting a large lay audience. Followers were told that they could practise Zen as they went about their daily lives. This approach, commonly known as 'unborn Zen', is currently undergoing a resurgence in modern Japan. (In 2000, Japan had 5,754 Rinzai temples.)

The third, and most influential of the great Rinzai masters, was Hakuin Ekaku. In addition to his systematization of *koan* practice into five levels, he also engaged in a lively criticism of the Soto school. This rivalry had its roots in the Chinese debates between the two schools.

SOTO ZEN
The Soto school, which utilizes silent seated meditation to gain enlightenment, was introduced into Japan by Dogen Kigen (1200–53) on his return in 1227 from a four-year visit to China. There, he had experienced the benefits of 'just sitting' (*shikantaza*). This led to what he called the 'unthinking of thinking', a process akin to that of maintaining mindful awareness in the present moment. He emphasized the importance of adopting a relaxed, wakeful posture, regular breathing, the proper alignment of the limbs and keeping the eyes open. He also stressed the importance of monastic discipline and ethical

Left A Kamakura-period sculpture of Zen master Muso Soseki (1275–1351). Soseki fostered the golden age of Rinzai, wrote poetry and influenced the development of Zen gardens.

living. For Dogen, a simple life, a vegetarian diet and regular meditation (*Zazen*) represented the sure and gentle road to awakening.

Under Keigan Jokin (1268–1325), often known as the second Soto patriarch, devotion to Kannon (Guanyin in China) and worship of Shinto deities were incorporated into Soto practice, which became jokingly known as 'farmers' Zen'. Soto monks also engaged in public-service works, such as road building and irrigation digging, as well as various kinds of healing. This helped the Soto to become the largest of the Japanese Zen schools, a position it still maintains today, with some 14,718 temples.

Below Morning service in the Dharma hall at Eihei-ji, founded by Dogen Kigen in 1228 and the head temple of the Soto school. Today, approximately 150 monks live and practise at this temple.

Above A seated Nyoirin Kannon, or Bodhisattva Avalokiteshvara, in a distinctive meditative pose, c. 1230–50. The figure of Nyoirin became popular in esoteric Buddhism in Japan from the 10th century onward.

OBAKU ZEN

Obaku Zen was brought to Japan in the 17th century by a Buddhist monk from China called Yinyuan Longqi (known as Ingen Ryuki in Japan, 1592–1673) at the request of his Japanese disciples. Its inclusion of devotions to Amida Buddha (Amitabha) and its commitment to the value of all Buddhist texts won it a substantial following. One of Ingen's disciples, Tetsugen Doko (1630–82), was the initiator of a huge project to create a Japanese canon of writings from all Buddhist schools on woodblocks; there are 6,956 printed volumes in all. Obaku masters are eclectic in terms of practice, encouraging the use of *koans* and *Zazen* alongside the chanting of the *nembutsu* (Chinese: *nianfo*): *Namu Amida butsu* ('Honour to Amitabha Buddha'). There were 460 Obaku temples in Japan at the turn of the last century.

POPULAR BUDDHISM

ZEN TOOK HOLD IN AMERICA THANKS TO THE COUNTRY'S LINKS WITH JAPAN VIA THE WEST COAST. THE PROMISE OF ENLIGHTENMENT THROUGH MEDITATION WAS TAKEN UP WITH GUSTO IN THE POST-WAR ERA AND TODAY ZEN METHODS ARE USED EVEN BY NON-BUDDHISTS.

Buddhism arrived in the Western world – essentially Europe and America – from two directions: in Europe, the main conduit was the colonial powers, while Americans received Buddhism mostly from across the Pacific via Hawaii. Because of this, Theravada remains the most well-represented Buddhist tradition in Europe. Americans were mainly exposed to Chinese and Japanese forms, which is why Zen Buddhism is better represented in North America. Initially, however,the main impetus for bringing Zen across the Pacific came from intellectuals.

ZEN REACHES THE USA

The World's Parliament of Religions, convened in 1893 as an adjunct to the world's fair being held in Chicago that year, had as one of its speakers the Rinzai master Soen Shaku. He made such an impression on Paul Carus of Open Court Publishing that Carus commissioned the Rinzai scholar D.T. Suzuki to write numerous works on nearly all aspects of Zen, many of which are still in print. Meanwhile, Chinese and Japanese immigrants had been making their way to Hawaii and the West Coast of the USA, though it was mainly devotional Buddhism that they brought with them. The first Zen temple was established in Hawaii in 1901.

American enthusiasts for Zen invited Soen Shaku back to the USA in 1905–6. One of his disciples, Nyongen Senzaki, subsequently founded a number of Zen groups on the West Coast, while another disciple, Sokei-an (Sasaki Shigetsu), formed the Buddhist Society of America, later renamed the First Zen Institute of

Above The Byodo-In temple on O'ahu, Hawaii, was built in the 1960s as a replica of the one in Japan to commemorate the centenary of the first Japanese Buddhist immigrant workers to arrive in Hawaii.

America. The first edition of the Institute's magazine, *Cat's Yawn*, was published in July 1940.

In the years following World War II, Zen engaged the minds of many young Americans through the extensive writings of D.T. Suzuki and Zen's popularization by 'beat' writers, such as Jack Kerouac and Allen Ginsberg. Baby-boomers started to experiment with Zen, and by the early 1970s, Occidental Zen masters were running major centres in San Francisco (Richard Baker), Rochester, New York (Philip Kapleau), Honolulu (Robert Aitken) and Shasta Abbey, near Dunsmuir in Northern California (Jiyu Kennett).

JIYU (PEGGY) KENNETT

The life of British-born Zen master Jiyu Kennett (1924–96) provides an example of some of the changes that took place within the Zen tradition after its arrival in the West – and also some of the

Left Hawaiians partake in a lantern-floating ceremony in 2004. This practice is part of the Obon festival in Japan, but in Hawaii has been adopted to honour war dead.

challenges it still has to address. In 1962, she took full bhikkhuni ordination in the Malaysian Lin-ji tradition and then went on to the Sojiji Soto temple in Japan to further her training. The following year, her insight (*kensho*) was acknowledged by master Koho Zenji. She received Dharma transmission from him and was then certified as a *roshi* (Zen master).

She implemented her teacher's desire for her to take Soto Zen to the West, initially visiting San Francisco in 1969, then founding Shasta Abbey the following year. Branch monasteries (now 23 in number) soon opened in other parts of the USA, as well as in Britain, Canada, Germany and the Netherlands.

The Buddhist establishment, however, did not welcome this female Zen *roshi*. She was shunned by the Buddhist Society in Britain, and the Soto hierarchy in Japan refused to endorse her Order of Buddhist Contemplatives or register her students.

CHALLENGING TIMES

Young Americans today seem to be less attracted to Zen than their baby-boomer parents. Indeed, many of the new recruits to Zen are older baby-boomers who are seeking spiritual enrichment in the second half of life rather than direction in the first.

Another challenge is the detaching of Zen from its Buddhist roots. Many of D.T. Suzuki's writings suggest that meditation is essentially independent of culture and tradition and is ultimately self-authenticating. Soto practitioners would not be entirely surprised at this line of argument, as they have always insisted that this is one of the greatest dangers that comes with the Rinzai approach. But in

ZEN IN THE ART OF ARCHERY

This delightful little book by Eugen Herrigel did much to make Zen accessible to the European mind, not only in his native Germany but also in the countries where it was disseminated in English, French, Italian and Scandinavian translations.

The book takes the reader through a six-year course of instruction under archery master Kenzo Awa. Readers share the frustration as Herrigel struggles to experience the Zen mind that allows for excellence in archery while not being a means to achieve excellence in archery: "The more obstinately you try to learn how to shoot the arrow for the sake of hitting the goal, the less you will succeed in the one and the further the other will recede". He is guided, when ready, through foundations in proper breathing and muscular relaxation to that state where 'right doing' is effortless and selfless, where there is no grief over bad shots nor rejoicing over good ones. One night, his master demonstrates the power of that selfless mind when, in the darkness, he releases two arrows. The first strikes the bull's-eye and the second splits the first. The final chapter explains how that same selfless mind underpins Japanese arts as diverse as flower arranging, painting and swordsmanship. Perfection in the art of swordsmanship is reached, he explains, "when the heart is troubled by no more thought of I and You".

Below Buddhists participating in kyudo *(Japanese archery, or 'the Way of the Bow'), which includes standing meditation practice, and combines the sacred and the spiritual in Japanese culture.*

America, this tendency may not be confined to Rinzai. Meditation teachers from all Buddhist traditions attend each other's retreats and workshops and even design jointly taught ones. Teachers from other religions also detach Zen methods from Zen teaching, employing them within the framework of their own philosophies. All this points to the danger of a dilution that may eventually rob Zen of any distinctive identity in Western culture.

BURMESE TEACHERS

A CENTRAL ELEMENT IN BUDDHIST TEACHING IS *VIPASSANA*, THE PALI WORD FOR 'INSIGHT'. THE INSIGHT IT REFERS TO IS THAT OF THE WORLD AS IT REALLY IS. IN MODERN TIMES, MEDITATION TEACHERS FROM BURMA HAVE LED THE WAY.

When Buddhists speak of *vipassana*, they are referring to an insight into reality based on 'right knowledge', which is sometimes listed as the ninth step of the path to liberation. But how is *vipassana* achieved? Of course, there are many routes to such a realization and understanding, but one approach is meditation. In recent times it has chiefly been meditation teachers from Burma who have given practical guidance in useful techniques. The two most influential of these teachers have been Mahasi Sayadaw, an eminent monk, and Sayagyi U Ba Khin, a highly respected layman.

In general terms, *vipassana* meditation is based on the Three Universal Truths, namely impermanence (*anicca*), suffering (*dhukkha*) and that there is no soul (*anatta*). The meditator finds a place to sit quietly and calms his or her mind. The aim is to observe the world and any inner feelings

Above Jack Kornfield, a prominent Buddhist, learned vipassana *meditation from Mahasi Sayadaw. Kornfield is the founding member of the Spirit Rock Meditation Center, in California.*

and thoughts that arise in a detached way. Sometimes the meditator contemplates or focuses on the body or the breath.

MAHASI SAYADAW

The respected teacher Mahasi Sayadaw (1904–82) was ordained in 1923 and went on to develop a special interest in the *Mahasatipatthana Sutta* and the *Satipatthana* method of meditation, which he studied under the guidance of Mingun Jetavan Sayadaw and began teaching in 1938. Throughout World War II, he lived at the Mahasi monastery at Seikkhun (hence the name Mahasi), where he gave instruction in what he called *satipatthana vipassana* meditation. In essence, this involves a mindful focusing on the breathing, especially in the

Left Mahasi Sayadaw leads a procession of monks at Oakenholt Buddhist Centre in Oxford, England, during one of his trips to Europe to spread the Dharma.

abdominal area, followed by a detached observation of whatever arises in the meditator's awareness.

In 1949, Mahasi Sayadaw took charge of the recently established Sasana Yeiktha Meditation Centre in Rangoon. Teachers from this centre were later invited to take the method to Sri Lanka, Thailand, Cambodia and Indonesia. He also taught meditation to Western lay people, notable among whom are the Americans Joseph Goldstein, Jack Kornfield and Sharon Salzberg, and the German Walter Kulbarz (Vimalo).

SAYAGYI U BA KHIN

A contemporary of Mahasi Sayadaw, Sayagyi U Ba Khin (1899–1971) became one of Burma's most famous meditation teachers, although he was never ordained. Indeed, he combined his meditation teaching with an active life as a government official and a father of six children.

His approach to meditation was strongly influenced by that of the eminent Burmese meditation master Ledi Sayadaw, and his practice was, in some ways, more traditional than that of Mahasi Sayadaw. His guidance on mindfulness (*sati*) encourages the meditator to focus attention on the breath as it passes over the upper lip, rather than on the rise and fall of the abdomen, as practitioners are encouraged to do in Mahasi Sayadaw's approach.

Perhaps more significant was Sayagyi U Ba Khin's emphasis on the importance of concentration (*samadhi*) in the development of insight and on impermanence (*anicca*) as the focus of *samadhi*.

Like Mahasi Sayadaw, Sayagyi U Ba Khin also offered his teachings to foreign students, most notable of whom are the Americans John Coleman and Ruth Denison, and the Indian

S.N. Goenka. Although all of these teachers have tended to downplay the importance of *samadhi* for the attainment of insight, there are some Western teachers who do continue to stress the importance of *samadhi*, one of the most prominent being the German nun Ayya Khema (Ilse Ledermann).

REACHING THE WEST

Since students of these Burmese masters first brought back their techniques to the West in the 1950s, they have tended to detach meditation practice from Buddhist teachings far more than their mentors ever did. They often present meditation as a universal method for promoting skilful living, rather than as a means of attaining liberation from rebirth.

They have also been more eclectic with regard to the kinds of practices that they include in their training, often weaving Tibetan and Zen techniques into their meditation courses.

The number of courses grew rapidly in the 1980s and 1990s, increasing from around a dozen in the mid-1980s to more than 100 by the mid-1990s. It remains to be seen whether this popularity will continue. Much will depend on whether people in the next generation find meditation a useful complement to their lives.

Below Meditation became popular in the West in the second half of the 20th century. Attention is given to the body and its posture, breathing and resting the mind.

DEVOTIONAL SCHOOLS

PRAYERS, PRAISES AND SUBMISSION TO A DEITY MIGHT SEEM TO HAVE
NO PLACE IN BUDDHISM. YET THE IDEA OF ENLIGHTENED BEINGS
THAT CAN OFFER HELP COMES FROM ONE OF THE EARLIEST
BUDDHIST TEXTS AND HAS LED TO SEVERAL DEVOTIONAL SCHOOLS.

*Above A Tibetan 19th-century
thangka of a Bardo mandala, showing
the period between death and rebirth.
Numerous deities exist in this 'in-
between' stage, and guide the deceased
individual toward liberation.*

The practice of praying to a deity had little prominence in early Indian Buddhism. Even so, there were some elements of a devotional approach. Pali texts contain many examples of the Buddha preaching a sermon or giving instruction, as a result of which someone acquires the *Dharma-caksus* – the eye that sees the Dharma – and is then able to embark on the Eightfold (or Tenfold) Path toward the eradication of suffering. The Buddha was there to help people on their spiritual journeys. So, too, were his awakened disciples. The Buddha was noted for his great compassion, for had he not postponed his own departure from this world in order to show men and gods how to escape from suffering?

A LESS PERSONAL PERSPECTIVE

As many monasteries were established and more monks and nuns began to map out their experiences of meditation, an emphasis on what might be called 'depersonalization' began to develop.

Buddhists believed the primary obstacle to spiritual progress is the subject–object distinction, with its roots in ignorance about the nature of the self. Buddhist meditators emphasized the compound nature of each person. A 'person' they taught, is really just the five aggregates (skandha), which are

themselves made up of dharmas, evanescent moments of existence. There is no self (*atman*).

While this can be useful for understanding the illusory nature of the subject–object distinction, it can promote a kind of detachment toward all phenomena, including the ignorant, suffering beings for whom the Buddha had postponed his own departure from the world. It can, that is, oppose the cultivation of compassion.

Many Mahayana sutras tried to balance the emphasis on the compound nature of all phenomena by renewing the focus on suffering beings and re-emphasizing the importance of compassion.

One of the earliest Mahayana texts, the *Lotus Sutra*, offers many examples of Buddhist compassion in action. There, the Buddha explains to his followers, often using parables, that his great compassion leads him to adopt a variety of 'skilful means' to help beings toward awakening. Thus, even though Shakyamuni has passed away, he still works to help suffering beings. To this end, he takes many forms and

*Left Avalokiteshvara, the Bodhisattva of
Compassion, from the Chinese Five
Dynasties period (907–60). Nowhere
is out of reach of the love and mercy of
this bodhisattva, who is often depicted
with 11 heads and 1,000 arms.*

Above This 15th-century Tibetan statuette is of Vajradhara, the primordial or Adi-Buddha, who is self-emanating and has no beginning or end. He represents enlightenment but also the void and emptiness.

appears in many places. The mechanics of how he could take form were later mapped out in the doctrine of the Buddha's three bodies (*trikaya*). These are the Dharma body (*dharmakaya*), the universal, awakened totality of things; the bliss body (*sambhogakaya*), the form he takes in heavenly realms when revealing the Dharma to their residents; and the transformation body (*nirmanakaya*), which he adopts when communicating the Dharma in earthly realms.

RECEIVING HELP

The message to Buddhists is clear: you are not alone. Advanced spiritual beings, such as bodhisattvas, are around to help. They do this through their

Right A Buddhist nun prays beside the large seated buddha at Wat Sri Chum in Sukhothai, Thailand. This Buddha touches the earth to call witness to his victory over Mara, the personification of desire.

teachings and also by using their great stores of merit to lift struggling beings up to a higher level.

In offering the follower salvation from suffering, Buddhism has to steer between two extremes: it is all up to the individual, or it is all done for you. The problem with the first is that the path can seem hard and progress slow. The solution is to provide some assistance. The problem with the second is that effort and morality become marginalized. If individuals make no contribution to their own awakening or salvation,

why should they not simply seek pleasure wherever they can? Why should they practise meditation? Why should they help others?

History shows, with some qualifications, that Buddhism began by stressing the importance of effort, and gradually came to offer more and more assistance to its adherents. The *Lotus Sutra* introduced the idea of awakened beings helping others. Other texts, such as the *Pure Land Sutras* and the *Meditation on Amitayus Sutra*, provided more details about how this could be achieved.

THE PURE LAND TRADITION

WHEN BUDDHISM REACHED CHINA A NEW SCHOOL OF THOUGHT DEVELOPED, KNOWN AS PURE LAND. IT ADDRESSED THE NEED FOR SPIRITUAL ASSISTANCE DIRECTLY, ALLOWING DEVOTEES TO CALL UPON THE HELP OF DEITIES FOR A QUICK PATH TO ENLIGHTENMENT.

The Buddhist school known as Pure Land is based on three early Mahayana texts that describe a 'pure land' free from suffering. The larger and smaller pure land (*Sukhavati-vyuha*) sutras are thought to have been composed during the 2nd century CE, while the meditation on Amitayus (*Amitayus-Dhyana*) Sutra was written later. The core ideas in these texts include the concept of a buddha-field (*buddhaksetra*); another is the practice of remembering the Buddha (*buddhanusmriti*).

BUDDHA-FIELDS

The teachings about buddha-fields are not entirely consistent, and different versions generate

different kinds of philosophical problems. Buddha-fields can be thought of as universes. Most of these have been created by the karma of the beings who inhabit them and are thus 'impure'. Buddhas arise in these worlds in order to 'purify' (awaken) them.

There are, however, some buddha-fields that are created from the merit of buddhas and bodhisattvas. These are 'pure lands', where it is easy to experience awakening. Some of the very earliest Buddhist texts refer to people who become 'non-returners' upon hearing and practising the Dharma. They achieve full awakening in a heavenly realm where there are few impediments to their progress. The idea of 'pure lands' is probably at least partly influenced by these references.

The *Larger Pure Land Sutra* describes how a bodhisattva called Dharmakara vowed to use all his merit to create a buddha-field that would be more conducive to awakening than any other, and explains that he would refrain from attaining buddhahood until his vow was realized. He now presides over the Pure Land of Sukhavati in the West as the Amitabha Buddha (the Buddha of

Left A representation of the 'Paradise of Amitabha', or the Pure Land, where it is believed to be easy to obtain enlightenment. Dating from the 10th century, this silk painting comes from Dunhuang, Gansu province, China.

Above A jade sculpture of Guanyin, the Chinese version of the bodhisattva Avalokiteshvara. In Buddhist philosophy, Guanyin is a companion bodhisattva to Amitabha, and they are sometimes depicted together.

Infinite Light), also known as Amitayus. All beings who have not committed any of the five great crimes (murdering a parent, murdering an arhat, harming a buddha, causing schism in the Sangha and slandering the Dharma) can be reborn in the Pure Land if they sincerely desire it and recite the name of Amitabha ten times.

PURE LAND IN CHINA

In China, the Pure Land texts and the meditation practices they promoted had an initially lukewarm reception. A few practising Pure Land meditations are mentioned during the 4th century CE. Images and paintings of Amitabha also appear in China around that time. However, it was not until the 6th century that an independent Pure Land tradition was established. Its most influential figures were Tanluan (476–542CE), Daochuo (562–645), Shandao (613–681) and Fazhao (9th century).

Tanluan distinguished between difficult and easy routes to awakening. The former involve the traditional Buddhist disciplines and practices; the latter are based on the vows of Dharmakara.

Below An image from the Meditation on Amitayus Sutra. *This important Pure Land text explains how to visualize Amitabha to reach the Pure Land within one lifetime.*

***Above** A large bronze statue of the Amida Buddha, the Japanese version of Amitabha. Believed to date from the 13th century, this well-known Japanese icon is part of the Kotoku-in Pure Land temple in Kamakura.*

Daochuo was the first to use strings of beads to help meditators keep track of their *nianfo* (repetition of Amitabha's name). He also promoted the Pure Land route as the one most suited to an age in which the Dharma was in decline. Shandao wrote a commentary on the *Meditation on Amitayus Sutra*, in which he argued that the principal Pure Land practice was the *nianfo*. Other practices, such as merit transfer, were deemed to be merely supplementary. This teaching enhanced the popular appeal of the Pure Land tradition. Fazhao developed a five-tone melody to help with *nianfo* recitation, which is still used by modern Japanese practitioners in the Jodo Shinshu tradition.

Innovation within the Chinese Pure Land tradition ground to a halt during the Song dynasty (960-1279), but by this time it had taken root in Japan.

THE JODO SHU SCHOOL

THE PURE LAND REACHED JAPAN IN THE 8TH CENTURY AND BY THE 12TH CENTURY HAD DEVELOPED INTO AN INDEPENDENT SCHOOL KNOWN AS JODO SHU. FOLLOWERS REPEAT SPECIAL MANTRAS EVERY DAY TO GAIN SPIRITUAL MERIT AND PREPARE FOR DEATH.

Genshin (942–1017) was one of the earliest Japanese advocates of Pure Land practices, especially the *nembutsu* (the recollection of the Buddha). By this time, two main types of *nembutsu* had been distinguished: the meditative and the recitative.

The meditative approach took a number of forms, often involving a combination of visualizing the Buddha (usually Amitabha, known as Amida in Japan) and meditating on his name. In all its forms, the meditative *nembutsu* was understood as a means, or method, for

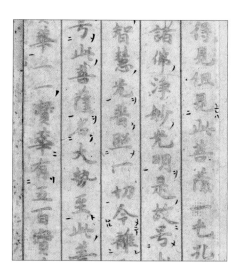

Above A section of the Meditation on Amitayus Sutra, *the most significant of the three major Pure Land sutras. This scroll dates from the late Heian period, 12th century.*

making spiritual progress toward rebirth in Amida's Pure Land. Recitative *nembutsu* – the simple recitation of the Buddha's name or a phrase containing it, such as 'Hail Amida Buddha' – was deemed by most practitioners, including Genshin, to be inferior to the meditative form. Indeed, Genshin referred to it as 'the practice of last resort'.

NEMBUTSU AND MAPPO

The low opinion of recitative *nembutsu* began to change when teachers started to think about it within the context of another doctrine that became increasingly prominent during the medieval period, that of *mappo*, the decline of the Dharma. Early Buddhist texts had referred to a decline in the Dharma on the occasion of the first female ordinations, but the idea that there were three stages in

Left It is believed that, after a period of mappo, *the Buddha will return to Earth, as shown in this depiction of the 'Buddha Descending from the Heaven of Thirty-three Gods', Cambodian, 19th century.*

its decline did not develop until the early medieval period in China. Saicho (767–822), the founder of the Tendai school, argued that each of the stages had practices that were most appropriate for it: meditation was suited to the first stage; recitation was appropriate for the final one.

For many Japanese Buddhists, the 12th and 13th centuries were clearly the time of *mappo*, which contemporary scholars believe began in 1052. Natural calamities and pestilence afflicted the countryside, the capital was destroyed by fire, uprisings were widespread and the emperor was unable to restore order. There was one monk, however, who saw the time of *mappo* as one of liberation and opportunity rather than degeneration; this was Honen.

THE BIRTH OF JODO SHU

Honen (1133–1212) was ordained as a Tendai monk at the age of 14. Like many other monastic groups, Tendai monks had organized themselves into small armies during the civil unrest, but Honen shunned the military life and sought a contemplative existence in a small Tendai monastery at Kurodani, near Mount Hiei. There, he engaged in Pure Land practices, particularly those of meditative *nembutsu*, under the guidance of master Eiko. However, he did not find satisfaction in this, and turned instead to what Genshin had called the practice of last resort: calling on the name of Amida Buddha with deep faith. This, he concluded, was the most appropriate practice for the time of *mappo*. Now that the monastic life had become spiritually inert, awakening had become available to all: monks and lay people, saints and sinners. This was attributable to the power of Amida's vow.

On the basis of this insight, Honen left the Tendai monastery and set up in Kyoto to teach recitative *nembutsu*. This move established an independent Pure Land school in Japan, the Jodo Shu. Honen offered his doctrine and practice to people from all levels of Japanese society, arguing that *nembutsu* recitation had been especially selected by Amida because it was available to all.

Traditionalists took umbrage at Honen's innovations and brought a number of charges against him in 1204. Unfortunately, his chances of weathering the storm that ensued were dashed when two of his disciples performed Pure Land rituals with some of the emperor's

Above A Japanese depiction of the monk Ippen on his travels, 19th century. Ippen (1239–89) spread the Pure Land teachings across Japan, in the tradition of Honen, and was an advocate of nembutsu.

women throughout the night. The disciples were promptly executed, and Honen was exiled to the provinces. He was allowed to return to the capital only in 1211, the year before his death.

By this time, however, Honen's innovations had sent spiritual ripples all across Japan. His disciples continued in his footsteps, and began to take Buddhism in new directions, ultimately establishing the new Jodo Shinshu school.

THE JODO SHINSHU SCHOOL

IN THE 12TH CENTURY A JAPANESE MONK CALLED HONEN FOUNDED JODO SHU, BUT HIS WRITINGS CONTAINED MANY AMBIGUITIES. UNABLE TO AGREE, HIS DISCIPLES SPLIT INTO A NUMBER OF SUB-SECTS THAT LED TO JODO SHINSHU, A POPULAR RELIGION TODAY.

Above The Jodo Mission spreads the Pure Land message in Honolulu. Jodo Shu, the forerunner of Jodo Shinshu, reached Hawaii in 1984, and there are now 14 temples serving the islands.

When the Jodo Shu school first fragmented, the most influential of the sects was the Chinzei-ha, founded by Bencho (1162–1238). He emphasized the importance of exclusive *nembutsu* (recitation of the Amida Buddha's name), stressing that it was to be performed as often as possible with a mind that was as calm as possible. Meanwhile another of Honen's disciples, Shoku (1177–1247), founded the Seizan-ha sect, which promoted *nembutsu* as complementary to other forms

Below Amitayus Buddha and Two Bodhisattvas Visiting the Monk Honen, Tosa Yoshimitsu, Kamakura period (1185–1333). The Pure Land sect was attractive during these particular years of upheaval in Japan.

of practice and was successful in getting it accepted by other Buddhist schools, Tendai and Shingon in particular. Despite their differences, Bencho and Shoku both understood the *nembutsu* as a method for gaining rebirth in Amida's Pure Land (a place without suffering and conducive to awakening as promised by Amida).

Other disciples were much more radical. Kosai (1163–1247), founder of the Ichinengi sect, argued that constant *nembutsu* was unnecessary because access to the Pure Land was granted in the instant that one true *nembutsu* was recited. This shift put more emphasis on the power of Amida's promise and considerably less on the idea of practice as an effective means of gaining rebirth in the

Pure Land. That interpretation was taken even further by another of Honen's disciples, Shinran (1173–1262), founder of the Jodo Shinshu (True Pure Land sect), which is now Japan's largest Pure Land school.

AMIDA'S POWERFUL VOW

For Shrinran, *nembutsu* was simply an expression of gratitude for the saving power of Amida's vow. Rebirth in the Pure Land,

Right The American Robert Clifton, dressed in ceremonial robes. In the 1930s, Clifton was the first foreigner to be formally recognized as a Buddhist priest by the Hongan-ji temple of Japan, of the Jodo Shinshu sect.

Right The American Robert Clifton, dressed in ceremonial robes. In the 1930s, Clifton was the first foreigner to be formally recognized as a Buddhist priest by the Hongan-ji temple of Japan, of the Jodo Shinshu sect.

according to Shinran, comes not from *nembutsu* practice but rather from the power of Amida's promise. All people can experience the fruits of this vow; all they need is faith in its efficacy. Once they have the faith, then they chant the *nembutsu* in gratitude. Such chanting has the benefit of conferring merit on the chanter, merit that can be used when the person returns from the Pure Land to help suffering beings.

Shinran's death in 1262 created divisions among his followers, who formed their own communities (*monto*) across Japan. Meanwhile, Shinran's youngest daughter, Kakushinni, built a mausoleum for her father's ashes. When presenting this to his disciples, she stipulated that its upkeep and the performance of any services there were to remain in the hands of her descendants.

Her son, Kakunyo, transformed the mausoleum into a temple, which he named the Original Vow Temple (Hongan-ji), and persuaded many of the *monto* to affiliate themselves with it. This marked the beginning of Jodo Shinshu as a distinct school.

NEW PURE LAND SECTS

When the 11th successor, Kennyo, died, his two sons contested the succession, and each established a separate school – the Western and

Right Devotees in Buddhist robes after a ceremony to enter the Buddhist priesthood at Higashi-Hongan-ji temple in Kyoto, 2003. Males have their heads shaved as part of the practice of the Otani branch of Jodo Shinshu.

Eastern Honganji – though there was little to distinguish them from each other doctrinally. Eventually, ten sects emerged: the two Honganji (by far the largest) plus the Bukkoji, Izumoji, Joshoji, Kibe, Koshoji, Sanmonto, Takeda and Yamamoto.

The Honganji sects have been more missionary-minded than their smaller relatives, taking Shinshu teachings outside Japan since as early as 1889. They have catered for the most part to the needs of Japanese immigrants to the USA. Under the title of the North American Buddhist Mission, the Western Honganji set up a centre in San Francisco in 1899. The disruption caused by World War II eventually led to the American branches claiming a de facto independence by ordaining their own priests and changing their name to the Buddhist Churches of America.

The popularity of the religion shows no sign of diminishing. At the start of the 21st century, the Jodo Shinshu was reckoned to have more than 13 million members, with more than 20,000 temples spread across the world.

THE LOTUS SUTRA

THE *LOTUS SUTRA* IS ONE OF THE EARLIEST MAHAYANA TEXTS. IT EXPLAINS THE MANY 'SKILFUL MEANS' OF THE BUDDHA, AND ITS TEACHINGS ON AWAKENED BEINGS WHO CAN HELP OTHERS WERE THE BASIS OF DEVOTIONAL SCHOOLS, SUCH AS TENDAI.

Above The lotus flower symbolizes mental and physical purity in Buddhist philosophy and art. The pink lotus is associated with the Buddha himself.

Scholarly consensus dates the oldest sections of the *Lotus Sutra* to the beginning of the Common Era, with most of the rest being added by the end of the 2nd century. The most influential version has been the one translated into Chinese by Kumarajiva and his team in 406, which has 28 chapters.

The contents of the *Lotus Sutra* are quite varied, though there are a number of particularly notable themes. Three of the most significant teachings are those on 'one vehicle' (*ekayana*), 'skilful means' (*upaya kausalya*) and compassion (*karuna*).

THE STATUS OF ARHATS

An issue that was disturbing the Buddhist world at the time that the *Lotus Sutra* was being written concerned the status of arhats (enlightened disciples). Were they fully awakened or could they fall

Below A richly embellished section of the Lotus Sutra, *entitled 'The Former Affairs of the Bodhisattva Medicine King'. This hanging scroll, which dates from the mid-12th century, has gold-leaf and silver-lead decoration.*

from their liberated state? The history of the issue is complex, though at the heart of it lay the criteria for achieving arhat status.

The early arhats seemed to have had the same awakening experience as the Buddha himself, albeit facilitated by his guidance. This included proficiency in accessing the four meditations of form (*rupa jhana*) and gaining the three (sometimes six) higher knowledges – of former lives, of the causes of rebirth and of the destruction of the defilements *(asava)*. Technically, only the last of these is essential for liberation, and it was not long before some monks started to claim that they had achieved the destruction of the defilements without proficiency in the *jhanas* or any of the higher knowledges. These arhats were called 'insight liberated' (*panna vimutta*). Their attainment seemed, in the eyes of many Buddhists, to be inferior to that of a buddha and it was argued that such attainment was fragile, and that such arhats could 'fall away'.

SKILFUL MEANS

Meanwhile, something else was stirring in the monasteries. Groups of monks started to proclaim a fresh interpretation of the Dharma, possibly based on visionary encounters with the Buddha. Moreover, they claimed that the teaching they were receiving had just as much, if not more, authority than the texts of the Tripitaka. One of these teachings, presented so eloquently

in the *Lotus Sutra*, was that debates about who is or is not a genuine arhat are unprofitable. Instead, beings should understand that the Buddha preaches the Dharma for one outcome: buddhahood for all sentient beings. Although it may seem as though the Buddha is teaching different things to different people, he is, in fact, simply adapting his message to their individual capacities. All who are moving toward that goal are bodhisattvas (buddhas-to-be, or enlightenment beings).

The *Lotus Sutra* presents this and other teachings via evocative parables. The one-vehicle message can be found in the parable of the burning house:

A father's children are playing inside a rambling, ramshackle old house, which catches fire. How can he save them without causing a potentially catastrophic panic? Knowing the preferences of each, he lures them out with the promise of various toys. When they have escaped, however, each receives the same toy, which is, nevertheless, completely satisfying.

Although the luring of the children with false promises is technically a lie, it is an example of the Buddha's skilful means. These are devices designed to facilitate people's awakening by meeting

Above A detail from a Heian-era painting depicting events from the Lotus Sutra. *The ancient text is often referred to by Mahayana Buddhists as the final teaching of the Buddha and, as such, is given great importance.*

them where they are, by offering teachings that they can understand as a preliminary to the full revelation of truth. This notion of skilful means proved to be particularly valuable when Buddhists introduced the Dharma to people from other cultures. Some Chinese, for example, found the doctrine of karma unintelligible without some notion of a self to carry its effects from one life to the next. Enterprising Mahayanists therefore taught the existence of a self (contrary to all Buddhist doctrine) until their students were ready to go beyond it.

The *Lotus Sutra* also taught compassion in action, again largely through the use of parables.

PROMOTING THE SUTRA

Finally, the sutra promotes its own status, claiming that a true rejoicing at hearing even a single verse will guarantee a person's attainment of buddhahood. It should be treated like a buddha and offerings made to it. Promoting the sutra will bring many benefits, including a favourable rebirth and even good looks; maligning it will lead to terrible consequences, including being attracted to animal births, being sickly and ugly if born human, and spending most of one's time in the lower hells. The sutra has such power, however, that it can save even the most grievous wrongdoer. These latter teachings were given particular prominence in the Tendai school and in the teachings of Nichiren (1222–82).

NICHIREN BUDDHISM

PROBABLY THE MOST FAMOUS FIGURE OF MEDIEVAL JAPANESE BUDDHISM, NICHIREN INFLUENCED JAPAN THROUGH HIS READING OF THE *LOTUS SUTRA* AND HIS INTERPRETATION OF THE CONCEPT OF *MAPPO*. HE PAVED THE WAY FOR MODERN JAPANESE BUDDHISM.

Born in 1222 in Kominato in the province of Awa, Nichiren began his study of Buddhism at the famous Seicho-ji temple and was ordained as a Buddhist monk at the age of 16. In 1253, after travelling to the main Buddhist sites of Japan, he expounded the *diamoku* mantra: *Namu-Myoho-Renge-Kyo* (Homage to the Lotus Sutra), for the first time. This showed the importance that he was giving to the teachings of the *Lotus Sutra* as the only correct Buddhist teachings. It was at this time that he took the name 'Nichiren' (*nichi* stands for Japan and *ren* is the character for lotus).

Because of the provocative nature of his teachings, especially his treatise on *mappo* (the age of decline of Dharma) issued in 1260, Nichiren was persecuted,

and, in 1264, almost assassinated. In 1271, he was sent to Sado island in exile, during which time he made the *gohonzon* (see box, opposite). Two years later he returned briefly to Kamakura, before choosing to live in solitary confinement on Mount Minobu, where he died in 1282.

Nichiren left a huge body of writings, including hundreds of treatises and letters. Some of them are criticisms of the other Buddhist schools, others expound his interpretation of the *Lotus Sutra* and his view of *mappo*.

THE END OF DHARMA

According to Buddhism, the existence of Dharma in the world is divided into three main phases. The first of these is the period of Correct Dharma, which coincides

Above Nichiren monks in the traditional robe of the school stroll outside the Sanjusangendo temple in Kyoto, Japan. Today, Nichiren Buddhism, founded in the 13th century, has a number of different forms and many followers.

Below This painting by Yoshimoro (Japanese school, 19th century) depicts the Buddhist monk Nichiren attempting to calm a storm with an invocation from the scriptures.

with the time of Buddha on Earth, his preaching, and the diffusion of Buddhism by the first generations of Buddha's disciples. However, over the course of time, the interpretations of the Buddha's teachings become more and more corrupted and the practice of Buddhism becomes increasingly distant from how it was in the Buddha's time. This is the period of Apparent Dharma. Finally, there is the third stage, the period of Final Dharma (*mappo*), when corruptions predominate among the Sangha (Buddhist community), there are no more valid teachers, and practice no longer bears any resemblance to that taught by the Buddha. It is at the apex of the Final Dharma that a new buddha is believed to descend to Earth, and the cycle restarts from the beginning.

Nichiren wrote a treatise on *mappo* in 1260, in which he claimed that the natural calamities and political disorder that were, at that time, afflicting Japan were the consequences of the corruption of Dharma. He argued that in order to re-establish a peaceful life in Japan, the correct teachings of Buddhism (which were embodied in the *Lotus Sutra*) must be restored and followed, and that other Buddhist schools should be repudiated. The treatise provoked harsh debates in both political and religious circles.

A GREAT SAGE
Although he was persecuted during his lifetime, Nichiren has received many titles and appellatives since his passing. Out of respect for the role he has played in the history of Buddhism, he is called 'Nichiren Daishonin' (Great Sage Nichiren) and 'Nichiren Shonin' (Reverend Master Nichiren). He started a new system of interpretation of the *Lotus*

***Above** Japanese women in a traditional summer ritual of Nichiren Buddhism at Ikegami Honmonji, Tokyo. The women hold a plate covering a talisman on their heads as they pray for overall good health.*

Sutra (which has been considered the most important scripture of East Asian Buddhism), as well as a new school. Nichiren Buddhism is very close to the Tendai school in its emphasis on the *Lotus Sutra* and the belief that it is possible to achieve enlightenment in this life.

After his death, Nichiren's main six disciples (Nissho, Niko, Nichiji, Nikko, Nitcho and Nichiro) reinterpreted the master's teachings and split the Nichiren school into six sects. Some have been absorbed by the others, but new sub-sects have also arisen. Today, the main two schools are the Nichiren Shu, which has its headquarters in Kuon-ji, and the Nichiren Shoshu, which is based at Taiseki-ji. Some new Japanese religious associations (*shin shukyo*), including the famous Rissho Koseikai and Soka Gakkai, have also been inspired by Nichiren's teachings. The former is rooted in Nichiren Shu while the latter is based on Nichiren Shoshu.

GOHONZON
Gohonzon is a general word indicating a Buddhist object of veneration, from a statue to a scripture. The *moji*-mandala (a mandala compiled with characters) is the form of *gohonzon* venerated in the Nichiren school. Nichiren wrote the first *moji*-mandalas, and his successors compiled others following his example.

Generally a *moji*-mandala includes the formula *Namu-Myoho-Renge-Kyo* in the centre, surrounded by names – of buddhas, bodhisattvas and the four guardians of the Dharma – that represent Buddhist teachings and suggest the correct doctrine.

***Above** Nichiren's* moji-*mandala* gohonzon. *The title of the* Lotus Sutra, *in the middle, is surrounded by the names of buddhas and bodhisattvas.*

Today, the practice of the Nichiren tradition includes the recitation of the formula *Namu-Myoho-Renge-Kyo*, the reading of the *Lotus Sutra* – with different sub-sects placing more emphasis on different chapters – the worship of Buddhist statues and images, and meditation on the *gohonzon*.

MODERN JAPANESE BUDDHIST ASSOCIATIONS

IN THE 20TH CENTURY, JAPAN WITNESSED THE FORMATION OF A NUMBER OF NEW BUDDHIST ASSOCIATIONS INSPIRED BY NICHIREN'S TEACHINGS, INCLUDING SOKA GAKKAI, RISSHO KOSEIKAI AND NIPPONZAN MYOHONJI.

The Meiji period (1868–1912) signalled the beginning of modernity in Japan, which in Buddhism brought clerical marriage and the abandonment of vegetarianism. The era was characterized by the establishment of several new religions, including new Buddhist associations. Some of these were founded by and formed of lay followers, others included monks and nuns as well. Most of the new Buddhist groups

Below A Buddhist monk offers prayers at the Nipponzan Myohonji temple in Mumbai, India. This new Japanese Buddhist group now has branch temples in many countries.

were inspired by the Nichiren school, and especially emphasized the recitation of the mantra *Namu-Myoho-Renge-Kyo*. With their headquarters in Japan, these associations have established branches worldwide, have their own media, publish magazines and organize social activities and religious meetings. All of these associations are also engaged in peace movements and educational activities.

SOKA GAKKAI

Tsunesaburo Makiguchi (1871–1944) founded Soka Gakkai in 1930. It means 'Society for the creation of values' and was based on Nichiren Buddhism. The aim was to revise the Japanese educational system in order to teach young people the values of independent thinking and self-motivation. Today, this lay Buddhist association has 12 million members from 190 countries.

The current president, Daiseku Ikeda (b.1928), maintains the original spirit of Buddhist humanism. A non-governmental organization, Soka Gakkai is formally linked to the United Nations and is involved in humanitarian campaigns, environmental protection, inter-faith dialogue, cultural activites (promoting the mutual understanding of different cultures), campaigns for peace and, above all, applying Buddhist teachings to daily life. Indeed, the back cover of *Soka Gakkai International Quarterly*, the

Above This statue of Nichiren is at Myokenji temple in Kyoto, Japan. The teachings of Nichiren Buddhism provide the doctrinal basis for most of the new Japanese Buddhist associations.

English magazine of the society, states the organization's mission: 'The Soka Gakkai International (SGI) is a worldwide association of 82 constituent organizations with membership in 190 countries and territories. In the service of its members and of society at large, the SGI centres its activities on developing positive human potentialities for hope, courage and altruistic action. Rooted in the life-affirming philosophy of Nichiren Buddhism, members of the SGI share a commitment to the promotion of peace, culture and education.'

RISSHO KOSEIKAI

Nikkyo Niwano and Myoko Naganuma founded Rissho Koseikai in 1938. Their aim was to create a group to study Nichiren's mandalas, gain and teach a correct understanding of the *Lotus Sutra* and recollect the figure of Shakyamuni Buddha. By 1941, the

Above These Buddhist monks of the Nipponzan Myohonji order are leaving Boston, along with other pilgrims, to retrace the route of the slave trade of the 17th and 18th centuries.

association had 1,000 members. Since its inception, Rissho Koseikai has been active in establishing collaboration with other religious and non-religious associations, including bodies of the United Nations. In the 1960s, Niwano founded the Brighter Society Movement, which organizes different services to the association. Niwano also chaired the first World Conference on Religion and Peace that was held in Kyoto in 1970.

Rissho Koseikai is well-known for holding the Niwano Peace Prize and for its involvement in inter-faith dialogue. The call for peace is usually accompanied by an appeal for bodhisattva practice. The members of the Rissho Koseikai take refuge in the Three Jewels (Buddha, Dharma, Sangha), practice sutra recitation and are involved in service to the community and in activities to promote world peace.

Norio Sakai, former chairman of Rissho Koseikai, summed up the history and spirit of the association and its founder: "Rev. Nikkyo Niwano, founder of Rissho Koseikai, concisely expressed the spirit of the encouragement Shakyamuni gave to his disciples when he said that 'every member is a disseminator of the

faith', and that we can 'learn through guiding others'. In this way he directed members to proceed on the same path that Shakyamuni indicated."

NIPPONZAN MYOHONJI

Nichidatsu Fujii (1885–1985) founded Nipponzan Myohoji after World War II. Inspired by Nichiren Buddhism and Mahatma Gandhi (whom he met in 1931), Fujii started promoting the value of peace, which he represented concretely through building 'Peace Pagodas'. The first ones were built in Hiroshima and Nagasaki, in memory of those killed by the atomic bombs in these cities. Later on, more pagodas were built throughout Asia, as well as in many European countries and the USA.

Below The Peace Pagoda at Milton Keynes in Buckinghamshire, England, is only one of many pagodas that has been built all over the world by monks and nuns belonging to the Nipponzan Myohonji Buddhist order.

CHANTING AND MUSIC

SINCE THE EARLY DAYS OF THE SANGHA, CHANTING AND THE RECITATION OF MANTRAS HAS BEEN PART OF THE DAILY BUDDHIST MONASTIC RITUAL. MEANWHILE, DRUMS, CYMBALS AND GONGS PLAY AN IMPORTANT ROLE IN TIBETAN BUDDHIST PRACTICE.

The seventh of the Eight Precepts observed on *posadha* (*uposatha*) days by lay Buddhists, and at all times by bhikkhus and bhikkhunis, states: "I undertake to refrain from dancing, singing, music, going to see entertainments, wearing garlands, using perfumes and beautifying the body with cosmetics". It is for this reason that music does not play as large a part in Buddhist practice as it does in many other religions.

CHANTING

Music is not absent, however. Teachings are still imparted to young monks and nuns in short verses memorized as rhythmic recitations and chants. The chanting of Buddhist monks may be accompanied by drums, gongs, bells, trumpets made from conch shells, or even human thigh bones, horns taller than the men who blow them, large standing drums, cymbals, flutes, or sticks.

Dharanis are phrases used in all Buddhist traditions to recall the meaning of, say, a sutra. Mantras are syllables or words, usually in Sanskrit, with a sacred meaning, that are used in many forms of Buddhist practice to promote concentration – a mantra is, in fact, part of a *dharani*. These special words or phrases are recited repeatedly to encourage deep concentration on the message of the sutra, and the recitation is believed to protect against harmful forces. Each syllable is pronounced in a prescribed way so that the sound resonates in the mind and deepens concentration.

Chanting takes many forms. In Theravada Buddhism, the *paritta* ceremony, usually held as a means

Below Tibetan monks play the gong and cymbals to ward off evil spirits. The ritual use of these instruments may have originated in the music of early shamanistic rituals.

Above The ringing of bells, symbolic of wisdom, punctuates the chanting of ritual texts. A dragon, protector of the Dharma, decorates the loop of this 14th-century bronze Korean bell.

of gaining magical protection, involves the chanting of 29 Pali sutras. This chanting is carried out by monks as an act of loving kindness or healing. Mahayana Buddhists may acquire merit by chanting sutras written for the purpose, which contain lists of the names of buddhas.

Mantras are recited to engage the body, speech and mind to effect mental transformation and develop the potential for buddhahood, which Buddhists believe resides in everyone.

DRUMS AND GONGS

Monks in Sri Lanka, who are not allowed to watch music or dance performances, may make offerings of drumming as part of their temple rituals to the Buddha. The drumming is performed in the temple by lay people.

Drums also have a role, as do cymbals and gongs, in Tibetan Buddhist ritual, which is partly rooted in the shamanism of Tibet's

ancient native religions. Drums and gongs transported the shamans to the spirit land, and their role in warding off evil spirits was adopted into Buddhist ritual. In Tibet, hand drums – some made of human skulls with a membrane of human skin stretched over them – are also used in meditation. These ritual objects, often donated to monasteries, serve as reminders of the impermanence of all things.

Many Japanese temples have a large drum beneath a thatched roof in the courtyard. These drums represent the 'commanding voice of the Buddha'. They are believed to sound through the universe and are used to herald important ceremonies.

Around many Thai temples are sets of bells for followers to strike for the forgiveness of an action that might bring bad karma as they circumambulate the temple. Further, in temple shrines and meeting halls, the sutras may be

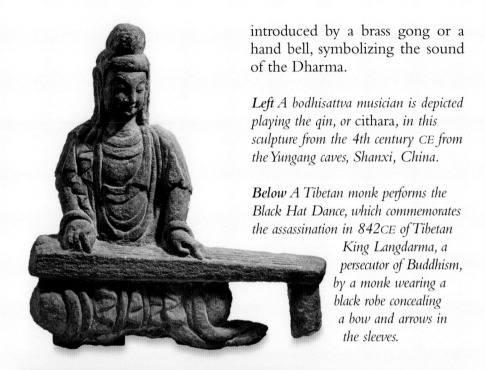

introduced by a brass gong or a hand bell, symbolizing the sound of the Dharma.

Left A bodhisattva musician is depicted playing the qin, or cithara, *in this sculpture from the 4th century* CE *from the Yungang caves, Shanxi, China.*

*Below A Tibetan monk performs the Black Hat Dance, which commemorates the assassination in 842*CE *of Tibetan King Langdarma, a persecutor of Buddhism, by a monk wearing a black robe concealing a bow and arrows in the sleeves.*

GATHAS

Lay Buddhists make the silent chanting of *gathas* part of their day. *Gathas* are short verses like these from the *Dhammapada* (Pali), or 'Way of Truth', a collection of Buddhist teachings, that recall steps on the path to enlightenment.

Not to do evil,
But to do what is right.
To keep the mind pure.
This is the teaching of the Buddha.

Better than one hundred years
*   lived*
With an unsettled mind,
Devoid of insight,
Is one day lived
With insight and absorbed
*   in meditation.*

THE KAGYU AND NYINGMA SCHOOLS

TIBETAN BUDDHISM HAS FOUR MAIN TRADITIONS: NYINGMA, KAGYU, SAKYA AND GELUK. KAGYU ('ORAL TRANSMISSION LINEAGE') AND NYINGMA ('THE ANCIENT ONES') BOTH EMPHASIZE MEDITATION AND ARE OFTEN REFERRED TO AS 'PRACTICE LINEAGES'.

Above A gilded 18th-century bronze statue depicting Padmasambhava, the Indian monk who introduced Tantric Buddhism to Tibet in the 8th century. Padmasambhava, on the central pillar, is flanked by his two wives.

The founder of the Kagyu school was Gampopa (1079–1153), who synthesized the monastic traditions of the Kadam school with the tantric teachings of Milarepa. His disciple Dusum Khyenpa (1110–93) created the Karma Kagyu lineage (whose spiritual leader is the Karmapa) and initiated the concept of re-incarnating lamas (*tulkus*) by giving instructions about the circumstances of their rebirth. However, the basis of the Kagyu school was determined less by its systematizers than by its precursors.

KAGYU

Gampopa's teacher, Milarepa (1040–1123), one of Tibet's best-loved masters of yoga, was a lay-man who had practised black magic in his youth and then sought salvation in tantric practices that could liberate a person in a single lifetime. Milarepa became a student of Marpa (1012–97), who was known as *lotsawa* ('translator'), a title accorded to Tibetans who had studied Indian languages, made the dangerous journey to India, and translated the texts with which they returned.

Marpa, also a layman, was a tantric master who had studied with the Indian *mahasiddha* Naropa (1016–1100) and undertaken similar ordeals to those the latter had experienced under Tilopa (989–1069). Marpa subjected Milarepa to a similar treatment, the aim of which was to secure the disciple's complete trust in the master, or guru – the fourth refuge of tantric Buddhists. The masters' lay status contributed significantly to the legacy of non-ordained lamas in Tibet.

The teachings of these tantric masters were both esoteric and controversial, particularly those based on texts known as 'supreme (*anuttara*) yoga tantras'. Many of these use explicit sexual language to introduce Buddhist teachings – "Thus I have heard: at one time the Lord reposed in the vagina of

Left This colourful thangka *depicts the Adi-Buddha Vajradhara surrounded by key figures from the Indo-Tibetan tradition, including Gampopa, Milarepa, Marpa, Naropa and Tilopa.*

MASTERS IN THE WEST

Modern Kagyu teachers who have disseminated the tradition in the West include Kalu Rinpoche, Rangjung Rigpe Dorje (the 16th Karmapa) and Chogyam Trungpa. Kalu Rinpoche (1905–89) was one of the first Tibetan masters to teach in the West, and his work continues at more than 100 centres dedicated to offering meditation retreats. The 16th Karmapa (1924–81) was a talented organizer who established a network of Kagyu centres across the world, offering traditional Kagyu meditation training and three-year retreats for the highly committed. Chogyam Trungpa (1939–87) co-founded the Kagyu Samye Ling monastery and Tibetan Centre in Scotland. His legacy also includes the Naropa University (a liberal arts college) and a network of *dharmadhatu* study centres.

Notable Nyingma teachers who have brought their tradition to the West include Kangyur Rinpoche, Khyentse Rinpoche and Sogyal Rinpoche. Kangyur Rinpoche (1897–1975), named after his great skill in reciting and explaining the Tibetan *Kangyur* (*Canon of Sutras*), was a noted *terton* (one who discovers *terma*, or hidden texts). He attracted many European disciples, though he never travelled to Europe. That journey was undertaken by his successor, Khyentse Rinpoche (1910–91), a *terton* and *tulku*. Sogyal Rinpoche (b. *c.*1950) received the traditional education of a *tulku*, as well as a Western version at the universities of Delhi and Cambridge. He established the Dzogchen Orgyen Choling in London during the early 1970s and later created Rigpa, a Nyingma fellowship that now boasts more than 100 affiliated centres in 23 countries. In 1992 he published his most famous and acclaimed work, *The Tibetan Book of Living and Dying*.

Above Sogyal Rinpoche, a Nyingma teacher, is the creator of Rigpa, an international network of Buddhist centres, and author of the acclaimed work The Tibetan Book of Living and Dying.

the Lady of the Vajra-sphere…" – as well as to describe the practices themselves – "positioning the great *vajra*-gem in the woman's pudenda and meditating on the great symbol (*mahamudra*), one achieves success (*siddha*)". The use of coded language (*Sandhabhasya*) in these texts has led some commentators to suggest that such references are symbolic and refer to meditational constructs rather than actual rites.

NYINGMA

The Nyingma masters traced their origins back to the first diffusion of Buddhism in Tibet and the tantric adept Padmasambhava. They preserved a number of texts that had been introduced at that time but were not recognized by the later schools, and also instituted a distinctive teaching about hidden texts (*terma*), many of which had been secreted by

Padmasambhava until the time was ripe for their dissemination. Perhaps the most famous of these is the *Bardo Thodrol*, or *The Tibetan Book of the Dead*.

The Nyingma practices known as *Dzogchen* ('Great Fulfilment') seem to include material on the innate purity of mind and sudden awakening that had been introduced into Tibet by Chinese masters. *Dzogchen* can be regarded as a synthesis of these and Indian *siddha* doctrines. The sixth and highest yoga in the Nyingma tradition, *atiyoga*, exemplifies this blend. Other schools were uncomfortable with *Dzogchen,* not so much for its sexual references as for the form of mind-only doctrine akin to that found in the Chinese text, *Awakening of Faith in the Mahayana*. Its practitioners, however, simply aim to access and abide in non-dual consciousness.

Above Sakyong Mipham Rinpoche is the head of the Shambhala Buddhist lineage, an offshoot of the Kagyu and Nyingma schools that developed in the 20th century. It now has many centres in the West.

235

THE SAKYA AND GELUK SCHOOLS

THE SAKYA ('GREY EARTH') AND GELUK ('MODEL OF VIRTUE') TIBETAN BUDDHIST TRADITIONS HAVE BEEN INFLUENTIAL. THE GELUK ORDER, THE MOST RECENT OF THE FOUR TIBETAN SCHOOLS TO BE ESTABLISHED, IS THE PREDOMINANT TIBETAN BUDDHIST SECT TODAY.

The founder of the Sakya order is Drogmi Shakya Yeshe (992–1074), but it was his disciple Khon Konchog Gyalpo who established the first monastery at Sakya in 1073. Sakya fortunes were given a boost in the 13th century when Godan Khan, grandson of Genghis Khan and de facto ruler of Tibet since 1240, chose the Sakya hierarch Sakya Pandita (1182–1251) to be his advisor in 1244. So impressed was Godan with his advisor's talents that he made him the temporal ruler of central Tibet. This appointment marked the beginning of ecclesiastical rule in Tibet that would last until the departure of the Dalai Lama in 1959.

Sakya Pandita's nephew, Phagpa, succeeded his uncle and continued to offer advice at the Mongol

Below The interior of Sakya monastery, Tibet. Founded in 1073, the monastery is the spiritual centre of the Sakya school.

court, by this time to Kublai Khan. He conferred tantric initiations on many of Kublai's ministers, being rewarded with further extensions of his temporal power and an appointment to the post of supervisor of the office regulating Buddhist affairs across the empire. He also enhanced his reputation by allegedly defeating Daoists and Christians in a contest of magic. However, as Mongol power began to wane in the 14th century, so too did the influence of the Sakya order. The Kagyus and, later, the Geluk order used the opportunity to extend their own influence.

A NOTABLE SAKYA MONK

Sakya monks also made significant contributions to the dissemination of Buddhism in Tibet. Most notable of these monks was Buton Rinchen Drup (1290–1364), who studied tantric ritual as a child under his grandfather and the Kagyu master, Trophupa. After

Above A Tibetan thangka *showing a lama of the Geluk sect, c. 1700–1825. In his right hand he holds a* dorje, *or* vajra, *a Tibetan Buddhist ritual object.*

being ordained as a novice when he was 18 years old, he studied under 28 different teachers from all traditions of Tibetan Buddhism. At the age of 30, he became abbot of Shalu monastery, where he remained for the rest of his life.

Among Buton's many achievements are a major history of Buddhism, the organization of Buddhist texts into the *Kanjur* and the *Tenjur*, and the creation of a fourfold categorization of tantric texts into Kriya (action), Carya (observance), *Yoga* and *Anuttarayoga* (supreme yoga). His classification became standard in all Tibetan Buddhist traditions except the Nyingma, which adopted a scheme that accommodated texts not recognized by other schools.

THE GELUK ORDER

The founder of the Geluk order was Tsongkhapa (1357–1419). Like Buton, he travelled widely in his youth and studied under teachers from different traditions. He absorbed the Kadam emphasis on monastic discipline and celibacy,

and incorporated these into the life of the monastery he founded at Ganden, near Lhasa, in 1409. His approach proved popular, and two other monasteries were established nearby. Eventually, the Geluk absorbed the Kadam order into itself and continued to found new monasteries. The manoeuvrings of Ngawang Losang Gyatso (1617–82), who became the 5th Dalai Lama, then ensured the subsequent domination of the Geluk order in the political life of Tibet.

GELUK TRAINING

Tsongkhapa's influence on the spiritual life of Tibet was profound. He divided a monk's training into two stages: Sutra and Tantra, the first of these being subdivided into practical and theoretical stages.

Practical students begin with texts such as Tsongkhapa's own *Lam-rim-chen-mo* and selected Indian texts, such as Shantideva's *Bodhicharyavatara*. In the theoretical stage, they study the five great texts: Maitreya's *Abhisamayalankara*, Candrakirti's *Madhyamakavatara*, Vasubandhu's *Abhidharmakosa*, Gunaprabha's *Vinaya Sutra* and Dharmakirti's *Pramanavarttika*. After this, students progress to tantric study, central to which is the *Guhyasamaja-tantra*.

Geluk teaching has been made available to Westerners by such notable figures as Geshe Rabten, who created the first geshe training programme in Europe, and Lama Thubten Yeshe, who established the Foundation for the Preservation of Mahayana Teachings (FPMT) in 1975. In partnership with the younger Lama Zopa Rinpoche, Yeshe travelled across Europe, America and Australia, setting up

Right The Gyantse Kumbum, in Tibet. Built in the 15th century as a perfect mandala, it has been an important place in Sakya history.

Above This Dalai Lama, made of gilded bronze, wears the distinctive pointed hat with long side-flaps of the Geluk order, which is often referred to as the 'Yellow Hat' school.

new centres. Once a centre was well established, he would appoint a Tibetan geshe to oversee the training. There are now more than 50 of these centres in the world, most of them in Europe.

A NEW TRADITION

In 1991, the Mañjushri Institute in England, under the supervision of Geshe Kelsang Gyatso, broke away from the FPMT to form the New Kadampa Tradition. Geshe Kelsang regards the teaching that formed the basis of the separation as being in keeping with those of Tsongkhapa. Others, including the Dalai Lama, are more sceptical, regarding the emphasis given to a protector deity, Dorje Shugden, as schismatic. The future of the New Kadampa Tradition will ultimately depend on whether Geshe Kelsang's Western successors can convince others that they represent an authentic Tibetan tradition.

THE DALAI LAMA

DALAI LAMA (MEANING 'OCEAN [OF WISDOM] TEACHER') IS A BLEND OF MONGOLIAN AND TIBETAN TERMS: *DALAI* IS MONGOLIAN FOR OCEAN, WHILE *LAMA* IS THE TIBETAN WORD FOR TEACHER – THE EQUIVALENT OF THE SANSKRIT WORD *GURU*.

The title 'Dalai Lama' was bestowed on the third head of the Geluk school, Sonam Gyatso (1543–88), by the Mongol leader Altan Khan in 1578. As Sonam Gyatso's two predecessors were also given the title posthumously, he became the 3rd Dalai Lama.

It is a position that is neither hereditary nor earned: on the death of a Dalai Lama, a formal procedure is adopted to identify his successor, who is regarded as an incarnation (*tulku*) of both his predecessor and the bodhisattva Chenrezi (Avalokiteshvara). The process begins about nine months after the demise of the previous Dalai Lama. Oracles are consulted, omens heeded and exceptional children identified. Candidates are subjected to a range of tests, which include identifying items belonging to the deceased Dalai Lama. If there is more than one successful candidate, names are placed inside a golden urn and the first one to be drawn out is chosen.

One problem with this system is the long period between the death of one Dalai Lama and the inauguration of his successor some 18 years later. During this time, a regent takes responsibility for the Dalai Lama's duties.

POLITICAL LEADERSHIP

It was the 5th Dalai Lama, Ngawang Losang Gyatso (1617–82), who manoeuvred to add political leadership of Tibet as a whole to that of the Geluk school. In an attempt to resolve the conflicts between the various aristocratic families and major regional monasteries, he sought the help of China's Mongol rulers. In 1642, a Mongol army under the leadership of Gushri Khan effectively conquered Tibet and handed power to the Dalai Lama. Three years later, he began the construction of the Potala Palace in Lhasa. The Potala mountain in southern India is by tradition the home of the bodhisattva Avalokiteshvara.

Above A figure of the bodhisattva Avalokiteshvara from Tibet. The Dalai Lama is believed to be an incarnation embodying both the previous Dalai Lama and Avalokiteshvara.

Mongol support for the Geluk school and the Dalai Lama continued during the following centuries. In 1706, after a *coup d'état* by Lhazan Khan, a descendant of Gushri Khan, Manchu forces returned power to the Geluks and replaced Lhazan's puppet Dalai Lama with the boy recognized as authentic by the Tibetans: Kelsang Gyatso, who became the 7th incumbent.

The Manchus retained a garrison in Lhasa until they were ousted by Republic of China forces in 1911. From that time onward, Sino-Tibetan relations became increasingly antagonistic. In 1950, the Chinese People's Liberation Army invaded Tibet, and the 14th Dalai Lama, Tenzin

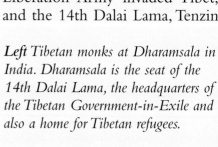

Left Tibetan monks at Dharamsala in India. Dharamsala is the seat of the 14th Dalai Lama, the headquarters of the Tibetan Government-in-Exile and also a home for Tibetan refugees.

Gyatso (b. 1935), who was just 15 years old, assumed full political power. The brutal crushing of a rebellion against Chinese rule in 1959 led the Dalai Lama and 80,000 other Tibetan people to seek asylum in India and other countries. Their exile continues to this day.

THE 14TH DALAI LAMA

Tenzin Gyatso was born in 1935 in the small north-eastern Tibetan village of Taktster. His parents, who were farmers, had six other children. The 13th Dalai Lama, Thubten Gyatso, had passed away two years before Tenzin was born, and the search for his successor had begun. Signs and visions directed the lamas to Taktster in 1937. The two-year-old boy they found there seemed to know who they were and passed all the tests he was set.

After extensive delays, caused largely by the fact that north-eastern Tibet was then controlled by the Chinese, Tenzin was taken to Lhasa. In 1950, the National Assembly of Tibet recognized him as a true reincarnation of the 13th Dalai Lama, and he was enthroned as the 14th Dalai Lama, the spiritual and temporal leader of the Tibetan people.

During the next ten years the young Tenzin led a dual life. On the one hand, he was the beneficiary of a rigorous education, which included traditional subjects, such as drama, music and composition, as well as an intensive study of Buddhist scriptures, logic and the methods of debate. He also had the opportunity to indulge his interest in engineering with the mechanical toys, models, watches and automobiles that were presented to him by foreign dignitaries. On the other hand, as the leader of his people, he was at the forefront

Above The 14th Dalai Lama, Tenzin Gyatso, in New Zealand. While he regards himself primarily as a monk, his role includes speaking tours and spiritual leadership around the world.

of dealings with the Chinese, who had invaded eastern Tibet that same year.

A LEADER IN EXILE

In 1951, an agreement was reached that gave Tibet some measure of autonomy, though the Chinese made it clear that their long-term aim was the eventual absorption of Tibet into a greater China. Chinese garrisons were stationed in Tibet, at considerable cost to the local people.

Conditions became intolerable for many native Tibetans, and so, in 1959, a rebellion broke out. The Dalai Lama, along with many of his people, sought refuge in India, where they were warmly and sympathetically received. Those who could not or would not flee were treated brutally.

Since 1959, the Dalai Lama has lived in exile. From his base in Dharamsala, in northern India, he has travelled the world, both as a spiritual teacher and as the leader of the Tibetan people. This work has involved ordaining Buddhist monks and nuns, attending interfaith events and introducing

Tibetan Buddhism to mainly Western audiences. Politically, he has been a persistent advocate of a non-violent return to Tibetan autonomy, proposing that Tibet be designated a zone of non-conflict (*ahimsa*). He has spoken out in support of universal human rights, rejecting claims by the leaders of oppressive regimes that they are merely Western cultural constructs. He was awarded the Nobel Peace Prize in 1989.

So far, however, the Dalai Lama's efforts have made little impact on the Chinese government, whose response to protests about human rights violations and the continued oppression of the Tibetan people has been dismissive. While the Dalai Lama remains optimistic about the possibility of a favourable outcome, other observers note Tibet's strategic importance for the Chinese, and fear that while Tibetan Buddhism may survive outside Tibet, the Tibetan people may never again be able to practise it in a country of their own.

Below In the months preceding the 2008 Olympic Games in Beijing, protests were held around the world in support of the Dalai Lama and against oppressive Chinese policies in Tibet.

THE TIANTAI MOVEMENT

CONSIDERED TO BE THE BEST REPRESENTATIVE OF THE CHINESE DEVELOPMENT OF BUDDHISM, THE TIANTAI SCHOOL CLAIMED TO BE ROOTED IN THE INDIAN MADHYAMAKA SCHOOL AND PROPOSED A THEORY OF MEDITATION THAT SPREAD THROUGHOUT EAST ASIA.

The Tiantai lineage could be said to have begun with Huiwen and Huisi, both of whom lived in the 6th century – Huiwen proposed a new theory of meditation, while Huisi emphasized the teachings of the *Lotus Sutra* – but it was Zhiyi (538–97) who combined these aspects and finally organized the Tiantai school.

Besides promoting the *Lotus Sutra* as the scripture of the perfect teachings, Tiantai highlighted the concept of 'Buddha-nature', which was defined as the potentiality of everyone to achieve buddhahood: every human being has the seed of 'Buddha-nature', but this needs to be nurtured through correct practice. It also promoted the

Above A seated Amitabha Buddha, enthroned on a lotus flower and flanked by statues of two bodhisattvas, at Enryaku-ji, Kyoto.

doctrine of the 'only vehicle' (*ekayana*), which avoids the common sectarian division between early Buddhism and Mahayana, encompassing both streams.

Tiantai declined in the Tang period, when it was replaced by the new Huayan school organized by Fazang (643–712).

NEW CLASSIFICATIONS
Zhiyi developed a complete and systematic classification of the Buddha's teachings into a hierarchical order that promoted the *Lotus Sutra* as the perfect teaching. Such a system of classification is named *panjiao* in Chinese. After Zhiyi, Xuanshou of the Huayan school proposed his own classification. Later on, other important Buddhist monks

Left The East Tower at Enryaku-ji, Mount Hiei. Enryaku-ji is the headquarters of the Tendai school, and also became well-known for hosting the sohei, *the ascetic-warrior monks.*

relied on Zhiyi's *panjiao* when compiling their own classifications of teachings, and attempted to relate their own conclusions to those of the Tiantai master.

According to Zhiyi, Buddhist doctrines can be grouped into five periods and 'eight teachings', the latter divided into two quartets. The five periods are considered in chronological order in accordance with the time of the teaching of the texts. These are the periods of the *Avatamsaka Sutra*, *Agama* scriptures, the fundamental Mahayana teachings, the Perfection of Wisdom scriptures (*Prajñaparamita*) and, finally, the *Lotus Sutra*.

These five periods are seen in parallel with the two fourfold classifications of doctrine. The first quartet includes sudden, gradual, secret and indeterminate teachings; the second quartet is divided into original, all-embracing, distinctive and round-and-perfect doctrine. The *Lotus Sutra* is identified with the last of these, and was also the final scripture that the Buddha preached to teach the *Ekayana* doctrine.

THEORY OF MEDITATION
Zhiyi's treatise on meditation is titled *Mohe zhiguan*. *Zhi* means 'calming (the mind)' and *guan*, 'contemplation', and these two terms – the Chinese equivalents of *samatha* (calming) and *vipassana* (insight) in early Indian Buddhism – are the two root elements of any tradition of meditative practice.

Zhiyi indicated four practices of *zhi*: sitting, walking, half sitting and half walking, neither sitting nor walking. This process helps prepare the mind, facilitating the achievement of insight and the consequent realization of wisdom. Zhiyi also wrote a list

of ten vehicles of *guan* that meditators should apply to their daily lives.

TIANTAI OUTSIDE CHINA
Eventually, the Tiantai movement spread beyond China and reached Korea, where it was called Cheontae, and Japan, where it became the famous Tendai.

Tiantai arrived in Japan via the Chinese monk Jianzhen in the 8th century, but it is the Japanese monk Saicho (767–822) who is credited as the founder of the Tendai movement. In 805, Saicho made a trip to China to collect other Tiantai texts and then founded Enryaku-ji on Mount Hiei, which is still the headquarters of the Tendai school. This school, especially its emphasis on the superiority of the *Lotus Sutra*, became the predecessor of the Nichiren school during the Kamakura period.

The Tendai order is still flourishing in Japan, and new Buddhist associations, such as Soka Gakkai, have embodied, and proposed, a reshaped version of its teachings.

Tiantai reached Korea only in the 11th century, via the Korean monk Uicheon. However, in recent years, Cheontae has been mostly absorbed by the stronger Chogye order.

Above Ryogen, also known as Gansan Daishi (912–85), depicted in this 18th-century painted silk scroll, was a Japanese Tendai monk and a Buddhist teacher at the Imperial Court. He was also chief abbot of the Enryaku-ji monastery and founder of the sohei *warrior monks.*

ZHIYI
Zhiyi (538–97) was the first patriarch of the Tiantai school. Originally from Jingzhou in the Hubei province of China, he became interested in Buddhism from a young age and was fully ordained as a Buddhist monk when he was only 20 years old. Three years later, he began studying the practice of meditation in the *Lotus Sutra* under the guidance of the senior monk Nanyue Huisi, and within a few years, he had become famous as a Buddhist teacher.

Zhiyi did not leave many writings, but most of his teachings were collected and edited by his disciple Guanding (561–632). His main works are two commentaries on the *Lotus Sutra* and the famous treatise on meditation: *Mohe zhiguan* (*Great Concentration and Insight*).

ESOTERIC BUDDHISM

THERE ARE TWO GROUPS OF TEACHINGS IN BUDDHISM: EXOTERIC BUDDHISM PROVIDES EASY ACCESS TO SPIRITUAL DEVELOPMENT, BUT BELIEVERS ARE REQUIRED TO UNDERGO SPECIAL INITIATION TO RECEIVE AND PRACTICE THE TEACHINGS OF ESOTERIC BUDDHISM.

Mikkyo is the Japanese translation of the Chinese term *mijiao*, which means 'secret teachings'. From the name of the tradition it is clear that access to its teachers and teachings is restricted. In fact, those who want to follow esoteric Buddhism have to pass through a sort of examination and be accepted by a teacher before they can receive an initiation to the teachings and practice, and the training they must follow is often strict and complicated.

East Asia (China, Japan and Korea) and Tibet have their own traditions of esoteric Buddhism. The Tibetan Vajrayana tradition is well known even in the West, but the Chinese Mijiao and Japanese Mikkyo are less popular outside Asia.

MIJIAO

Esoteric Buddhism appeared in China in the 3rd–4th centuries. At this early stage of the Mijiao, practice consisted of the recitation of mantras and *dharanis*. It was heavily influenced by the esoteric tradition of Indian Mahayana, from which it inherited both texts and

methods of cultivation. During the following centuries, Mijiao became enriched with the arrival and translation of new Buddhist texts from India, and the integration of elements of Daoism.

The Tang dynasty (618–906) represented the golden age of the esoteric tradition in China and witnessed the flourishing of the Zhenyan school, whose practice emphasized the recitation of mantras, and spiritual progression through the use of mudras and mandalas, meditation and visualization. It especially highlighted the study of the *Mahavairocana Sutra*, which is one of the most important scriptures

Above *The embroidered white jacket and religious objects shown here are worn and carried by pilgrims on the Shikoku pilgrimage in Japan.*

in Chinese Buddhism, especially in the esoteric tradition. The main Zhenyan centres were Chang'an and Luoyang, and Anguosi and Qinglongsi were among the most important Mijiao monasteries founded at that time. Mount Wutai, one of the sacred Buddhist mountains in China – well known for being considered the abode of the bodhisattva Mañjushri – became the most favoured pilgrimage site for practitioners of Mijiao, and many temples were established there.

The persecutions that Mijiao was forced to endure in the 9th century were not an obstacle to the survival of the school, which later grew even stronger in the provinces of Sichuan and Yunnan.

From the Yuan (1279–1368) and Ming (1368–1644) dynasties onward, a new form of esoteric Buddhism, Tibetan Buddhism,

Right *This object, which is used in esoteric Buddhist rituals, is a gilt-bronze katsuma – a crossed three-pronged vajra (a stylized thunderbolt). This example most likely dates from the Japanese Kamakura period (1185–1333).*

Above A monk on the Shikoku pilgrimage, wherein followers visit the 88 temples associated with Kukai, the founder of Shingon Buddhism.

arriving with the Mongols, brought new Mongolian and Tibetan texts into China. In the Republican period, as well as in recent times, communities of Chinese monks and nuns practising the esoteric doctrine have arisen in Sichuan province, in particular.

MIKKYO

The esoteric tradition arrived in Japan from China during the 6th century. However, it was during the Tang dynasty (especially from the 9th century onward) that Japanese monks travelling to China began to bring new texts into Japan and systematized the Japanese tradition of Mikkyo. This stream includes two main schools, Shingon and Tendai, and has two leading figures in the founders of these schools: Kukai and Saicho. During the Kamakura period (1185–1333), the Buddhist monk Nichiren proposed an esoteric reading of the *Lotus Sutra* as well.

Today, the doctrine of Mikkyo is a combination of different religious phenomena and includes aspects of Tibetan Vajrayana, Chinese Mijiao, Chinese Daoism and Japanese Shinto, and is also linked to Shugendo. Mikkyo is characterized by the practice of visualization, which is a form of meditation and therefore based on the process of calming the mind and then achieving wisdom.

Followers of the Vajrayana tradition, besides evoking the deities venerated in the esoteric tradition, also visualize themselves becoming these deities. This process of meditation ends with the practitioners emptying themselves, and then the deities, in order to experience the realization of emptiness and the impermanence of life.

SHINGON

Founded by the monk Kukai in the 9th century, the Shingon ('true word') school still survives today as one of the main traditions of esoteric Buddhism. The followers of Shingon are initiated on Mount Koya, study the Vajrayana scriptures and ascetic practices, and utilize mandalas and visualization.

SHUGENDO

Shugendo, which literally means 'the path of practice and experience', includes elements of Buddhism, Daoism and other Japanese local beliefs. It is based on Kukai's teachings and therefore is affiliated to Mikkyo. Practitioners of Shugendo aim to obtain a union with nature through the recitation of spells and ascetic practices.

Shugendo was subject to persecutions during the Meiji period (1868–1912), when it was accused of being a superstitious belief system and thus in opposition to the rationalization and secularization movement in vogue at that time. Despite this, the practice survived, and today Shugendo has a large number of followers. Disciples of the esoteric tradition of Tendai and Shingon Buddhism also continue to practice Shugendo.

Below A Japanese woman prays as she stands beneath a waterfall for purification during a Shingon Buddhist ritual at Inunaki Mountain in Japan.

ENGAGED BUDDHISM

ONE OUTCOME OF THE MODERNIZATION OF ASIA HAS BEEN THE RISE OF ENGAGED BUDDHISTS, WHO, ACTIVE IN RELIGIOUS, POLITICAL AND SOCIAL SPHERES, ARE CHALLENGING BOUNDARIES BETWEEN THE LAITY AND MONKS AND NUNS AND ADVANCING A NEW ROLE FOR BUDDHISM.

Although Buddhism has been considered socially engaged since its inception, the phrase 'Engaged Buddhism' refers to a recent phenomenon. It originated during the second half of the 20th century, and was formed largely by a group of Asian Buddhist leaders who were involved not only in the religious world but also active in the political arena.

The term 'Engaged Buddhism' is said to have been coined by the Vietnamese monk and peace activist Thich Nhat Hanh in the 1960s in his attempt to save the country from war. Originally meaning 'Buddhism into-the-world', the phenomenon of Engaged Buddhism has developed and expanded in the last decades to include any sort of social concern undertaken by Buddhists.

KEY CHARACTERISTICS

Engaged Buddhism manifests itself in different ways, depending on the region and the historical and political climate at the time of its origination, but there are a number of aspects that are shared by all of the various forms of Engaged Buddhism.

Above It was Buddhist monk Thich Nhat Hanh who first coined the term 'Engaged Buddhism' in the 1960s in opposition to the Vietnam War.

Below Monks at the Pha Luang Ba Tua Buddhist temple in Kanchanaburi, Thailand, undertook the task of protecting the endangered Indo-Chinese tiger from extinction.

First of all, there is an emphasis on the human being – human rights, educational initiatives and social welfare in particular. This often includes a concern for environmental protection and ecological isues. Second, there is invariably a charismatic figure leading the movement.

Any revision of Buddhism implies the restatement of Buddhist doctrine, which has always been subject to selection, modernization and, sometimes, simplification. Based on the Mahayana tradition, Engaged Buddhism appeals for the concrete practice of the bodhisattva path in daily life. The laity plays an important role, co-operating with the Sangha and sometimes replacing the Sangha in entire activities and sectors. Because of this, Engaged Buddhism has sometimes been accused of rationalizing and secularizing the religious sphere.

REPRESENTATIVE FIGURES

Thich Nhat Hanh (b.1926), who coined the term 'Engaged Buddhism', was in opposition to the war in Vietnam in the 1960s. Expelled from his country at the end of the 1960s, he was nominated for the Nobel Peace Prize in 1967 and became famous in the West, where he founded several centres of meditation, for teaching mindfulness in daily life. He established the Tiep Hien Order (the Order of Interbeing) between 1964 and 1966.

In India, B.R. Ambedkar (1891–1956) established the Buddhist Society of India in 1955, to fight for the rights of the 'untouchables'. In Burma (Myanmar), Aung San Suu Kyi (b.1945) was awarded the Nobel Peace Prize in 1991 and has been under house arrest for fighting in defence of human rights and democracy, and for opposition to

Left Aung San Suu Kyi, the famous Burmese activist for human rights and democracy, who was put under house arrest. She was awarded the Nobel Peace Prize in 1991.

the government. In Sri Lanka, A.T. Ariyaratne (b.1931) founded the Sarvodaya Shramadana Movement, a self-governance movement that assists in village development. The first political party of Buddhist monks, the National Heritage Party (JHU), has also been active in Sri Lanka since 2004.

The International Network of Engaged Buddhists (INEB) was founded in 1989 as the result of a meeting of modern Buddhist figures, including Sulak Sivaraksa (b.1933), which was held in Thailand. The network aims to facilitate connections among lay Buddhists, monks and nuns, and Buddhist scholars in a number of missions that address social issues and promote human rights, as well as the correct diffusion of Buddhism.

ENGAGED NUNS

Another page in the history of Engaged Buddhism was written in China and then Taiwan. The reformer monk Taixu (1890–1947) and his Humanistic Buddhism signalled the beginning of this movement, and the legacy of Taixu's teachings can be found in the activities of several Buddhist nuns in Taiwan today. For instance, the nun Zhaohui is a campaigner for human rights and animal rights, and founded the Life Conservationist Association.

A second noteworthy individual is the nun Lianchan, who in 1987 established the Chinese Buddhist Library for the Blind, accredited by the Taiwanese government. In June 1990, the library was extended and developed into the Chinese Buddhist Cultural Centre for the Blind.

BUDDHADASA BHIKKHU

A Theravada monk in Thailand, Buddhadasa Bhikkhu (1906–93) attempted to restore the Buddha's original teachings in modern Southeast Asia, and to propose an inclusive view of all religions into one Dharma. Founder of Wat Suan Mokkh (1932) and the Dhamma Hermitage Center (1993), Buddhadasa became well known for his efforts to integrate Buddhism and socialism in a period when Western political and cultural sytems, including socialism, were undermining religion in Thailand. In his work *Dhammic Socialism*, Buddhadasa explained that Karl Marx's socialism was just a manifestation of anger, whereas, if it were guided by the principle of Buddhism – and thereby become 'Dhammic' (Buddhist) – socialism could become the correct philosophy for the world. Buddhism, Buddhadasa reasoned, embodies the essence of socialism through its concern for the suffering of humanity.

ACTIVE ENGAGEMENT

SCHOOLS AND HOSPITALS, TV CHANNELS AND PUBLISHING HOUSES, NEWSPAPERS AND JOURNALS, BUSINESSES AND CHARITIES – THESE ARE BUT A FEW OF THE CREATIONS OF ENGAGED BUDDHISM IN ASIA. SUCH ENTERPRISES ARE PARTICULARLY PREVALENT IN TAIWAN AND KOREA.

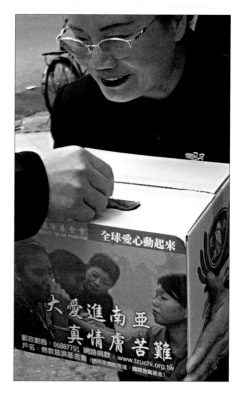

The main facets of Engaged Buddhism in Taiwan include close co-operation between monks, nuns and the laity, the practice of the bodhisattva path in daily life, and the focus on establishing a 'pure land' on earth, instead of aiming at a rebirth in Amitabha's Pure Land.

Active engagement has seen an increasingly important place given to lay Buddhists, as well as a secularization of the role that monks and nuns had previously played in the religious scene, and has developed a variety of activities, ranging from educational initiatives to missionary propaganda, humanitarian campaigns and medical assistance. Another feature of active engagement has been the global spread of the various movements and social initiatives, which has led to Taiwanese Buddhism becoming well-known and appreciated, but also sometimes criticized, all over the world.

HUMANISTIC BUDDHISM

The most widely accepted translation of the Chinese *renjian fojiao* is 'Humanistic Buddhism'.

Below An attempt by Fo Guang Shan to recreate Amitabha's Pure Land, this 32m (105ft) high statue of the Buddha surrounded by 480 smaller statues stands in Gaoxiong county, Taiwan. Followers gather on the patio to do walking and sitting meditation.

Above The Tzu Chi Foundation organizes fundraising to provide relief to victims of natural disasters all over the world. This volunteer is collecting donations for refugees of the tsunami that affected South-east Asia in December 2004.

Renjian fojiao literally means 'Buddhism for the Human Realms', and is said to derive from the formerly theorized *rensheng fojiao* ('Buddhism for the Human Life'). As these denominations indicate, the movement focuses on life on Earth, rather than aspiring to otherworldly realms, and aims to realize the so-called *renjian jingtu* ('Pure Land on Earth').

The Chinese reformer monk Taixu (1890–1947) is recognized as the first theorizer of Humanistic Buddhism, which is a product of the process of modernization of Buddhism in Taiwan. According to Taixu, Buddhism was a philosophy and a science that needed to be purged of all its superstitious features. With this objective, he proposed the threefold reform of the Sangha, teachings and institutions. These plans were theorized in mainland China during the first half of the 20th century, but put into practice only after the 1950s in Taiwan.

FO GUANG SHAN

In 1967 the Chinese monk Xing Yun founded Fo Guang Shan in Gaoxiong, Taiwan. Born in Jiangdu (Jiangsu province, China) in 1927, and fully ordained in 1941, Xing Yun was among the monks who fled to Taiwan in 1949. Claiming to be a follower of Taixu's programme, Xing Yun became one of the main promoters of Humanistic Buddhism in contemporary Taiwan.

With branch temples all over Taiwan as well as across the world, Fo Guang Shan has the largest monastic community on the island as well as a considerable lay association – Buddha's Light International Association – which co-operates with the Sangha.

Similarly to all other Engaged Buddhist groups, Fo Guang Shan lists four main objectives: charity, culture, education and Dharma propagation, placing particular emphasis on the last two of these. Fo Guang Shan has established colleges for monks and nuns, as well as secular higher education institutions, and has published a new version of the Chinese Buddhist Canon. The University of the West in California was also established under the umbrella of Fo Guang Shan.

THE TZU CHI FOUNDATION

Zheng Yan was born as Wang Jinyun in 1937 in a small village in the centre of Taiwan. After the death of her father, who taught her the principle of impermanence, Jinyun shaved her head and followed the nun Xiudao and the traditional practice of Buddhism. Her move toward Humanistic

Buddhism was driven by three events: becoming a disciple of the monk Yinshun (1906–2005), who gave her the Dharma name Zheng Yan and taught her to work 'for Buddhism and for all living beings'; an encounter with three Catholic nuns who blamed Buddhism for not being committed to social welfare; and the sight of a poor woman dying in a hospital because she could not afford medical care.

Zheng Yan established the Tzu Chi Foundation in 1966. The organization, which is dedicated to the four missions of charity, medicine, education and culture, founded the Tzu Chi General Hospital in 1986 and the Tzu Chi College of Medicine in 1994. Starting with only five lay women, Zheng Yan now has millions of followers – mostly lay women, and not necessarily Buddhist – in Taiwan as well as abroad. Dubbed the 'Mother Theresa of Asia', Zheng Yan was a candidate for the Nobel Peace Prize in 1993, and she has become a symbol of Taiwan both at home and abroad.

Above Fo Guang Shan has opened branch temples in different countries throughout the world. This is the main hall of the branch in London. Chinese Buddhists as well as those of other nationalities attend activities at the temple.

Above The Buddhist nun Zheng Yan is the most famous and charismatic Buddhist figure in Taiwan. Working 'for Buddhism and for all living beings', Zheng Yan emphasizes the practice of compassion and the wisdom of the bodhisattva path.

GLOSSARY

ABHIDHARMA The third part of the **Tripitaka** of the Pali canon.

ADI-BUDDHA In the **Mahayana** and **Tibetan** traditions, the primordial buddha, who came into being before anything else existed.

AMITABHA In the **Mahayana** and **Vajrayana** traditions, the **bodhisattva** of infinite light and Buddha of the Western Paradise, where devout Buddhists hope to be reborn.

ANATMAN (Skt; P: *anatta*) Non-self, the Buddhist doctrine that sentient beings do not have an immortal soul (**atman**), or core self that lives on after death.

ANITYA (Skt; P: *anicca*), Impermanence. The idea that all 'conditioned phenomena', ie all things that come into being through cause and effect, are transient phenomena.

ARHAT (Skt; P: *arahant*) One who has achieved **nirvana** by following the Buddha-Dharma and will not be reborn.

Below A Tibetan Buddhist monk circumambulates a stupa and walks past hundreds of prayer wheels on his journey.

ASCETICISM Abstinence from worldly pleasures; an extreme path to **enlightenment** tried and rejected by the Buddha in favour of the **Middle Way**.

ATMAN The Hindu concept of a timeless, unchanging reality, which implies the existence of a permanent, unchanging soul.

BHIKKHU/BHIKKHUNI A fully ordained Buddhist monk/nun.

BHUMI One of the ten stages of spiritual advancement that a **bodhisattva** goes through.

BODHI Enlightenment; to know the ultimate reality; the opposite of ignorance.

BODHI TREE *Ficus religiosa*, tree of **enlightenment**.

BODHICITTA In **Mahayana** Buddhism, the 'enlightened mind' of a bodhisattva; a bodhisattva's intent to become enlightened for the salvation of all sentient beings.

BODHISATTVA In **Mahayana** and **Vajrayana** Buddhism, an ideal state attainable by everyone, in which an enlightened being commits to help others attain **enlightenment**. Buddha Shakyamuni was a bodhisattva before his enlightenment.

BRAHMAN One of the highest Hindu caste, originally a priest.

BUDDHA An 'awakened being'

Above A gilt bronze statue of the Bodhisattva Avalokiteshvara, from the Yuan dynasty, 14th century.

who has achieved **enlightenment** in one lifetime, without the guidance of a predecessor.

BUDDHAHOOD In the **Mahayana** tradition, the freedom from greed, hate and delusion; **enlightenment**.

CHAITYA A shrine containing a **stupa**. A *chaityagriha* is an assembly hall containing a stupa, often used for prayer.

CHAKRAVARTIN (Skt; P: *cakkavatti*) An ideal universal king, who rules righteously.

CHAN The meditation school of Chinese Buddhism (**Zen** in Japan, **Son** in Korea). Chan rejects textual study in favour of meditation and intuition as the most effective ways of attaining **enlightenment**.

CHEDI A Pali term used in Thailand meaning **stupa**.

CHORTEN The term for a **stupa** in Tibet, Ladakh, Bhutan and other countries where Tibetan Buddhism has been influential.

CONDITIONED PHENOMENA All entities that come into being through cause and effect.

COSMIC BUDDHA In **Mahayana** Buddhism: the primordial buddha, who manifests in human form; the compassionate buddha, who is eternally omnipresent. In **Esoteric Buddhism**, the Cosmic Buddha is represented as Vairocana, who is the personification of wisdom and the truth of the universe.

DAGOBA A Sri Lankan **stupa**, derived from the Sanskrit *dhatu-garbha*, meaning 'repository', having a distinctive dome shape.

DANA Selfless giving, generosity, which brings **merit**.

DEVA In the Hindu pantheon, a divine being, literally 'the Shining One'; a benevolent deity. The female form is devi.

DHARMA (Skt; P: *dhamma*) The universal law, the truth. The teachings of the Buddha Shakyamuni are called the Buddha-Dharma.

DHYANA Mental states reached during meditation.

DHYANI BUDDHAS The five buddhas who evolved from the **Adi-Buddha**.

DUHKHA (Skt; P: *dukkha*) 'Unsatisfactoriness'; suffering in all its forms, from discomfort and unease to physical and mental pain and agony.

ENLIGHTENMENT Nirvana, spiritual awakening.

ESOTERIC BUDDHISM A name applied to the teachings of the **Tantric, Vajrayana** and **Tibetan** Buddhist schools, which are made known only to those who have been initiated.

HINAYANA 'Lesser vehicle'; a term, now seen as pejorative, once used by followers of later schools to describe earlier schools such as the **Theravada**.

KARMA The consequences of all intentional actions, which build up **merit** (*punya*) or demerit (*papa*). The balance of karma at death determines into which of the six realms of the Buddhist universe a person will be reborn.

KARUNA Compassion.

KLESHAS Thoughtless reactions that cause beings to commit misdeeds intentionally and accumulate *papa*, or negative **karma**.

KOAN A question intended for contemplation and to inspire insights and, through them, sudden **enlightenment**. Koans use language to move an individual beyond language.

LAMA In **Tibetan Buddhism**, a monk who has mastered tantric meditation and ritual; a guru, teacher or spiritual leader.

LOSAR The New Year festival in **Tibetan Buddhism**.

MADHYAMAKA A Buddhist school founded on the ideas concerning *sunyata* (emptiness) put forward by the 2nd century CE philosopher Nagarjuna.

MAHASAMGHIKA 'Adherents of the Great Order'; one of the early schools of Buddhism, which split off from the first **Sangha** during the 4th or 3rd century BCE, in what may have been the original schism.

MAHAYANA 'Great vehicle'; the second major Buddhist tradition, founded around the 1st century BCE. It emphasizes the value of compassion and teaches that all beings can achieve buddhahood.

MANDALA A diagram designed to aid the visualization of spiritual realms in meditation.

MANTRA A word or phrase with a powerful meaning, chanted to discipline the mind as an aid to meditation or as an incantation.

MERIT (*punya*) Positive **karma** accumulated by beings during their earthly existence.

MIDDLE WAY The Buddha's path to **enlightenment**, which rejects self-indulgence and asceticism.

MIND-ONLY (*cittamatra*) The **Yogacara** school of Buddhism; the idea that the world of objects does not exist, that consciousness is the only reality.

MUDRA Symbolic hand gesture.

NICHIREN A **Mahayana** sect founded during the 13th century in Japan by Nichiren, who aspired to purify **Tendai** Buddhism of **esoteric** practices.

Below Guanyin, the Chinese Bodhisattva of Compassion, and the most popular of the Mahayanist Buddhist deities.

NIRVANA 'Extinction'; liberation from **samsara**; emptiness; supreme **enlightenment**.

ONE-POINTED CONCENTRATION A state of deep trance, intense concentration and higher consciousness.

PAGODA A **stupa**, especially in East Asian countries. The word is a European corruption of **dagoba**. A Chinese pagoda is usually a hollow stepped tower of 3, 5, 7, 9 or 11 storeys. Inside there may be buried relics or sacred texts.

PALI CANON The Buddha's teachings, written down in Sri Lanka during the 1st century BCE.

PANCASILA The five ethical precepts observed by Buddhists.

PARAMITAS The perfections cultivated by a **bodhisattva**.

PARINIRVANA (Skt; P: *parinibbana*) 'Complete **nirvana**'; the complete extinction of the individual, characterized by freedom from the effects of **karma**.

Below The interior of a cave temple at Luoyang, China. The original paint, dating from the 5th–6th centuries CE, still adheres to the walls.

POSADHA (Skt; P: *uposatha*) Observance days on which **bhikkhus** and **bhikkhunis** confess to each other their infringements of the rules.

PRAJNA Wisdom, insight.

PRANG In Thai architecture of the 13th–18th centuries, a Buddhist temple tower.

PRATIMOKSA The rules of monastic discipline.

PRATITYA-SAMUTPADA 'Dependent arising'; the idea that an event takes place as part of a chain of causation that began in the past and extends into the future, and leads from rebirth to death.

PRAYER WHEEL A hollow wheel containing **mantras**, **sutra** quotations, or prayers inscribed on paper. Tibetan Buddhists turn the wheel to create **merit**.

SAMADHI A practice where the meditator becomes absorbed in the object of meditation, leading to **one-pointed concentration**.

SAMSARA The cycle of birth–death–rebirth in which beings are trapped as a result of negative **karma**; the opposite of **nirvana**.

SANGHA The Buddhist Order, or monastic community.

SARVASTIVADA One of the early schools of Buddhism, the name of which stems from the doctrine that everything exists (*sarvam asti*).

SATORI A sudden spiritual awakening, an intuitive understanding of the nature of reality, achieved in **Zen** Buddhism.

SHINGON 'True word'; an **esoteric** Japanese sect, a branch of **Vajrayana Buddhism** founded in the 9th century by Kukai, a Japanese monk. It emphasizes the direct experience of personal buddhahood.

SHRAMANA A religious seeker; a person who practices **asceticism** in the quest for spiritual knowledge, usually as a mendicant and homeless wanderer.

SILA Morality.

SKANDHA Any of the five aggregates, the physical and mental components of a human being.

SKILFUL MEANS (*upaya paramita*) The ability to teach in a way that is perfectly adapted to be understood by those who receive it.

SON The Korean version of the Chinese Buddhist meditation school **Chan**.

STHAVIRAVADA One of the early Buddhist schools, which supported the Buddha's original teachings.

STUPA A monument built to enshrine relics, or raised to commemorate significant events.

SUNYATA Emptiness, the idea that the universe is empty of a permanent essence, since everything changes.

SUTRA (Skt; P: *sutta*) A summary of one of the Buddha's observations prepared in verse form so that it is easy to memorize.

TANTRAS Buddhist scriptures on which Tantric (or **Vajrayana** or **Tibetan**) Buddhism is based.

TANTRIC BUDDHISM An offshoot of **Mahayana** Buddhism

Above Tibetan monks carry a yak butter sculpture during a festival. Butter sculptures have been part of the Tibetan Buddhist tradition for centuries.

based on scriptures called **tantras**, which emphasize techniques to effect rapid **enlightenment**.

TATHAGATA Literally 'one who has thus gone', an honorific title of a **buddha**. The Buddha Shakyamuni referred to himself as Tathagata.

THERAVADA The most conservative of the three main Buddhist traditions that still exist. The Theravada preserves the Buddha's original teachings, written down in the **Pali canon**.

TIANTAI A Chinese Buddhist sect founded during the 6th century CE, which recognizes the influence of the *Lotus Sutra*.

TIBETAN BUDDHISM An offshoot of **Mahayana** that evolved in Tibet from Indian

Vajrayana teachings combined with the Tibetan Bön religion.

TRIPITAKA (Skt; P: *Tipitaka*) 'Three Baskets'; the **Pali canon**, the earliest written form of the Buddha's teachings that has been preserved in its entirety.

TRISHNA (Skt; P: *tanha*) Thirst or desire; considered one of the major causes of suffering.

UPANISHADS Sacred Hindu texts written *c*.800–200BCE.

UPASAKA A male lay member of the **Sangha**; an *upasika* is a female lay member.

USHNISHA Protruberance on the crown of the head of an image of a **buddha** or **bodhisattva**.

VAJRAYANA BUDDHISM 'Diamond Vehicle'; the third major tradition, which evolved from **Mahayana** during the 8th century CE, and influenced the development of **Tibetan Buddhism**.

VEDAS Ancient sacred hymns and other writings of the Brahmanic religions, first written down in 1500–1200BCE and believed to be divine revelations.

VIBHAJJAVADA One of the early Buddhist schools, which evolved into **Theravada**.

VIHARA 'Dwelling'; a Buddhist monastery or temple.

VIPASSANA 'Inward vision'; meditation techniques to promote a clear understanding of the nature of reality.

YOGACARA A Buddhist school founded in the 4th century CE, which emphasizes the practices of yoga and meditation.

ZAZEN Sitting meditation; a **Chan** and **Zen** practice.

ZEN A Mahayana Buddhist school, the Japanese form of **Chan**, that emphasizes meditation as the path to *satori*, or **enlightenment**.

INDEX

Above A bodhisattva statue in the Greco-Buddhist style, Peshawar, 4th century CE.

Above Monks at Bumthang monastery, Bhutan.

*Above The Buddha descending to his
last incarnation, 3rd–4th-century relief.*

Above A giant Maitreya statue in Leshan, Sichuan Province, China.

This edition is published by Hermes House, an imprint of Anness Publishing Ltd
Hermes House, 88-89 Blackfriars Road, London SE1 8HA
Tel. 020 7401 2077; fax 020 7633 9499
www.hermeshouse.com;
www.annesspublishing.com

Anness Publishing has a new picture agency outlet for images for publishing, promotions or advertising. Please visit our website www.practicalpictures.com for more information.

ETHICAL TRADING POLICY
At Anness Publishing we believe that business should be conducted in an ethical and ecologically sustainable way, with respect for the environment and a proper regard to the replacement of the natural resources we employ.

As a publisher, we use a lot of wood pulp to make high-quality paper for printing, and that wood commonly comes from spruce trees. We are therefore currently growing more than 750,000 trees in three Scottish forest plantations: Berrymoss (130 hectares/320 acres), West Touxhill (125 hectares/305 acres) and Deveron Forest (75 hectares/185 acres). The forests we manage contain more than 3.5 times the number of trees employed each year in making paper for the books we manufacture.

Because of this ongoing ecological investment programme, you, as our customer, can have the pleasure and reassurance of knowing that a tree is being cultivated on your behalf to naturally replace the materials used to make the book you are holding.

For further information about this scheme, go to www.annesspublishing.com/trees

© Anness Publishing Ltd 2009

For Anness Publishing Ltd:
Publisher: Joanna Lorenz
Editorial Director: Helen Sudell

Produced for Lorenz Books by Toucan Books:
Managing Director: Ellen Dupont
Editor: Anne McDowall
Project Manager: Hannah Bowen
Designer: Elizabeth Healey
Cartographer: Julian Baker
Picture Researcher: Tam Church
Proofreader: Marion Dent
Indexer: Michael Dent

The publishers have made every effort to trace the photograph copyright owners. Anyone we have failed to reach is invited to contact Toucan Books, 89 Charterhouse Street, London EC1M 6HR, UK.

akg-images 241, /British Library 73b, 178t, /Hervé Champollion 107t, /Mark De Fraeye 144 t and bl, 151b, 158t, /Nimatallah 1, 190t, /Jean-Louis Nou 12b, 15t, 26t, 30, 39t, 66t, 69, 96b, /Gilles Mermet 19t, 41t, /ullstein bild 190b, /Werner Forman 212b, 232t. Alamy /Jim Allan 94t, Kenneth Garrett/ DanitaDelimont.com 101. Ancient Art & Architecture Collection /C.M. Dixon 22b, 52t, /J.F. Kenney 71t, /T Paramjit 24b, /Ronald Sheridan 68. Arkreligion.com /Martin Barlow 147t, /Joan Batten 106b, /Rafael Ben-Ari 239t, /Anthony Bloomfield 182b, /Tibor Bognar jacket back tl, 3t, 47, 57t, 80b, 91b, 93t, 115t, 126t, 155b, 157b, 199b, 210t, 212t, 228t, /Dinodia Photo Library 14b, 33, 76bl, 77b, 79t, 89t, 92t, /Malcolm Fairman 64b, /Andrew Gasson 4l, 96t, /Fiona Good 53t, /Michael Good jacket back tmr, 110b, 159b, /Jeff Greenberg 182t, /Richard Hammerton 61t, /Jean Hall 231b, /Sally Hunt 130b, /Warren Jacobs 111t, 126b, /Nobby Kealey 62t, /Mel Longhurst 162b, /Tim Morse 215, /Robin Nichols 84t, /Janet Pugh 105t, /Resource Foto 185b, /Jan Roberts 78b, /Helene Rogers 23l, 77t, 132t, 220t, /David Sutton 167l, /Jane Sweeney jacket front bl, 83t, 103r, 112t, 116t, 136b, 232b, /Trip 238t, /Adina Tovy 221tr, /Brian Vikander 48, 70b, 90t, 166t, /Joan Wakelin 115b, 174t, /Maciej Wojtkowiak 21r, 34t, 45, 85t, 93b, 102t, 116b, 117b, 120t, 122b, 123b. The Art Archive /Atami Museum Kanagawa/Laurie Platt Winfrey 46b, /Bibliothèque des Arts Décoratifs, Paris/Gianni Dagli Orti 42t, 150t, /British Library 92b, /British Museum 89b, 138b, /Stephanie Colasanti 81br, /Collection Antonovich /Gianni Dagli Orti 252, /Genius of China Exhibition 20bl, /Gianni Dagli Orti 95t, /Imperial Household Collection Kyoto/Laurie Platt Winfrey 148t, /Jobon Rendaiji Temple Kyoto/Laurie Platt Winfrey 18b, /Koyasan Wakayama prefecture/Laurie Platt Winfrey 35t, 149t, /Mohammed Khalil Museum Cairo /Gianni Dagli Orti 135t, /Musée Cernuschi, Paris /Gianni Dagli Orti 140t, /Musée Guimet, Paris /Alfredo Dagli Orti 19b, /Musée Guimet, Paris /Gianni Dagli Orti back flap, 3b, 16t, 35b, 43tl, 56t, 58t, 88t, 97t, 112b, 124t, 131t, 136t, 139b, 192t, 201t, 218b, 233t, 234t, 237t, 253, /Museo Nazionale d'Arte Orientale Rome/Gianni Dagli Orti 22t, 208b, /Private Collection Paris/Gianni Dagli Orti jacket back tm, 6, 75, 91t, 137b, 192b, /Sylvan Barnet and William Burto Collection 44b, 88b, 134bl, 152b, 222t, 226b, 242b, /Mireille Vautier 12, 82t, 150b, /Victoria & Albert Museum London/Eileen Tweedy 102br. Aruna Publications (www.ratanagiri.org.uk) 196b. The Bridgeman Art Library 27t, 74t, 76br, 78t, 110t, 209b, /Ashmolean Museum, University of Oxford 248t, /The Barnes Foundation, Pennsylvania 145r, /Bibliothèque des Arts Décoratifs, Paris /Archives Charmet 224b, /Bibliothèque Nationale, Paris 54b, 138t, /British Library 17, 36b, /British Museum 203, /Bulguksa Temple, South Korea 145l, /Trustees of the Chester Beatty Library, Dublin 9m,

148b, /Christie's Images 152t, 199t, /The Detroit Institute of Arts, USA 200t, /Fitzwilliam Museum, University of Cambridge 97b, /Paul Freeman 52b, 208t, 219t, /Glasgow City Council (Museums) 198t, /Lauros /Giraudon 74b, /National Museum, Ayutthaya, Thailand 34b, /National Museum of India 27b, /National Museum of Karachi 13b, /National Museums of Scotland 40b, 41b, 56b, 234b, 236t, /National Museum, Seoul 176t, /National Palace Museum, Taipei 141t, 205b, /Musée Cernuschi, Paris/Archives Charmet 223, /Musée Guimet, Paris 15b, 16b, 20br, 249, /Musée Guimet, Paris/Bonora 18t, 222b, /Musée Guimet, Paris /Giraudon 60, /Musée Guimet, Paris /Lauros /Giraudon 38t, 194t, 204t, 220b, /Musée National de Phnom Penh, Cambodia/Giraudon 23r, /Museum of Fine Arts, Boston 40t, 205t, /Museum of Fine Arts, Houston 134br, /Royal Geographical Society, London jacket front tm, 25, 142b, /Victoria & Albert Museum, London 218t, 228b, /Walters Art Museum, Baltimore, USA 162t. Corbis /Alinari Archives 184t, /Tiziana and Gianni Baldizzone 236b, /Dave Bartruff, Inc. 63t, /Remi Benali 142t, /Bettmann 20t, 117b, 177t and bl, 159t, 225t, /Bohemian Nomad Picturemakers 198b, /Tibor Bognar 113b, /Christophe Boisvieux 58b, 61b, 73t, 90b, 124b, 153b, 191b, 240t, /Horace Bristol 80t, /Bruce Burkhardt 248b, /Burstein Collection/The Munch Museum/The Munch-Ellingsen Group 46t, /Demetrio Carrasco /JAI 99t, /Angelo Cavalli/zefa 156b, /Christie's Images 193t, 202br, 227, /Sheldan Collins jacket front tl, 70t, /Pierre Colombel 99b, /Richard A. Cooke 98b, /Cordaiy Photo Library Ltd. 186t, /John Dakers /Eye Ubiquitous 86b, /epa 66b, /Ric Ergenbright 154t, /Michele Falzone/JAI 82b, /Werner Forman 146t, /Michael Freeman jacket front tml, 14t, 83br, 161b, 166b, /Jose Fuste Raga front flap, 118br, 132b, /Goebel/zefa 237b, /Lynn Goldsmith 235b, /Peter Harholdt 221bl, /Blaine Harrington III 9l, 81bl, 127l, 143t, 195b, /Lindsay Hebberd jacket front tr, 11, 26b, 51t, 114t, 219b, 233b, /Jon Hicks jacket front tmr, 29b, 62b, 146b, /So Hing-Keung 44t, /Angelo Hornak 13t, /Jeremy Horner 59l, 169l, /Rob Howard 60r, /Lee Jae-Won/Reuters 67b, /John R. Jones /Papilio 72b, /Catherine Karnow 171b, /Kimbell Art Museum 39b, 202tr, 213b, /Manjunath Kiran/epa 53b, /Earl & Nazima Kowall 127r, /Stephanie Kuykendal 151t, /Kim Kyung-Hoon/Reuters 144r, /Frank Leather/Eye Ubiquitous 210b, /Charles & Josette Lenars 21l, 118t, 175t, /Yang Liu 140b, /Craig Lovell 106t, 129t, /Araldo de Luca 153t, /Colin McPherson 179b, /Kevin R. Morris 185t, /Tom Nebbia 251, /Kazuyoshi Nomachi 184b, /Abraham Nowitz 98t, /Fred de Noyelle/Godong 160t, 187b, /Diego Lezama Orezzoli 100t, 191t, /Tim Page 79b, /Micheline Pelletier/Sygma 245, /Reuters 7t, 169r, /Reuters/Muzammil Pasha 119, /M.A. Pushpa Kumara/epa 72t, /David Samuel Robbins 104t, 131b, /Anders Ryman 157t, /Sakamoto Photo Research Laboratory 200b, /Sangdao Sattra/epa 163b, /Phil Schermeister 63b, /Smithsonian Institution 211b, /Southern Stock Corp 216t, /Keren Su 38bl, 100b, /Riko Sugita/Reuters 243b, /Jane Sweeney/Robert Harding 130v, /Sygma 235t, /Luca I. Tettoni spine bottom, 24t, 37r, 48t, 108, 156t, 164t and b, 170b,

/John Van Hasselt 137t, /Julian Abram Wainwright /epa 244t, /WEDA/epa 174b, /Nevada Wier jacket back tr, 51b, /Nik Wheeler 107b, 224t, /Adam Woolfitt 32, /Alison Wright spine top, 4r, 5l, 30b, 42b, 59r, 121t, 193b, 204b, 242t, 243t, /Michael S. Yamashita 86t, 230t, /Liu Yu/Redlink 246b, /Liang Zhuoming 104bl. Dharma Realm Buddhist Association 186b, 206t and b, 207t and b. Getty Images 55t, /AFP 158b, /Alison Wright/Lonely Planet Images 87b, /Ami Vitale 178b, /The Bridgeman Art Library 105b, /Paula Bronstein 120b, /Frederic J. Brown/AFP 177br, /Jan Bruggeman 95b, /Dean Conger/National Geographic 176b, /Sebastian D'Souza/AFP 230b, /Eliot Elisofon/Time Life Pictures 43tr, /Tim Graham 5r, 121b, /David Greedy 167r, /Henry Guttmann/Hulton Archive 179t, /Ernst Haas 135b, /Tony Hallas 45b, /Hulton Archive 76t, /Liu Jin/AFP 49, /Robert W. Kelley/Time Life Pictures 36r, /Saeed Khan/AFP 244b, /Leelu/Hulton Archive 31, /Patrick Lin/AFP 246t, /Lonely Planet Images /Keren Su 133, /Tatyana Makeyeva/AFP 50t, /Hector Mata/AFP 64r, /John Moore 118bl, /Francoise De Mulder /Roger Viollet 173b, /National Geographic /Maria Stenzel 29t, /Kazuhiro Nogi/AFP 225b, /Christopher Pillitz 102bl, /Robert Harding 71b, /Robert Harding/Gavin Hellier 194b, /Robert Harding/Jochen Schlenker 28b, 147b, /Robert Nickelsberg/Time Life Pictures 65b, 188, /Manpreet Romana/AFP 143b, /Dibyangshu Sarkar /AFP 9r, 87t, /Sharon Smith /Photonica jacket front mr, 37t, /Tang Chhin Sothy/AFP 55b, 168t, /Tom Stoddart 238b, /Stone/Jerry Alexander 160b, /Stone /Hugh Sitton 84b, /Stone/Pete Turner 94b, /Justin Sullivan 239b, /Taxi Japan/Karin Slade 155t, /Travel Ink /Gallo Images 165b, /Lakruwan Wanniarachchi /AFP 50b, /Choi Won-Suk/AFP 83bl, /Michael S. Yamashita /National Geographic 154b. Paul Harris 109, 125t and b, 128t and b, 129b, 134t, 149b, 172t, 189, 226t. Manar Hussain 111b. The Library of Hsu Yun Temple, Honolulu, Hawaii 201b. London Fo Guang Shan 247t. PA Photos 183b, /Malcolm Browne 67t, /Misha Japaridze 178b, 103l, /David Longstreath 57b. Photolibrary.com /Imagestate /Steve Vidler 171t, /Japan Travel Bureau 170t, 139t, 240b, /Jon Arnold Travel/Peter Adams 168b. Photoshot.com 10. REUTERS /Lucy Pemoni 214b, /Brian Snyder 231t, /Eriko Sugita 229t. Robert Harding /Richard Ashworth 113t, /D. Beatty 8, 114b, /James Emmerson 187t, /Alain Evrard 81t, /Ursula Gahwiler 7b, 211b, 213b, /Gavin Hellier 141b, /Bruno Morandi jacket front ml, 38br, /Christopher Rennie 2, /Jochen Schlenker jacket back tml, 65t, 122t, /Eitan Simanor 123t, /Luca I. Tettoni 175b, /Tony Waltham 28t. shutterstock.com /Bruce Amos 165t, /Robert O. Brown Photography 183t, /Buddhadl 250, /Chee Choon Fat 172b, /Juha Sompinmäki 163t, 254, /TAOLMOR 161t, 195t, /charles taylor 85b, /Christophe Testi endpapers, /Harald Høiland Tjøstheim 255, /Andy Z. 214t. Roy Brabant Smith of the Lay Buddhist Association 216b. Spirit Rock Meditation Center 217t. Topfoto .co.uk 180t and b, 181. Stefania Travagnin 247b. Werner Forman Archive 173t, 212b, 232t. www. kwanumzen.org 209b. www.nichirenscoffeehouse.net 229b. www.watnongpahpong.org 196t, 197t and b.